# MUSIC PUBLISHING IN CHICAGO BEFORE 1871

DETROIT STUDIES IN MUSIC BIBLIOGRAPHY

.......... Bruno Nettl, General Editor

REFERENCE MATERIALS IN ETHNOMUSICOLOGY, by Bruno Nettl  Rev ed
    1967  40p  $2.00 — Number 1

SIR ARTHUR SULLIVAN: AN INDEX TO THE TEXTS OF HIS VOCAL WORKS,
    compiled by Sirvart Poladian  1961  91p  $2.75 — Number 2

AN INDEX TO BEETHOVEN'S CONVERSATION BOOKS, by Donald W.
    MacArdle  1962  46p  $2.00 — Number 3

GENERAL BIBLIOGRAPHY FOR MUSIC RESEARCH, by Keith E. Mixter  1962
    38p  $2.00 — Number 4

A HANDBOOK OF AMERICAN OPERATIC PREMIERES, by Julius Mattfeld  1963
    135p  $3.00 — Number 5

MEDIEVAL AND RENAISSANCE MUSIC ON LONG-PLAYING RECORDS, by
    James Coover and Richard Colvig  1964  122p  $3.00 — Number 6

RHODE ISLAND MUSIC AND MUSICIANS, 1733-1850, by Joyce Ellen Mangler
    1965  90p  $2.75 — Number 7

JEAN SIBELIUS: AN INTERNATIONAL BIBLIOGRAPHY ON THE OCCASION
    OF THE CENTENNIAL CELEBRATIONS, 1965, by Fred Blum  1965
    114p  $3.50 — Number 8

BIBLIOGRAPHY OF THESES AND DISSERTATIONS IN SACRED MUSIC, by
    Kenneth R. Hartley  1967  127p  $3.00 — Number 9

CHECKLIST OF VOCAL CHAMBER WORKS BY BENEDETTO MARCELLO, by
    Caroline S. Fruchtman  1967  37p  $2.00 — Number 10

AN ANNOTATED BIBLIOGRAPHY OF WOODWIND INSTRUCTION BOOKS
    1600-1830, by Thomas E. Warner  1967  140p  $3.00 — Number 11

WORKS FOR SOLO VOICE OF JOHANN ADOLPH HASSE (1699-1783), by Sven
    Hostrup Hansell  1968  110p  $3.00 — Number 12

A SELECTIVE DISCOGRAPHY OF SOLO SONG, by Dorothy Stahl  1968  95p
    $2.50 — Number 13

*Detroit Studies in Music Bibliography - 14*

# MUSIC PUBLISHING IN CHICAGO BEFORE 1871: THE FIRM OF ROOT & CADY, 1858-1871

*by Dena J. Epstein*

*Information Coordinators, Inc. Detroit, 1969*

Copyright 1969 by Dena J. Epstein

Printed and bound in the United States of America

Price $6.00

INFORMATION COORDINATORS, INC.
1435-37 Randolph Street
Detroit, Michigan 48226

TABLE OF CONTENTS

INTRODUCTION . . . . . . . . . . . . . . . . . . . . . . . . . . . . . . . . . . . . . . . . . . . . . . ix-x

| | | | |
|---|---|---|---|
| Chapter | I | CHICAGO MUSIC PUBLISHERS OTHER THAN ROOT & CADY . . . . . . . . . . . . | 3-13 |
| Chapter | II | THE PARTNERS . . . . . . . . . . . . . . . . . . . . . . . . . . . . . . . . . . . . . . | 17-30 |
| | | George Frederick Root, 1820-1895 . . . . . . . . . . . . . . . . . . . . . . . | 17-20 |
| | | Ebenezer Towner Root, 1822-1896 . . . . . . . . . . . . . . . . . . . . . . . | 20-23 |
| | | Chauncey Marvin Cady, 1824-1889 . . . . . . . . . . . . . . . . . . . . . . . | 23-30 |
| Chapter | III | ROOT & CADY PRIOR TO THE CIVIL WAR . . . . . . . . . . . . . . . . . . . . . . | 33-39 |
| Chapter | IV | THE CIVIL WAR PERIOD . . . . . . . . . . . . . . . . . . . . . . . . . . . . . . . . . | 43-53 |
| Chapter | V | THE POST-WAR YEARS, 1866-1868 . . . . . . . . . . . . . . . . . . . . . . . . . | 57-73 |
| Chapter | VI | THE END OF THE FIRM, 1868-1871 . . . . . . . . . . . . . . . . . . . . . . . . . | 77-84 |
| Appendix A | | ROOT & CADY PUBLICATIONS . . . . . . . . . . . . . . . . . . . . . . . . . . . . . | 87-146 |
| | | I. Checklist of Plate Numbers . . . . . . . . . . . . . . . . . . . . . . . . . | 91-130 |
| | | II. Chronological List of Copyrighted Works Found Without Plate Numbers . . | 133-135 |
| | | III. Copyrighted Works Not Found . . . . . . . . . . . . . . . . . . . . . . . . | 139 |
| | | IV. Music Books . . . . . . . . . . . . . . . . . . . . . . . . . . . . . . . . . . . . | 143-146 |
| Appendix B | | COMPOSER INDEX TO SHEET MUSIC PUBLICATIONS . . . . . . . . . . . . . . . . | 149-164 |
| Appendix C | | SUBJECT INDEX TO PUBLICATIONS OF EXTRA-MUSICAL INTEREST . . . . . . . | 167-177 |
| Appendix D | | DIRECTORY OF THE MUSIC TRADE IN CHICAGO BEFORE 1871 . . . . . . . . . . | 181-211 |

BIBLIOGRAPHY . . . . . . . . . . . . . . . . . . . . . . . . . . . . . . . . . . . . . . . . . . . 215-220

INDEX . . . . . . . . . . . . . . . . . . . . . . . . . . . . . . . . . . . . . . . . . . . . . . . . 223-243

INTRODUCTION

INTRODUCTION

This study approaching mid-nineteenth century music in the United States from the viewpoint of the publisher was begun as a master's thesis at the University of Illinois Library School. A collection in the University of Illinois Library of over 800 sheets of music published in Chicago before 1871 served both as a starting point and a basic source of information, providing a lively demonstration of publishing practice. When the work began, no information was available as to the extent, volume or importance of the trade, and it was tacitly assumed to have been fairly small. As the search of contemporary newspapers and other sources progressed, however, it became apparent that the number of active firms was larger than had been supposed and that the importance of some of them was considerable. While a number did not attain any prominence, at least three had extensive catalogs and more than local influence. To keep the study within reasonable limits, my thesis director and I decided to outline the development of music publishing in pre-fire Chicago and to discuss in greater detail the most important and interesting house, Root & Cady. The thesis, based almost entirely on sources found in Urbana and Chicago, was completed in 1943 under the title <u>Music Publishing in Chicago Prior to 1871: The Firm of Root & Cady, 1858-1871</u>.

At just about this time Richard S. Hill was assuming editorship of Music Library Association <u>Notes</u>, transforming it from a mimeographed bulletin into the printed quarterly which remains his most enduring achievement. Earlier I had offered the directory of the music trade in Chicago for publication in <u>Notes</u>, but months passed without reply. When one finally came, it was a proposal from Mr. Hill to publish the whole thesis, which he had borrowed through inter-library loan. Perhaps a few improvements might be made in later chapters, said he, but right now he needed copy for Chapter I in a week. To allow some time for consideration, I suggested that Chapter I be an independent survey of music publishing in Chicago before 1871. It was printed with almost no material which had not appeared in the thesis.

Three months later Chapter II appeared, the biographies of the three partners, rewritten in a more readable style, but again incorporating very little new material. Beginning with Chapter III, however, the copyright records entered the picture. Since I was then living in New Jersey, I was able to consult materials in the Library of Congress which I had not previously seen, especially the manuscript copyright ledgers in the Rare Book Room and the files of copyright deposit copies in the Music Division. Without fully appreciating the magnitude of the task, I enthusiastically set about assembling a complete list of Root & Cady publications with their plate numbers, supplementing the copyright deposits with the collections of the New York Public Library.

But Dick Hill was not the sort of editor who quietly waited for copy to arrive. When time ran short or he became impatient, he would make changes in the copy himself. Not until Chapter III appeared in print did I realize that he had added comments and filled in gaps without consulting me. But, when I suggested that his name be added as joint author, he refused, saying he did not wish to have his name both as author and editor. Succeeding chapters held their surprises for me when I saw them in print, culminating in Chapter V, where he supplied most of the history of the Boston group of publishers and the interpretation of their series of plate numbers. Again and more strongly I remonstrated with him that he should take credit for his work, but he was unmovable. Only now can I make clear his contributions to the articles in <u>Notes</u>. Since we rarely disagreed on interpretations, the supplementary material which he added did not change the essential structure of the history.

Because the articles represented a growing body of material, much of it uncovered after the early chapters were in print, it was necessary to do some thoroughgoing revision before reissuing them in book form. In the present edition, Chapter I has been completely rewritten to include material uncovered during the work on later chapters as well as that found since the articles were published. The biography of George F. Root in Chapter II has also been completely rewritten, and new material has been inserted wherever appropriate. The list of plate numbers which originally appeared in several installments has been consolidated into one sequence, with the addition of about 100 numbers previously lacking. Appearing for the first time is the Directory of the Music Trade in Chicago Before 1872, with full listings for all music printers, publishers and dealers, instrument manufacturers and dealers, and those lithographers and engravers whose names have been found on music publications.

My grateful thanks is due many individuals and institutions who generously gave their help: William Lichtenwanger, Reference Librarian, Music Division, Library of Congress; Frank C. Campbell and George R. Hill, of the Music Division, New York Public Library; Margaret Mott, Grosvenor Library, now part of the Buffalo and Erie County (N.Y.) Public Library; and Donald Krummel, The Newberry Library. Other collections whose staffs were of great assistance include the University of Illinois Library, the Chicago Historical Society Library, the Chicago Public Library, and the University of Chicago Library. Several private collectors kindly volunteered missing plate numbers from their own collections, notably W. N. H. Harding, of Chicago, and Edith Wright and Josephine McDevitt, of Washington, D.C. Mr. Harding later was most gracious in allowing access to his collection and in sharing his knowledge and experience. The late Harriette Cady, daughter of C.M. Cady, and Ralph Root, grandson of George F. Root, were generous with reminiscences and encouragement. A very special debt of gratitude is owed to Professor Emerita Anne Morris Boyd, of the University of Illinois Library School, who advised and guided the work on the thesis from which this study developed. Above all I am beholden to the late Richard S. Hill, who encouraged, stimulated, inspired, and nagged that thesis into published form, inserting material himself when time ran out and deadlines had to be met. No fledgling librarian ever had a better teacher, a more demanding task master, or a truer friend.

Dena J. Epstein

The University of Chicago Library

CHAPTER I

CHICAGO MUSIC PUBLISHERS OTHER THAN ROOT & CADY

## CHICAGO MUSIC PUBLISHERS OTHER THAN ROOT & CADY

The history of Chicago is divided by its greatest catastrophe into two periods -- before and after the fire of October, 1871. Although the fire stunted the city's growth only temporarily and a rebuilt Chicago forged ahead to become the colossus of the middle west, certain charming aspects of the city's life died with the fire. The trees which had lined the business streets were not replanted; no longer could Chicago be described as the Garden City. The thriving music trade of pre-fire days was crippled by overwhelming losses and many of the firms disappeared. Although the trade in instruments and musical merchandise revived and expanded with the city, Chicago's music publishing never regained the leading position it had assumed during the Civil War.

The music trade came to Chicago early. By 1836 one could buy from Osbourn and Strail, dealers in dry goods, groceries and crockery, "flutes, violins, clarinets, flageolets, accordions, violin strings and bridges, clarinet reeds, tuning forks, and brass post horns" as well as "the latest and most fashionable Songs for the Piano and Guitar, for 1, 2 and 3 voices, together with a variety of the latest Marches, Waltzes, arranged for the Piano."[1] The market for such wares was demonstrated by the formation of the Old Settlers' Harmonic Society in 1835, described by George Upton in his Musical Memories (Chicago, A. C. McClurg & Co., 1908, p214-16).

Chicago's first music store, "Brainard & Mould, Music Salon, Fancy Goods and Confectionery" was listed in Norris' Chicago directory of 1847/48 [p17 (adv)]. Both partners, Brooks K. Mould and Henry Mather Brainard, came from Cleveland where, ten years earlier, another house of Brainard & Mould, dealers in music and musical instruments, had done business at 34 Superior Street. Unfortunately, J. P. B. MacCabe's Directory of the Cities of Cleveland & Ohio, 1837/38, did not give the names of the partners, but the membership of the Harmonic Society [p107] included Silas Brainard and Henry J. Mould. Mr. Mould, a native of Chertsey, England, and later of London, had at least four children, Emily, Laura, Brooks and Edmond. In 1840, Emily married Silas Brainard, the rising young music merchant.[2] The next available city directory for Cleveland, Peet's General Business Directory ... 1845-6, listed Henry Brainard as a clerk in his brother Silas' music store, while H. Mould & Sons (B. K. and E. C.) prospered as "manufacturers of candies, confectionery and wholesale dealers in foreign fruits, preserves, pickles, &c." [p7 (adv)].

Henry Mather Brainard, born on June 6 or 8, 1823, in Lempster, N.H., married Laura V. Mould on April 20, 1847, further cementing relations between the two families. During 1847 he and his brother-in-law, Brooks, moved to Chicago, setting themselves up in business at 196 Lake Street in the Merchants' Exchange, where they combined their respective specialties, music and confectionery. No evidence has been found that Brainard & Mould did any publishing, although the firm was in business for several years. A vestige of its career is a rubber stamped phrase "Sold by Brainard & Mould, Chicago" found on a copy of Oh! Share My Cottage Gentle Maid, by R. G. Shrival, published by Frederick D. Benteen, Baltimore. The firm was last listed in Danenhower's Chicago city directory for 1851, although it is likely that it was then out of existence, for the same directory also listed the Chicago Music Store at the same address. H. M. Brainard disappeared from the Chicago scene with this listing, returning to Cleveland and his brother's more prosperous business. Throughout his Chicago career, his ties with Cleveland had remained strong, as indicated by the births of his daughter Alice there in July, 1849, and his son Alfred Henry in August, 1851. Since the only source of information on his movements, the city directories, did not list married women and children, it is not known whether Mrs. Brainard remained in Cleveland during this period or returned home from Chicago for her confinements.

In any case, Knight & Parsons' Cleveland directory for 1853 placed Henry Brainard once more behind the counter of S. Brainard & Co. He died at the age of 31 on May 3, 1855, leaving his widow, two sons and a daughter.

\* \* \*

[1] Chicago American, December 17, 1836, quoted by Bessie L. Pierce, A History of Chicago (New York, A. A. Knopf, 1937) I, 303

[2] Apart from directory information, all facts about the Brainards and their relations with the Mould family were found in Lucy Abigail Brainard's The Genealogy of the Brainerd-Brainard Family in America, 1649-1908. (Hartford Press, 1908) I, 188, 327

When Henry Brainard returned to Cleveland, Edmond Mould joined his brother Brooks in Chicago. His name first appeared in Danenhower's directory for 1851, listing the successor to Brainard & Mould: Chicago Music Store. E. C. Mould, no. 98 Lake Street, dealer in music, musical instruments, music books, etc., piano fortes & patent melodeons [p154 (adv)]. Abandoning the confectionery department, the Mould brothers kept Chicago's first store devoted exclusively to music of which a record has been found. No publications of this firm have been found, and E. C. Mould did not play a conspicuous role in the musical life of Chicago. The exact length of his stay is unknown, but two years later, he was back in Cleveland. Knight & Parsons' directory for 1853 listed him once more with H. Mould & Son, Confectioners, and Boyd's directory for 1857 listed Edmund [sic] C. Mould as senior partner of Mould & Numsen, confectioners. Since there is no evidence that he had any subsequent interest in music or publishing, he need not concern us further.

Brooks K. Mould meanwhile remained in Chicago, continuing a music store at 98 Lake Street and sponsoring a concert series in cooperation with one of Chicago's pioneer musicians, Julius Dyhrenfurth. The first announcement of this project appeared in the Chicago Daily Journal for July 17, 1851 [3:1]. As his music store prospered, B. K. Mould began to publish music, probably the first Chicagoan to do so.

Earlier music had been registered for copyright in Illinois, but none that originated in Chicago. Possibly some of the titles registered were never published, for only one, Peter Long's Western Harp, was listed in Cecil Byrd's Bibliography of Illinois Imprints, 1814-58. Nevertheless the copyright ledgers for the District Court for Illinois listed music books, beginning with The Western Sunday School Psalmody, in Patent Notes, by I. L. (?) Stewart, registered Aug 6 1833. No place of publication or publisher was named. Later came The Melodious Songster ... edited and published by the Rev. E. Knox (no place) registered Dec 17 1836; Evangelical Hymns, arranged by the Rev. Joel Knight (no place) registered Dec 12 1839; The Western Harp, or Hymns, Spiritual Songs and Sacred Poems ... by Peter Long, Greenville, Ill., registered July 12 1848 (copy in the Illinois State Historical Society, Springfield); The Numerical Harp, A Philosophical System of Music Containing A Collection of Choice Church Music ... by W. A. Vertrees (Knoxville, Ill., Winter & Collins) registered Dec 18 1849; and A Collection of Pslams [sic] Hymns and Spiritual Songs, adapted ... by William H. Willeford (printed & published by W. H. Willeford, Williamson County, Ill.) registered Apr 10 1850. The first individual musical composition listed in the copyright records of Illinois was The Song of Night, Quartette by one E. C. Davis (no place) registered Sept 5 1854.

Before discussing B. K. Mould's career as a music publisher, we should consider claims made for other firms to the title of Chicago's first music publisher. In his dissertation, A History of Music Publishing in Chicago, 1850-1960 (Northwestern University, 1961) Theodore W. Thorson claimed priority for S. C. Griggs and Co. on the basis of two songbooks by William B. Bradbury, The Alpine Glee Singer, 1850, and The Singing Bird or Progressive Music Reader, 1852, copies of which bearing S. C. Griggs and Co. imprints are in the Newberry Library. The most comprehensive work available on S. C. Griggs and Co., Jack C. Morris' The Publishing Activities of S. C. Griggs and Company, 1848-1896 ... with lists of publications (Ms. thesis, University of Illinois, 1941) identified both books as courtesy imprints, i.e., indications of firms acting "only as agents for the publisher," handling "the publication in large quantities by special arrangement with the original publisher," whom Mr. Morris identified as "the New York firm of M. H. Newman & Co. (up to 1851), Newman & Ivison (1852-53), Ivison & Phinney (1854-59) ..." [p317]. Earlier Mr. Morris stated unequivocally: "At no time ... did the Chicago firm ever produce the books; the contracts with printers and binders were always carried out in New York; usually the publications were electrotyped by Thomas Smith & Son, and printed by J. D. Bedford & Co., both of New York City," [p24] names appearing on the copy of The Alpine Glee Singer which Mr. Thorson examined. Mr. Morris' list of S. C. Griggs publications included no music whatever.

A more recent work, Cecil K. Byrd's Bibliography of Illinois Imprints, 1814-58 (Chicago, University of Chicago Press, 1966) lists as Item 1766 [p340] a Root & Cady publication, George F. Root's Rock Me to Sleep Mother with a copyright date of 1851. This is either a misreading or a misprint for 1861, the date on copies in the New York Public Library and the Buffalo and Erie County (N.Y.) Public Library. Mr. Byrd's statement: "Chauncy [sic] Marvin Cady and Ebenezer Towner Root were Chicago music publishers as early as 1850," is unsupported here by evidence and is not borne out by any contemporary account that I have seen. As will be shown in the pages to follow, Cady came to Chicago in 1856, Root followed in 1858, and they began publishing in 1859.

The earliest appearance I have seen of B. K. Mould's name in an imprint was on a song arranged by H. Augustus Pond, The Buttonwood Tree at the Door, written by A. E. Drake. Louisville, Ky., F. W. Ratcliffe; Chicago, B. K. Mould [etc., etc., c1851]. The deposit date on the copy in the Library of Congress is June 22, 1852, but it is of little significance for Chicago publishing since a secondary imprint of this kind indicated arrangements for the sale of copies rather than an active publisher.

On January 5, 1854, the Daily Democratic Press of Chicago reported: "We have received from the publisher, B. K. Mould, of this city, a new polka, composed and dedicated to the ladies of the Chicago Philharmonic Society, by it[s] leader and director, C. Plagge ... the 'Garden City Polka' ... The same publisher has also issued a new song, composed by L. D. Hoard, for words by Mrs. M. A. H. ... " The title of the song was not given, but the words were quoted, beginning "Long years have passed since in autumn time." Not entered in the copyright records for Illinois, Christoph Plagge's polka was registered for copyright by B. K. Mould on Dec 27 1853 in the District Court for Southern New York, possibly the location of its engraver. The deposit copy in the Library of Congress with the date of deposit written on its cover is the earliest music publication from Chicago which has been found. Another copy is in the collection of W. N. H. Harding of Chicago.

Mr. Harding also has a copy of L. D. Hoard's Long Years Have Passed, with no copyright claim, although the composer was a local man, apparently the same one who signed legal notices as Clerk of the Cook County Circuit Court. The imprint reads: Chicago, Published by B. K. Mould; Philada, J. E. Gould; Boston, T. T. Barker; Cincinnati, D. A. Truax; Boston, C. C. Clapp & Co.; New York, T. S. Berry. Apparently Mould's standing as a dealer was an asset when he began to publish. The absence of a copyright date makes it futile to attempt to prove that Mr. Hoard's song preceded Mr. Plagge's polka. Another, probably later, edition issued by Oliver Ditson, Boston, also without a copyright claim, is in the Library of Congress; Oliver Ditson was listed as the publisher in the Complete Catalogue of Sheet Music and Musical Works Published by the Board of Music Trade of the United States of America, 1870.

About five weeks after the announcement of the publications, a notice of co-partnership appeared in the Daily Democratic Press [2:7 (adv)] announcing a reorganization of the firm of B. K. Mould:

The undersigned have this day associated themselves in partnership for the transaction of a wholesale and retail business in all kinds of musical merchandise, and for the manufacture of Carhart's Patent Melodeons.

Chicago, Feb. 14, 1854　　　　　　　　　　　　　　　　B. K. Mould
　　　　　　　　　　　　　　　　　　　　　　　　　　R. G. Greene

Mr. Greene was described as "a gentleman well known among the musical profession of this city" in the Tribune for February 22 [3:2], but information about him prior to his entering the firm is sketchy. The Daily Democratic Press for February 1st [3:1] reported his nomination as corresponding secretary of the Young Men's Association, but he was not elected. On May 2, the same paper told of his re-election as secretary of the Chicago Philharmonic Society [3:1]. A notice of his wedding on September 27 to Agnes E. Calder of Providence, appearing in the Democratic Press for October 3 [3:2] serves as convincing identification with the Robert Gorton Greene, mentioned in Louise Brownell Clarke's The Greenes of Rhode Island (New York, 1903, p694). He was born in Providence on September 23, 1829, but no further details of his early life are given.

Mould & Greene made an excellent start. On March 7 an advertisement appearing in the Democratic Press [2:7] made use of four bars of music from Rossini's Semiramide, an innovation for Chicago advertising. On May 8 the Press mentioned a publication from the new house, La Corinna, a song without words by a local man, Henry E. Lippert [3:1] and, on July 19 [3:1] the Rescue Grand March by the same composer. The extent of the business was indicated in an article on August 14 [3:2] describing the store which occupied the whole of the three story building at 98 Lake Street, except for a "small part of the second."

The first or ground floor ... is devoted to the retail and jobbing department for sheet music, books, violins, violoncellos, &c. ... On the second floor is the wareroom for melodeons ... The third story which is tastefully fitted up, and hung about with choice engravings ... the portraits of a number of noted musicians and composers, is wholly filled with a splendid stock of piano fortes ...

Within a short time, however, the partners seem to have modified their relationship. In the Tribune for April 25, 1855 [2:7], an advertisement for piano fortes was signed: R. G. Greene, 98 Lake Street. On the 30 of April, B. K. Mould advertised pianos to rent from the same address [2:8], while on May 1, tickets were "sold at Mould & Greene" [3:1]. Although no formal announcement of the dissolution of the partnership has been found, Mould was listed as clerk for R. G. Greene in Hall's Chicago directory for

5

1855. Beginning with the issue for May 3, 1855 [3:3], the Tribune printed a number of notices of new music received from "R. G. Greene, 98 Lake Street." A confusing item in the Tribune for June 25 [3:2] announced that Mould & Greene had just published two pieces, Dearest, Good Night, by L. D. Hoard and Lilly Day, by George P. Graff. Nor was this editorial nodding, for the copy of Lilly Day, no. 4 of the series, Melodies of the Moonlight Harmonists, in the Library of Congress, bears the imprint of Mould & Greene. Since no later reference to that firm has been found, it seems at least possible that these pieces were prepared earlier. At any rate, on August 20, the Democratic Press announced that R. G. Greene, then of 74 Lake Street, had issued a catalogue of the music he "has on hand."

With R. G. Greene finally established as head of the firm, the business became increasingly active. On June 25, the Tribune commented that Mr. Greene, on an eastern visit, was making arrangements to have his music printed in Chicago. It is possible that the three publications announced on November 8 in the Democratic Press were home products in manufacture as well as in composition. One was a Valse Brillante by Franz Staab, Chicago pianist and teacher, and two were by L. D. Hoard.

During 1855, R. G. Greene also began to manufacture melodeons, employing twenty workmen in his factory.[3] Another ambitious project was the launching of Volume I, Number 1 of the Western Journal of Music, edited by William H. Currie, published on Saturday, May 31, 1856. It was described as a bi-weekly, published on alternate Saturdays in issues of eight pages by the New York Musical Review and Gazette [7 (June 14 1856) 178]. Three issues were deposited for copyright on June 30, the last dated June 28, but the deposit copies have not been found. As late as September, The Evangelist, a religious paper published in New York, referred to it as if it were still being published: "... subscription price one dollar a year ... Each number contains also one or more pieces of well printed music, besides articles of criticism and instruction in various matters pertaining to music. So far the Journal seems to be well sustained ..." [27 (Sept 25 1856) 154]. It is not certain whether this was the first musical journal published in Chicago, for Higgins Brothers issued the first number of The Flower Queen [cf p8] at about the same time. No issues of the Higgins magazine were deposited for copyright, but its publication was announced in the Daily Chicago Times for May 28, 1856 [3:1], as promised "in a few days," and a long review appeared in the Times for June 4 [3:2]. No copies of this journal have been found either.

In 1856, R. G. Greene was elected president of the reorganized Philharmonic Society. He was a man of energy, who might have occupied an important position in the musical history of Chicago had he not died at the age of 28 on November 23, 1857. The listing in Cooke's Chicago directory for 1858 for Robert G. Greene, real estate, may refer to another man or may be the only indication found that he left the music trade before his death.

In 1854, a competitor to Mould & Greene was opened by one Herbert Brabant, as Brabant & Co., music and fancy goods, 70 Lake Street, successor to S. W. Marsh, a short-lived dealer who did no publishing. During Brabant's short career of approximately two years, he published some music, although none of his titles were registered for copyright in Northern Illinois. Two of his publications were mentioned in the Tribune for February 3, 1855 [2:3], The Light Guard Polka and Schottisch, both by Franz Staab. I have not found copies of either of these, but Do They Love Us Yet? by A. Marechal (another local musician, recently arrived from France in 1855) is in the University of Illinois Library. It bears the imprint: Published by H. Brabant, Chicago; G. P. Reed & Co., Boston; Wm. Hall & Son, New York; and a copyright claim for 1855 in the District Court of Illinois. These three titles are the only Brabant publications of which a record has been found. The disposition of his plates could hardly have been a big transaction. The Board of Music Trade Catalogue, 1870, did not list the Marechal title, and the Staab pieces were listed as publications of Root & Cady. No connection between Brabant and Root & Cady should be presumed; it is quite possible that the composer acquired the plates and later disposed of them. After 1856, Brabant disappeared from the Chicago scene; no information of his subsequent career has been found.

Following R. G. Greene's withdrawal from the music trade, B. K. Mould opened a new store at 83 Lake Street. Gager's Chicago City Directory for the Year Ending June 1st, 1857, listed B. K. Mould & Co. at that address, while Case & Co.'s directory for the same period located the firm at 70 Lake Street. Notices of his publications appearing in the Times in November and December, 1856, support the address at 83.

*   *   *

---

[3] Fourth Annual Review of the Commerce, Railroad, and Manufactures of Chicago for the Year 1855. (Chicago, Democratic Press Steam Printing House, 1856) p41

Probably his most interesting publication in its associations was the Wau-Bun Galop, by Antonio de Anguera, issued in 1856, dedicated to Mrs. John H. Kinzie, the authoress of Wau-Bun, or Early Days in the North-west, a classic reminiscence of pioneer Chicago. In 1858, Brooks K. Mould's music store was at 104 Lake Street. After that year his movements are difficult to chart, since we are dependent on city directories which give incomplete and sometimes contradictory information. The Chicago directories did not list him, 1859-61; Brooks Mould, book keeper, was listed in J. H. Williston & Co.'s Cleveland directory for 1861/62, boarding with his brother Edmund [sic] at 54 Ontario. In 1862, one B. R. Mould, commission merchant, was listed in Chicago; since the surname was fairly uncommon and Brooks K. Mould was listed in 1863, it seems safe to assume the R. a misprint. His last appearance in the Chicago directories was in 1866: B. K. Mould, bkpr.

The plates which had belonged to R. G. Greene, B. K. Mould, and Mould & Greene must have been sold piecemeal. One title bearing a B. K. Mould copyright claim, Antonio de Anguera's Soldier's Dream Polka Militaire, is found in the New York Public Library with the imprint of Higgins Brothers. Another, Florence Whitmore's Emerald Schottisch, with an H. M. Higgins imprint, is owned by W. N. H. Harding, of Chicago. Several titles were listed in the Board of Music Trade Catalogue, 1870: the Wau-Bun Galop as the property of D. P. Faulds, Louisville; L. D. Hoard's Nocturne and Franz Staab's Valse Brillante, Oliver Ditson, Boston; and George Graff's Lilly Day and Staab's Amelia Mazurka, John Church, Cincinnati. Other titles apparently did not sell well enough to justify their being in print in 1870, and no information of their disposition is available.

In 1855 while R. G. Greene was arranging to have his music printed in Chicago, a new firm, Higgins Brothers made its first appearance on the Chicago scene. Whether Mr. Greene appreciated the significance of this event is doubtful, but Higgins Brothers and its successors, A. J. Higgins and H. M. Higgins was to prove second only to Root & Cady in importance among the pre-fire music publishers of Chicago. The history of the family, sketched in Katharine Chapin Higgins' Richard Higgins ... and His Descendants (Worcester, Mass., Printed for the Author, 1918, p591-2) begins with Seth Higgins "ancestry undetermined," who was born about 1796 at Sherburne, N.Y. He and his wife (name unknown) lived first at Warsaw, N.Y., where four children were born, moved to Laona, N.Y., where eight more children were born, and then moved to Palmyra, Wis. The dates on which the various children were born were not given; Hiram Murray was the second, Thomas Metcalf, the fifth, Adoniram Judson, the sixth, and Elizabeth (or Libbie) the eighth. The others need not concern us.

The earliest contemporary notice of the Higgins family which I have found dates from January, 1850. Organized into a concert troupe of the type so popular at that time, two brothers and two sisters known as the Higgins Family or the "Columbians" were touring Kentucky. Reviews from the Lexington Statesman for January 28 and the Louisville Courier for January 31, praised their manner of execution and the elevating and refining influence of their "exhibition." [Quoted in The American Monthly Musical Review, and Choir Singers' Companion, 1 (July 1 1850) 70 and (Sept 1 1850) 103]. The identity of the four is uncertain; probably the brothers were Adoniram Judson and Hiram Murray. One of the sisters must have been Elizabeth, who was musical; the other might have been either Sarah, the third child, or Harriet, the seventh. In any case, neither Sarah nor Harriet reappeared in the musical history of the Higgins'.

Three years later the New-York Musical Review and Choral Advocate [5 (Feb 2 1854) 44] reported: "A. J. Higgins has several large music classes in the vicinity of Harrodsburg, Ky. He is enterprising and capable. Success to him!" In April a dispatch from Lacon, Ill., dated the 10th, spoke of him as being "one of the best teachers they have ever had. He came here about a year ago, and taught one course of twenty lessons..." From this it seems that the concert troupe had disbanded. The dispatch reported further: "Some of our Western teachers are now on their way to New-York to attend the Musical Institute. Among the numbers are Messrs. A. J. and H. M. Higgins. T. M. Higgins is already there" [5:139]. While her brothers were studying with Lowell Mason and George F. Root in New York, Miss Libbie Higgins, "recently one of the popular troupe called 'Columbians,'" was married in Milwaukee on July 20, to James E. Browne, Esq., of Quincy, Ill. [Ibid 5:277]. Libbie did not long remain only a housewife, however. In 1858, Higgins Brothers, Chicago, published The Valentine; or, The Spirit of Song, by Miss Libbie Higgins. Eleven years later, Root & Cady published for the composer numbers 5 and 6 of her Songs of Affection, a series begun by De Motte Brothers. These two songs, My Barefoot Boy and Thy Spirit Will Ever Be Near (dedicated to my much loved brother, A. J. Higgins, lately deceased), she published as Mrs. E. H. Jackson. In 1874, Brainard's Musical World [11 (Oct 1874) 150] praised her ability as a vocal teacher and her skill in drilling and organizing choirs and teaching harmony and thorough bass. She had two children, Ernest Higgins Jackson and Leonora Jackson, a pupil of Joachim and a violinist of some reputation at the turn of the century. Elizabeth Higgins Jackson died in Brooklyn in June, 1916, aged 85.

To return to 1855, sometime during that year, Adoniram Judson and Hiram Murray Higgins settled in Chicago and opened a music store at 54 Randolph Street. An advertisement for Higgins Brothers first appeared in the Democratic Press for July 28 [2:6]. Before the end of the year the firm began to publish music, depositing I Have No Mother Now, by Franz Staab for copyright on October 29. Two months later, on December 28, four more compositions were deposited, one by T. M. Higgins and two by Joseph Philbrick Webster, the clergyman from Elkhorn, Wis., who was to write some of Higgins' most successful songs. His first Higgins publications bear typical titles: Oh Scorn Not Thy Brother and They Buried Her under the Old Elm Tree.

An advertisement in the Daily Chicago Times for January 1, 1856 [3:8], first inserted on September 19, 1855, stated that Higgins Brothers were "Dealers in all kinds of musical instruments, sole agents for Light [sic] Newton & Bradbury's piano fortes ... a large assortment of Instruction Books for all ... musical instruments; also, Guitar and Violin Strings ... Melodeons, Guitars, Violins, Accordeons, Flutinas, Flutes and Brass Instruments ... Piano Stools ..." The vigor with which Higgins Brothers pushed their instruments was demonstrated in a story from the Times for April 18, 1856 [3:1], telling of the enthusiasm of the brothers for the Lighte, Newton & Bradbury piano:

> One of these pianos has recently been subjected to a most severe test. Four or five months ago, it was placed in the parlor of one of our wealthy citizens, where it has ever since been exposed to the heat of a large grate on one side, and a hot air furnace on the other. All the other furniture in the room felt and showed the effects of this heat. The cracks of the door parted more than a quarter of an inch. Tables and chairs cracked and shrank. But the piano is intact! Not the slightest crack is discernible. The reason is evident. It was made by ARTISTS ...

On May 16, the arrival in Chicago of William C. Webster, a successful music teacher from Buffalo was announced in the Times [3:1]. His headquarters was at Higgins' store, a normal arrangement for those days when music stores were centers for all sorts of musical activity, receiving mail for itinerant teachers and selling concert tickets as well as sheet music. If Webster had no previous acquaintance with either Higgins, they lost no time in planning a joint undertaking. Less than two weeks later, the Times told of Messrs. Higgins' plan to issue a new monthly paper, with Mr. Webster as editor. It was to be called The Flower Queen, after George F. Root's popular cantata [cf p18]. "It will be in quarto form, and devoted to the interests of music, the dissemination of musical knowledge, and the cultivation of correct musical taste" [May 28 1856 3:1]. A year's subscription was to cost only 50 cents. The editorial evangelism of Mr. Webster was illustrated in a quotation reprinted in the Times of June 4:

> ... let our children be taught to sing songs full of pointed meaning, illustrated from nature, the grand inspirer of pure and living thought! Let us have songs of the sunset and the sunrise; songs of the stars and gentler moon; songs of the warbling birds, the lowing herds, the humming insects, and the fragrant breathing flowers; ... songs of the ever varying seasons, and each adapted to convey some pointed moral to the heart. Let us have songs reproving evil passions; and songs alluring to the sweeter practice of every virtue; songs of reproof, of counsel and instruction, with grateful hymns of praise and adoration ... [3:2].

In anticipation of a ready market for such sound sentiments, the publishers had 10,000 copies of the June number printed [New-York Musical Review and Gazette 7 (June 14 1856) 178].

Higgins Brothers was fast becoming Chicago's most successful music dealer and publisher. In July the firm advertised that it was sole wholesale and retail agents for the publications of Nathan Richardson, Boston [Daily Chicago Times, July 11 1856 3:2 (adv)]. The extent of the business was indicated by its expansion from a store to a four-story building, formerly occupied by a livery stable. The news of the remodeling of the building appeared in the Times for October 17, 1856 [3:1], but an announcement of the firm's removal to the new quarters did not appear until March 31, 1858 [2:3 (adv)].

While still in the old store at 54 Randolph Street, Higgins Brothers further demonstrated the firm's growing importance, by reorganizing its monthly paper, The Flower Queen, into the more pretentious magazine its new name indicated - The Chicago Musical Review and Flower-Queen, under a new editor. As with Webster, it is difficult to decide whether the new editor, C. M. Cady, came to Chicago to edit Higgins' magazine or whether they engaged him after his arrival. The earliest he is known to have been in Chicago was September 20, 1856, the date of an issue of the New-York Musical Review and Gazette, announcing that he had moved to Chicago. "His address at present is: 'Care of Higgins Brothers, Chicago, Ill.'" [7 (Sept 20 1856) 289]. The change in editor and the plans for putting the magazine on a permanent basis were approved by the Times for October 26 [3:2]. Previously editor of the New York Musical Review, Cady must have been regarded as a desirable addition to the firm's staff.

Around April 1, 1858, Higgins Brothers moved into the "splendid iron-front" store at 45 Lake Street, between State and Wabash Avenue. From all indications, their retail and wholesale trade was prosperous, and their publications were selling well. J. P. Webster's Lorena, published in 1856, was a national favorite, and continued to be so popular in the South during the Civil War that pirated editions were published in the Confederacy. [Cf Confederate Literature: A List of Books and Newspapers, Maps, Music and Miscellaneous Matter Printed in the South During the Confederacy ... Prepared by Charles N. Baxter and James M. Dearborn. (Boston, The Boston Athenaeum, 1917)]. The general level of Higgins' publications was comparable to that of other publishers in the South and West. With the exception of a few songs by Schubert and similar non-copyright pieces, the Higgins catalog consisted entirely of sentimental or comic ballads, patriotic and topical songs, dances, marches and reveries for piano. Although the Chicago press usually approved of this type of music, the Times on one occasion deplored those "flat, stale and unprofitable productions, yclept sheet music ... from Higgins Brothers ... which ... bear a corresponding relation to music that the 'yellow covered' publications of the day bear to literature" [Oct 10 1858 3:1].

Early in 1859, without warning, the dissolution of Higgins Brothers was announced in the Tribune [1:7 (adv)]:

> The Co-partnership heretofore existing between H. M. Higgins and A. J. Higgins under the name and style of Higgins Brothers is this day dissolved by mutual consent. H. M. Higgins assumes all the liabilities of the late firm, and to whom all debts must be paid.
>
> Chicago, February 1, 1859      H. M. Higgins
>      A. J. Higgins
>
> H. M. Higgins returns his thanks to his customers for past favors and hopes by strict attention to business to merit their future patronage.
>      My stock is by far the largest and most complete in the Northwest.
>      New music received weekly from all the eastern publishers.
>      My catalogue of my own publications is now the finest of any published in the United States, to which I am constantly adding from the best composers in the Eastern and Western states.
>
>      H. M. Higgins
>      45 Lake Street

A. J. Higgins was not listed in D. B. Cooke & Co.'s City Directory for the Year 1859-60, but the Tribune for November 6, 1860 [1:7], told of his publishing and selling music at 49 Clark Street. The disposition of the assets of Higgins Brothers is unclear. Only an inference can be drawn from a comparison of catalogs appearing as advertisements on the back covers of the publications of the two succeeding firms. In the University of Illinois Library a "Select Catalogue of Music Published by A. Judson Higgins" is to be found on the verso of p5 of Mabel Clare, by A. J. Higgins (Chicago, A. J. Higgins, c1861) and a similar "Select Catalogue of Sheet Music Published by H. M. Higgins" is on the verso of p5 of H. C. Work's Brave Boys Are They! (Chicago, H. M. Higgins, c1861). These catalogs list so many of the same titles that one is forced to conclude the brothers must have had some arrangement for issuing the same songs and piano music under separate imprints.

The Tribune for November 19, 1861 [1:7 (adv)], carried the first advertisement of the successor to A. J. Higgins, E. H. Patterson. Ezra H. Patterson was listed in Halpin & Bailey's directory for 1861/62 as bookkeeper for A. J. Higgins; the following year he was listed as accountant to Woodruff & Rosseter, Commission Merchants, so his career in the music trade was short. There is no evidence that he owned, even temporarily, the plates which had been Higgins'. A few titles copyrighted by A. J. Higgins have been found with the imprint of H. M. Higgins, giving a clue as to the disposition of his plates. Halpin & Bailey's directory for 1862/63 listed A. Judson Higgins as a commission merchant, and in 1865 "A. J. Higgins, physician" was listed. Doubts as to the identity of the physician are removed by the listing of Adoniram Judson Higgins in Richard Higgins ... and His Descendants as a physician who lived in Chicago "at one time." No mention is made of his music publishing activities. He died in Martinsburg, Mo., in 1869.

H. M. Higgins, meanwhile, prospered as a music dealer and publisher. Early in 1860 he moved to a new and presumably larger store in the Kingsbury Block at 117 Randolph Street. The Tribune for April 19 [1:2], observed that the "elegant" new building was nearly finished and about to be occupied by tenants which included, besides Higgins, "Peugeot as a Fancy and Variety store ... Oakley as a Tobacco and Segar store. The beautiful Concert Hall will be opened and dedicated next week." H. M. Higgins continued in this location through 1867. George P. Upton's statement in his Musical Memories [p271] that Root & Cady were "successors to H. M. Higgins" can be accepted only as applying to his position as the leading music dealer and publisher in the Northwest.

Five years after the formation of Root & Cady, H. M. Higgins was its closest competitor. The Tribune for April 2, 1863 [4:2], told of his new catalog, "a handsome pamphlet of thirty-two pages, giving a sketch of the enterprise itself; a brief biography of J. R. [sic] Webster, whose compositions are the exclusive property of this house, and a list of one hundred and fifty other composers, whose pieces are issued and copyrighted by Mr. Higgins ..." Possibly the catalog so described was the Quarterly Circular of H. M. Higgins Music Publishing House, a copy of which is bound with The Patriotic Glee Book, c1863, in the New York Public Library. This Circular includes a biography of Webster [p[3]-5], a puff of the firm, and a list of publications. Over a year later, the Tribune for July 3, 1864 [4:1], described the complete redecoration of the Higgins store, "increasing the facilities of his extensive trade. He is now the oldest music house in the city ..."

Not until 1867 did Higgins cease publishing, and then he did not sell his stock and plates to Root & Cady, but to J. L. Peters, of St. Louis. The announcement in the Tribune for May 29, 1867 [1:7 (adv)], read:

> Notice is hereby given that I have sold my stock of sheet music and books to Mr. J. L. Peters of St. Louis.
>
> I shall continue the sale of pianos, organs, melodeons, guitars, violins, accordeons, flutinas, drums, violincellos [sic] and all kinds of instruments, strings, &c., at the old place, 117 Randolph St. ...
>
> Send 75 cents, and get a copy of Higgins' Musical Review for one year ... Pianos to rent.

During the period from 1866 to 1868, H. M. Higgins acted as supervisor of the community of Hyde Park, where lived the Roots, the Cadys, and the Works. [A. T. Andreas, History of Cook County, Illinois ... (Chicago, 1884) p514-16].

The sale of the Higgins catalog was later described in The Presto [12 (Sept 19 1895) 23]:

> ... members of the Chicago trade will remember Mr. DeMotte as one of the two rosy-cheeked young men who came from New York in '68 to succeed the old house of H. M. Higgins. J. L. Peters, then at the zenith of his success as a music publisher, had bought the Higgins stock and catalogue, and the DeMotte Bros., in turn purchased the stock from Peters. The firm of DeMotte Bros. was then established at 91 Washington Street, where it continued for several years.

In an advertisement on p63 of T. E. Zell & Co.'s Guide to the City of Chicago, 1868, DeMotte Brothers called themselves "Successors to H. M. Higgins, music publishers, wholesale & retail dealers in all kinds of sheet music, books and musical instruments."

As for Higgins, he continued to sell pianos and other instruments for several years after the sale of his music catalog. His last listing in a Chicago directory was in Edwards' Annual Directory for 1869, where he was designated "piano mnfr. and wine mer." The usually dependable George Upton stated that he "became so engrossed with table tipping and spooks that his business was soon at loose ends. I met him many years afterwards at his ranch in Southern California where he was experimenting with seedless lemons" [Musical Memories, p271].

After leaving Chicago, Higgins eventually settled in San Diego. His residence there in 1879 was recorded when he contributed 40 acres to the subsidy offered the Atchison, Topeka and Santa Fe Railroad as an inducement to make San Diego its western terminus. [Cf William E. Smythe's History of San Diego, 1542-1907 ... (San Diego, The History Company, 1907) p396-8]. He died in San Diego on July 6, 1897, according to an obituary in the Musical Visitor [26 (Aug 1897) 221].

The DeMotte brothers first announced their purchase of the "large stock of Sheet Music formerly owned by Mr. H. M. Higgins" and the opening of their store at 91 Washington Street in the Tribune of

August 23, 1867 [1:9 (adv)]. Evidently Higgins' plates were not included in this sale. Two songs by J. P. Webster, copyrighted by Higgins, Lorena and Don't Be Sorrowful, Darling, were reissued by J. L. Peters with a secondary imprint for DeMotte Bro's., Chicago. Copies of these editions are in the University of Illinois Library. The secondary imprints on other Peters publications appear in two forms: DeMotte Bros. and T. G. DeMotte. DeMotte Bros. registered a few titles for copyright, the first being Farewell False Heart, by Jas. E. Haynes, filed October 22, 1868. In all probability the few plates they issued were later sold to J. L. Peters, with their stock.

Two brothers were listed in the directory for 1868, A. Huyler and Thomas G., and a third, Edgar M., joined them in 1869. During the two years the firm was in business, it frequently had secondary imprints on the publications of J. L. Peters, for whom it seems to have been the Chicago agent. In November, 1869, Peters' Musical Monthly published an announcement from J. L. Peters that he had purchased the "Stock of sheet-music, music-books and musical instruments owned by DeMotte Brothers, of Chicago, Ill., and have removed the same to No. 599 Broadway, New York ..." [4 (Nov 1869) 200]. The Peters firm was going through a period of rapid expansion at this time, absorbing other firms in quick succession. The previous February, Peters' Musical Monthly had announced the purchase of the plates belonging to A. E. Blackmar and J. J. Dobmeyer & Co., together with the stock of Blackmar's New York store and Dobmeyer's St. Louis store.

Two of the DeMotte brothers remained in the music trade after the closing of their Chicago store. Thomas eventually became manager of the New York office of the John Church Co., a position he occupied at the time of his death in 1886 [The Musical Visitor 15 (Oct 1886) 260]. In 1883 Edgar was employed by the Roe Stephens Music Co. in Detroit, after a period with S. T. Gordon & Son, New York, according to the Musical People [7 (June 1 1883) 13]. Later in 1895, The Presto reported his movements in California, where he had just left Waldteufel's music department to go to the Pacific Music Co. [12 (Sept 18 1895) 23].

The only music publisher of pre-fire Chicago to survive into the twentieth century was Lyon & Healy. Its importance merits far more attention then can be devoted to it here, but, since most of its career came after 1871, it may fairly be considered beyond the scope of this work. All that will be attempted here is an outline of the events before the fire.

In Lyon & Healy's anniversary brochure, Seventy-five Years of Everything Known in Music, c1940, the story is told of how Oliver Ditson sent for two of his clerks, Patrick Healy and George Washburn Lyon, offering to set them up in business in Chicago, St. Louis, or San Francisco as an outlet for Ditson publications. Having chosen Chicago, the partners were discouraged on their arrival in May, 1864, by the "muddy country village with its ramshackle business section rising from the mire on stilts." The attempt to raise the level of the city which had impressed George F. Root in 1858 [cf p33] was still in progress. While Lyon grew nostalgic for the amenities of Boston, Healy assembled the stock for their "little shop." So runs the official story.

The Tribune for 1864 spent little space in heralding the new firm. Occasional advertisements of Oliver Ditson & Co., offering to sell direct by mail continued to appear, one each on October 13 [1:6] and October 25 [3:7], neither of them mentioning Ditson's new outlet, which (according to the official story) opened its doors on the morning of October 14. A notice of Smith & Nixon, with whom Lyon & Healy shared the "little shop" appeared on the 15th [1:6] and, on the 20th, Lyon & Healy advertised 100 new pianos for rent, describing themselves as agency for Steinway's piano [1:7]. Actually, Smith & Nixon were the Steinway agents.

Finally, on November 4, Lyon & Healy published an advertisement describing the scope of the "NEW MUSIC STORE."

> ... Lyon & Healy, music publishers, importers and dealers in sheet music, musical works and musical merchandise of every description. Northwestern agency and wholesale depot for the musical publications of Oliver Ditson & Co., Boston. Their publications furnished to the trade without any advance whatever on the net Boston prices ... the issues of all the American music publishers ... foreign music and musical works.... musical instruments and strings ... melodeons, harmoniums and cottage organs ... [1:7].

The impression one receives from the Tribune is that Smith & Nixon was the more affluent firm of the two, and that Lyon & Healy was fortunate to acquire such an important connection. "The elegant store forming the entrance to the new Music Hall of Messrs. Smith & Nixon," extolled the paper for December 12 [4:1], "with premises extremely elegant and well-lighted." The "little shop" seemed not so little in 1864.

Beside acting as Ditson's western agent, Lyon & Healy began to publish independently almost immediately.  On December 30, 1864, the firm registered its first piece for copyright, <u>Dear Mother the Battle is Over</u>, Song & Chorus, by Henry Foutrill.  It is beyond the scope of this work to unravel the intricacies of the relationship between Lyon & Healy and Oliver Ditson.  Apparently Lyon & Healy never joined the Board of Music Trade, although this publication was listed in the Board's <u>Catalogue</u> of 1870 as a Ditson product.  Possibly Ditson listed all Lyon & Healy publications because of the close relationship between them.  In any case, Lyon & Healy was certainly an active publisher as late as 1871, as witness numerous advertisements for publications in the firm's house organ, <u>The Musical Independent</u> for 1871.

In 1869, the store outgrown by the expanding business, Lyon & Healy and Smith & Nixon, still closely associated, moved to a new location in the Drake Block at the corner of Washington Street and Wabash Avenue.  Lyon & Healy's sales now amounted to about half a million dollars for the year, according to <u>The Musical Independent</u> for April, 1870 [2 (Apr 1870) 55].  Then came a devastating fire, foreshadowing the disaster of 1871.  In September the Drake's Block was reduced to a heap of ruins, destroying the entire stock of sheet music and books, valued at $200,000 and only partially covered with insurance.  While the fire was still in progress, telegrams were sent to Boston and New York, ordering new stock to be shipped immediately.  Both firms moved into the store at 150 Clark Street, lately occupied by H. M. Higgins, and "so forbidding that one would scarcely imagine that any beauty could be developed in such a soil" [op cit 3 (Jan 1871) 9 and 2 (Sept 1870) 134-5].  Root & Cady came to the aid of the distressed firm, placing its own stocks at Lyon & Healy's disposal, to assist in filling orders.  The setback proved only temporary, and, in the spring of 1871, the firm was able to absorb the business of Smith & Nixon, becoming Steinway & Sons' sole representative in the area.

Forbidding or not, Lyon & Healy remained at 150 South Clark Street until the Great Fire of October, 1871.  More fortunate than their competitors, Lyon & Healy were able to empty their safe of all its valuable contents - money, bills receivable and insurance policies - before the building went up in flames.  "So shrewdly had the insurance been placed that the house of Lyon & Healy realized practically all the face of the policies and the comparatively new concern was able to go on where scores of old established firms were swept away."  Here the official brochure can be supplemented by accounts in contemporary periodicals.  <u>Church's Musical Visitor</u> reported that Lyon & Healy's loss was total.  "All their valuable plates and stock ... being completely swept away.  For the present their business is transferred to their parent house (Oliver Ditson & Co., of Boston).  These gentlemen have our most sincere sympathy, and we trust they will be able ere long to resume business."  This misfortune was contrasted with Root & Cady's luck in being able to salvage its music and book plates.  A similar story appeared in <u>The Metronome</u> for November, 1871 [1 (Nov 1871) 58].  The transfer of the business to Ditson's home office must have been a very temporary arrangement, for the "Fire edition" of Edward's Chicago directory, with listings as of December 12, 1871, gave Lyon & Healy's new address, 287 W. Madison.  The movements and successes of the firm from 1872 on are part of the post-fire period beyond the scope of this history.

There remain a number of minor firms to consider.  Hiram T. Merrill, a native of New Hampshire, first came to public notice as a music teacher in Galena, Illinois.  Notices of concerts by his pupils appeared in the <u>New-York Musical Review and Gazette</u> [10 (Jan 22 1859) 18 and 10 (July 23 1859) 225].  An invention of his, the "Gamut-Board," an aid to the would-be pianist, was described in the issue of July 9 [10 (July 9 1859) 210].  He was first mentioned in the Chicago <u>Tribune</u> on August 8, 1862, the day after he had registered a song, <u>Corn Is King</u>! for copyright.  At that time he was principal of an Academy of Music as well as a music dealer.  Between April 11, 1865, when the last advertisement for H. T. Merrill appeared, and May 9, he formed a partnership with John H. Brennan, as Merrill & Brennan, music publishers and dealers in musical instruments.  The details of the firm's publishing career will be given later [cf p61]; but by 1866, Edwards' directory listed John H. Brennan as a piano forte manufacturer, while H. T. Merrill & Co. continued to deposit publications for copyright.  By 1870 Brennan had abandoned the manufacture of pianos for the proprietorship of a saloon.  Merrill's new partner was not identified in the city directories.  Late in 1868 or early in 1869, H. T. Merrill sold his plates to Root & Cady, concentrating thereafter on teaching, leading choirs, and playing the organ.  In March, 1870, his work at the Clark Street M. E. Church received favorable notice in the <u>Musical Independent</u> [2 (Mar 1870) 43].  Eight years later his application for relief in bankruptcy was mentioned by the <u>Music Trade Review</u> [6 (May 3 1878) 24].  No further information about him has been found, save the negative fact that his heirs claimed renewal of his copyrights in 1891.

Sometime during 1863 Alanson Reed began to sell music and instruments at 88 & 90 Randolph Street.  A. T. Andreas' claim in his <u>History of Chicago</u> [2:595-6] that Reed's business was established in 1842 has not been born out in contemporary newspapers, periodicals or directories.  Andreas' account, written during Reed's lifetime, stated that Alanson Reed was born in Warren, Mass., on November 13, 1814.  After being apprenticed to a cabinet-maker, he went to work in the Chickering factory in Boston, and "mastered everything connected with the manufacture of pianos." In 1837, he left Chickering's and began activities as a dealer. His name first appeared in the Chicago directories in 1863 as Alanson Reed, piano dealer, changing in 1864 to Reed's Temple of Music. In 1866, his two sons, Alanson H. and John Warner Reed were admitted into the partnership, the firm becoming Alanson Reed & Sons, which it remained through 1875, the last year for which directories were checked. An advertisement appearing in the Chicago Tribune for November 8, 1864 [1:7], announced: "We have added a sheet music department to our establishment and are now PUBLISHING NEW MUSIC daily." The story of Reed's publishing activities and his relations with Florenz Ziegfeld, Ziegfeld & Willson and Ziegfeld & Gerard will be told later in Chapter V.

Still another minor publisher, John Molter, was born on April 4, 1832, at Treves (Trier).[4] After a traditional German musical education in the musical school of the local cathedral and the teachers' seminary in Bruehl, he was appointed principal of a public school and leader of church music in a small country town. Wishing for speedier advancement than Germany could offer, he emigrated in 1856, first to Canada, where he spent a year teaching singing schools and giving concerts. In the spring of 1857, he arrived in Chicago, and soon he was busy as a music teacher, leader of several German singing societies and organist of the First Unitarian Church.

On October 13, 1863, the Chicago Tribune published an advertisement announcing the opening of a new music store under the management of John Molter [1:8]. The Chicago directory for 1864 listed John Molter, dealer in pianos and musical instruments, at 104 Randolph. Before the next directory was issued, Molter had entered into a partnership with Rudolph Wurlitzer, of Cincinnati, as Molter & Wurlitzer, importers and dealers in musical instruments, and on May 9, 1865, the Tribune told of the firm's moving from 136 Clark Street to 82 Dearborn [1:9 (adv)]. Subsequent addresses for the firm were 111 and 117 Randolph. Sometime before the fire of 1871, the partnership was dissolved, for the directory for 1871 listed only "John Molter, piano fortes" at 117 Randolph. Although the store was listed in the directories for 1872-74, it was a declining enterprise, and Andreas stated unequivocally that Molter lost all his profits in the fire.

Publications bearing the imprint of Molter & Wurlitzer were registered for copyright, beginning with Molter's The Famous Grecian Bend, filed October 29, 1868. John Molter published some works, notably an edition of Beethoven's Adelaide, but none of his publications were registered for copyright in Northern Illinois. Possibly they were all in the public domain. Molter & Wurlitzer's catalog was largely composed of music in the German tradition by such men as Otto Lob, Julius Huneman, and John Molter himself, plus titles by George W. Brown, who wrote under the pseudonym of Geo. Persley. A good many, if not all, of the plates were acquired by Root & Cady in 1871, if the evidence of the plate numbers assigned by the new owner can be trusted. Molter & Wurlitzer copyrights have been found with Root & Cady plate numbers between 6121 and 6167, immediately preceded by 6117, filed July 5, 1871, and followed by 6169, filed June 6, 1871.

After he left the music trade in 1879, Molter remained active as an organist and teacher of voice, organ, and piano. His compositions published by his own firm, Root & Cady and H. M. Higgins were piano pieces and vocal music, including the Patriotic Glee Book, which he compiled during the war. Before leaving Germany, he had written a number of masses, "Manner choruses" and school songs which apparently remained unpublished as were a group of his later compositions, psalms and sacred music for quartet choir with English, German and Hebrew text.

The music publishers of pre-fire Chicago had much in common with their competitors in other cities of the United States. The difficulties in communication between various parts of the country encouraged the growth of local publishers who served primarily the immediate neighborhood. The types of publications issued will be discussed in more detail in connection with the firm of Root & Cady, the most important of the pre-fire firms and yet fairly typical in its interests. In the chapters that follow, the career of Root & Cady will be examined in detail, giving a rounded picture of a mid-nineteenth century music publisher in the United States.

\*   \*   \*

[4] This account is based on that in A. T. Andreas' History of Chicago (Chicago, A. T. Andreas Co., 1886) III, 640, published while Molter was still living.

## CHAPTER II

### THE PARTNERS

THE PARTNERS

Among the firms which published music in Chicago before 1871, Root & Cady was outstanding in the volume of its business and the quality of its publications. A major factor contributing to the influence and success of the firm was the character of the partners who composed it. An account of their careers is therefore an appropriate prologue to the history of the firm.

### GEORGE FREDERICK ROOT, 1820-1895

The facts of the life of George Frederick Root, composer of *The Battle Cry of Freedom*, *Tramp, Tramp, Tramp* and *The Vacant Chair*, are too well known to require detailed retelling. Since his autobiography and numerous shorter biographical sketches are available, only a brief account of his career, emphasizing aspects pertinent to the firm of Root & Cady, will be given here.[1]

He was born in Sheffield, Massachusetts, August 20, 1820, the first child of Sarah Flint and Frederick Ferdinand Root. The Roots and their eight children were all musical, despite the isolation at Willow Farm in North Reading to which they moved in 1826. Young Frederick became adept at picking out tunes on any instrument he could find in the neighborhood. "At thirteen I figured I could 'play a tune' upon as many instruments as I was years old. ... in our isolated village, and in those days, it was regarded as something rather wonderful" [p3].

In 1838 a member of A. N. Johnson's choir in Boston vacationed in the neighborhood, giving Root a first-hand report of the musical life in Boston. When a happy accident sent him to Boston, young Root presented himself at the studio of A. N. Johnson, applying both for piano lessons and a job. Fortunately Johnson needed a helper, so an agreement was soon reached: Root was to tend the fires, sweep the studio, and be on hand to answer questions during the absence of Mr. Johnson, who gave most of his lessons at the homes of his pupils. In return he would receive lessons, board, room, three dollars a week, and the use of the studio piano.

It is difficult to find much information about Artemas Nixon Johnson, Root's first music teacher.[2] The Library of Congress has established that he was born in 1817, which would make him only three years older than his pupil - 21 when, according to Root, he was already a choir leader, organist, and conductor of the Musical Education Society. Later in his career he compiled a number of tune-books, conducted musical conventions, and edited and published two short-lived musical periodicals, *The Boston Musical Gazette*, 1846-48, and *The Boston Musical Journal*, 1853-55.

His arrangement with Root was "a veritable bonanza" wrote W. S. B. Mathews, a former Root & Cady employee in his obituary eulogy of Root [op cit, p503-4]. Mathews continued:

> ... he entered upon his duties with such zeal that in spite of a phenomenally intractable hand a still less advanced pupil was assigned to him within six weeks from the time of his beginning. Another advance was made when he had reached the ability to play Hebron through several times in succession without missing chords. Another tune was assigned for a lesson, and he was ordered to prepare them to play at the prayer meeting two weeks later. ... The notable advances made ... bring out in very strong light the imperfect standard of teaching qualifications at that time prevailing in Boston ... in one sense the position of our young musician was little above that of the accompanist of gospel songs in an evangelizing service ...

\*   \*   \*

[1] Quotations attributed to George F. Root in this and succeeding chapters are from his autobiography, *The Story of a Musical Life* (Cincinnati, John Church Co., c1891). The more interesting sketches of his life include: Birdseye, George W., "America's Song Composers, II: George F. Root," *Potter's American Monthly*, 12 (Feb 1879) 145-8; Coonley, Lydia Avery, "George F. Root and His Songs," *New England Magazine*, 19 (Jan 1896) 554-70; Mathews, William Smythe Babcock, "Geo. F. Root, Mus. Doc.," *Music*, 8 (Sept 1895) 502-9; and the article in *Biographical Sketches of the Leading Men of Chicago. Written by the Best Talent of the Northwest* (Chicago, Wilson & St. Clair, 1868).

[2] Not Benjamin Franklin Baker, often named as Root's first teacher.

When auditions were held for new members for the Boston Academy of Music Chorus, Root applied and was accepted. He studied flute, and then took voice lessons from George James Webb. The musical life of Boston in the early 1840's, at least that part concerned with musical education and choral music, was led by Lowell Mason and George James Webb, but opportunities were opening for younger men. Mason's success with singing classes for children had led to an experimental class in the Boston public schools which convinced the School Committee of its effectiveness. When instruction was extended to other schools in 1839, Mason hired assistants, including A. N. Johnson and George F. Root.[3] Root was then 19 and had been studying music for about a year. That same year Johnson took him into partnership under the terms of which he assisted both as teacher and organist, playing alternately at each of the two churches for which Johnson was responsible. Root himself wrote:

> If my getting on so fast in a city like Boston seems unaccountable, I must explain again that music was in a very different condition then from what it is now. It was just emerging from the florid but crude melodies and the imperfect harmonies of the older time. Lowell Mason had but just commenced what proved to be a revolution in the "plain song" of the church and of the people, and his methods of teaching the elementary principles of music were so much better and so much more attractive than anything that had before been seen that those who were early in the field had very great advantage. We had no competition and were sought on every hand. ... such very moderate players as we were, got on, because our choirs produced the new kind of simple, sweet music that went to the hearts of the people ... [p26-7].

The activities of Mason and his group, however, were largely confined to the Boston area. When, in 1844, Jacob Abbott invited Root to become music teacher at Abbott's School for Young Ladies in New York, he pointed out that Root would have the field to himself, nothing like Mason's work having been attempted there. Root did not hesitate long, and within a short time he was also teacher of music at Rutgers Female Institute, Miss Haines' celebrated School for Young Ladies, and the New York State Institution for the Blind, besides leading the choir at the Mercer Street Church.

In every sense a man of his time, Root thought of music largely in terms of classroom singing, the church and the parlor. While he was increasingly aware of the "advanced" music performed in Europe and brought to America by touring virtuosos, he assigned more importance in his thinking to the musical needs of the vast unsophisticated American public. It was to meet his needs as a teacher that he compiled his first book, The Young Ladies' Choir. "I did not ask anybody to publish it but just had copies enough made for my own use. I don't think I even copyrighted it ... " [p53]. The Library of Congress has a copy, and it was copyrighted by Leavitt, Trow & Co., New York, the publisher. The title-page reads:

> The Young Ladies' Choir: a Collection of Sacred Music, Arranged in One, Two and Three Parts, for Ladies' Voices, with an Accompaniment for the Piano Forte ... Composed and Arranged by George F. Root, Professor of Music in the "Rutgers' Female Institute," and "Institution of the Messrs. Abbott," and other Schools in the city of New York. New York: Leavitt, Trow & Co.; Boston, George P. Reed; 1846.

When the ladies had mastered the secular music in this volume, "my brother and I began the plan of getting up pamphlets of such music as I needed, still seeking no publisher, and thinking only of my own wants" [Ibid].

In the winter of 1850, Root took a year's sabbatical from his various labors and went to Paris to study piano and singing. He met Gottschalk, heard Berlioz conduct, and such singers in concert as Sontag, Viardot, Lablache, and Sims Reeves, but his religious scruples at that time prevented him from entering a theatre or opera house. His interests centering around teaching, he did not study composition, nor is there any evidence that he considered it.

On his return home in the fall of 1851 he wrote his first cantata, The Flower Queen; or, The Coronation of the Rose, planned as to subject, difficulty and distribution of parts to suit the resources of a young ladies' academy. The plot, if one may call it that, concerned a gathering of flowers

\* \* \*

---

[3] Rich, Arthur Lowndes. Lowell Mason, the Father of Singing among the Children. (Chapel Hill, University of North Carolina Press, 1946) p27

in a forest glen to choose their queen. Enter a recluse (sung by the teacher, male or female) in search of repose and solitude. After many short simple songs in which each flower set forth her own virtues, the recluse awarded the crown to the rose, an accomplished lady who could sing a high B flat. A more innocent and innocuous tale would be hard to imagine. Again Root had written with the needs of his classes in mind, but The Flower Queen, published by Mason Brothers, New York, seemed to fill a real need, and soon audiences in many states were treated to performances by pretty young misses in suitable floral surroundings.

In 1852, stimulated by the success of Stephen Foster and men like him, Root tried his hand at writing a "people's" song. To prevent this experiment from affecting his career as a teacher and choir leader, he published the song, Hazel Dell, under the pseudonym, G. Friedrich Wurzel. His publisher was Wm. Hall & Son, the firm that employed his younger brother, E. Towner Root. Far from being a failure, Hazel Dell was a resounding success, convincing Root that the field of "people's" songs was educationally sound, aesthetically satisfying and financially profitable. Soon afterward he again demonstrated his competence in writing more "serious" music with The Academy Vocalist, a book for schools, and the cantata, Daniel. In January, 1853, The Musical Review and Choral Advocate announced that he had been called to take charge of instruction in sacred music at Union Theological Seminary [4:11]. Later in the year he was instrumental in the establishing of the first Normal Musical Institute, a three-month training class for teachers in the techniques of Lowell Mason.

From 1853 to 1855 the Normal Musical Institute met in New York City. Between sessions Root taught in the city and conducted conventions wherever he was invited. In 1855, he decided to give up his schools and devote himself wholly to "conventions, Normals and authorship" [p101]. His attitude toward composition was pragmatism itself. "I am simply one, who, from such resources as he finds within himself, makes music for the people, having always a particular need in view. This, it seems to me, is a thing that a person may do with some success, without being either a genius or a great composer" [p98]. His cantata, The Haymakers, 1857, further demonstrated his ability in judging the taste of the American public [cf p35].

When the firm of Root & Cady was founded in 1858, G. F. Root took a "small pecuniary interest" in it [p122]. He came west frequently to hold conventions, visiting the store and watching it grow. "This playing at business ... and the new and adventurous life of Chicago were so attractive to me that early in 1859 I took a room in the building in which the store was, and occupied it as a library and working-room between convention engagements" [p129]. By December, 1860, he had moved to Chicago. The prestige he brought with him was indicated in the comment made by the Tribune for December 3 [1:4]:

> We are glad to learn that Mr. Geo. F. Root is to become a resident of Chicago. While establishing himself as a composer, he devoted himself largely to teaching in New York, in which few, if any, have ever been more successful. Having established by his Normal Musical Institute, his music books and popular ballads, a world-wide reputation, it is doubtless a matter of little importance to himself where he resides, since he is hereafter to devote himself mainly to the compilation of music books ... the writing of songs, ballads, etc., which he may reasonably expect will circulate all over the Union ... As an indication that he has really cast anchor here, we may be allowed to say that he became a partner in the music house of Root & Cady on the 1st inst., which was the second anniversary of that firm's successful business.

The outbreak of the war in April, 1861, and the enormous expansion of the firm's business due to its succession of effective war songs demanded more and more of Root's energies. "I saw that it could no longer be regarded as a secondary matter or a recreation. ... My department now demanded nearly all the time I could spare from writing, and to attend to that properly I must give up conventions ... So in 1863 I moved my family to Chicago" [p144]. As the member of the firm in charge of publications, Root selected, criticized and edited the work of other composers, his own experiences and his beliefs on the place of music in American life determining his judgments. Around himself he gathered a group of young men who wrote the type of music he felt was "useful" - Henry Clay Work, Philip Paul Bliss, the writer and singer of gospel hymns, and B. R. Hanby, composer of Darling Nelly Gray. Those colleagues who respected his opinions and accepted his advice spoke highly of his kindness and friendly criticism. There may have been composers who disagreed, but their views have not been reported.

His approach to publishing can be surmised from his discussion of another firm:

> About the time that I began to be known as a successful song-writer Nathan Richardson (afterward author of "The Popular Piano Instructor") started a music publishing house in

Boston. He had lived some years in Germany, and had come home filled with a strong desire to improve the musical tastes of the benighted people of his native land. ... he determined that he would publish nothing but high-class music. I doubt if there was an American then whose compositions he would have taken as a gift. He had an elegant store on Washington street, fitted and furnished in an expensive manner ...

All went well for a few months. Musicians met there and greatly enjoyed a chat amid the luxurious surroundings, and they occasionally bought a piece of music when they found what their pupils could use. Some of the comparatively few amateurs of the city, who were advanced, also patronized the establishment, but it did not pay. At length both Nathan and the rich brother became convinced that they could not make people buy music, however fine, that they could not understand nor perform, and ... calling the music that the common people liked, "trash," did not help the matter at all [p110-11].

Throughout his career, Root remained a layman's musician, writing music to suit the tastes and purposes of the widest public. As he grew older, he became more defensive, writing in 1892:

... it is an axiom that people can be benefitted musically only by music that they like ... not only are Patti's simple songs a benefit to the "people" but her dealings with them are on an honest business basis - she gives them what they pay for ... If the simple music that prevails is not good enough, let the advanced musicians make better, for simple music people in elementary musical states must have and if they can't get the best, they will take what they can get ["Madame Patti and the Old Songs," Music, 1 (Mar 1892) 429-31].

Root, Lowell Mason, and their school have been severely criticized for their lack of appreciation of the native music which preceded them, for their commercial approach to composing, and for their belief that they alone had the right approach to music education. Would it have been possible, one wonders, within the cultural milieu of the mid-nineteenth century United States, to have maintained a sympathetic appreciation of earlier American music and to have provided universal musical education without diluting natural musical taste or weakening oral traditions? These questions are also relevant to other areas of cultural history, but have yet to be answered.

Despite the severe limitations of range and difficulty he imposed on his music to insure its being accessible to wide sectors of the population, Root was capable of writing infectiously rousing marching songs with texts equally universal in their appeal. During the Civil War, he produced inspired rallying songs, perfectly suited to the moment. His hymns and sacred songs, although no longer found in many hymnals, were widely sung during his life, the expressions of a deeply religious man. In 1864 he and his wife signed the constitution of the Chicago Society of the New Jerusalem, remaining throughout the rest of their lives followers of Swedenborg. [(Rudolph Williams) The New Church and Chicago, a History. (Chicago) W. B. Conkey Co., 1906. p50 et seq].

After the dissolution of Root & Cady, Root devoted himself to writing and editing music and musical literature. As conventions were outmoded, he concentrated on normal teaching institutes and the writing of material suitable for public school music teaching. From 1872 to 1875 he was president of the Chicago Musical College, teaching choral singing and the normal department. He died on August 6, 1895, a man honored and respected throughout the country. The Presto, a journal of the music trade, eulogized him as "unquestionably the foremost writer of truly American songs ... His versatility was marvelous ..." [12 (Aug 8 1895) p(9)].

## EBENEZER TOWNER ROOT, 1822-1896

The senior partner of Root & Cady, Ebenezer Towner Root, was born in Sheffield, Massachusetts, on August 5, 1822, the second son of Frederick Ferdinand and Sarah Flint Root.[4] In 1826 the Roots moved

\* \* \*

[4] The chief sources of information on E. T. Root are the articles in Biographical Sketches of the Leading Men of Chicago (Chicago, Wilson, Peirce & Co., 1876) p77-8; and A. T. Andreas, History of Cook County, Illinois (Chicago, A. T. Andreas, 1884) p553. All statements not otherwise documented are drawn from these articles.

to North Reading, where he spent his boyhood. At the age of fourteen he went to Buenos Aires, staying three years because of his health, according to his brother, George F. Root [p27]. Before his trip young Towner probably had the same education as his brother, that offered by the local country school. On his return he found George had left the farm and established himself as a musician in Boston.

> It was not long ... before he decided to make music his business as I had done. So we sent a piano up to the old red house, and he went home and gave himself wholly to practice. He was always the singer of the family. Before his voice changed it was a beautiful soprano, and after the change a smooth, sympathetic tenor [p27-8].

After learning the rudiments, E. T. Root taught music in Boston for several years and then in 1846 followed his brother to New York as his assistant. Three years later he went to Alabama to teach, remaining there until 1851. On his return from the South

> ... becoming tired, as he said, of being as a teacher only "Mr. Root's brother," he decided to learn the music business and was then a clerk in the [Wm.] Hall [& Son] establishment. The Messrs. Hall were the publishers of Gottschalk's and Wm. Vincent Wallace's music at that time, and I frequently met those gentlemen there.... Hall's was a famous rendezvous for musical people [p91-2].

Outside of business hours, Towner Root continued his singing. A performance of Daniel, composed and conducted by George F. Root, in which Towner Root sang the part of Azariah, was reviewed in the New York Musical Review and Choral Advocate for March 16, 1854. It could not have been his first public appearance for the critic wrote, "Mr. E. T. Root ... did not seem to be in as good voice as usual...." [5:91].

About this time the Root brothers came to know C. M. Cady, both as a student at Union Theological Seminary and as editor of the Musical Review and Choral Advocate. The meeting was recalled in the Chicago Tribune's notice of Mr. Cady's death, printed June 18, 1889:

> Mr. E. T. Root said last night that he first met Mr. Cady in New York thirty-three years ago. Mr. Cady came west about that time and took editorial charge of the [Chicago] Musical Review. In 1858 Mr. Root again met Mr. Cady in Chicago. The result was the organization of the firm of Root & Cady.... [3:1].

E. T. Root remained with Wm. Hall & Son until 1858, when he left for Chicago. Of the reasons leading to his decision to move to the West, nothing is known, but since Mr. Cady had preceded him by several years, it is possible that Mr. Cady suggested to him the promising future in the new city of Chicago for two experienced and well-trained musicians and businessmen.

In the Chicago Daily Press & Tribune for December 24, 1858 [1:5], was announced the new firm of Root & Cady. The division of responsibility between the partners in the early years is not known. After 1860 when George F. Root entered the firm, he stated that E. T. Root "attended to the business detail in all the departments" [p140]. Although G. F. Root was in charge of publications, his brother's opinion apparently carried some weight in such matters, as shown in the following incident:

> ... we published a New Year's extra [of the Song Messenger of the Northwest] in those days.... I used to write a song for it.... December was now approaching and I was very much interested in something I was working at ... and had put off the song for the coming extra. One day my brother said, "We must have that song or we can not get the paper into the hands of the people by New Year's Day; go write it now while it is on your mind." In two hours I brought him the song. We tried it over and he said, "I must confess I don't think much of it, but it may do." ... The song was Tramp, Tramp, Tramp, the Boys Are Marching [p140-41].

E. T. Root supplemented his business life by taking an active part in the musical and social life of the community. On January 21, 1859, less than a month after the first public announcement of the formation of Root & Cady, he sang in the Musical Union concert at Metropolitan Hall. The Tribune for January 24 commented:

> Mr. E. T. Root sang Schubert's Serenade so charmingly that he was rapturously encored and obliged to repeat it. His voice is an exceedingly pleasant tenor, and his style and manner that of the artist, entirely at his ease [1:4].

On June 17, 1859, he took part in a "Grand Concert" at Metropolitan Hall, one of seven soloists [1:9]. In the Musical Union's highly successful production of George F. Root's The Haymakers on January 10, 1860, he sang the role of Snipkins, "a city youth unused to rural affairs" [1:8]. Nine days later his election as an officer of the Musical Union Academy was announced [1:2]. When he sang in one of the Classic Concerts at the Briggs House, a pioneer venture in chamber music, the Tribune of February 20 was friendly if cautious in its comments:

> Mr. Root did credit to himself by the rendering of a song by Robert Franz, but the main effect in this song -- as in nearly all the songs of this composer -- being in the harmonious modulations, it requires more acquaintance, before it can be duly appreciated [1:2].

At the second Classical Concert, announced on February 24, he sang the trio from Rossini's William Tell with Messrs. Lumbard and De Passio [1:7].

The Tribune for June 7, 1860 [1:5], told of his appointment to a committee with his colleagues, H. M. Higgins, W. W. Kimball, Nathaniel Goold, and Julius Bauer, to organize a Grand Benefit Concert at the Wigwam for the relief of the unfortunate sufferers from a recent tornado. The entire musical forces of the city were to be drafted. The ensuing concert was described on June 14 [1:3]. One hundred and fifty performers entertained an audience of 7,000, and many more were turned away. "Chicago has never beheld such an immense turnout ... excepting at a Fourth of July celebration, or a National Republican Convention."

From these notices it is apparent that E. T. Root was concerned with all aspects of musical life in Chicago. His taste in music, as reflected in his concert offerings, as well as his frequent appearances, were worthy of note. As the years passed, however, he confined his efforts more to the music trade. That he retained the respect due a pioneer is shown by his appointment in 1889 to the music dealers' committee to prepare for the approaching World's Columbian Exposition.[5]

In 1855 he married Almira R. Kimball, a pupil of his brother George at Rutgers Institute.[6] Both Mr. and Mrs. Root joined the Church of the New Jerusalem (Swedenborgian) in 1864. "They were very devoted and active, and reared their children with the knowledge of, and faith in the New Jerusalem."[7] Moreover, Mr. Root was a Mason, a charter member of the South Park Lodge, No. 662, chartered October 3, 1871. Mrs. Root, for her part, was on the Executive Committee of the Union Charitable Society. From these few facts it appears that the Towner Roots participated in community affairs to a limited extent. In a booklet describing the suburbs of Chicago, Out-of-town (Chicago, Western News Co., 1869), their home was mentioned:

> ... among the places that are especially noticeable for handsome grounds or appropriate residences ... Towner Root, whose barn ... has a golden violin for indicating the direction of the wind [p13].

After the dissolution of the firm of Root & Cady, Towner Root remained in the music trade of Chicago. In 1873 he formed a partnership with William Lewis, a prominent violinist and former employee of Root & Cady. Root & Lewis were music dealers only, leaving publishing to the firm of George F. Root and Sons, but neither of these firms was very successful. On January 1, 1875, the Root & Sons Music Co. was established, amalgamating the firms of Root & Lewis, George F. Root & Sons, and Chandler & Curtiss. E. T. Root withdrew from this firm in 1880, and with his sons, Frank K. and Walter R. Root, formed the firm of E. T. Root & Sons, general music dealers. Until his death at the age of 74 on October 10, 1896, he was active in the music trade. The Presto for October 15 said:

\*     \*     \*

[5] The Presto, 6 (Aug 15 1889) 8. The other members of the committee were W. W. Kimball and Geo. W. Lyon, cf Lyon & Healy. For undiscovered reasons, Root was soon replaced by I. N. Camp. Cf Ibid (Aug 30 1889) 12

[6] J. P. Root, Root Genealogical Records, 1600-1870 (New York, Anthony & Co., 1870) p486, and G. F. Root, op cit, p122

[7] Randolph Williams The New Church and Chicago (Chicago, W. B. Conkey Co., 1906) p395

The firm of E. T. Root & Sons was successful and absorbed the close attention of the late E. Towner Root up to within three weeks ago, his last visit to the office being on September 23 [8:20].

Although the career of E. T. Root was overshadowed by those of his famous brother and his energetic partner, C. M. Cady, his contribution to the music trade of Chicago in the days before the fire was recognized by all who knew him. In his quiet way he served the cause of music well.

## CHAUNCEY MARVIN CADY, 1824-1889

The junior partner of the firm, Chauncey Marvin Cady, is today almost forgotten although during an incredibly active life, he participated in every branch of musical activity as teacher, editor, business man, publisher, conductor, choir director, and amateur singer. He was the first teacher of music at Illinois State Normal University, the first conductor of the Chicago Musical Union, and the first president of the village of Hyde Park, Illinois.

Born in Westport, New York, on May 16, 1824, he was the seventh child and fifth son of Abigail Brainerd and Oliver Cady, who were "prominent in church work and gifted with more than ordinary ability."[8] His childhood was spent in an orthodox Congregationalist family, two of his brothers entering the ministry. His daughter recalled that many years later he told his children how hard the quiet Sundays had been to an active, healthy boy, who sat behind his Bible, catching flies to relieve the monotony. He did not learn to dance until after his marriage in 1855.

In 1843 he was enrolled as a preparatory student at Oberlin, Ohio, where his brother, Cornelius Sidney Cady, was studying at Oberlin Seminary then a "hotbed of abolitionism." After a year of prep school, he entered Oberlin College, but remained only one year.[9] It was possible for him to study music at Oberlin for the Triennial Catalogue of ... Oberlin Collegiate Institute, 1848-9 stated on p34: "Systematic and thorough instruction in Music is given to all who desire it." Whether Mr. Cady took advantage of this opportunity to study music is not known. His daughter stated that, so far as she knew, he had no formal musical training although he possessed a fine baritone voice and loved to sing. In view of his work as a conductor and a teacher of music, however, it seems likely that he studied music at some time in his career, either at Oberlin or later at the Union Theological Seminary, possibly under George F. Root.

From Oberlin, Mr. Cady must have transferred to the University of Michigan, for on July 15, 1851, the Regents of that institution voted to confer on him the degree of Bachelor of Arts pro merito. The course of study at Michigan included mental philosophy, German, chemistry, Greek Testament, declamation, and composition, but no music.[10]

From 1851 to 1853 he was a student at the Union Theological Seminary in New York. Perhaps he may have planned to enter the ministry and later changed his mind. At any rate he did not graduate; the Alumni Catalogue ... 1836-1926 of the Seminary listed him as a former student, not as an alumnus [p79]. During his stay there he came to know George F. Root, who taught music at the Seminary. When Mr. Root decided to write a cantata for his choir, the words were entrusted to Chauncey Cady and Frances Crosby, a pupil of Root's at the Institute for the Blind, later a famed writer of gospel hymns.

While still a student at the Seminary, Mr. Cady made his entrance into the music trade. A notice in the Musical Review and Choral Advocate for January 1, 1852, said:

\* \* \*

---

[8] O. P. Allen, The Descendants of Nicholas Cady of Watertown, Mass. (Palmer, Mass., C. B. Fiske, 1910) p153. Letter from Miss Harriette Cady, his daughter, verified the date of birth.

[9] Oberlin College, General Catalogue of Oberlin College, 1833-1908 (Oberlin, O., The College, 1909) p149

[10] Michigan. University, Regents' Proceedings ... 1837-1864 (Ann Arbor, The University, 1915) p494-5; Courses for the first term, 1850-51, p485. While at Michigan he joined the Alpha Delta Phi fraternity in 1851. Cf Alpha Delta Phi, The Alpha Delta Phi, 1832-1882 (Boston, By the Fraternity, 1882) p293

C. M. Cady selects and forwards sheet and bound music of every description, as well as all kinds of musical instruments, to every part of the country, without charge above the lowest retail price. All orders must be pre-paid. Address him at the office of the Musical Review and Advocate [3:10].

The same journal for May 1, 1852, reprinted Clear Cold Water (Temperance song and chorus). Words by C. M. Cady, Music by George F. Root, c1852 by Wm. Hall & Son [3:76-7]. Mr. C. M. Cady was announced as the winner of the prize essay contest for the "best treatise on Music in America" on August 1, 1852 [3:113]. His essay, printed in two parts, [3:113-16; 130-33] included references to Greek, Latin, Egyptian and Chinese mythology and quoted Quintillian as well as a speech by Fétis reported in the Revue et Gazette Musicale de Paris. Part I traced the origins of music and Part II described its progress in the United States. Further recognition appeared in the November issue with the announcement that, beginning with Volume IV, "The paper will be under the editorial charge of Mr. C. M. Cady, author of the Prize Essay on Music in America, &c., and already known to many of our readers as one to whom they are mainly indebted for whatever of editorial ability characterized the present volume of the Review & Advocate...." [3:168].

The magazine which Mr. Cady edited was published by F. J. Huntington and Mason & Law, having as contributing editors such musical men of note as Lowell Mason, Isaac B. Woodbury, Thomas Hastings, William B. Bradbury and George F. Root. Frequent communications from abroad, reviews and comments on music in all parts of the United States, notices of new publications, and selected pieces of music were to be found in its pages. The standards of preceding years were maintained during Mr. Cady's year as editor.

After the December, 1853, issue of the Musical Review, however, Mr. Cady's name no longer appeared on the masthead as editor. Beginning with January, 1854, the publisher's name alone was printed above the editorials although no change in editorship was announced. No mention was made of C. M. Cady's whereabouts until April 27, 1854, when a dispatch reported that he was holding musical conventions in the West -- Monroeville, Ohio, April 4-7; Oxford, Ohio, May 3-5; Indianapolis, Indiana, May 7 (a lecture on church music); and Racine, Wisconsin, May 9-12, the convention in Racine being the first of its kind in that city [5:140, 188]. Although he returned East to hold a convention in Sag Harbor, L. I., on November 15-17, 1854 [5:388], he was in Cleveland in July, 1855, serving as a conductor with Lowell Mason and William B. Bradbury at the first meeting of the Ohio State Musical Association. "Mr. Cady devoted a small portion of each day to chorus drilling, questions of taste, etc., and on Thursday delivered an address which was well received" [6:252]. Perhaps his approaching marriage to a young lady from Sag Harbor led him to make New York his base of operations for the coming winter. At any rate he had inserted in the September Musical Review this notice:

> Owing to engagements lately made in New York, Mr. Cady will be able to attend only the two following conventions this fall: Elgin, Ill., commencing Oct. 10th, continuing three days ... Sandusky, Ohio, commencing Oct. 16th, continuing three days.... [6:324].

The engagements which kept him in New York must have been highly gratifying for he apparently succeeded George F. Root as vocal instructor at Mr. Abbott's school. The Musical Review and Gazette for February 9, 1856, noted:

> The pupils of Mr. Abbott's Young Ladies' Institute gave a musical soirée at their chapel, Spingler Institute ... assisted by their teachers, Messrs. C. M. Cady and C. C. Converse, and also by William Mason.... [7:34].

An item of May 31, 1856 [7:161], referred to him as still teaching at the Abbott school, but by the 10th of June, he was in Canton, Ohio, directing a four-day convention [7:178]. His stay with the Abbott school was officially over by July 26 when he announced: "C. M. Cady takes this opportunity to inform his friends that he has terminated all engagements in New York, that prevent his attending Musical Conventions" [7:232]. Although he presided at a convention in Orient, L. I., in late July [7:247], by September 20 he was settled in Chicago receiving his mail "Care of Higgins Brothers, Chicago, Ill." [7:289].

His duties were described on November 29, 1856:

> The Flower-Queen, a musical journal started some six months since in Chicago, Ill., by the Messrs. Higgins Brothers, comes to us with both a change of title and in the editorship. The paper is now called, The Chicago Musical Review and Flower-Queen, and Mr. Wm. C. Webster has relinquished his chair to Mr. C. M. Cady, formerly of New York City [7:371].

His friend, William B. Bradbury, passed through Chicago on a convention-holding tour late in 1856. He wrote in a letter published in the December New York Musical Review and Gazette (and later reprinted in the Song Messenger for October, 1871 [9:145-6]), "... and here, too, is our old friend, Cady, ready with pen, voice and heart for every good musical word and work, editing Musical Review Junior (Chicago Musical Review), holding musical conventions, etc...." [7:405]. Unfortunately no copy of this Review during the period of his editorship has been found.

Other good musical works were soon under way. On April 7, 1857, the Chicago Musical Union gave its first concert, which he conducted.[11] His Minnehaha Glee Book, published by Higgins Brothers, has a preface dated September 12, 1857. From the same year were Cady's Popular Home Songs, a series also published and copyrighted by Higgins Brothers. On the cover of O'er the Billow were listed ten songs, one of which at least was successful. It was reissued after January 1, 1859, by H. M. Higgins as "The Universally Popular Song, Three Angel Visitants," song or quartette with piano or guitar accompaniment.

Mr. Cady was first listed in a Chicago city directory in 1858 as "Cady, Chauncey M., editor Musical Review, 84 Randolph," the address of Higgins Brothers. His connection with that firm ended, however, when the Chicago Musical Review was sold to Oliver Ditson of Boston, as announced in the following letter, printed in Dwight's Journal of Music for August 7, 1858:

> To the subscribers of the Chicago Musical Review.
> 
> While I regret to part company with my readers, I gain, by this release from editorial labors, more time to devote to musical conventions and other professional duties that have of late increased so rapidly upon my hands. In the meantime, let me assure my friends that the Northwest is still my field of labor; that Chicago continues to be my headquarters, and that, though I relinquish to one abler than myself the pleasing duty of furnishing them with stated supplies of musical pabulum, I shall always ... be happy to hear of their prosperity....
> Yours truly,
> 
> C. M. Cady
> Chicago, August 1, 1858 [13:150-51]

While he was still associated with Higgins Brothers, Mr. Cady was engaged as music teacher by the newly organized Illinois State Normal University, as noted in the New York Musical Review and Gazette for November 28, 1857 [8:270]. When his connection with the University began, the school was in its infancy with its buildings under construction. According to Gen. C. E. Hovey, the first president of the school, Mr. Cady played a part in its early financial life. McLean County, Illinois, where the new school was to be located, had set aside certain county lands, the sale of which would provide funds for the University. The Illinois Board of Education authorized the sending of an agent east to effect, if possible, a sale of the county lands, expecting that an impressive and established business man would be sent. General Hovey reported that when he could find no "honorable" or "rich" man to undertake the journey, he concluded to try "Young America." Cady was sent, and found an interested speculator. Legal complications developed in transferring the deeds. To simplify matters, Hovey himself bought a large tract of land with the intention of re-selling it to Cady's prospect. The prospect, meanwhile, grew cold and Cady could find no other. Hovey would have been left in a very embarrassing position, had it not happened that his purchase became noised about as a big speculation. Others took heart and bought lands on a gamble, and Hovey managed to extricate both himself and the University's building program. Cady's part may not have been altogether glorious, but it is significant to note that Hovey was willing to trust his "music teacher" with so important an assignment.[12]

As teacher of vocal music, Mr. Cady was a special instructor on the original staff, for music was a required subject in the general course, due to efforts of Lowell Mason and his colleagues. A contemporary account of the situation in which Mr. Cady found himself is most amusing:

\* \* \*

[11] G. P. Upton, Musical Memories (Chicago, A. C. McClurg & Co., 1908) p271

[12] C. E. Hovey, "A Schoolmaster's Story," The Schoolmaster, 2 (Nov 1869) 83. Quoted in J. W. Cook and J. V. McHugh, A History of the Illinois State Normal University, Normal, Illinois (Normal, Ill., Pantagraph Printing and Binding Establishment, 1882) p43-4

Another theory was tested to the satisfaction of the school ... and this was the idea that each and every person can be made a musician, or a teacher of music. Some of the members of the State Board went so far as to refuse to believe a pupil should be allowed to graduate unless he was able to teach music and lead in singing. Prof. C. M. Cady, of Chicago, was employed, with strict instructions to spare no pains to prove the correctness of the theory of the existence of universal musical ability. He divided the school into four sections. "A" was made up of good singers, those who had good voices, and also could read music readily by sight. "B" included moderately well-informed singers, and those who were capable of being rapidly advanced. "C" comprised all with a natural ear for music; those whose voices needed training to fit them for a place in the upper classes. According to popular report, section "D" was made up of "birds that couldn't sing, and that could never be made to sing." This class was small, but desperate. It labored zealously to grasp the rudiments of the grand art, but its best efforts were failures, and it became, in the course of a year or so, the laughing stock of the entire school. Being an early and constant member of this class, I have a right to mention its woes and tribulations, and to observe that it finally graduated from the pursuit of knowledge under these difficulties, by rising in a body and leaving the hall when the music hour arrived -- no permission being asked or given -- it being tacitly conceded that the pet theory of universal music training had broken under the strain.[13]

There is no evidence that Mr. Cady himself subscribed to the theory of universal music training, but undoubtedly he did his best to give all his pupils good instruction. The Chicago Daily Press and Tribune for December 20, 1859, reported: "... C. M. Cady, Esq., of our city, has created so much musical interest in Bloomington by his connection with the State Normal University, that, besides the hundred pupils under his charge in that institution, the citizens have lately organized a select singing class of about one hundred ladies and gentlemen under his instruction" [1:3]. During the Anniversary Week of 1860, he again received favorable notice for the quality of his work. The Tribune for June 30 referred to his leading "the entire school in well executed singing. This branch of instruction is not a mere form, but the students of both sexes are diligently and carefully trained to sing" [3:3].

The course laid out was ambitious, lasting nine terms and including "oratorio and solo singing, harmony and musical composition, but there is no evidence that the entire course was ever taught." Mr. Cady remained on the faculty only until 1861, and by 1868 vocal music was no longer taught, not being resumed before 1899.[14] Since his work was apparently satisfactory, he left the school probably because of the pressure of other work.

While his duties at the University must have demanded that he spend at least part of each week in Normal, he nevertheless found time for many other activities, most of them in Chicago. Among these was the direction of music at the First Congregational Church of Chicago. No record has been found of the beginning or end of this association; the sole report of it was an item in the Press and Tribune for November 15, 1858:

> A systematic effort is being made in the First Congregational church ... to prepare all its attendants to join the choir in the plain songs of the sanctuary. To accomplish this, Mr. Cady, the director of music in the church, meets every Saturday afternoon the children of the Sabbath schools ... to teach them the elements of music and to drill them in church music. Last Saturday there were present in this class about 400 children. In the evening, Mr. Cady meets the adults of the congregation. The first part ... is devoted to the elements of music, and the latter part to the practice of tunes to be sung the following day... [1:3].

A major project was the Chicago Musical Union, which gave its first concert under his direction on April 7, 1857. In the fashion of that day the program was a miscellaneous assortment of numbers with many soloists. By November 28, 1857, the New York Musical Review and Gazette was able to report:

\*   \*   \*

---

[13] Cook and McHugh, op cit, p160-61

[14] Illinois State Normal University. Semi-centennial History of the Illinois State Normal University, 1857-1907 (Normal, Ill., 1907) p57-61

> We are glad to learn that the commercial revulsion has not affected the lately formed Musical Union at Chicago, under the direction of our old friend, C. M. Cady, Esq. This society now numbers more than one hundred active members, is out of debt, and during its brief existence of ten months, has accumulated funds, library, and other property, to the amount of $700. Pretty well for Chicago, that it thus sustains music [8:270].

On October 6, 1858, the Press and Tribune reported the re-election of Mr. Cady as conductor [1:4], and on December 16, he was put in charge of the Musical Union Academy, "an instruction department designed to take learners where the elementary class leaves them and carry them forward to the hights [sic] of music attainment" [1:4]. Membership was open to "ladies and gentlemen possessing some knowledge of music and wishing to perfect themselves in sight singing, taste, &c." The first meeting as reported on December 23 was "well attended and ... gave promise of an interest ... which can but make it of great value to our community" [1:3].

On April 29, 1859, the Musical Union celebrated the Centennial of Handel's death with Chicago's first performance of the Messiah. Two of the soloists, Mrs. J. H. Long and Mr. C. R. Adams, were brought from Boston for the occasion; Mr. Cady conducted and A. J. Vaas led the orchestra. Enthusiastically the Tribune said on April 29:

> ... we cordially thank the Musical Union for the opportunity they gave us, to listen to one of the most sublime compositions ... ever ... written.... The Union have merited the confidence and support of our entire community.... [1:3].

The New York Musical Review and Gazette for May 14 indicated that progress could still be made. "The choruses were from fair to middling. The orchestra lacked precision to a lamentable degree" [10:148].

Mr. Cady remained conductor of the Union until his resignation in January, 1860. On January 25, the Tribune reported that the Musical Union "passed a series of resolutions highly complimentary and flattering to their late conductor, C. M. Cady, Esq., who has resigned his post, from a pressure of other duties, and voted him the sum of one hundred dollars in acknowledgment of the obligations of the society to him...." [1:3].

For the period immediately following his resignation as conductor, he held no office in the Union. On June 11, 1862, however, the organization was completely reorganized to form a new society with Hans Balatka as musical conductor. At the last meeting of the old Union, a committee of three was appointed, consisting of Dr. L. S. Boone, ex-mayor of Chicago, W. Hansbrough, and C. M. Cady, "to transfer the property of the old society as a donation to the new organization as soon as it is perfected" [4:2].

The officers of the new Musical Union were announced on June 18, 1862, including C. M. Cady, treasurer [4:3]. In this position he continued for several years, at least until 1865, and probably until the dissolution of the society. That he fulfilled his duties well was shown by his repeated election to the office and by such comments as that appearing in the Tribune, July 20, 1863, following the annual meeting for 1863: "The report of the treasurer, C. M. Cady, was eminently satisfactory, showing that the finances have been excellently well managed" [4:2]. His record in this position was another evidence of his sound business ability.

The Musical Union was pictured by George P. Upton, music critic of the Tribune, in his Musical Memories:

> ... of this society I can speak from personal experience.... The best singers in Chicago were members of the Musical Union, and there were no dissensions in the ranks. They were a very happy family, and their principal objects were public entertainment, personal enjoyment, and social hilarity. They succeeded in all of them.... The society lasted eight happy years; it disbanded because other societies offered dangerous competition, and also because of the pressure of business interests which claimed the time of members [p271].

To get some idea of the variety of Mr. Cady's musical activities, let us consider a particularly active week in 1859. On April 28, he conducted the music at the first anniversary exercises of the Chicago Theological Seminary as reported in the Tribune on the next day [1:3]. On the 29th, he led the Musical Union in their performance of the Messiah. In addition to his duties in the newly opened music store of Root & Cady and his teaching in Normal, he must also have been preparing his courses for the

Chicago Musical Institute which was to begin its term on Monday, May 2, and continue in session every day for six weeks according to an advertisement in the Tribune for April 16, 1859 [1:9].

As the years passed Mr. Cady's interest in things musical did not lessen although he was more often to be found behind the scenes making the arrangements than on the podium itself. For example, in the Fall of 1859, he was on a committee with the composer, William H. Fry, and the two publishers, D. P. Faulds of Kentucky and W. C. Peters of Ohio, to arrange a contest between "brass and orchestral bands" at the Fair in Chicago held by the U. S. Agricultural Society.[15] The Tribune for April 20, 1861 [4:3], reported that he was a member of the Committee on Music to make arrangements for the Grand Rally of Freemen held at the Wigwam on that day. On January 5, 1867 [4:4-5], his appointment was announced to a committee of three to purchase a "monster organ" for the Y.M.C.A. These official duties, however, did not replace his love of making music himself in his home. His daughter, Miss Harriette Cady, in a letter dated July 20, 1944, recalled his delight in singing the lieder of Schubert and Schumann to her accompaniment; and the Tribune for August 12, 1865 [4:1], prints a brief social note describing an evening in his rooms at the Hyde Park Hotel when the musical élite of Chicago took turns performing.

Do not think, however, that his time was confined to musical activity for he also was a leader in commercial, cultural and civic affairs. Less than two years after the formation of Root & Cady, he was named by the Mercantile Association as one of a committee of six "to represent the Association on making arrangements for the funeral obsequies [of Senator Stephen A. Douglas] ... and to invite the merchants of the city to unite ... in paying respect to the memory of the illustrious dead," according to the Tribune for June 5, 1861 [4:3]. Although no record has been found of his work in the Congregational church, other than as a musical director, it is likely that he took an active interest in its affairs, since in 1867 he was instrumental in the establishment of the Congregational paper, The Advance. The organizational meeting of the stockholders was held on July 2, 1867, in the store of Root & Cady, and Mr. Cady was chosen as one of the directors as reported in the Tribune for the next day [4:1]. The breadth of his interests is indicated by his subscription of $500 to become a life member of the Chicago Academy of Sciences, announced on January 18, 1866 [1:8].

Probably Mr. Cady's outstanding service as a citizen was to the community of Hyde Park, Illinois, which he served as president of the Board of Trustees. He was elected in 1868, when the community amended its town charter to provide for a board of trustees, and continued in the same office after Hyde Park became a village on August 13, 1872. His name last appears as president for the electoral year 1873-74,[16] and shortly thereafter he left for New York.

Hyde Park at this time was a pleasant residential district with an unusually rich cultural life.[17] Its growth was particularly rapid after the Great Fire of 1871 when many people moved "to the country" to rebuild their lost homes. A description of it in Out-of-town, published in 1869, says: "Hyde Park, with an area big enough for a department to be divided into arrondissements, or a city with numerous wards, is still regarded simply as a township, and is governed by a board of trustees, C. M. Cady, president...." [p5].

There is no evidence that Mr. Cady had any motive other than public service when he accepted office. Apparently there were no political contests involved, and the salaries mentioned in the annual reports of Hyde Park were negligible. He took his duties seriously spending much time inspecting roads under construction and planning for needed public works. Miss Cady believes that the South Park system of Chicago today owes much to her father's foresight and intelligent planning.

The variety and interest of Mr. Cady's avocational interests must not be allowed to obscure the major aspect of his career -- the house of Root & Cady. That his services were valuable to the firm and profitable to him cannot be doubted. His responsibility was finance as distinguished from business detail which was under the charge of E. T. Root. "Mr. C. M. Cady is the financial man of the firm -- a position

\* \* \*

[15] The Press and Tribune, Aug 19 1859 [1:5]. The results of the contest were announced on September 17, 1859 [1:1].

[16] A. T. Andreas, History of Cook County, Illinois (Chicago, 1884) History of Hyde Park, p514-16. Hyde Park must have been proud of its musical town officials. In 1864 Henry C. Work, the composer of Kingdom Coming, was elected Town Clerk. The following year, Work was re-elected and Hiram M. Higgins, a competitor of Root & Cady, was elected supervisor. In 1868 Higgins was made a trustee and Cady became president of the Board.

[17] Mrs. B. F. Ayer, "Old Hyde Park," in Chicago Yesterdays; A Sheaf of Reminiscences, ed. by Caroline Kirkland (Chicago, Daughaday and Co., 1919) p179-92

in which shrewdness, integrity and a deep and varied knowledge of human nature is absolutely necessary for success."[18] The entire music trade recognized his leadership by electing him president of the Board of Music Trade of the United States for more than one term as the Song Messenger proudly pointed out in September, 1870 [13:137].

After the failure of Root & Cady, Mr. Cady became a partner of the reorganized firm of Root & Cady[19] which was itself dissolved shortly. The financial worries occasioned by tremendous losses in the fire and the struggle to pay the debts of Root & Cady in full, despite nonpayment of insurance and debts due to the firm, told very heavily on him. Threatened with brain fever, he was weakened for a long time.[20] Edwards' ... Directory ... of the City of Chicago ... for 1873 does not list his name which may indicate that he left the city for a time. The following year, however, he was listed in The Lakeside Annual Directory of the city of Chicago ... 1874-5 as vice-president of the Chicago Post & Mail Co., of which one Woodbury M. Taylor was business manager, but nothing further is known of this phase of his career.

About 1875 Mr. Cady began a new publishing venture under the name of C. M. Cady at 107 Duane Street, New York City. With acumen typical of his earlier days, he persuaded Henry Clay Work to leave his retirement and write songs again. Work's Grandfather's Clock, copyrighted by C. M. Cady in 1876, was the greatest success of this house selling hundreds of thousands of copies.[21] The organization of this firm is not known, but a catalog issued by it offers much insight into Mr. Cady's personality and business methods. Significantly it was called the Telephone, a new word in 1878.

CADY'S TELEPHONE 107 DUANE STREET, NEW YORK, DECEMBER, 1878.
CONFIDENTIAL.

I send this Telephone only to the most influential of the musical profession, in every place of importance in the United States and the Dominion of Canada. I place it in your hands in order to make to you certain confidential propositions, which I trust you will find it as much to your interest as mine to seriously consider....

If you will obtain such of my new publications as are likely to be useful and interesting to yourself and your friends, and make them known in concerts and parlor entertainments and by other practical means, I will furnish you now and hereafter, any of the 2000 sheet music publications mentioned in this Telephone, in any quantities you may order ... on receipt of half the retail price.[22]

The firm of C. M. Cady published some successful songs, but Mr. Cady no longer had the strength to carry on an active publishing house by himself. The good connections made by the firm were shown by its advertisement in Brainard's Musical World for February, 1880: "Three new songs by ... Henry C. Work ... Cleveland and Chicago, S. Brainard's Sons, publishers; Cincinnati, Brainard Bros.; New York, C. M. Cady" [17: inside front cover]. Note that Cady is listed last of the firms indicating his declining vigor since he almost certainly was the original publisher. In May, 1880, C. M. Cady's name did not appear in this advertisement. The firm was dead.

Mr. Cady felt himself too old to regain his former position. In August 1880 Brainard's Musical World announced that he had moved to Atlanta, Georgia, as manager for the agency of the Estey Organ Co. [17:127]. He remained in the music trade of Atlanta until his death on June 16, 1889, at the age of 65, while on a short trip to Asheville. The Atlanta Constitution for June 17 said in part:

\*     \*     \*

---

[18] Northwestern Insurance and Mercantile Journal quoted in The Song Messenger of the Northwest, 4 (April 1867) Extra
[19] The Weekly Trade Circular, 1 (Jan 18 1872) 12
[20] Letter from Miss Harriette Cady
[21] George W. Birdseye, "Henry C. Work," Potter's American Monthly, 12 (April 1879) 286
[22] Photostat lent by C. A. Swoyer, Columbus, Ohio

29

> ... Mr. Cady came to Atlanta from Chicago seven or eight years ago to take charge of the Estey organ depot here. In Chicago he had owned one of the largest musical establishments in the country. This was destroyed by fire and the loss was uncovered by insurance, leaving Mr. Cady a comparatively poor man.
>
> He was recognized in Atlanta as a man of sterling business capacity and as a successful manager. After holding his position with the Estey Organ Company, Mr. Cady resigned ... to accept a position as general superintendent of the southern agencies for the Kimball organs and Wheelock pianos. He was holding this position at the time of his death [p7].

The same paper in its issue of June 19 described his last illness:

> ... Mr. Cady left the city last Saturday, and was ill with cholera morbus when he went away. He continued to grow worse until the train reached Spartanburg, where a wait of four hours aggravated his already enfeebled condition.
>
> After his arrival at Asheville Mr. Cady continued to grow worse, and, although the physician did everything that could be done to save him, he expired at 8:40 o'clock Sunday morning....
>
> During the last few years he has been agent for the Kimball Piano and Organ Company for the southern states, with headquarters in Atlanta. He made many friends here, and his sad death is universally lamented [p4].

His wife and two of his three daughters were with him when he died, and they took his body to Sag Harbor, L.I., Mrs. Cady's girlhood home, for burial.

CHAPTER III

ROOT & CADY PRIOR TO THE CIVIL WAR

ROOT & CADY PRIOR TO THE CIVIL WAR

The Chicago of 1858 to which Chauncey Cady welcomed the Root brothers was a far cry from the metropolis of today. Many of the streets were still unpaved proving to be almost impassable in bad weather. In a valiant effort to improve the drainage, the entire level of the city was being raised several feet. Arriving in the midst of the city's attempt to pull itself out of the mud, the Roots found some of the buildings at the new level and some at the old. A stroll along the flimsy wooden sidewalks was a continuous climb up and down stairs. The crinolines dictated by prevailing fashion made a shopping expedition along the streets a hazardous adventure for the ladies. Though the boosters might call it the cultural and business center of the Northwest, there was still much of the frontier about Chicago.

The year had almost ended when the formation of the new firm was announced. In the Chicago Daily Press and Tribune for December 9, 1858 [1:3], was the first printed notice that Root & Cady had taken "an elegant and finely located store in Larmon Block" to be fitted up as a music store. Excepting only the Sherman House and the Baptist Church, the Larmon Block was the most prominent building on the four fronts facing Court House Square, at that time the center of Chicago's life. A four-story building on the northeast corner of Washington and Clark Streets, it housed Bryant & Stratton's Business College on the upper floors and, on the street level, J. T. & E. M. Edwards, jewelers; Julius Bauer, pianos; J. M. Loomis, hatter; Root & Cady's music store, and Buck & Raynor's drug store.[1]

On the day before Christmas the Tribune [1:5] noticed that the store, although not completed, was open in some departments and sharing the holiday trade. Three weeks later all preparations had been completed. The firm's first advertisement appearing in the Tribune of January 15, 1859 [1:7], was a portent of the vigor and enterprise of the new house. It read in full:

> New music store. - / 95 Clark Street / Opposite the Court House, Chicago, at the sign of [bar of music] The Star Spangled Banner / MESSRS. ROOT & CADY / take this opportunity to respectfully inform the music buyers of Chicago, and the North West, that they are now receiving one of the largest and most attractive assortments of Musical Merchandise to be found West of New York, consisting in part of
> 
> The freshest, newest, and best sheet music of the day / instruction books of all kinds / Church music, glee and juvenile books. / Steinway & son's / gold medal piano fortes. / Prince's & co's. / improved patent melodeons & organs. Wm. Hall & son's / celebrated guitars, flutes and banjos. /
> 
> Also, just imported from Europe, Violins, Violoncellos, Cornopeans, Cornets, Accordeons, Flutinas, Concertinas, Tamborines, Pitch Pipes, Rosin, Bows, etc.
> 
> Best Italian, English, French, German, and American Strings for Violin, Violoncello, Double Bass, Guitar, Banjo, Harp, etc., etc., etc.
> 
> Such are the facilities of this House that Dealers, Teachers, and Seminaries in the Northwest may here obtain the best of everything musical as cheaply and with much greater dispatch than from the Eastern cities.
> 
> Organs, Pianos, Melodeons and all kinds of Musical Instruments tuned and repaired in the most reliable manner.
> 
> E. T. Root                                   Root & Cady
> C. M. Cady                                   No. 95 Clark Street, Chicago

Nevertheless the business was begun on a modest scale with a capital investment of twelve hundred dollars[2] and a shop which measured only 20x65 feet.[3] No doubt the Eastern connections of the two partners helped

\*     \*     \*

[1] F. F. Cook, Bygone Days in Chicago (Chicago, A. C. McClurg, 1910) p175. A contemporary woodcut of the building is given in I. D. Guyer's History of Chicago; Its Commerce and Manufacturing Interests and Industry (Chicago, Church, Goodman & Cushing, 1862) p48.

[2] G. W. Birdseye, "American Song Composers: George F. Root of Chicago," New York Musical Gazette, 1 (July 1867) 65

[3] J. S. Wright, Chicago: Past, Present, Future. (Chicago, Western News Co., 1868) p279, quoting the Chicago Courier of April 1. Wright does not specify the year, and no Couriers have survived. The quotation begins by referring to the founding of Root & Cady "ten years ago," and thus the year must have been 1868 or possibly 1867.

in establishing the new venture. To the satisfaction of everyone concerned, Root & Cady was so well received by Chicago that it expanded almost immediately. Early in 1859, G. F. Root took a room in the Larmon Block for his personal use between convention engagements. Soon thereafter, according to the Tribune for August 15 [1:6], a wholesale wareroom was established with C. L. Watkins, 124 Lake Street.

From the beginning of the firm, the sale of instruments was pushed while a tuning and repair service was organized. In the Tribune for July 1, 1859, Root & Cady announced the engagement of

> a corps of Musical Repairers and Tuners whose work they can confidently recommend. Organs, Melodeons, Accordeons, Violins, Piano fortes, Seraphines, Flutinas, Guitars, Flutes, &c., &c. [1:6].

By September, Root & Cady assumed the rank of Chicago's foremost music store outstripping the others in awards at the U.S. Agricultural Fair. In Class 123, Musical Instruments, the firm received two silver medals, a bronze medal and a diploma while its closest competitor, H. M. Higgins, was awarded two bronze medals according to the Press and Tribune for September 23 [3:7].

As the presidential campaign of 1860 approached, "Wide Awake Clubs" were organized throughout the North to support the candidacy of Abraham Lincoln by meetings, torchlight parades, and other means. No meeting nor parade could be successful without a brass band as the Wide Awake Clubs soon realized. While the other music dealers in Chicago advertised pianos and melodeons, Root & Cady called upon the Wide Awakes to examine "the largest and best assortment of Piston Valve Saxhorns, Equitone Valve Saxhorns, Rotary Valve Saxhorns, Cornets, Drums, Cymbals, Fifes, &c., &c., west of New York" [July 21 1860 (1:7)]. Russell & Tolman of Boston also advertised saxhorns in their house-organ, The Boston Musical Times, so that this may also be taken as further evidence of the business ties between the two firms -- a point which will be returned to often in what follows.

Instruments, of course, were not the only successful department. Each proud new owner of a Steinway piano or a Prince melodeon was a potential buyer of untold quantities of music sheets and books. The partners may well have estimated the increased market for music when they read in the Tribune for March 27, 1860 [1:2]: "Of the large stock of Steinway & Sons' pianos, which Root & Cady had a few days ago, not one is now left." Certainly the firm was well equipped to supply the demand. Within the first year of its existence, it advertised for sale music issued by Russell & Tolman, Reed & Co., and J. P. Jewett & Co., of Boston; Mason Brothers, Wm. Hall & Son, and Delisser & Procter, of New York; and Novello of London. From these houses came a steady stream of songs and ballads, both sentimental and humorous, marches, polkas, schottisches, variations, and other types of instrumental music. Besides sheet music, Root & Cady carried juvenile books for day and Sunday schools, music instruction and glee books, Episcopal church music, and hymn books such as the Wesleyan Sacred Harp, the New Temperance Melodist, and Lowell Mason's best-selling Sabbath Hymn and Tune Book, of which eighteen different styles were kept constantly on hand. In the popular Novello cheap edition were stocked standard oratorios, organ voluntaries, masses and Catholic music.

The business prospered. The friendly Tribune was never tired of informing its readers that Root & Cady's stock was surpassed by none west of New York although on occasion it made the same claim for other music dealers as they appeared on the Chicago scene. Typical of the items printed in its local news column was one for November 23, 1859:

> ... It is a proof of the fitness of both gentlemen for their position, and the happy conjunction here following the antecedents of each in connection with music matters in New York, and in this city, that the Music House of Messrs. Root & Cady has attained in so short a time since its establishment its present prominent place in its department of trade. At present it may almost be said that the bulk of musical wares and literature from the great primary sources at the east for the Northwest comes through their hands. They are daily filling bills for wholesale houses in all parts of the West [1:5].

It cannot be assumed, however, that the pre-eminent position of Root & Cady in the music trade of Chicago was a mirage dreamed up by an over-enthusiastic newspaperman. The unquestioned growth of the firm must have been based on a steady flow of profits; moreover, other contemporary comments substantiate in general the Tribune's picture. For example, a dispatch from Chicago to the Musical Review and Musical World of New York [11 (Nov 24 1860) p355] mentioned Root & Cady as "doing the largest music business of any in Chicago, and, perhaps, in the Northwest." It is difficult, however, to support these glittering claims with cold figures. Only on rare occasions did estimates of sales or profits appear.

One such statement appearing in the Tribune for November 24, 1859 [1:7], claimed that 25,000 copies of W. B. Bradbury's Jubilee, a book of sacred music, had been sold that fall.

Since E. T. Root and C. M. Cady had fingers in many musical pies, they must have had help in running their store almost from the first. For the early years of the firm, no facts have been found as to the number or kinds of employees, but tuners and draymen must have been hired for specific jobs, if not regularly. A significant change in organization occurred on December 1, 1860, when George F. Root came into the firm as a partner bringing with him both capital and prestige. Having already established himself as one of the best known composers in the country as a whole, there was no disputing his position in 1860 as Chicago's top-ranking musician. He suited the city then as he was to suit the Union during the war. Chicago, despite its visiting opera companies and frequent concerts, was not a sophisticated city any more than most of the other growing communities scattered across the country. The Tribune praised the operas, but like many others, found George F. Root's Haymakers more to its liking:

> The Italian Opera walks on stilts, deals in exaggeration, and treats largely of kings, queens, dukes and nobles. This is purely democratic, exalts labor, ridicules the useless city dandy, and holds up for your admiration the sturdy Farmer and his household.... [Jan 9 1860 (1:4)].

Root & Cady's numerous advertisements are the only available means for recapturing the character of the firm and its business methods. Other music houses of Chicago were -- to say the least -- conservative in their advertising. Higgins Brothers, for instance, ran an advertisement intermittently in the Daily Press and Tribune from August 25, 1858, until January 20, 1860, without altering one word. Except for the standard advertisement of W. W. Kimball with its stock cut of a square piano and the inconspicuous "card" of Julius Bauer, the firms which dealt largely in musical instruments advertised infrequently. Root & Cady, on the other hand, used progressive advertising techniques from the beginning of its career. This is particularly apparent in the Tribune where the advertising copy was changed every few days. In the less important papers, such as the Daily Chicago Herald and later The Daily Times and Herald, the firm apparently signed contracts to repeat an advertisement for a month or longer, and one advertisement of Mason Brothers' publications appeared once a week for nearly a year. Even so, compared to other firms, the design of the advertisements was likely to be distinctive. The initial insertion in the Tribune, which ran from January 15th to 25th, 1859, featured the firm's "trade mark" -- a brief musical phrase extracted from The Star Spangled Banner. For a firm that was soon to become nationally famous for its patriotic songs, the choice of trademark is apt enough to border on witchcraft. Copies of the Herald for 1859 have not been available, but judging by the "key," which was always run at the foot of each box, a very similar advertisement was run there daily from April 3rd, 1859 to April 17th, 1860. Following the original notice in the Tribune, there appeared an advertisement for the melodeons manufactured by Prince & Co., which concluded: "Preserve this advertisement for the next one will be about something else." On March 3rd appeared the firm's motto, "One price, small profits, and quick returns."

Because of the limited number of type styles available and the fact that illustrations were almost invariably printed from a few stock cuts, advertisers of that day had to exercise ingenuity to make their layouts attractive or even eye-catching in the dreary monotonous pages of small type that made up a typical nineteenth century newspaper. Root & Cady knew all the tricks for getting away from it and used them. An eight or twelve inch column would be taken and a very few words and phrases scattered down its length. The relatively white space amidst all the black type must have given somewhat the same impression as a single diamond necklace glittering in Tiffany's big window. From the earliest days, advertisers had used another method of gaining emphasis, but the device seems not to have been common in the West until Root & Cady made it so. It consisted merely in using a number of short phrases, each reprinted three times. The first use of the method by Root & Cady was in a pianoforte advertisement in the Tribune [3:1] on November 15, 1859. Later, from August 17 to September 18, 1860, they combined the two styles in a half-column advertisement of the fancy sixth edition of their Zouave Cadets Quickstep in The Daily Times and Herald with the various groups of phrases staggered and separated by wide spaces.

Another advertising device, unusual in the music trade, was the use of a full column to sum up all current matters of interest to customers. "Root & Cady's Column" appeared in the Tribune on May 7, 1860, prompting the editor to comment:

... In "Root & Cady's Column" will be found matters of interest relating to Mason & Hamlin's celebrated Harmoniums and Melodeons ... Root & Cady, the wholesale agents, are of late so often applied to for descriptive price lists that they take this method of placing before the public the information usually desired... From the manner in which Root & Cady advertise, our readers need not be told that they are doing an immense business [1:3].

Although they may not have issued price lists or catalogs at this time, the partners were resourceful in using their public performances to promote interest in Root & Cady's stock. E. T. Root sang Robert Franz's O Wert Thou in the Cauld Blast at a Briggs House Classical Concert just ten days after the Tribune announced that Root & Cady had received the song from Russell & Tolman of Boston [Feb 7 1860 (1:3)].

---

Many and various sources have been drawn upon to reconstruct the early ventures of the firm in the field of publications. Advertisements in newspapers and magazines, such as the Chicago Tribune and the New York Musical Review, have yielded many titles and dates although strangely enough there must have been a goodly number of compositions issued for which a diligent search has turned up no advertisements. The original copyright records have been checked over carefully, but unfortunately two factors have made them less useful than might be supposed. Many of Root & Cady's earlier publications were re-issues of the popular hits of the day, and except where Root could claim copyright on an arrangement or translation, they could not be registered. Secondly, the firm was particularly careless in sending in for deposit even those original works for which they were entitled to claim protection. Advertisements are constantly found saying that a composition has "just been published" with dates that precede the copyright registration by anything from two months to a year and a half. Since the serial order of the plate numbers almost invariably bears out the advertisements rather than the copyright registration, the order of publication has been established as a rule from the plate numbers, and the year given in the printed copyright claim on the title-page or at the foot of the first page of music has been preferred to the manuscript note giving the exact date of registration found on many of the copies still preserved in the Library of Congress.

The Root & Cady plate numbers have a peculiarity rarely found in those used by other firms. They consist of two sets of figures separated by a hyphen or a few dots. The first figure is the plate number proper, and the second indicates the number of printed or engraved pages in the piece in question. No doubt the feature was of assistance in assembling the correct number of plates whenever the composition was to be reprinted.

As the volume of Root & Cady's sales increased, eastern music publishers added its name as a secondary imprint to their publications. As early as May 26, 1859 [1:5], Lowell Mason's Sabbath Hymn and Tune Book was advertised as published by Mason Brothers, New York; Root & Cady, Chicago. The close association with Russell & Tolman, referred to above, is witnessed once more on July 15 of the same year [1:4] when ten sheets of music were announced as published by the Boston firm with Root & Cady given as a secondary imprint.

Two months later, on September 26 [1:3], the Tribune noted the first publication by Root & Cady, Oh, Are Ye Sleeping, Maggie, arranged by George F. Root.[4] Copies have been found with

\* \* \*

[4] A fuller description of the piece is as follows:

Oh, are ye sleeping Maggie. Scotch song as sung by J. G. Lumbard esq. Arranged by Geo. F. Root. Chicago, Root & Cady, c1859. Plate number: 3690 or 1-5

In the imprint, "Russell & Tolman, Boston" is added to "Chicago, Root & Cady, 95 Clark St." The publisher's copyright claim appears on the title-page. The music is on pp3-5 with the verso of p5 blank. Title-page and music engraved. Figure $2\frac{1}{2}$ in 7 pointed star. Deposited for copyright October 29, 1859.

two different plate numbers: 3690 or 1-5. Their next publications, a set of six ballads by George F. Root, also have two sets of plate numbers in different copies:

1. Only Waiting         3737   2-4
2. Softly She Faded     3733   3-4
3. The Forest Requiem   3738   4-4
4. My Mother She is Sleeping  3761   5-4
5. Lilly Brook          3760   6-4
6. My Home is on the Prairie  3762   7-4

    The ten sheets of music, mentioned above gave Russell & Tolman as the primary imprint and Root & Cady as the secondary; these seven pieces reverse the process. And although Russell & Tolman, presumably on the basis of the secondary imprint, advertised the seven titles in the <u>Boston Musical Times</u> as their own publications [1 (May 19 1860) 112], Root & Cady was the rightful owner since it was the latter firm that deposited them for copyright in the District Court of Northern Illinois. Probably, following along in the procedure set up for the earlier ten works, Russell & Tolman either through oversight or because no other provision had been made allowed the engraver to stamp the plates with numbers from their own series. Unquestionably, the higher numbers belong to that series since numerous publications have been found which fit into it. The point in the Russell & Tolman series reached at the beginning of 1859 can be determined from two songs by Root himself. <u>Kind friends one & all</u>, with the plate number 3292, was copyrighted in 1858; <u>Low in the dust</u>, with the plate number 3297, in 1859. Towards the end of 1859 appeared Root's <u>The quiet days when we are old</u>, PN 3660, and two songs by James G. Clark: <u>I love my Home</u>, PN 3685, <u>The Bob-o-link</u>, PN 3730. This would indicate that within the course of the single year, Russell & Tolman had published at least 433 compositions. Among them, there is ample room for the seven works they had engraved for Root & Cady. There is also no doubt that the copies with the larger plate numbers were issued earlier than those with the low Root & Cady numbers since the copies deposited for copyright in every case but one bear the larger number. The first song was registered on October 29, 1859, and with it the first three titles from the set of six Root songs; the fifth and sixth songs were deposited on April 13, 1860. For some unknown reason -- more than likely because the partners had too many other tasks to occupy their attention -- the fourth song, <u>My Mother, She is Sleeping</u>, was not deposited until January 26, 1861. It is therefore significant that the plate number on this copy is 5-4. Publication of the piece was not delayed until this date since the <u>Tribune</u> for December 1, 1859 [1:7], advertises it as "just published," and it must have appeared at least with, if not before, the fifth and sixth songs in the series. Furthermore, the copy of the fourth song in the University of Illinois Library bears the number 3761, so that we may presume that like the others it was originally issued with the Russell & Tolman plate number. The late registration makes it possible to deduce that the first supply of these songs had been exhausted before the beginning of 1861 and that in subsequent printings Root & Cady's own series of plate numbers had been substituted.

    If more evidence is needed to show that the new firm used the facilities of an established house to get started, it may be found in the fact that Mr. Root's six ballads were manufactured in Boston. They had in common an ornamental title-page with a harvesting scene, stacks of grain, farm implements, and a border of plants engraved by Greene & Walker, Boston. The music was engraved by F. G., possibly F. Göckerwitz, also of Boston.

    The eighth and ninth publications issued by Root & Cady, <u>We meet Upon the Level</u> by Chauncey M. Cady, and <u>The Pet Polka</u> "composed" by George A. Florance and arranged by Charles MacEvoy, bear no indication of where or by whom they were engraved. Perhaps they were manufactured in Chicago as were most of Root & Cady's subsequent publications. Next came a series of three polkas celebrating popular Chicago hotels, a laudable display of civic pride. Written by A. J. Vaas, leader of Chicago's Light Guard Band, the polkas have plate numbers 10, 11, and 12, and were all deposited for copyright on April 13, 1860. Number 11, however, bears the copyright date 1859 while 10 and 12 are dated 1860. Each of the three has on its title-page a small engraving of the appropriate hotel, the Richmond House (11) signed Baker, the Briggs House (10) signed S. A. Ward, printer, and the Tremont House (12) attributed in the lower margin of p5 to J. G. Osbourn, engraver, Ward, printer, all Chicago firms. Succeeding publications during 1860 bore out the <u>Tribune's</u> proud announcement on February 1, 1860 [1:4], "The mechanical portion of the work is entirely done in Chicago, and that too, in a style that would do credit to any city in the Union."

    The fifteenth publication issued by Root & Cady was its first national success, the <u>Zouave Cadets Quickstep</u>, written by A. J. Vaas for the famous regiment organized and trained by Elmer E.

Ellsworth. At least eight editions of undetermined size appeared, the copy in the University of Illinois Library being from the eighth, with a handsome colored lithograph of the cadets in uniform. Judging by the advertisement mentioned above from the <u>Daily Times & Herald</u>, however, the lithographed cover was used as early as the sixth edition. On August 20, 1860, the <u>Tribune</u> gave vent to its enthusiasm:

> Zouave Cadets Quickstep. -- Perhaps nothing of the kind before published in Chicago ever began to have the success that this piece of music is now having. Messrs. Root & Cady, the publishers, are daily receiving orders by the hundred, from all the principal cities of the Union. Three causes combine to give it this success. 1st. The music is brilliant. 2d. The popularity of the corps to whom it is dedicated and by whose band it has been played on their late tour, and 3d. The beautiful lithograph title page, done by Mendel [of Chicago] and pronounced by Eastern publishers equal to anything of this kind that has been done in New York. To the Zouaves, to the composer, Mr. Vaas, to the lithographer, and to the enterprising publishers, it is alike creditable, and its success shows that some things can be done in Chicago as well as others [1:4].

The success of the <u>Zouave Cadets Quickstep</u> marked the coming of age of Root & Cady as a publisher whose grasp of the public's taste and interests in 1860 presaged its understanding of the nation's needs from 1861 to 1865.

    A clue to the relations between Root & Cady and other music publishers throughout the country can be found in the secondary imprints on the sheets of music already mentioned. Russell & Tolman is the sole secondary imprint on the first seven publications, and from this and other indications it seems clear that they had the closest connections with Root & Cady when the new firm began publishing. The titles printed in Chicago, however, including <u>The Pet Polka</u> by George A. Florance, have all or most of these firms as secondary imprints: Boston, Russell & Tolman; New York, Wm. Hall & Son; Cincinnati, W. C. Peters & Sons; Louisville, D. P. Faulds & Co.; Milwaukee, H. N. Hempsted. (Cady's <u>We Meet Upon the Level</u> does not enter this discussion because the publisher's address, 67 Washington Street, indicated that the copy examined was issued after 1865.) If it can be assumed that a secondary imprint indicated an active dealer, it would appear that by 1860 Root & Cady had a ready outlet for its publications as well as widespread and well-placed business connections.

    At the beginning of 1861 Root & Cady was still housed in the confined quarters where the business had begun. In March, despite uncertainty in the future and the possibility of war, the firm took over the second floor above the store as a piano room. The faithful <u>Tribune</u> reported on April 1 [1:3] that the addition relieved the pressure on the crowded store, commenting: We are glad to see them "making broad their phylacteries" for it indicates that even in a dull time the influence of music is not lost, nor is it being willingly spared by the community, who are not willing while bank notes disappoint, and other notes go to protest, that there shall be any suspension of discounts in the musical way.

    A wood-cut of these salesrooms appeared in I. D. Guyer's puff of Chicago business houses[5] signed "Baker, Chicago," a signature which appeared on Root & Cady title-pages as early as 1859. The picture is consistent with the available descriptions of the store and may have been drawn from life. A "General Salesroom" was shown on the first floor with a business office in the rear behind a railing and counters on both sides, one for music and the other apparently for instruments and musical goods. A square piano or melodeon stood in the rear, bugles and drums hung from the wall. The "Piano and Melodeon Salesroom" on the second floor displayed seven instruments to several customers, one of whom was seated before an instrument playing. Carpet on the floor, many pictures on the walls, and an elaborate chandelier gave the room an appearance of prosperity and luxury.

*   *   *

[5] I. D. Guyer, <u>History of Chicago: Its Commercial and Manufacturing Interests and Industry: Together With Sketches of Manufacturers and Men Who Have Most Contributed to Its Prosperity and Advancement</u> ... (Chicago, Church, Goodman, & Cushing, 1862) p179

    This book was described by F. F. Cook in <u>Bygone Days in Chicago</u>, op cit, p232: "... in 1862, one I. D. Guyer took it into his head to publish a 'History of Chicago' ... The historical part was exceedingly brief, and for the rest the publication was a sort of literary and illustrated business directory, in which such firms as were willing to pay for the luxury were written up for all they were worth."

The story in the _Tribune_, which told of the new salesroom, also mentioned another milestone in the history of Root & Cady, a printed catalog. Since no copy has been found, we must depend on the _Tribune's_ description: "a compact and closely printed catalogue of over one hundred pages which in itself is a very complete directory to music lore, literature and wares ... sixty odd closely printed pages of Sheet Music, classified and grouped ... Instruction Books, Classic Music, Religious Hymn and Tune Books, &c."

In spite of the fact that the catalog must have listed all the titles carried by the store and not merely the firm's own publications, it would have been a decided boon in putting together the lists of publications for this period if a copy of it had been available. Although all the pertinent newspapers and music magazines have been searched, insufficient titles have been found to fit all the available plate numbers from 1 to 71 -- those issued before the outbreak of the Civil War. The 39 titles listed in _Notes_ for December, 1944, have increased to 47 with two additional numbers assigned with confidence although the pieces have not been found leaving still a number of plate numbers in excess of titles of which a record has been found. One possible explanation is that the firm published a few works for amateur composers at their own expense (as is known to have been done later). Although Root & Cady plate numbers may have been punched on the plates, the firm neither advertised nor copyrighted the works. Other pieces probably were editions of perennial favorites from the public domain printed for local consumption. With only 9 plate numbers unassigned, it seems reasonable to assume that the missing publications did not differ markedly in character from those which are known. Any great departure from its normal publishing practice would not only have been foreign to the policies of Root & Cady but should have been noticed by the local press.

CHAPTER IV

THE CIVIL WAR PERIOD

## THE CIVIL WAR PERIOD

During the Civil War, the publishing activities of Root & Cady expanded on a rising tide of war songs to include music books and a monthly magazine, <u>The Song Messenger of the Northwest</u>. While issuing war songs that have never lost their flavor, <u>The Battle Cry of Freedom</u>, <u>Tramp, Tramp, Tramp</u>, and <u>Kingdom Coming</u>, Root & Cady also published many songs and instrumental pieces which had no discernable connection with the war. This chapter will attempt to cover the high spots of this exciting period, by inter-relating the many types of publications and services offered by Root & Cady to Chicago, to the Northwest, and to the Union.

A year or two after our entry in World War II, when there had been time to note the peculiar phenomenon that this war had produced no patriotic songs worthy of the name, several writers started looking to the past for songs that had moved the people. Lehman Engel, in <u>Modern Music</u> [19 (March-April) 149] and Earl Robinson at the Writers' Congress held at the University of California in Los Angeles in October, 1943, agreed that the songs written during the war to preserve the Union and free the slaves had never been equaled. In the past, however, these songs were better appreciated by the political historian and the G.A.R. veteran than the musician. Reminiscences of the sixties frequently pay tribute to the inspiration and enthusiasm with which they were sung by soldier and civilian alike. Contemporary accounts leave little doubt that these songs were consciously produced to help fight the war by writers, composers and publishers, whose sympathies for the most part were wholeheartedly with the Union cause, while the men who sang them at recruiting rallies and mass meetings chose them for the message they carried to the people. As one writer put it,[1] the more successful songs had been "the white caps of popular feeling."

Within the firm of Root & Cady, Union sentiment was general. As early as January 4, 1861, three months before the inauguration of Lincoln, when South Carolina alone had seceded, Root & Cady, among other firms, signed a call printed in the <u>Chicago Tribune</u> [1:5] asking the people of Chicago "without distinction of party, who are in favor of standing by the Constitution and the Union and the enforcement of the laws" to meet in Bryan Hall the following day. Never one to chase an elusive inspiration, George F. Root wrote his songs to fit the times. In his autobiography, <u>The Story of a Musical Life</u> [p136], he gives his approach to the war song: "... when anything happened that could be voiced in a song, or when the heart of the Nation was moved by particular circumstances or conditions caused by the war, I wrote what I thought would then express the emotions of the soldiers or the people." The firm's other star composer, Henry Clay Work, was the son of Alanson Work, anti-slavery advocate and operator on the Underground Railroad. In the preface to the collected edition of Work's songs,[2] Bertram G. Work claimed that Alanson Work helped nearly 4,000 slaves to reach freedom before he was imprisoned for his activities. His father's sufferings and the contacts with runaway slaves must have contributed fervor and authenticity to many of Henry Work's songs. Benjamin Hanby, the composer of <u>Darling Nelly Gray</u> and <u>Ole Shady</u>, who worked for Root & Cady for a time after the war, also had a father, the Rev. Mr. William Hanby of Rushville, Ohio, who like Alanson Work was listed as a station master or operator in Wilbur H. Siebert's classic study, <u>The Underground Railroad from Slavery to Freedom</u> (New York, The Macmillan Co., 1898). Another associate of the firm, James R. Murray, volunteered and served in the Union forces throughout the war. While in the army, he composed the widely successful sentimental ballad, <u>Daisy Deane</u>, which Root & Cady published. A not inconsiderable number of other songs in their catalog appeared with the name of the author or composer proudly prefaced with his commission and followed by the name of his regiment while still others are dedicated to some friend in the service or to the national hero who inspired the composition.

On April 12, 1861, the bombardment of Fort Sumter sounded the beginning of war. While the news was still coming over the telegraph wires, George F. Root must have started writing Root & Cady's first war song, <u>The First Gun is Fired! May God Protect the Right!</u> Three days later it was in print and had been deposited for copyright in the District Court for Northern Illinois. The <u>Tribune</u> for April 16 [4:1] confirms this by reporting that on the previous day it had been sung at a patriotic rally in Metropolitan Hall by "the Messrs. Lumbard and other gentlemen in excellent style, the audience who had been supplied with copies, joining in the chorus." As luck would have it, a copy of the broadside supplied to the audience

\*   \*   \*

[1] <u>The Song Messenger</u>, Aug 1867, p72
[2] H. C. Work, <u>Songs</u> ... compiled by Bertram G. Work ... (New York, J. J. Little & Ives Co., [188-?]) p3

has survived since it was deposited at the same time as the regular sheet music edition and bears the legend across its back in the hand of the County Clerk: "Filed & entered April 15, 1861." It is a fairly crude affair, printed from a stereotype plate on thin paper, giving only the melody and three stanzas of the words. The white heat of Mr. Root's creative faculties and his firm's presses is further borne out by an advertisement in the Tribune for April 19 [4:4] saying that copies of both forms were available for sale -- the one with pianoforte or organ accompaniment at 25 cents and the broadside at 50 cents a dozen. On April 23, the Tribune [4:3] reported that the song had been sung at a mass meeting in the Wigwam after 10,000 people had taken the oath of fealty. The chorus "was given with a will, and with the finest effect by the immense throng." Although it was soon to be superseded by other, more successful songs, The First Gun is Fired! stands as the first of many rallying and recruiting songs.

> The first gun is fired!
> May God protect the right!
> Let the freeborn sons of the North arise
> In power's avenging night;
> Shall the glorious Union our fathers made
> By ruthless hands be sunder'd?
> And we of freedom's sacred rights
> By trait'rous foes be plunder'd?
>
> Arise! Arise! Arise!
> And gird ye for the fight.
> And let our watchword ever be,
> "May God protect the right!" ...

During the first exciting weeks of the war, Root & Cady concentrated on recruiting songs. By May 23 five were available, and advertised in the Tribune [1:7]. "To All who Love Union and Freedom, Root & Cady's Patriotic Songs." Three of them were by Root, The First Gun Is Fired!, God Bless Our Brave Young Volunteers, and Forward, Boys, Forward; and one each by Henrie L. Frisbie, The Stars and Stripes, the Flag of the Free, and E. C. Saffery, The Union Volunteers. The excitement was soon tempered by mourning for the first great tragedy of the war was Illinois' own. On May 24, Col. Elmer E. Ellsworth, leader of the famous Zouaves, was killed at Alexandria, Virginia. His death was commemorated with the Ellsworth Requiem, by A. J. Vaas, the local bandmaster who had had such a success with the Zouave Cadets Quickstep in 1860. The Light Guard Band under Mr. Vaas played the Requiem at the Ellsworth funeral services at Bryan Hall which were reported at length in the Tribune for June 3 [1:3]. Its publication was a unique instance of cooperation between Root & Cady and a local competitor for the Ellsworth Requiem shared its lithographed title-page design with Sadly the Bells Toll the Death of the Hero, by A. B. Tobey, published by A. J. Higgins.

On September 16 [4:1] the Tribune announced the publication of the "Army Regulations for Drum, Fife and Bugle, being a complete manual for these instruments, giving all the calls for camp and field duty," by William Nevins, drum major of Gen. McClellan's body guard, the Sturges Rifles, and formerly associated with the Light Guard Band of Chicago. The western army, however, was not satisfied by the music of drum and bugle; each regiment wanted a band -- and the trade in instruments consequently soared. Root & Cady, reported the Tribune for September 26 [4:1], were receiving brass and German silver instruments at the rate of $1,000 worth a day. The next day [4:7] a notice appeared asking musicians who wished to form a band for the 19th Regiment Illinois Volunteers to call at Root & Cady's or at Julius Bauer's. By October 22 [4:1] the band had twenty-two members, equipped with instruments from Root & Cady.

The sale of instruments was of course restricted to the Northwest, but the war songs were beginning to attract attention in the East. One of the songs published early in 1862 spoke for the loyal wives, H. T. Merrill's Take Your Gun and Go, John:

> Don't stop a moment to think, John
> Your country calls, then go,
> Don't fear for me nor the children, John,
> I'll care for them, you know!
> Leave the corn upon the stalk, John,
> The fruit upon the tree,

44

> And all our little stores, John
> Yes, leave them all to me.
>
> Then take your gun and go, John,
> Take your gun and go,
> For Ruth can drive the oxen, John
> And I can use the hoe ...

In later stanzas the wife tells John that she will do her best for the children if he does not return. And then, commending him to God's care, she finishes

> Be our beloved country's shield,
> Till war shall pass away.

Not fine poetry, these verses give a straightforward portrait of an unassuming heroine who had little in common with the sentimental Victorian lady who has graced so many novels and motion pictures.

When Root & Cady had a good song on hand, Mr. Cady, in charge of advertising, knew well how to promote it. For a week before the publication of Kingdom Coming, Henry Work's first national hit, the mysterious words "Kingdom Coming!" stared at the citizens of Chicago from newspapers and street posters causing all kinds of speculation according to the Tribune for April 19, 1862 [4:1]. The song was at last introduced by Christy's Minstrels in a production named in its honor which opened April 23. By May 2 the Tribune predicted for it the fame of Dixie adding

> The Negro melodists, theatre orchestra and rural concert givers are producing it in every part of the country. The composer has worked himself into a popularity which must have astonished him [4:1].

Climbing onto the band wagon, H. M. Higgins acknowledged the success of Kingdom Coming by announcing a new song, The Kingdom Has Come, on May 7 [4:1].

Three months after publication the Tribune for July 10 [4:1] stated that the sale of Kingdom Coming had already reached 8,000 copies, and by November 18 [4:3], it had passed the 20,000 mark. More impressive than its sale, however, was the speed with which it traveled throughout the country reaching even the illiterate slaves behind the Confederate lines. A correspondent of the New York Evening Post with Gen. Banks' army in western Louisiana was quoted in the Chicago Tribune for June 10, 1863 [2:2], as saying of the slaves: "Everywhere they flocked out to welcome us.... They give us full particulars as to the sentiments and history of their masters, and in other ways manifest their friendship, acting as if they could not do enough for us. One of the songs which they are in the habit of singing runs as follows:

> " 'Massa run away, hi, hi!
> Nigger bound to stay, ho, ho!
> I tink dat now de Kingdom come,
> Dat dis de year of Jubilo!' "

The resemblance between this chorus and the official version of Kingdom Coming is very strong.

> De Massa run? ha, ha!
> De darkey stay? ho, ho!
> It mus' be now de kingdom comin'
> An' de year ob Jubilo!

Still another version is given under the title The Contraband as an authentic song of the Mississippi Negroes sung during the Vicksburg campaign:

> Massa run away,
> Darkie stay a home;
> It must be now dat de kingdom's coming
> In de year of Jubilum.[3]

Curiously enough, Mrs. Staton interpreted this joyous welcome of freedom as an amusing expression of loyalty to the Confederacy. She pictured the master in hiding from the Yankee raiding parties, but made no attempt to explain the reference to the coming kingdom, nor does her version include the third and fourth stanzas found in the official editions, concluding with

> De whip is lost, de handcuffs broken,
> But de massa'll hab his pay;
> He's old enough, big enough, ought to know better,
> Den to went an' run away.

It is possible that Work based his composition on a folk song, but no versions earlier than his have been found, nor has his claim to authorship ever been disputed. The music which accompanies these words is a rollicking tune, full of folk flavor and spirit. It has been used by Robert L. Sanders as thematic material for the final movement of a string quartet, and in 1945, served as the music which introduced the radio program of Edgar Bergen and Charlie McCarthy.

Following <u>Kingdom Coming</u> by four months, <u>The Battle Cry of Freedom</u> became almost at once the great rallying song of the war. George F. Root, in his autobiography, <u>The Story of a Musical Life</u>, gave the traditional story of its composition and introduction:

> I heard of President Lincoln's second call for troops one afternoon while reclining on a lounge in my brother's house. Immediately a song started in my mind, words and music together:
>
> > "Yes, we'll rally round the flag, boys, we'll rally once again,
> > Shouting the battle-cry of freedom."
>
> I thought it out that afternoon, and wrote it the next morning at the store. The ink was hardly dry when the Lumbard brothers ... came in for something to sing at a war meeting that was to be holden immediately in the court-house square just opposite. They went through the new song once, and then hastened to the steps of the court-house, followed by a crowd that had gathered while the practice was going on. Then Jule's magnificent voice gave out the song, and Frank's trumpet tones led the refrain ... and at the fourth verse a thousand voices were joining in the chorus. From there the song went into the army, and the testimony in regard to its use in the camp and on the march, and even on the field of battle ... made me thankful that if I could not shoulder a musket in defense of my country, I could serve her in this way [p132-3].

It is not surprising that Root writing in 1891 did not clearly remember the details of his story. The meeting to which he referred was held on July 26, 1862, while the song had been sung for the first time two days earlier at the Board of Trade War Meeting, according to the <u>Tribune</u> for July 25 [4:3]: "Following the speech of Mr. Arnold was the singing of <u>The Battle Cry of Freedom</u>, words and music composed by Geo. F. Root, Esq., of this city, after attending the great war meeting of last Saturday night [July 19]..." The meeting mentioned by Mr. Root was headlined in the <u>Tribune</u> for July 28 [4:1] as "The Great War Meeting / Immense Uprising of the People / The Enthusiasm Increasing / Speeches from Three Stands at Once / Twenty Thousand People Celebrating / The Court House Square Crowded / Stirring Music -- Patriotic Songs ..."

In the circumstances of the singing at this gathering lie conclusive evidence that the song could not have been sung from the manuscript with the ink hardly dry. The <u>Tribune</u> [4:1] went on to say that it "was sung by a well trained chorus of voices, J. G. Lumbard sustaining the solo and the band furnishing

\* \* \*

[3] Kate E. Staton, comp. <u>Old Southern Songs of the Period of the Confederacy: the Dixie Trophy Collection</u> (New York, S. French, c1926) p101

the accompaniment." In the same issue appeared the first advertisement of the song [1:9].

From its introduction until the end of the war, no meeting was complete without The Battle Cry of Freedom.[4] During the spring election campaign of 1863, the Tribune for April 21 separated its news items with slogans, including "Rally round the ballot box for the old flag, the Constitution, and the Union" and "The Battle Cry of Freedom at the ballot box today." On November 4 [1:1] the results of the presidential election were headed with the chorus of The Battle Cry of Freedom as a masthead. When the news of Lee's surrender reached Chicago, popular emotion found release in music reported the Tribune for April 10, 1865:

> A large crowd gathered in front of the Tremont House, and made the night musical with their cheers and shouts of joy. "John Brown," the "Battle Cry of Freedom" and "Praise God from Whom All Blessings Flow" were sung by the multitude with great fervor... Bonfires were lighted in all the principal streets ... As we write (1 A.M.) a band is promenading the streets playing national music, and all along our thoroughfares resound the shouts and cheers of an enthusiastic and excited multitude ... [4:2].

In the army as well as on the home front, The Battle Cry of Freedom was tremendously effective in creating enthusiasm and maintaining morale.

> Yes, we'll rally 'round the flag, boys, we'll rally once again,
>   Shouting the battle cry of Freedom.
> We will rally from the hill-side, we'll gather from the plain,
>   Shouting the battle cry of Freedom.
>
> The Union forever, Hurrah! boys, hurrah!
>   Down with the traitor, Up with the star;
> While we rally 'round the flag, boys, rally once again,
>   Shouting the battle cry of Freedom ...
>
> We will welcome to our numbers the loyal, true and brave,
>   Shouting the battle cry of Freedom,
> And altho' they may be poor, not a man shall be a slave,
>   Shouting the battle cry of Freedom ...

In The Century Magazine for December, 1887 [35:320] a letter from a G.A.R. veteran recalled the black days at Murfreesboro just after the battle of Stone's River when the losses on the field were augmented by resignations of officers from the border states who disapproved of the Emancipation Proclamation. When morale was at its lowest, a glee club came down from Chicago bringing a new song, The Battle Cry of Freedom.

> The effect was little short of miraculous. It put as much spirit and cheer into the army as a victory. Day and night one could hear it by every camp fire and in every tent. I never shall forget how the men rolled out the line, "And although he may be poor, he shall never be a slave."

Widely varying estimates of the total sale of this song have been found; two years after the war the firm claimed a sale of 350,000 copies, and in later years, the figure continued to mount to "between five

\* \* \*

[4] Cf Chicago Daily Tribune, Aug 2 1862 4:4; Oct 23 1862 4:1; Apr 10 1863 4:1, and July 13 1864 4:2-3

and seven hundred thousand."[5] Since these figures apparently include publications of the song in book form, they are high but perhaps not impossibly so.

With The Battle Cry of Freedom, Root & Cady got into their stride as the country's chief purveyor of patriotic songs, a role of which they continued to boast in various little articles and notes in The Song Messenger until long after the war was over. Quite obviously, they felt that their publications were as much "munitions of war" as bullets, and headed one of their advertisements in the Tribune, September 1, 1862 [1:8], with that phrase. This was not simply shrewd business. They felt their patriotic and political duties keenly and took an active and responsible part in helping to shape opinions and events in their community. While many loyal supporters of the Union, in Illinois as elsewhere, were still strongly opposed to emancipation by proclamation, the names of C. M. Cady and G. F. Root appeared in an appeal to the President calling for a decree of emancipation as "a sign of national repentance as well as a military necessity [Tribune Sept 4 1862 (4:6)].

As the controversy on emancipation continued, Root & Cady brought out the first music book to be printed in Chicago, The Silver Lute, which was manufactured on the Tribune's presses as that paper proudly stated on September 24 [4:1] designating it "The first music book ever prepared, stereotyped and printed in Chicago." An earlier music book, C. M. Cady's Minnehaha Glee Book, published by H. M. Higgins in 1857, was printed in New York by Miller & Curtis, Music Printers, cor. White & Center Sts. according to the notice on the verso of the title-page. The Silver Lute was deposited for copyright on September 26; a month later [1:6] Root & Cady advertised that the first edition of 10,000 copies was nearly exhausted. Had the book been printed a decade earlier, George F. Root would have promoted its sale by using it as a text at the musical conventions and normal schools he held throughout the country. By 1862, although conventions were still held, music was recognized as part of the public school curriculum, and the school board, by adopting a book, could assure its sale to every child within the school district. Six weeks after publication, The Silver Lute was proposed for adoption by the Chicago Board of Education. Judging from the discussion reported in the Tribune for November 6 [4:3], the provision made for instruction in music was lamentable.

At the regular monthly meeting of the Board, Mr. Steele, of the Committee on Text Books, moved that The Silver Lute be adopted as the music book for the schools. His speech in support of the motion was not reported, but the opposition pointed out that there was no music teacher employed in the schools and that the books compiled by Mason and Bradbury now in the possession of the children, though old, were still

\*   \*   \*

[5] Lydia A. Coonley, "George F. Root and His Songs," New England Magazine, 19 (Jan 1896) 564 "At one time his publishers had fourteen printing presses at work on 'The Battle Cry of Freedom,' and could not supply the demand. A single house often ordered twenty thousand copies...."

Cf a report of the annual meeting of the Board of Music Trade in the Chicago Tribune, July 21 1865 2:4: "It is no uncommon thing for successful songs to reach a sale of from 30,000 to 50,000 each. 'Lilly Dale,' published by Oliver Ditson & Co., Boston, for example, reached, I am told, a sale of 65,000. 'Rosalie, the Prairie Flower,' published by Tolman & Co., Boston, reached the extraordinary figure of 129,000 in the course of only three or four years. 'Tramp, Tramp, or the Prisoner's Hope,' published only last January by Root & Cady, of your city, has already reached an issue of nearly 100,000 and I heard some of the oldest Boston publishers ... predict that it would reach 200,000 thus beating everything known in the history of the trade."

The "Extra" issue of The Song Messenger, published in April, 1867, cites sales figures for some of the firm's more popular songs. The two entries for The Battle Cry of Freedom may explain some of the discrepancies in the different calculations. Root & Cady included the song in most of their methods, collections, and singing books, so that if figures on sales of these are worked into the grand total almost any number, if it were of sufficiently astronomical proportions, could be justified.

| 1862 | Kingdom Coming. By Henry C. Work | 75,000 |
| --- | --- | --- |
| 1862 | Battle Cry of Freedom, in sheet form | 100,000 |
| 1862 | Battle Cry of Freedom, in book form | 250,000 |
| 1863 | Vacant Chair [by Geo. F. Root] | Nearly 100,000 |
| 1864 | Just Before the Battle, Mother | 100,000 |
| 1865 | Tramp, Tramp, Tramp | 150,000 |

The statistician in the compiler caused him to add: "Total weight of above, thirty-three tons." A more extended history of the song is given in the author's "The Battle Cry of Freedom," Civil War History, Special Issue: Civil War Music, 4 (Sept 1958) 307-18.

serviceable. In support of the motion, Mr. Sheahan said no one had purchased a book by Mason or Bradbury in recent years unless they were green [sic], and Mr. Taft demanded a text-book to assist the classroom teacher who was required to teach music. Running a middle course, Mr. Holden agreed to support the motion if the publishers would take in exchange whatever singing books were now in use. "He did not know much of the book named, but thought if the compiler had selected more and written less, it would have been an improvement." After much acrimonious discussion, the motion was passed, and the children of Chicago became potential purchasers of The Silver Lute.

With the successful publication of The Silver Lute, Root & Cady soon began to extend its activities in the field of books and instrumental methods. The war songs bearing its imprint were known and sung throughout the country, including the Confederacy where several songs were available in pirated editions. Richard B. Harwell's checklist of "Sheet Music Published in the Confederate States" in his Confederate Music (Chapel Hill, University of North Carolina Press, c1950, p101-56) included The Battle-Cry of Freedom, Just Before the Battle, Mother, Kingdom Coming, and The Vacant Chair. Upon the firm foundation of a prosperous trade in instruments and musical goods, Root & Cady felt ready as a publisher for open competition with the older publishing houses of the east. Its aim was to take over the music trade of the Northwest while selling as much as possible to the Eastern states. To provide a regular means of communication with its customers and the public generally, Root & Cady established in April, 1863, a monthly magazine, The Song Messenger of the Northwest, Henry C. Work, editor.

At this time several musical periodicals were issued in the East, for example, Dwight's Journal of Music in Boston and the Musical Review and Musical World in New York. Previous to Root & Cady's effort, there had been several attempts in that direction in Chicago which were listed in F. W. Scott's Newspapers and Periodicals of Illinois, 1814-1879, (Rev. and enl. ed. Springfield, Ill., The Trustees of the Illinois State Historical Library, 1910): the Western Journal of Music, 1856-1857, a semi-monthly paper "devoted to literature and art ... to the advancement of musical knowledge and interest, in the western states, particularly," edited by William H. Currie and published by R. G. Greene [p71]: and the Flower Queen, 1856-1857, edited by William C. Webster and published by Higgins Brothers which, after six months, became the Chicago Musical Review, edited by Mr. Cady. None of these lasted more than a year, however, while Root & Cady's venture was destined to continue until 1875, surviving the Chicago fire and two reorganizations of the firm.

The Song Messenger of the Northwest resembled in style and content most of its contemporaries, excepting always Dwight's Journal of Music. Like the others, it was primarily a house organ accepting advertisements from no other publisher. Although it was copyrighted, the publishers reserved the rights of the music only inviting editors to copy the articles [1:9]. In the first issue were a dedicatory poem, "The Song Messenger" by G. F. Root, two sketches, "John Prosy's Talks by the Fireside" and "Frank Whiteside's Introduction to Society," by the Editor, musical chit-chat, and five vocal quartettes by Mr. Root. The first editorial [1:8], setting its tone, was a characteristic blend of regional pride, musical uplift and democratic patriotism, ending, "Our aim -- is simply this: While making a musical paper especially for 'the people,' to furnish one which shall be of interest and value to the most highly-cultivated artist."

At the end of the month marked by the first issue of The Song Messenger, Root & Cady had ready for sale a low-priced collection of fifty war songs including The Battle Cry of Freedom, Flag of the Fearless and Free, Brave Boys Are They (for which H. M. Higgins held the copyright), Kingdom Coming, and many others. Priced at $3.00 a dozen, sample copies, 25 cents, The Bugle Call was quite a bargain in comparison with Higgins Patriotic Glee Book, published in the same year containing thirty-six songs, which sold at $8.00 a dozen, 75 cents a copy. The purpose of The Bugle Call was clearly stated in its Preface for all to see:

> This book is designed for use in all gatherings of loyal people, whether around the campfire, or the hearth-stone, whether in the Union meeting, or in the Loyal Leagues, wherever the fire of patriotism burns, there may its tones, like the bugle-call arouse every true heart to a greater love for the Union, and a sterner determination to protect it to the last.

Including many of the hit tunes of the day and priced attractively for a mass market, The Bugle Call should have been widely circulated. In the annual "Extra" of The Song Messenger for April, 1867, it is claimed that a total of 50,000 copies had been sold.

In The Bugle Call, the songs of George F. Root and Henry C. Work stand out for vigor of thought and language and for their rousing tunes. In all likelihood there was close, if unvoiced, agreement between the two composers as to the role and qualities of a good war song. On other matters, however, dissension was soon apparent. In <u>The Song Messenger</u> for July, 1863, Henry C. Work voiced strong disapproval of the alterations made in old tunes by modern compilers of hymn and tune books. This attack was answered the following month by George F. Root, himself. In a most serious column [1:67] headed "TO ALL READERS OF THE SONG MESSENGER," Mr. Root stated that Mr. Work had spoken for himself, not for the publishers, who believed that the faults and untasteful places in the old tunes caused them to be outmoded, regardless of how many people still clung to them. "... if they do not like the improvements, let them sing in the old way -- I am sorry for the temporary inconvenience these changes cost, but I must put forth my work to the world as well as I can make it, and not entail upon the younger singers the faults and false tastes of their fathers ... Is it possible ... that none of the tunes of past time can be improved in the light and greater knowledge of this age with its new and improved circumstances? ..."

Taken as a whole, the paragraphs reveal the least attractive side of Mr. Root's personality. Like other public educators before and after him, he could be a zealot with little appreciation for anyone's ideas but his own. Undoubtedly, he had been too often guilty of Mr. Work's charges, and although his "improvements" may never have been as tasteless as the example which Work cited, he must have felt that the criticism could be applied to him, and he was not willing to accept it. As editor, Work could include his own answer to the rebuttal in the same issue -- again, apparently, without Root's prior knowledge. Designed as an amplification and further explanation of an arguable point, it has the natural modesty characteristic of a man of broad emotional experience and deep human sympathies.

> ... Mr. Root speaks of the progress in arts and sciences, and asks if it can be possible that music is left behind. Now I am not opposing improvements in music. I believe in all kinds of real improvement. For instance, I believe that we ... are making advancement in the art of Painting; but does it follow from that, that all our old pictures should be altered? that each time-honored canvas should be retouched each year, in order to keep pace with the improvements ...?
> 
> ... It is a false notion that <u>everything</u> should be put through the mill of improvement. The people don't want the portraits of their fathers improved.... They wish their family relics left undisturbed.
> 
> In conclusion, let me address a question or two to those who alter our tunes; and, be assured, I do it not in anger.
> 
> Tell me, was it kind for that rich man who had an abundance of flocks and herds to seize his poor neighbor's one little ewe lamb, and slaughter it for his guest? Is it kind, is it brotherly, is it right then, for you, while having in the works of the great masters and other sources, an almost endless treasury from which to draw materials to experiment on -- is it right for you to appropriate the old tunes which are treasured up almost entirely by sincere worshipers, and which form, with many, in clusters of two, three or half a dozen, their only means of uniting in the worship of song? Is it right?

The debate ended there. Mr. Work was so manifestly correct that there was nothing left which Mr. Root could say in words. The interests of Root & Cady in general and of G. F. Root in particular, however, rested on the sale of music books written in the didactic tradition, and therefore with the November issue Henry Work's name disappeared from the masthead. A few months later, he was called upon to write the leading editorial, but only because Mr. Root was too busy and Mr. Cady indisposed. He develops the point at some length, and then rounds out his "essay" with such non-controversial subjects as how a man should get plenty of good, nourishing food, lots of out-door exercise, and at least eight hours of sleep each night. Later, from time to time, he wrote other articles, but until January, 1871, when James R. Murray took over formally, no editor was specified. Where Work's name had appeared in the masthead stood: "Root & Cady, Publishers."

Meanwhile, business was good. <u>The Silver Lute</u> was officially adopted as "the singing book best adapted to the wants of public schools" by the Minnesota State Teachers' Convention, meeting on the 26th and 27th of August, according to the Tribune for September 17, 1863 [4:4]. Orders were coming from all parts of the country. By October 16 [4:3-4], the sale exceeded 1,000 copies a day, and the books were not printed and bound fast enough to keep up with the demand.

A card game called "Musical Celebrities" was filed for copyright on May 11, 1863. It consisted of ninety-six cards with the names and short biographical sketches of eminent composers and performers, modeled on the old game of "Authors." Thereafter, a steady stream of books, mostly small but occasionally larger, began to appear from their presses at intervals. A check list of the books published will be given in

Appendix IV.

Meanwhile, Root & Cady continued with their primary occupation -- the publishing of sheet music. Much of it was completely unwarlike. They are said to have obtained the sheet music rights to two Stephen C. Foster songs originally written for Clark's School Visitor. Mine Is the Mourning Heart will be found in the appended list under plate number 290; no copy of Beautiful Child of Song, however, has been located. During 1863, they also published Henry Work's The Days When We Were Young, Tarantelle, by Albert Loeschhorn, and Love, Sweet Love Is Everywhere, by J. M. Hubbard, besides a steady stream of war songs. The last song of 1862 was Work's Little Major, followed in 1863 by '63 Is the Jubilee, by D. A. French; Work's Song of a Thousand Years; Root's Just Before the Battle, Mother, his Within the Sound of the Enemy's Guns; and Work's Babylon Is Fallen! a "sequel to Kingdom Coming." Babylon Is Fallen! was a graphic picture of Negroes in the army.

> Don't you see de black clouds risin' over yonder,
>   Whar de Massa's ole plantation am?
> Nebber you be frightened, dem is only darkeys,
>   Come to jine and fight for Uncle Sam.
>
> Look out dar, now, we's agwine to shoot,
>   Look out dar, don't you understand,
> Babylon is fallen, Babylon is fallen!
>   And we's agwine to occupy de land ...

In contrast, Little Major was typical of the sincere sentimentality of the nostalgic songs of love, mother, home, and mourning for those lost in battle which were so popular, North and South, during the war. These songs have aged more than their martial contemporaries, but the best of them, Just Before the Battle, Mother and The Vacant Chair, still have appeal today. Little Major, however, may fairly be called a period piece.

> At his post, the "Little Major"
>   Dropp'd his drum, that battle day;
> On the grass, all stain'd with crimson,
>   Through that battle night he lay --
> Crying "Oh! for love of Jesus,
>   "Grant me but this little boon!
> "Can you, friend, refuse me water?
>   "Can you, when I die so soon?" ...
>
> Now the lights are flashing round him,
>   And he hears a loyal word,
> Strangers they, whose lips pronounce it,
>   Yet he trusts his voice is heard.
> It is heard -- Oh, God forgive them!
>   They refuse his dying pray'r!
> "Nothing but a wounded drummer."
>   So they say, and leave him there ...

A contradiction in the nineteenth century personality which the twentieth century cannot fathom was the combination of limp sentimentality and the most vigorous action. The ladies who wept over the sad fate of Little Major accomplished miracles in supplying the needs and comforts of the armies in the days before the Red Cross. When the ladies organized a great Northwestern Sanitary Fair in the fall of 1863 to raise money for their work, Root & Cady was happy to cooperate. The Tribune for October 30 [4:3] announced that a Vose piano from Root & Cady's would be raffled at the Fair, five dollars a ticket. Enterprising but unsuccessful was its bid for the purchase of the original manuscript of Lincoln's Emancipation Proclamation, described by the Tribune of November 18 [4:3] as "liberal and generous." Messrs. Root & Cady offered twenty-one hundred dollars, stipulating that the firm should issue facsimiles to be sold by the United States Sanitary Commission "at a price that will afford said Commission a profit of one hundred per cent, and also afford us a per centage of profit on the cost of manufacture." When Root & Cady were fully reimbursed for the outlay, the manuscript was to be presented to the Chicago Historical Society.

The year 1863 was prosperous for the music trade of Chicago judging from the few statistics that have been found. The Song Messenger for April 1864 [2:8] proclaimed that Root & Cady alone during that year issued over 258,000 pieces of sheet music "which if stretched out sheet by sheet would bridge the entire State of Illinois from Chicago to the Mississippi River" besides nearly 100,000 music books. "The plate punching, engraving, lithographing, stereotyping, printing and binding were all done in Chicago, and nearly all of them in their own establishment." That most dependable index to a firm's prosperity, the incomes of the partners, was given in the Tribune for January 7, 1865 [4:2], in a "List of incomes above and including $3,000 ... for the year ending Dec. 31, 1863": C. M. Cady, $6,100; G. F. Root, $7,345; and H. M. Higgins, $6,282. The return for 1864, printed July 4, 1865 [4:3], showed upward trends for Root & Cady and the reverse for Higgins: C. M. Cady, $8,965; E. T. Root, $9,154; G. F. Root, $10,188; and H. M. Higgins, $3,701. In Chicago's music trade, the highest income for 1864 went to Alanson Reed, of Reed's Temple of Music, a dealer who did little publishing -- $19,832.

As the business grew, an expansion of the plant was in order. In The Song Messenger for November [2:120] the publishers announced: "We have now purchased and just got in operation, two steam power presses: a cylinder press, which gives us 1,200 impressions an hour ... to print our stereotyped sheet music, and a six roller Adams press, such as the Harper's use for their finest book and wood cut work, to print Silver Lute, Bugle Call, Musical Curriculum, Song Messenger, &c." By the end of 1864 [2:133, i.e., 143] the firm's paper consumption had reached nearly one ton a week on the average.

1864 also saw the publication of one of the most tearful ballads the world has ever known, Henry Clay Work's Come Home, Father, called widely by its first line, "Father, dear father, come home with me now." This sad saga of the drunkard's child showed that Work was capable of writing the worst kind of tear-jerker as well as fine war songs and a simple ballad like Grandfather's Clock. With solemnity, real or assumed, Root & Cady reprinted the lugubrious words of Come, Home, Father in The Song Messenger for June offering a free copy to the hardy soul who could read it without weeping. The July issue [2:57] carried the news that ten people had claimed free copies. Estimating its readers at more than ten thousand, the editors stated that only one in a thousand had read the poem with dry eyes.

As the war approached its close, the presses of Root & Cady were hard at work. January, 1865, saw the publication of Henry Work's Marching Through Georgia in the midst of the first success of Root's Tramp, Tramp, Tramp; or, The Prisoner's Hope. Of Tramp, the Tribune for January 14 declared it "has all the elements of a wonderful success. It has been sung all the week at the Academy of Music and other places of amusement, and has at times won a double encore, the company being compelled by the audience to sing it three times" [4:1]. A wonderful success it was; by July it was reported to have sold almost 100,000 copies. A dispatch from the annual meeting of the Board of Music Trade at Niagara Falls to the Tribune for July 21 [2:4] said "some of the oldest Eastern publishers ... predict that it would reach 200,000, thus beating everything known in the history of the trade." Although the end of the war cut its career short, the martial roll of Tramp has made it a perennial favorite with the American people. Let no one assume, moreover, that its fame was restricted to the United States; across the Pacific the Japanese soldier is said to call it his own. In Le Monde Moderne [1 (Apr 1895) 571], Motoyosi-Saizau, writing of "L'Armé Japonaise," quoted a marching song of the Japanese army, the music of which was Tramp, Tramp, Tramp with only minor changes in rhythm. Do the Japanese still sing it? And did any Americans in Philippine prison camps recognize it and remember the original?

> In the prison cell I sit, thinking, mother dear, of you,
> And our bright and happy home so far away,
> And the tears they fill my eyes, spite of all that I can do,
> Tho' I try to cheer my comrades and be gay.
> Tramp, tramp, tramp, the boys are marching,
> Cheer up, comrades, they will come,
> And beneath the starry flag, we shall breathe the air again,
> Of the free-land in our own beloved home.

Throughout the war Root & Cady's catalog, so far as is known, consisted entirely of music for voice, piano or guitar. No chamber music of any kind, not even violin with piano accompaniment, is to be found in it, no orchestral scores nor parts. The composers represented in the list were for the most part members of Root & Cady's staff, professional and semi-amateur musicians of Chicago or the vicinity, a few visiting virtuosos and a sprinkling of the more popular song writers of the nation, lured from their regular publishers for a number or two. There were but few foreign composers, and those few never of the best in spite of the fact that the firm could have had its pick since none but resident Americans enjoyed copyright protection in this country at that period.

To give a more comprehensive picture of the productions of the firm from the out-break of the Civil War through December, 1865, a check list, arranged by plate number, has been appended. It is not complete, particularly for the first year and a half. Having rushed <u>The First Gun Is Fired</u> to the clerk's office in record time, the firm deposited a single piece -- Hambaugh's <u>Stars and Stripes S'chottisch</u>, PN 129 -- on November 20, 1861, but did nothing further about registering their publications until the appearance of Root's book, <u>The Silver Lute</u>, provoked a house cleaning. By this time, they had reached PN 247 in their series of sheet music publications which means that 175 pieces had been published since the appearance of their first war song. Nonetheless, on September 26, 1862, only 66 musical works were registered for copyright, of which nine had already appeared before the period under discussion. Of the remaining 57, copies of 46 have been found, not all of them in Washington. If the clerk for the Northern District of Illinois transferred all the compositions which had been deposited with him to Washington when the central depository was set up in 1871, a most diligent search has not located them. To make up for this in some degree, seven works which bear a printed claim of copyright on their covers but which were not registered in the copyright ledgers have turned up, as well as nine additional publications of works which were in the public domain and which therefore could not be registered. Many such pieces are listed in advertisements and on the back covers of other publications. They include popular salon pieces by contemporary European favorites like Theodore Oesten, Brinley Richards, Lefébure-Wély and Adolph Le Carpentier. Others were the "hit" songs of previous years, such as <u>The Cork Leg</u>, a number of which were grouped in <u>Root & Cady's Collection of Popular Songs, Duetts, Trios, &c. by various composers</u>. Aside from PNs 82, 100, 130, and 247, the series included H. G. Barrus' <u>Lament of the Irish Lover</u>, Kucken's <u>Barcarole</u>, Balfe's <u>Then You'll Remember Me</u>, a vocal-polka without composer, called <u>O My Charming Elfie May</u>, Thomas Haynes Bayly's <u>No, Ne'er Can Thy Home Be Mine</u>, and the three sections of Charles W. Glover's <u>Jeannette and Jeannot</u>.. Naturally, none of these could bear a claim of copyright. There is evidence to indicate that the vast percentage of the missing and unaccounted for publications from this rather brief period would fall into this category -- uncopyrighted public domain compositions. Presumably, if they were worth republishing, they must have been reasonably popular. Many of them, however, would have to be sold in competition with other editions, and their distribution would consequently tend to be localized in the Chicago area. Whatever the explanation, they have turned out to be excessively scarce. There is one satisfaction to be drawn from the fact; although it would obviously be desirable to locate more of these pieces, if only to show how a publisher larded his list, considerable checking and cross-checking has begun to show that in spite of all the gaps in the plate number list very few important original publications of the firm are missing. This is particularly the case if one takes into consideration the two groups of titles appended at the end of the main list -- the publications which have turned up without plate numbers and the few copyrighted works which are still missing.

Fortunately, after this preliminary period of dereliction, the firm soon "reformed" and instituted a policy of registering their publications regularly and with increasing frequency. Instead of registering fifty or sixty at one time, they deposited sometimes only two or three and came back a few days later with two or three more. The result is that the plate numbers and the filing dates begin to run in two parallel series. Usually when some minor irregularity takes place it can be explained by a quite obvious deduction -- a particularly large work has taken longer to get through the shop or, on the other hand, some important new song by one of the partners has been given a little special attention. The only times that the dates of filing begin to jump around in seeming disorder are when the plate numbers of a particularly large series were all assigned at once in advance, but the individual works were fed to the engraving shop by degrees.

CHAPTER V

THE POST-WAR YEARS, 1866-1868

THE POST-WAR YEARS, 1866-1868

As the Civil War neared its close, the commercial North, confident of victory, entered upon a period of expansion. The industries which had languished during the war began to hope for better times, while those which had thrived looked to the future with unbounded optimism. Among the latter, Root & Cady was an exception only in the degree of its exuberance. The unparalleled success of the war songs convinced the members of the firm that they understood the public taste and knew best how to please and educate the United States in all things musical. To carry into the post-war period the prominent position the firm had achieved, Root & Cady needed more room. An attempt to open a branch store in St. Paul, Minnesota, was announced in The Song Messenger Extra dated "New Years, 1865." The manager, M. L. Temple, was drowned in the Mississippi River on February 16, 1865, while on his way to meet his family and bring them to St. Paul. In announcing his death, The Song Messenger for March, 1865 [2:185], stated that the new store would be under the management of William A. Root, youngest brother of George F. Root, and D. H. Elliott. Although it was entered elaborately in McClung's St. Paul Directory and Statistical Record for 1866, it had disappeared entirely from the issue for 1867 and could not have been a conspicuous success.

Of more lasting importance in the life of the firm was the decision to move to more spacious quarters. It was inevitable that the new home of Root & Cady should be in the Crosby Opera House, Chicago's newest cultural center, housing an opera house, art gallery, and studios of music teachers, painters and sculptors. Erected by an enterprising Chicago citizen, Uranus H. Crosby, the four-story building was considered a model of convenience and beauty. It was located on the north side of Washington Street, between State and Dearborn Streets, with a music hall on the State Street side. Facing Washington Street on the ground floor were four stores occupied eventually by Julius Bauer & Co., Root & Cady, Kinsley, the caterer, and W. W. Kimball.

After its inauguration on April 20, 1865, with a gala performance of Il Trovatore under the baton of Carl Bergmann, the Crosby Opera House became Chicago headquarters for Jacob Grau's Italian opera troupe, Grover's German opera, and various other touring opera and concert companies. George Upton in his interesting Musical Memories (Chicago, A. C. McClurg & Co. 1908 p237-52) told of the place of the opera house in Chicago's musical history, and of its chequered career. Although it was generally believed that the house was a financial as well as an artistic success, it became apparent that Mr. Crosby's inexperience had brought him to the verge of bankruptcy. To extricate himself, he resorted to a lottery in which the Opera House itself was to be the Grand Prize. At a time when lotteries and gift schemes were very popular, national advertising of such an enterprise created a sensation. The chromo which was sent to every ticket holder, "Mercy's Dream," is still to be found hanging in some homes, the only souvenir of a now forgotten dream of waking up some morning the owner of an opera house. On the day of the drawing, January 23, 1867, thousands crowded the Opera House. There were two hundred and ten thousand numbers, of which a quantity remained in Mr. Crosby's hands. Under the supervision of a committee of well-known citizens, the drawing for the pride of Chicago took place. To the crowd's disappointment, the owner of the winning ticket was not present, and it was several days before he was identified as one A. H. Lee of Prairie du Rocher, Illinois. The rest of the story is shrouded in mystery with only a few details undisputed. A writer in The Song Messenger [4 (Feb 1867) 169] claims to have seen Mr. Lee "in propria persona" and says that he "had the good taste to sell the Opera House to the original proprietor, Mr. U. H. Crosby, for $200,000, the 26th ult." But whatever happened, Mr. Crosby soon retired to a New England village, and his brother Albert somehow obtained the management of the house.

In the days before the opening of the Opera House, however, it seemed certain to usher in a new era in the artistic life of Chicago. Root & Cady announced its intention of moving to the new building a month before its inauguration, advertising in the Chicago Tribune for March 20 [1:5] a miscellaneous stock of pianos at "very low prices." The store at 95 Clark Street being rented, Root & Cady had to move on May 1st although the new store was far from ready. In The Song Messenger for June, 1865 [3:40], was a frantic description of the difficulties of doing business in a half-finished store surrounded by a chaos of music and instruments.

When order was achieved, the new store seemed spacious after the cramped quarters on Clark Street for the retail salesroom alone at 67 Washington Street was thirty by one hundred eighty feet.[1] Its

* * *

[1] All descriptions of the store agree on these dimensions. Cf among others, The Chicago Tribune, Oct 5 1865 4:5; J. S. Wright, Chicago, Past, Present, Future (Chicago, Western News Co. 1868) p279; and the various accounts in The Song Messenger

decorative scheme was considered the height of elegance and taste. "The counters, desks, shelf-fixtures, and even the very floor, are composed of oak and black walnut in alternate panels, pilasters, etc., fluted and carved in the highest style of art, and all reveling in native beauty, unaided by pencil or brush," marveled The Song Messenger for April 1865 [5:67]. The impression made upon the music trade lasted for many years; as late as 1881, The Musical People for July said that the S. Brainard's Sons retail store in Cleveland was "fitted in a style which for convenience and elaboration has never been approached in the trade since the time when Root & Cady fitted up their new store in the ill-fated Chicago Opera House...." (Quoted in Brainard's Musical World [18 (Aug 1881) 127].

The readers of The Song Messenger Extra for August, 1868, were treated to a conducted tour of the store:

> ... On the left hand, as you enter, is the retail sheet music department, where are to be found over thirty thousand different pieces.... On the right hand is the retail department for imported goods, such as violins, strings, &c. About the center of the front half of the store are two enclosed desks, one on each side. That on the left is the Cashier's, while the one on the right is devoted to ... the SONG MESSENGER....
>
> In the center of the room, dividing it into two equal portions, are the private offices of the heads of the firm, bookkeeper's desk, and the mail order department.
>
> The entire rear portion of the room is devoted to pianos, organs and musical instruments....
>
> On one side of ... [the basement] you see in triple lines of shelving the wholesale music department ... nearly six thousand different pieces of sheet music, and from ten to fifty copies of each. As we go towards the rear of the store we come to ... the shipping clerk's department. Do you see that table ten feet long and six feet wide, piled full of music and books, marked "Hands off, Ready to pack?" Those are a part of today's orders.... Here are daily tied up, marked and shipped from two to three wagon loads ... of parcels. This is exclusive of pianos and organs which are shipped in the rear....
>
> Now cross the alley with us, and we enter our printing office. Here are four steam presses ... seven plate presses ... while on this side an army of compositors are busy with dexterous fingers setting the types for the next "MESSENGER," or some music book or other....

Such was the store where Root & Cady carried on a large retail and wholesale trade in addition to its publishing. An awe-inspiring notice in the Tribune for August 4, 1865 [4:1], described a single order given to Mason Brothers, New York, for 8,050 music books, including 2,000 copies of the Key Note by Wm. B. Bradbury. Several months later on December 18 [1:8] an advertisement called attention to the foreign music offered for sale by Root & Cady: "... two and four hand arrangements of the symphonies, string quartettes, &c., of Beethoven, Schumann, Mendelssohn, Gade, Rubenstein, and others. Duetts for violin and piano, and flute and piano, from the best authors. Organ music by Bach, Battiste, Hesse, Rink, and others. Also, the best German, Italian & French operas...." Only on rare occasions during the post-war period did Root & Cady thus call attention to European music; still less frequently if at all did they publicize American editions of the more serious music from abroad.

In addition to music, Root & Cady did an extensive trade in pianos, cabinet organs, and other instruments. Violinists and would-be violinists must have been attracted to the store by the presence of William Lewis, one of Chicago's most promising performers, who many years later founded the firm of Wm. Lewis & Son. On occasion, too, the firm could experiment. In May, 1867, it displayed the "Dynamicon," an improved type of cabinet organ made by Mr. M. O. Nichols of Laporte, Indiana, which enabled the performer "to exercise his fancy on new combinations and effects including the string tremolo, trill, clarionet, etc." according to the Tribune for May 24 [4:1].

The full extent of Chicago's music trade immediately after the war was shown in the figures for sales upon which the dealers paid license tax for the year 1865 as reported in The Song Messenger [4 (Sept 1866) 89]:

| | |
|---|---|
| Root & Cady | $260,000 |
| Lyon & Healy | 180,000 |
| Alanson Reed & Sons | 150,000 |

| | |
|---|---|
| Julius Bauer & Co. | 144,000 |
| Smith & Nixon | 125,000 |
| W. W. Kimball | 95,000 |
| H. M. Higgins | 50,000 |
| N. Gould | 25,000 |
| Merrill & Brennan | 25,000 |
| Ziegfeld, Gerard Co. | 25,000 |
| Grand total of musical merchandise sales in Chicago in 1865 | $1,079,000 |

A figure for 1866 was given in a letter written to the Orchestra, an English musical paper, by John Holt, bandmaster of the 2d Battalion, 17th Regiment, British Foot, and reprinted in the Tribune for June 3, 1867 [4:3-4]. Mr. Holt said that in 1866 Root & Cady sold 334,758 copies of sheet music and books paying a Government license on sales amounting to over $282,000. "This shows the magnitude of a general music business in America and how general some degree of musical taste must exist among the communis populi to support such an establishment."

At this time Root & Cady's reputation as a publisher was well established, but the market for the firm's most popular commodity, the war songs, had disappeared. The firm was now faced with the problem of retaining its public with other kinds of music. It should have been possible to build a catalog based on teaching material, as well as the best compositions by Americans and the European masters, with plenty of simple songs to satisfy the country folks. But Root & Cady chose to continue publishing music for the unsophisticated. As an examination of the check-list of the firm's publications will show, the quality of its output declined after the war. With very few exceptions Root & Cady's publications were sentimental ballads, humorous songs, vocal quartettes, both sacred and secular, and for piano, marches, polkas, schottisches and variations and fantasias on the popular songs or operas of the day. A few arias from familiar operas and an occasional song from the pen of Robert Franz or Schumann, these were the high points of the catalog. It must not be assumed that Root & Cady was backward in comparison with its competitors. No music publisher in the West or South was any better, and only a few prominent houses in the East, Henry Tolman & Co. and Oliver Ditson of Boston, for example, issued any fair amount of music with lasting value. Root & Cady, through its music books and sheet music, sought to educate the American public to a knowledge of and a love for music, but the firm concentrated on the elementary stages of instruction and taste to the exclusion of all else.

The standard excuse for not printing "better" music was (and is) that it would not sell. It seems, however, that the type of music Root & Cady did publish sold none too well either. In The Song Messenger for April, 1867 [5:8], an editorial, "The Music Trade of Chicago," discussed the closing of several music stores, not because the trade had fallen off but because it was "more concentrated in the large houses." The leading article in the Extra for May, 1869, however, reflected the true state of affairs.

> During the year, in fact since the war, neither we nor any other American publishers, have made any great hits in sheet music.... Our imprint is probably worth something, and our many channels for introducing new things a great deal more, but when these do not suffice to make good piquant songs upon new subjects go with anything like the rush that favored us during the war, how are we going to foist into favor new songs that travel in old ruts?...

Five months earlier, the Extra for January had referred to the same problem in its leading article, "The New Year and the Old":

> Since the intense excitement attendant on the war ... the natural reaction of general torpor has prevented any astonishing successes in this line [sheet music]. We have, however, issued a great deal of sheet music the past year all of which has met with reasonable success. In our books, however -- Educational, Recreational and Devotional -- our success for this period has been most satisfactory.

The postwar prosperity of Root & Cady then was based on the music books issued by the firm rather than its sheet music. The list seems limited to twentieth century eyes, but apparently neither Root & Cady or the public they served found it so. The Song Messenger Extra for May, 1869, preens itself: "SONGS FOR THE NEW LIFE ... will round out our book publications so as to meet almost all needs."

Meanwhile, the firm had started out on a program which during the course of 1867 and 1868 very nearly increased its sheet music publications sevenfold. It was accomplished through a procedure which, although it is found in other countries, has been carried to even greater extremes by American publishers. As in the animal kingdom, large publishers gain much of their growth by swallowing up smaller publishers, only after the passage of a few years to be themselves swallowed by a still larger publisher. The result is that the ultimate origins of a publisher's stock of engraved plates can be traced back through a complicated pyramid of roots spreading out and interlocking with earlier publishers until the story of one publisher necessitates the unraveling of a dozen firms. To attempt to trace to their source the several thousands of works which Root & Cady bought during the course of these two years would obviously be impossible here. But to arrive at any understanding at all of Root & Cady, some general discussion of the tributary firms is essential and will be undertaken with this preliminary explanation of its inadequacies.

The first purchase was made quietly and with no publicity sometime before April, 1867. It included the entire catalog of Ziegfeld, Gerard & Co. whose publications, with revised covers and Root & Cady plate numbers, begin to appear in their list with PN 678. Along with Root & Cady's own publications, the purchased plates are mixed thickly through the list down to PN 732. A few, such as PNs 922 and 2452, may have been added much later, but conceivably even these might once have had earlier numbers on interim editions.

As so frequently happens, the Ziegfeld, Gerard catalog was not itself a simple unit, but rather was a link in a short-lived chain. It started when Alanson Reed added music publishing to his flourishing business in musical instruments at his "Temple of Music" at 88 & 90 Randolph Street and 69 Dearborn Street. On May 21, 1864, he registered for copyright three pieces by Florence Ziegfeld and a patriotic song by one "Pip Winkle." By February 2, 1865, he had registered eleven more, five by A. E. Wimmerstedt, two by N. Cawthorne, the organist of the Grace Methodist Episcopal Church, a <u>Hero's March</u> by Charles M. Lindsay, an <u>Andante and Scherzo</u> by Paul Becker, and songs by Chas. G. Degenhard and G. G. Goodfellow.

By April 13, 1865, Alanson Reed seems to have made some sort of deal with Ziegfeld & Willson since this firm deposited three compositions with the imprint: "Chicago, Published by Ziegfeld & Willson at Reed's Temple of Music, 69 Dearborn and 88 & 90 Randolph St." On the back cover of one of them -- Edward Lilly's <u>Little Ella's Song to Her Angel Brother, Charlie</u> -- are lists of "New Vocal Music" and "New Instrumental Music," which include all but two of the fifteen pieces Reed had registered for copyright, as well as seven additional titles which he apparently published but did not register. At the foot of the two columns are two songs and three instrumental pieces which Ziegfeld & Willson registered on April 13th and May 6th. Alanson Reed, it seems, had decided to devote himself entirely to his instruments, allowing Ziegfeld and Willson to handle the publishing with the "Temple of Music" used as quarters. A total of fourteen compositions were registered under these auspices by August 19, 1865.

The next four publications were registered on October 19, 1865, and February 13, 1866, giving Florence Ziegfeld as the sole claimant; and on copies of the music the address is usually given simply as 69 Dearborn St., with no mention of Reed or his double address. Ziegfeld soon found another partner, however, and the next group of seven registrations appear with either "Ziegfeld, Gerard & Co.," or "Ziegfeld & Gerard" as claimants. The addresses in the imprints on the publications are not as specific as they might be. Sometimes "Dearborn St.," is given without any number, a <u>Skating Waltz</u>, arranged by Fred. Freiberg, has no address at all, and finally on the last piece, Otto Lob's song, <u>A Curious Circumstance</u>, the address changes to 133 Dearborn St.

One more publication was deposited on February 18, 1867, using this same address, and by this time Gerard had apparently left the firm. The claimant in the copyright records and the publisher on the copy deposited is given as "F. Ziegfeld & Co." Since the piece was included in Root & Cady's purchase, the deal must have been closed with the firm after it had reached this transformation and not with Ziegfeld, Gerard & Co., as Root & Cady later stated. The publication -- Boulanger's <u>Opera House Drawing March. Composed and dedicated with the sympathy of a fellow sufferer to all the unfortunate ticket holders</u> -- is otherwise chiefly notable for a well-executed satirical sketch on the cover showing a complicated revolving winch hooked up to the Opera House, preparatory to moving it off to the winner's backyard. The reason for the sale may be deduced from a story in <u>The Song Messenger</u> [5 (April 1867) 8] on <u>The Music Trade of Chicago</u>. It included the sentence: "We are sorry to say that some of these houses are finding business unprofitable, and are either being closed out by the sheriff, or are 'selling off at cost, or less than cost,' with a view of entering something more lucrative." Presumably, Root & Cady picked up the four dozen odd sets of plates for little more than a song.

This was barely the beginning. The Song Messenger Extra for January, 1869, later had as its lead article a puff of Root & Cady which referred to additional purchases:

> Up to January, 1868, business had increased so greatly that the demands upon us for musical merchandise were getting too great for our resources. The better to meet these demands, negotiations were entered into, which, about February 1st, resulted in our becoming the owners of the "Tolman Catalogue," previously belonging to Henry Tolman & Co., of Boston ... Previous to this "annexation" we had purchased the list of the select music for Cabinet Organ, published by Mason & Hamlin, of Boston [and New York]; and since that event the entire catalogue of Ziegfeld, Gerard & Co., H. T. Merrill & Co., and H. R. Palmer, of Chicago.

The temporal sequence is so specific that it is tempting to accept it at its face value, but if it is true that the Mason & Hamlin purchase preceded the Ziegfeld, it can only have been on a contractual basis, not the real basis of actual possession of the plates. The New York Musical Gazette carried frequent advertisements for the Mason & Hamlin cabinet organ publications down through the beginning of 1868. Close relations were obviously maintained between the two firms. The Gazette carried a Mason & Hamlin advertisement in its issue for November, 1867 [p7], which included several Root & Cady titles without indicating their owner; and when the set of six Fireside Harmonies ... for the Mason & Hamlin Cabinet Organ [PNs 800-805] were published by Root & Cady in January, 1868, the Gazette carried a brief notice of them with the statement that they could be had from Mason & Hamlin. Nonetheless, the few Mason & Hamlin publications which have turned up with plate numbers from the Root & Cady series all fit into the sequence late in 1868 or early in 1869 (cf PNs 4152, 4160, 5050, 5089, 5173, 5190, and 5319), and it seems only reasonable to suppose that Root & Cady did not take possession of the plates until well after the Ziegfeld sale had been negotiated and the proceeds thoroughly digested. It is doubtful if Root & Cady ever realized any considerable profit from either purchase. Although slightly larger than the Ziegfeld catalog, the Mason & Hamlin publications were mostly arrangements and transcriptions by Gustav Blessner, Julius Eichberg, and Charles Fradel for the cabinet organ, and although Root & Cady pushed them with all their skill, no single copy has been found with a Root & Cady imprint. Five of the seven plate numbers referred to above were taken from the renewal copies deposited by Brainard after they had purchased the major portion of Root & Cady's plates; the other two are from Brainard editions in the possession of W. N. H. Harding, of Chicago. Horatio Richmond Palmer (1837-1907) was a relatively young man when he sold out to Root & Cady, with most of a very active career ahead of him. There are minor signs of his potentialities in his Chicago efforts, but they are distinctly in the bud. He tried his hand at a magazine, The Concordia, but it lasted for only the first three months of 1866. In May, he published his song, My Father's Fireside, and at the end of the year, he arranged and published F. Stevens Chandler's They Blossom There Up There. The cover gives his address as 91 Washington Street, but the following year the address is given as 38 Crosby Opera House on three small books which he published -- The Song Queen: A Collection of Music for Singing Classes; The Elements of Musical Composition; and Palmer's System of Teaching the Rudiments of Vocal Music in Classes. Root & Cady thought highly enough of The Song Queen to bring out a "revised and enlarged" edition in 1868, but Palmer's total productions could not be said to have added much to their list, and there is no trace at all of his two sheet music publications, so that we have no way of dating the approximate time of the purchase.

If their plate numbers can be taken as evidence, however, the H. T. Merrill purchase was again consummated before the Mason & Hamlin deal but not until some months after the Ziegfeld purchase. At any rate, the publications seem to have been worked into the Root & Cady series in the range around PNs 1127, 1143, 1492, 2011, and 2848. Merrill gave himself as sole claimant for a series of works deposited between August 7, 1862, and December 24, 1866, in spite of the fact that the clerk recorded the imprint of one of these deposits as "Merrill & Brennan." Registration of five works on October 26, 1864, and on December 24, 1866, enter H. T. Merrill & Co. as claimant, and an extensive series of deposits between May 26, 1865, and December 17, 1868, are credited to Merrill & Brennan. The natural deduction from this overlapping is that Mr. H. T. Merrill ran the business, no matter what form the firm's name might currently take. It is a reasonable deduction. Merrill had done some publishing earlier in Galena, Ill., and when he came to Chicago, it was as the principal of the Academy of Music rather than as a mere publisher. In fact, his first Chicago publication was "Corn Is King!" from the Continental Monthly. Music by H. T. Merrill. Published by the Author at the Academy of Music, No. 164 Clark St. Curiously, the plate number on this piece in its original state looks surprisingly like a Root & Cady number, and considering that Merrill had no facilities, perhaps they engraved it for him. There is still a blank at 227 3, where the piece could fit.

If the purchase was made after the last deposit by Merrill & Brennan on December 17, 1868, Root & Cady acquired at least 44 titles, and they probably got some few titles in addition which Merrill failed to register. Merrill himself was responsible for the bulk of the output: he had edited the March, June, and October 1865 issues of The Seven Sounds; he compiled Merrill's Sabbath School Songs, The Golden Crown, and The Music Teacher's Register; and he had composed In Memoriam, Quartette on the Death of Abraham Lincoln, as well as eight miscellaneous songs and three instrumental pieces. The other compositions were six of the innumerable songs by Frank Howard; a duet, two songs, and three dances by Charles P. Hubbard; a song and three instrumental numbers by A. E. Wimmerstedt; two piano pieces by Theodore Moelling; four songs, one each by Thos. P. J. Magoun, W. A. Ogden, Bisco [!] and Thornton; and lastly three dances -- schottisches by Mrs. Minnie A. Phelps and Mrs. D. C. Johnson, and The City Railway Galop by Edwin H. Longman, Professor of Music.

The policy behind the purchase of these smaller firms is important, but considered as additions to Root & Cady's catalog, they all shrink to insignificance with the purchase for an undisclosed sum of the aggregation of Boston publishers which ended up as Henry Tolman & Co. When a comparatively young firm absorbs the catalog of an old and well-established competitor, a certain amount of pointing-with-pride is to be expected. In the Chicago of the sixties, where the gospel of "Bigger and Better" was universally accepted, the reticence of Root & Cady with respect to the purchase of the Tolman catalog would seem phenomenally mysterious were it not that music publishers since early in the 18th century had been notorious for their practice of hiding the date and origins of their engraved plates. The new plates bulked too large for the deal to be kept from business associates, but obviously if the public was not informed, they would have no reason to suspect these fine new copies, all bearing Root & Cady's imprint on the redesigned covers, of being as much as twenty-five years old. As a consequence, no announcements of the purchase can be found in the newspapers or in The Song Messenger until the "Extra" for August, 1868, at which time a curt "Correction" may be found buried on page 7:

> The facts in relation to the sale of Messrs. Henry Tolman & Co's. catalogue of sheet music and books having been grossly misrepresented by certain parties, we deem it advisable to put our readers right in the matter.
>
> All the plates of the sheet music published by the above firm prior to February 1st, 1868, were purchased and are now in possession of Messrs. Root & Cady, Chicago.
>
> S. T. Gordon, Esq., of New York, purchased all the music books, formerly published by the same firm.
>
> O. Ditson & Co., of Boston, purchased the plates of the sheet music published since February 1st, 1868.

There will be occasion to refer back to this statement from time to time in what follows to amplify some of its bare facts.

The purchase of the Tolman catalog came as a natural development. Root & Cady long had had close personal and business relations with all the members of the chain of Boston publishers who had contributed in building it. The first of these with which we will have occasion to deal directly was G. P. Reed, although his catalog, too, had prior antecedents and included numerous plates from Dubois & Stoddard, a few from William Oakes, some from William Hall, and doubtless still more from others. He was followed by George D. Russell, Nathan Richardson, a gentleman named Fuller, whose first name has not been determined, and finally Tolman himself. All of them found themselves in strenuous competition with Boston's dominant music publisher, Oliver Ditson, and consequently there was a tendency for them to look outside of Boston for alliances. From the time in 1845 when Reed had published George F. Root's See the Sky Is Darkling and E. Towner Root's Slumber Gentle Lady until the Roots set up in business for themselves, the Boston firms brought out many of their best songs including "Wurzel's" biggest pre-War hit, Rosalie, the Prairie Flower. When Root & Cady was founded, it was Russell & Tolman that saw to the engraving and printing of their first publications, and throughout the 1860s the two firms served as reciprocal outlets for each other. At the meetings of the Board of Music Trade, C. M. Cady usually represented his firm, and judging by the enthusiastic letters he sent back to The Song Messenger about sailing on the Cape and week-end parties in Boston with Henry Tolman, the two men did their utmost to continue and strengthen the friendly relations between their firms. Even if Oliver Ditson's was the normal graveyard for most Boston firms, it is not in the least surprising to find Henry Tolman preferring to turn to his old friends in the West.

To assay the size of the purchase and to understand its effect on the Root & Cady catalog, the interrelations of the conglomerate of Boston firms must be blocked out in some detail. The copyright records furnish a temporal schema on which such an edifice can be hung. In addition, the copies deposited at the time of making the registrations are readily available in the Library of Congress; in unscrambling the constantly changing imprints with their plate numbers altered or added later, it has been invaluable to have this foundation of guaranteed first editions. At the same time, it was apparently customary during the 1840s for a publisher to register with the county clerk a relatively small proportion of his works, even when he printed a copyright claim on a far larger number; thus it has not always been possible to call the turn of the year or furnish the exact plate number when some new procedure was instituted. On the whole, however, the records have served the present purpose well and have made possible certain deductions which might otherwise have remained complete mysteries.

The history of the group of Boston firms starts, therefore, for our purposes with the registration by G. P. Reed on November 18, 1839, in Vol. 14 of the Massachusetts's records, item no. 260, of:

> The Dennis Quick Step. As performed by the Boston Brigade Band respectfully dedicated to Major Louis Dennis, officers and members of the Hancock Light Infantry (performed for the first time at their Anniversary, Oct. 28th, 1839) composed and arranged for the piano-forte and flute by B. A. Burditt.

A long silence follows, until on April 23, 1842, a second march by Burditt -- Major Train's Quick Step -- was registered. On October 21st of the same year, Reed deposited William R. Dempster's The Lament of the Irish Emigrant. A Ballad. Poetry by The Hon. Mrs. Price Blackwood. These pieces were not the total of Reed's output as is shown by the discovery of other compositions, such as Edward L. White's The Musical Gift, not registered but bearing a printed claim for 1842. His publishing venture seems nonetheless to have begun slowly.

The tempo continued deliberate with only one registration on December 29, 1843, and two in 1844. The following year, however, it jumps to nineteen falling off again in 1846 to four. In 1847, Reed either radically changed his policy with regard to registrations, or his output jumped tremendously. The copyright records list 36 titles, and the rate is raised in 1848 to 37. It falls to 24 the following year, but is back to 33 in 1850. From this point onward, the registrations drop off markedly: 1851 (17), 1852 (9), 1853 (3), 1854 (6), 1855 (6, all on February 27th), and 1856 (12).

Had Reed used plate numbers regularly, we would have had a better measuring stick of the significance of these figures. Actually, he engraved no consecutive numbers on his plates before late in 1847. On December 15th, he registered four compositions, one of which still bore no plate number; the other three, however, bore the numbers 1005, 1006 and 1010. Somewhere he had learned about the usefulness of plate numbers for keeping track of his large stock of plates and decided to try out the system. Probably he picked out the good, round number of 1000, with which to start. It may have represented his rough estimate of the number of sets of plates in his vault, but it would be dangerous to take the figure too literally. On January 12, 1848, he registered pieces with the numbers 1015 and 1016, and from this point onward to November 9, 1848, every sheet music deposit bore a plate number with the series progressing for the most part in reasonable order. One of the three pieces deposited on November 9th bore the PN 1110; the other two and the four remaining deposits in 1848 were without numbers in the deposit copies, although there is reason to suppose that this was a mere oversight which was soon rectified.

The first deposit of the following year on May 16, 1849, still carries no number, but it does introduce one very significant change -- G. P. Reed has become G. P. Reed & Co. Reed had taken his chief clerk, George D. Russell, into partnership. No further registrations were made until fall, but then on nine different dates -- September 12 and 19, November 27, and December 18, 19, 20, 21, 22, and 31 -- 23 compositions were deposited. At first glance, the plate numbers seem to be nonsensical since the order of publication has not been preserved. It would seem as if Reed had suddenly realized that he had registered few works, and that it behoved him to get them on the books before the year changed. Unscrambled, the numbers fall into what appears to be two limiting series plus five compositions without plate number: 1111, 1186, 1189, 1191, 1194, 1198, 1205 -- 1507, 1509, 1510, 1514, 1516, 1518, 1519, 1520, 1522, 1524 and lastly, 1531. The five pieces without plate numbers may fit in anywhere along the line; PN 1111 must have appeared quite early in the year, or possibly late the previous year, since it doubtless followed along after PN 1110, registered on November 9, 1848. The numbers from 1186 to 1205 would then have appeared after a discrete interval allowing for the publication of 75 compositions in the interim. The jump to the higher series, however, can hardly be explained on the theory that Reed issued 302 new works in only a few months. What probably happened is something that we shall find the Boston publishers doing time and time again. Both Reed and Tolman began to use plate numbers at a period when they had already published large quantities of compositions, and in order to put their house in order, they would periodically add plate numbers to a group of publications which had been brought out long before. It should be remembered that there is nothing inherently chronological about a plate number. Publishers used them not to tell the date on which they had published a particular work but merely as a convenient method of identifying a set of plates, and for that purpose the numbers could be assigned in any order the publisher chose. For the cataloger trying to use plate numbers as a temporal clue, therefore, it becomes just as important to know when a particular series means nothing as to know what it means when it has some significance. Here, then, is one series of numbers -- from 1205 to 1507 -- which must be used with extreme caution. Plenty of later editions have been found which fall within the range although naturally no attempt has been made to identify even a substantial part of them. Those which have been found -- including Reed's PN 1400, which turns out to be a reissue of Edward L. White's *The popular national melody of "Yankee Doodle" with variations* originally copyrighted by Wm. H. Oakes in 1841 -- are all of earlier or indeterminate vintage, and thus unless some other criterion can be found to substantiate it, any previous date chosen at random would be preferable to 1849.

One puzzle follows upon the other in studying Reed's plate numbers. Having established a seemingly satisfactory series, he abruptly stops using plate numbers entirely during 1850 and 1851, and then just as abruptly starts using them again in 1852. The most surprising part is that the series which ended in 1849 with PN 1531 starts off in 1852 with the deposit of PN 1559:

> February 14, 1852: PNs 1559, 1563, 1567
> April 6, 1852: PNs 1598, 1599, 1627, 1630
> July 24, 1852: PNs 1703, 1717

Fifty works had been registered for copyright during the two blank years, not to mention all of the other pieces which Reed characteristically failed to register, and yet there is a gap of only 28 numbers between the last work registered in 1849 and the first in 1852. Although it certainly could not have bridged the entire period, without question, the series was filled in from one end or the other before or after it was broken. In all probability, this would still leave a group of 200 or more publications without plate numbers.

This poses the second problem. We know that Reed issued approximately a thousand pieces before he first attempted to establish a plate number series. Now we have roughly two hundred more waifs issued in 1850 and 1851. Some three hundred of the earlier publications were probably given numbers in 1849. But what happened to the rest? Hundreds of Reed publications have been examined which bear plate numbers below 1000. Among them are some of the pieces known to have been published in 1850 and 1851, and thus if some one plate numbering project was undertaken for stamping numbers on all of the plates which had none, it probably took place after the series was started up for the second time. A terminal date for the other end may be found in the type or style of plate number used. The numerals on all the early plates are large and full; sometime shortly before PN 1627 the style is changed to a neat, small figure which remains characteristic of all the Boston firms right through to the end of Henry Tolman & Co. Since all the plate numbers below 1000 are stamped with the larger punches, the numbers must have been affixed before PN 1627 was copyrighted on April 6, 1852. This delimits the probable period to the Spring of 1852. It is a very logical time for it since it follows immediately on the re-inauguration of the system of assigning plate numbers. And who can tell, with nearly a thousand sets of plates to stamp, perhaps the punches were worn out in the process and had to be replaced thus occasioning the new style of plate number.

One thing, however, is quite certain. None of the low numbers nor the ones between 1205 and 1507 can be used for calculating the date of publication. What, if any, system was used in assigning the numbers has not been discovered, but assuredly it was not chronological. Judson Hutchinson's *If I Were a Voice*, copyrighted in 1850, has the PN 200, whereas a piece by William R. Dempster, copyrighted in 1843, was given the PN 203. Likewise, there seems to be no possibility that the plates were arranged alphabetically either by composer or by title and then given a serial number. It would almost seem as if the numbers had been stamped on purely at random just as the boy happened to pick them off the shelf in the storeroom. Fortunately, after 1852, Reed learned to mind his ways, so that the series continues with perfect regularity and at a reasonable pace. Under the circumstances, the figures given in the table on an adjoining page can finish the story.

Compared to Reed, Nathan Richardson presents no problems at all. During the autumn of 1853 he registered two books -- his *The Modern School for the Pianoforte* on September 8th, and

Elements of Music at Sight on October 5th.  The first registration of a sheet music publication did not take place until January 9th of the following year.  It was a Funeral March by W. B. Babcock, dedicated to Jonas Chickering, and was brought to the county clerk's office together with a newly engraved portrait of the famous piano manufacturer.  Chickering had died in Boston on December 8, 1853, and apparently there was some haste attached to the manufacture of his funeral march, since it bears the PN 14, whereas Mollenhauer's Spharen Polka with PN 1 was not registered until February 13th.  For the most part, however, the numbers proceed henceforth in a reasonably close approximation of a chronological order.  The last assortment of sheet music to be registered was taken to the clerk's office on July 10, 1856. It included two earlier plate numbers, 253 and 274, but its characteristic center lies in the series 299 followed by 302-305.  Unregistered compositions with plate numbers as high as 310 have been found, but except for J. C. D. Parker's collection of concerted numbers from operas, entitled The Musical Drama, deposited on December 30, 1856, Nathan Richardson copyrighted nothing further in his own name.

William Arms Fisher writes [4]: "In 1859 [!], Mr. Russell left Mr. Reed to go into partnership with Nathan Richardson, who had owned a 'Musical Exchange' since 1854, as Russell & Richardson at 291 Washington St."  Christine Merrick Ayars seems to agree, at least in part [5]: "In 1856 Mr. Russell left Mr. Reed to go into partnership with Nathan Richardson."  Judging by the table of plate numbers for the Boston firms, perhaps it would be more correct to say that Mr. Reed retired, leaving Mr. Russell in charge of their large catalog of books and music, and making it necessary for him to find a new partner.  Exactly what became of Mr. Reed is difficult to discover.  None of the more likely books has anything to say on the point, and the Boston directories contribute no more.  The entries for G. P. Reed, with a store at 13 Tremont St. and a house at 49 Eliot cease to appear after 1856.  A new entry for a Geo. P. Reed is to be found in the 1857 directory with what at first seems to be a town house at 20 Court St. and a country home at Roxbury; but by following the gentleman through to 1860, he turns out to be a manufacturer of coal oil and a different character altogether.  The musical G. P. Reed simply disappears.

It is true that Russell did not remain at the old address, but neither did he simply move in with Richardson.  An article in the Boston Morning Post for February 23, 1857, reprinted in an advertisement in Dwight's Journal on March 7th, begins: "The well known music publishers, Russell & Richardson, have removed from No. 17 Tremont Row and 282 Washington Street, to a new store at No. 291 Washington Street, in the granite building recently erected by Mr. Burnett."  Apparently, both men had to move.

On setting up in their new quarters, one of the first things they did was to work Richardson's plates into the Reed series by assigning them new numbers.  The process might be expected to take some time, and since the partners were busy issuing new works, they apparently set aside a section of their series to be used for this purpose as time permitted.  At least, this seems to be the most sensible explanation of the jump shown in the table from PN 2577, deposited on March 11th, to PN 3077, deposited on December 18th.  The jump is much too large to be encompassed in the course of a single year, and furthermore, a fair quantity of the renumbered Richardson pieces have been seen with plate numbers falling in this range.  It has usually not been possible to match them up with a copy bearing the original Richardson imprint and number, but three samples to illustrate the process can be submitted:

|  | Richardson | Russell & Richardson |
|---|---|---|
| Mason, William: Amitié pour Amitié | 121 | 2635 |
| Root, G. F.: 6 Songs, No. 1, Glad to get home | 217 | 2340 |
| Rossini, G.: Sombre Forêt, Romance from Wm. Tell | 229 | 2744 |

Although the new numbers on the samples get progressively larger, their relationship to each other is not the same as that of the original numbers, and again we must conclude that they were not assigned in a chronological series but merely in the order in which there was some occasion for withdrawing them from the storeroom. What is more, as will develop later, some of the plates were never renumbered at all.

During 1858, Nathan Richardson became ill, and if the implications are credited, his mind was affected.  It thus became necessary for Russell to find a new partner.  For a short time, he joined forces with Fuller, and two groups of compositions were registered on September 21 and November 9, 1858.  The over-all range of the plate numbers was from 3221 to 3247.  The partnership must have been a frankly transitional affair since on the same date that Russell & Fuller deposited PN 3247, Russell & Tolman brought

\* \* \*

[4] Fisher, William Arms: One Hundred and Fifty Years of Music Publishing in the United States (Boston, Oliver Ditson Co, Inc, 1933) p117

[5] Ayars, Christine Merrick: Contributions to the Art of Music in America by the Music Industries of Boston, 1640 to 1936 (New York, H. W. Wilson Co, 1937) p15

65

## DATED TABLE OF PLATE NUMBERS USED BY BOSTON PUBLISHERS*

| | G. P. Reed & Co. | Nathan Richardson | Russell & Richardson | Russell & Fuller | Russell & Tolman | Henry Tolman |
|---|---|---|---|---|---|---|
| 1852 | 1559 Feb 14<br>1598 Apr 6<br>1630 Apr 6<br>1717 July 24<br>1681 Dec 29<br>1728 [c1852] | | | | | no PNs |
| 1853 | 1746 Sept 9<br>1909 [c1853]<br>2074 Aug 24<br>2085 Sept 26 | Book Sept 8<br>Book Oct 5 | | | | no PNs |
| 1854 | 2095 [c1854]<br>2143 Mar 18<br>2180 [c1854]<br>2230 [c1854] | 1 Feb 13<br>14 Jan 9<br>121 Oct 13 -- becomes 2635<br>131 Nov 11 | | | | no PNs |
| 1855 | 2248 Feb 27<br>2293 Feb 27<br>2346 [c1855]<br>2384 [c1855] | 112 Jan 19<br>144 Jan 19<br>217 Oct 1 -- becomes 2640<br>229 Dec 1 -- becomes 2744 | | | | no PNs |
| 1856 | 2388 Feb 26<br>2476 Apr 3<br>2490 June 12<br>2526 June 12 | 245 Jan 19<br>259 Apr 2<br>305 July 10<br>Book Dec 30 | | | | no PNs |
| 1857 | | | Book Jan 29<br>2577 Mar 11<br>2581 Mar 11<br>3045 Dec 18<br>3151 Dec 18 | | | no PNs |
| 1858 | | | 3146 Jan 4<br>3076 Feb 3<br>3098 Feb 3<br>3093 Sept 13<br>3192 Sept 13<br>3213 Sept 13 | 3221 Sept 21<br>3247 Nov 9<br>3312 [c1858] | 3257 Nov 9<br>3284 Dec 12 | no PNs<br>[last regis-<br>tration made<br>Sept 14] |

| 1859 | 1860 | 1861 | 1862 | |
|---|---|---|---|---|
| | 3292 Feb 12 | | | |
| | 3383 Feb 12 | | | |
| | 3646 Aug 9 | | | |
| | 3685 Aug 27 | | | |
| | 3759 Dec 16 | | | |
| | 4004 Dec 16 | | | |
| | 3676 Feb 7 | | | |
| | 4043 Feb 7 | | | |
| | 3811 Feb 18 | | | |
| | 3944 Feb 18 | | | |
| | 4104 Mar 15 | | | |
| | 3842 July 19 | | | |
| | 3884 July 19 | | | |
| | 3973 Oct 15 | | | |
| | 4201 Oct 15 | | | |
| | 4268 Dec 31 | | | |
| | | 2466 Jan 29 | | |
| | | 4275 Jan 29 | | |
| | | 2866 Feb 5 | | |
| | | 4299 Apr 15 | | |
| | | 3366 June 11 | | |
| | | 4134 Nov 1 | | |
| | | 4140 Dec 28 | | |
| | | 2855 Dec 28 | | |
| | | 2864 Dec 28 | | |
| | | | 2866 Feb 5 | 2871 Feb 18 |
| | | | 2874 Feb 18 | 3193 Apr 5 |
| | | | | 4259 Apr 26 |
| | | | 2921 Sept 4 | 3501 June 12 |
| | | | | 2901 June 12 |
| | | | | 2926 Sept 4 |
| | | | | 2939 Nov 21 |

\* For a discussion of the earlier plate numbers used by G. P. Reed, cf p63-4 ff.; for those of Henry Tolman, cf p68 ff., and for a schedule of Tolman's later plate numbers, cf p69.

in a very considerable group of publications bearing the plate numbers 3257, 3262-3266, and 3282-3283.

So large a deposit would normally be quite impossible on the first day of a partnership, but it must be remembered that Henry Tolman was no raw recruit. He had set up in business with Elias Howe Jr., the well-known Boston publisher of music collections and the future inventor of the sewing machine.[6] Only one composition, however, was deposited by the firm of Howe & Tolman on March 12, 1845: Over the Sea, from the Romance of Angela. Words by F. A. Dunivage, Esq. Melody by N. G., Arranged for the Piano Forte. The volume for 1846 contains no record of a work published by either Tolman or Howe, and when a deposit is finally made on December 3, 1847, of two works by H. G. Barrus and two songs by B. F. Baker and I. B. Woodbury, Tolman's name alone is given as claimant. Like Reed, Tolman was not a frequent depositor. Three works were registered in 1848, none in 1849, and three each in 1850 and 1851. The year 1852 saw a considerable increase to fifteen registrations. The record for the next years runs along at about the same level: 1853 (18), 1854 (16), 1855 (8), 1856 (15), and 1857 (23); finally in 1858, two groups were registered, four pieces on March 19th and five on September 14th. Quite possibly, the eight pieces deposited by Russell & Tolman on November 9th came for the most part from Henry Tolman's shop engraved in the interim since September 14th.

Although Henry Tolman between 1847 and 1858 registered 118 compositions and published an unknown quantity in addition, there is no plate number problem since not a single piece bears one. Eventually, most of the plates found their way to Chicago. Of a hundred titles checked in the Board of Music Trade's catalog for 1870, only 22 titles could not be found. Doubtless, some of these are actually given there but were missed since the catalog, which is broken down into numerous classifications and lists works only under title rather than composer, is not always the safest tool imaginable. The very first piece registered by Howe & Tolman, however, is included -- Over the Sea by N. L. G. -- so that it seems safe to assume that substantially the entire list went to Root & Cady except for a small percentage of lesser compositions jettisoned along the way for lack of popular appeal and an occasional work sold earlier to some other publisher -- C. J. M. Bradley's Ben Bolt's Reply turns up in the Board of Music Trade's catalog credited to D. P. Faulds of Louisville although it was filed by Tolman on August 6, 1852. The disposition that was made of them in the interim must largely be guessed. Only two of the pieces Tolman copyrighted before 1858 have been found with Root & Cady imprints. One is the piano version of T. Paine's The Old Cabin Home, originally registered on February 12, 1857. Instead of being engraved, however, the Root & Cady edition seems to have been printed from new stereotype plates without a plate number and hence is of no assistance in solving the riddle. The other, in the New York Public Library, is A. F. Winnemore's The Gum Tree Canoe, c1847 by H. Tolman & Co., bearing PN 109. Brainard renewed the copyright on three other publications, and these furnish our only clue. Two were issued in the series, A Collection of Ballads, Duetts and Quartettes, Sung by Ossian's Bards, Poetry and Music Composed and Arranged for the Piano by James G. Clark. The first, Rock of Liberty, Quartette, has now been given the plate number 3518, and the second, Indian Mother's Lullaby, Song & Quartette, has 3420. The third piece is J. P. Thomas's Shades of Evening; Nocturne, and has the plate number 2740. The fact that there is a gap of nearly a hundred between the two Clark quartets, in spite of the fact that they were issued as two consecutive numbers in a series, and furthermore that the second of these has the lower number, implies very strongly that the new plate numbers were assigned in no regular and logical order but again were added to the plates at random whenever it became necessary to print a new batch of copies. Turning to the schedule of plate numbers used by Russell & Tolman, it would seem at first that in averaging six or seven hundred numbers per year they were producing an almost unbelievable quantity of new publications. The two Clark quartets, however, fit into the series in 1859, and the Thomas nocturne in 1861. Apparently, the explanation of this tremendous output is simply that Russell & Tolman was gradually working all of the earlier Tolman plates into their main series as opportunity presented itself. As a consequence, it may never be possible to determine exactly how many works Russell & Tolman themselves engraved during their short partnership nor how many Tolman had published by himself before 1858. Worse still, no plate number in this range can be trusted implicitly, since it is always possible that the piece was actually issued by Tolman much earlier.

The whole problem is further complicated by the double series of numbers which Russell & Tolman start using early in 1861. Having reached the lower four thousands in a fairly consecutive fashion, they suddenly jump back to numbers which normally would belong to Reed or to Russell & Richardson. Obviously, a much more detailed study of this and the following few years will be necessary before the reason can be

\* \* \*

[6] Ayars, Christine Merrick, loc cit p12-15

safely determined, but basically it is a question of filling gaps in the earlier sections of the list. It is more difficult, however, to determine what produced the gaps. Dichter and Shapiro[7] say that in 1861 part of the Russell & Tolman catalog was taken over by Henry Tolman and part by S. T. Gordon. The split between Russell and Tolman did not take place until 1862, but it is conceivable that a sale of a section of the catalog to S. T. Gordon may have been arranged in 1861. No evidence to this effect has turned up during the course of the present study, and no sheet music compositions copyrighted by Reed, Richardson or Russell have been found with S. T. Gordon imprints. The statement is therefore open to the suspicion that it is a misdated account of the sale of Tolman's books to Gordon in 1868 at the same time that Root & Cady bought the sheet music. Tolman's plate number pattern for the next few years would seem to favor the theory that he and Russell had determined to go over their complete list filling all gaps that had been left by accident or intention, or which had developed during the course of time through the occasional sale of a set of plates to some other publisher or finally to the gradual obsolescence and discard of some unimportant work which had ceased to attract the public.

Aside from an occasional number in the Reed section of the list, the first consistent attempt to fill a gap centered in the twenty-eight and twenty-nine hundreds. In 1857, Russell & Richardson had used numbers scattered over a range of nearly six hundred. Even if we suppose, as was mentioned above, that approximately three hundred of the numbers went to re-numbering the works published by Nathan Richardson during the three previous years, this still leaves a superfluity of plate numbers. The publisher who in those days had the energy and capital to engrave much more than a hundred sets of plates in any one year was rare. Furthermore, we can not be certain from the very scanty available evidence that all of Nathan Richardson's previous publications were given new numbers. A Russell & Tolman reprint of Richardson's edition of the first of Mendelssohn's six two-part songs has turned up still bearing the plate number 48. Possibly, instead of going to the trouble of re-numbering them all, some of Richardson's publications were allowed to fit into gaps in the early Reed list, and thus less than the estimated quantity of numbers would be required from the section set aside for this purpose.

In any case, there can be no doubt that Russell & Tolman and later Henry Tolman found sufficient numbers available in this range to take care of most of their publications down to the Spring of 1863, with the exception of single numbers, selected apparently at random from a very wide range. The situation can best be illustrated by giving a more numerous sampling of the Tolman numbers than could be fitted into the main table above.

PLATE NUMBER LIST FOR HENRY TOLMAN & CO., 1863-1868

| Year | Date | Number | Year | Date | Number |
|---|---|---|---|---|---|
| 1863 | Sept 26 | 2907 | 1865 | Feb 18 | 5032 |
|  | July 31 | 2991 |  | May 22 | 5047 |
|  | Nov 21 | 3018 |  | Nov 27 | 5056 |
|  | June 12 | 3019 |  | Nov 27 | 5107 |
|  | May 5 | 3174 |  | Dec 4 | 5121 |
|  | Aug 12 | 3391 |  |  |  |
|  | June 12 | 3416 | 1866 | Jan 12 | 5115 |
|  | July 31 | 3472 |  | Jan 12 | 5132 |
|  | Sept 26 | 3530 |  | June 14 | 5167 |
|  | Oct 14 | 3602 |  | Sept 22 | 5195 |
|  | Dec 31 | 3690 |  | Dec 18 | 5237 |
| 1864 | Jan 21 | 3348 |  |  |  |
|  | Jan 21 | 3697 | 1867 | June 29 | 5244 |
|  | Jan 21 | 3709 |  | Oct 2 | 5331 |
|  | Mar 21 | 3737 |  | Oct 2 | 5361 |
|  | May 17 | 3754 |  | Dec 14 | 5407 |
|  | May 17 | 3920 |  | Dec 21 | 5427 |
|  | [c1864] | 3993 |  |  |  |
|  | June 28 | 4982 | 1868 | Jan 7 | 5408 |
|  | Dec 20 | 4995 |  | Jan 17 | 5432 |
|  | Dec 20 | 3066 |  | Feb 7 | 5436 |
|  | Dec 20 | 5020 |  | Mar 12 | 1503 |
|  | Dec 20 | 5026 |  | June 8 | 1590 |

\* \* \*

[7] Harry Dichter and Elliott Shapiro, Early American Sheet Music, Its Lure and Its Lore, 1767-1889 (New York, R. R. Bowker Co., 1941) p228; repeated in substance, p237

Although the plate numbers have been arranged in progressive order from lowest to highest, it is clear from the scattering of the dates of filing that they were not assigned in any regular succession. PN 3018 was deposited on November 21st and PN 3019 over five months earlier on June 12th. After Tolman had settled down to a regular series, the quantity of publications varies from 90 to 180, but in 1863 he used plate numbers scattered over a range of 783, and in 1864 the range jumped to 1678. It is quite inconceivable that anything like this quantity of publications was issued, and the only alternative seems to be that Tolman was systematically filling all the gaps. He apparently left one fairly significant space unfilled between PNs 4800 and 4978, as will be explained in due course when it comes time to show how Root & Cady used the numbers for their own publications, and it is not altogether clear just how or when he covered the ground from PN 4299, filed on April 15, 1861, and PN 4995, filed on December 20, 1864. Except for the aforementioned gap, however, he seems to have completed his task of filling out the entire series by the end of 1864 since otherwise there would be no reason for him to continue so logically and regularly through the first half of the five thousands. The point will receive further confirmation later. It is naturally of considerable importance with regard to Root & Cady since it now becomes possible to determine fairly accurately just how many sets of plates they received.

This is all the more possible because the point which Tolman had reached when the sale was consummated can be set with quite satisfactory exactitude. Tolman made deposits on six different dates in January, 1868 -- on the 2nd, 7th, 10th, 16th, 17th, and 28th. There is a considerable scatter in the plate numbers filed on these dates. PN 5424, for instance, was deposited on December 11, 1867, whereas PN 5408 was not deposited until January 7, 1868. In addition, a fair number of the compositions issued during this period were not deposited at all, and it has not been possible to determine their titles. Of those which were deposited, however, the following have a bearing on the case.

```
5430   VASCHETTI, C.  The Flower Girl.  Filed January 10.  BTC-7
5431   CRAMER.  Il Desiderio [varied]  Filed January 16.  BTC-7
5432   KELLER, M.  Unbidden tears.  Filed January 17.  BTC-7
5416   FIELD, WM. A.  Comedy Galop.  Filed January 28.  BTC-7
5436   KELLER, M.  Grief and Song.  Filed February 7.  BTC-1
5415   WYMAN, ADDISON P.  The Alps.  Marche de Bravoura.  Filed February 7.
       BTC-1
1503   EMERY, STEPHEN A.  Apfelblüthen Walzer.  4 hands.  Filed March 12.  BTC-1
1510   No. 2.  Menuet.  Filed March 17.  BTC-1
1511   No. 1.  Polonaise.  Filed March 17.  BTC-1
```

The abbreviation, BTC, refers to the catalog of the Board of Music Trade, where the symbol 7 stands for Root & Cady and 1 for Ditson. Thus the "Correction" in The Song Messenger "Extra" for August, 1868 [cf p62] is completely justified in saying that the sale was dated as of February 1st, and although the identity of Tolman's PNs 5433 and 5434 is not known, reference to the list of Root & Cady plate numbers at the end of this chapter will show that the Chicago firm after a considerable gap started their main series again with PN 5436 taking up with the number of the first piece Tolman deposited after February 1st.

After the lapse of a month, Tolman starts publishing music once more with a new series of plate numbers beginning suspiciously close to 1500, a figure which may easily be sheer artifice and be strictly the equivalent of 1. He could not have issued 1500 pieces in a month; he apparently did not retain them from the old stock since Root & Cady obviously got them all; and no purchase of 1500 pieces from another publisher can be traced. Perhaps because he had to start from scratch, his activities during the next few months are unexampled. A series of 30 arrangements by Adolph Baumbach under the general title Beauties of the Opera were issued with plate numbers ranging from 1519 to 1588. Another series -- Tolman seems always to have thought in terms of "sets" or "series" -- of Selections from La Belle Hélène by Offenbach was soon up to No. 6. Additions were made to the series of Concerted Pieces and to Sacred Pieces. On June 8th, A. E. Warren's Dew Drop Mazurka was deposited with the PN 1590. On June 1st, a song by Edward Saxton had the PN 1591. Finally, on June 25, 1868, two additions were made to the series Gems from France and Italy with English translations. They were his last publications to be deposited for copyright. The sale to Ditson must have taken place very soon thereafter since otherwise the rumor which Root & Cady corrected in August would not have had time to get started in Chicago. If Ditson acquired something less than a hundred sets of plates, it is easy to see why Root & Cady with their 5435 sets should feel that the misconception should be righted. The sale marked the end of Tolman's publishing career. The Boston directory for 1868 gives him as selling "musical instruments" at 291 Washington St.; in 1869, he has moved to 289 Washington St., where he is given as selling only pianos. In 1870, he retired, and in 1871 the directory supplies no business address at all and has him comfortably settled at "13 East Brookline."

Very little of the story for this period remains to be told except for a brief survey of the plate number list which follows and a description of the effect which the purchase of the Tolman catalog had upon that list. Only five of the Root & Cady sheet music publications deposited for copyright have not been found. Any gaps which remain therefore must belong to compositions of three types -- reprints by Root & Cady of public domain compositions, numbers assigned to plates purchased from other publishers, and lastly to a fairly large group of works which Root & Cady published and copyrighted but on which no plate numbers are printed in the deposit copies although numbers were apparently reserved for them and were sometimes added in later printings. Between January and June, 1868, Root & Cady copyrighted 24 titles without plate numbers compared with eight for the preceding six months and two for the following six months. Many of these have the initials of the title instead of a plate number or, in the case of stereotyped plates, give a few complete words from the title. Enough of these present a sufficiently different general appearance to suggest that during the turmoil resulting from the Tolman purchase, the preparation of some of the plates had had to be sub-contracted to other shops which did not know the Root & Cady plate number system. A separate section of such publications has been appended to the main list.

This main list itself proceeds with admirable regularity, particularly admirable when we consider the state of affairs in Boston. There is one minor unexplained upset starting with PN 588 and coming to a climax with the assignment of PNs 613-616 and 618 each to two compositions. During this range, the advertisements in The Song Messenger bear out the dates of registration, so that something either drastic or merely inadvertent must have happened to the method of allocating plate numbers. The resulting confusion finally came to the attention of someone in authority, so that starting with PN 619, a new system of assigning numbers was organized, and except for the unfortunate blanks produced when the small Chicago publishers were worked into the list, the numbers and dates progress with fair regularity until PN 839 is reached.

With PN 840 comes the abyss. Previously, Root & Cady had been easily able to digest the smaller publishers whose stocks they had bought, and work these into their own series of plate numbers. With the purchase of the Tolman catalog, it would have become a question of the tail trying to wag the dog. Strictly on the basis of least effort and with no sign of false sentimentality about their own publications, Root & Cady accepted the Boston series as its new base and worked their own series into it. Two or three Boston publications have been noted with altered plate numbers, but these were presumably changed as an afterthought or as a later adjustment, since the vast mass of Boston plate numbers were taken over unaltered. Obviously, this necessitated changing any Root & Cady number conflicting with an early G. P. Reed number. All of these changes have not been recorded for a number of reasons. Editions of Root & Cady publications with the original number crossed off with a thin line and a new number added in the center are relatively scarce since they could only have been sold during the succeeding three years. After Brainard and John Church acquired the plates, they issued copies in so much greater quantities that during the early stages of this study it was supposed that Brainard had instituted the new system, and therefore no record was kept. Later, it did not seem necessary as long as the general procedure was established. Brainard and Church both frequently deposited these revised editions when applying for renewal of the copyright, and most of the statistics given below were acquired from such copies. Nonetheless, a sufficient number of pieces with revised plate numbers have been found bearing the Root & Cady imprint to prove beyond all reasonable doubt that the labor of remarking all these plates was largely accomplished between June 1868 and January 1869.

The system employed can be made clearer with a few examples. Apparently, it was quite arbitrary. John Church got most of George F. Root's songs and in renewing the copyright on his Six Ballads sent in copies of at least five of them. These were the songs which Root & Cady had issued as almost their first venture and which Russell & Tolman engraved for them giving the plates of the first edition numbers from the Russell & Tolman series. They now turn up with some of the numbers the same and some changed:

1. Only waiting, PN 2 shifts to PN 1831
2. Softly she faded, PN 3733, the original Russell & Tolman number
3. The Forest requiem, PN 4 ... 4, unchanged
4. [Missing]
5. Lilly Brook, PN 6-4, shifts to PN 1339
6. My home is on the prairie, PN 7-4, unchanged

Presumably, Reed had published compositions with the PNs 2 and 6, and Root & Cady consequently changed the number on their own publication. One would normally suppose that for the sake of keeping the plates of a series together, all numbers in the series would be changed if one of them had to be. Quite obviously, this is not what happened. Series are constantly broken and their component parts scattered broadcast over all five thousand plate numbers. If it meant more work for the man who had to assemble the plates for a new edition, it nonetheless saved time and trouble by avoiding the remarking of many plates. Similarly, Root's <u>My Cottage Home</u>, <u>Dear Mother</u> is available in the original Root & Cady deposit copy and in Brainard's renewal copy, both bearing the PN 88 4; but his <u>Mother, Oh Sing to Me of Heaven</u> turns out to have the original number, 78 4, crossed out in the Brainard imprint and PN 1380 substituted. Some of the shifts seem just a little senseless. P. P. Bliss' <u>Mr. Lordly and I</u> was shifted from 605 4 to 1371, only to have C. P. Hubbard's <u>Come Where the Morning Is Breaking</u>, originally published by Merrill & Brennan, assigned to 605. It would seem simpler to have given the Hubbard piece the PN 1371 in the first place, but possibly Root & Cady thought they were going to use the Reed publication with the PN 605 and after shifting their own, decided to jettison the Reed publication and consequently found themselves with a blank into which they fitted Hubbard's song.

Although space does not permit the discussion of many single cases, it may be of interest to list a group of the other shifts largely as a witness to the large number of alterations which were made and to illustrate the seemingly hit-or-miss fashion in which the new numbers were assigned.

| | | | | | | | |
|---|---|---|---|---|---|---|---|
| 33 8 to 1358 | 371 4 to 3876 | 635 8 to 675 | 755 4 to 2055 |
| 128 4 - 4915 | 380 4 - 4905 | 658 4 - 1240 | 756 4 - 3149 |
| 134 3 - 1822 | 381 4 - 4943 | 664 6 - 470 | 758 5 - 1872 |
| 135 4 - 812 | 397 7 - 1097 | 665 8 - 4913 | 767 3 - 3870 |
| 188 4 - 483 | 408 - 3582 | 668 4 - 476 | 775 4 - 3874 |
| 189 4 - 934 | 418 5 - 995 | 682 8 - 2408 | 785 5 - 1839 |
| 196 4 - 3923 | 432 4 - 3868 | 683 6 - 850 | 790 5 - 3447 |
| 211 4 - 2599 | 433 4 - 3569 | 686 5 - 2674 | 798 4 - 580 |
| 215 8 - 1179 | 434 6 - 463 | 689 4 - 3141 | 799 6 - 2777 |
| 270 4 - 816 | 450 8 - 4940 | 701 4 - 2137 | 806 5 - 2648 |
| 271 4 - 3587 | 454 4 - 3865 | 705 6 - 1273 | 818 3 - 1406 |
| 274 8 - 557 | 460 4 - 343 | 707 4 - 2141 | 821 4 - 1930 |
| 278 4 - 992 | 467 4 - 3803 | 708 6 - 1021 | 826 4 - 4867 |
| 304 4 - 3959 | 471 2 - 3924 | 722 5 - 835 | 827 4 - 1138 |
| 340 4 - 3747 | 546 8 - 1355 | 725 6 - 2949 | 828 3 - 2542 |
| 342 4 - 3867 | 552 5 - 664 | 728 4 - 2717 | 833 3 - 4933 |
| 348 3 - 1263 | 564 6 - 909 | 729 5 - 2685 | 834 5 - 4932 |
| 350 4 - 3871 | 603 7 - 2657 | 732 4 - 1764 | 835 6 - 335 |
| 354 4 - 2563 | 605 4 - 1371 | 736 6 - 616 | 836 11 - 1140 |
| 362 3 - 1791 | 606 5 - 2444 | 738 10 - 623 | 837 5 - 4867 |
| 363 4 - 1078 | 622 13 - 690 | 749 5 - 910 | S - 2738 |
| 368 4 - 2705 | 623 10 - 766 | 752 5 - 3523 | Title - 5498 |

The shifts obviously have a double meaning: the original Root & Cady number would not have been cancelled if G. P. Reed had not furnished an acceptable composition with the same number; on the other hand, the <u>new</u> number in most cases would not have been selected if plates from one of the Boston publishers already bore that number. Although the shifts above represent only about one-tenth of the ones that might have been made, they were collected entirely at random and probably represent a chance or average distribution. It is a little surprising therefore to find that the largest number of shifts were made to numbers in the region below 1000 and that of these 23 shifts, 17 were to numbers under 839 or within the range of Root & Cady's own series. Three of these went to numbers which are currently blank -- 816, 463, 675 -- but there is no reason to suppose that Root & Cady had not used them previously. Somewhat too often to be sensible they shifted the number of one of their own compositions, only to fill it later with another. Once, even, they moved 552 to 664, 664 to 470, and 470 must have gone to some undetermined number, since it was No. 2 of Root's popular series of arrangements, <u>Camps, Tramps, & Battlefields</u>. Nineteen shifts were made to plate numbers in the ranges of both the 1000s and the 3000s whereas seventeen were made to the 2000s. Probably these would be statistically equivalent. But except for the 4800s and the 4900s, which were used largely for new Root & Cady publications, only nine shifts were made to other numbers in the 4000s. Had Tolman actually left a substantial section from 4300 to 4800 blank, Root & Cady's obvious move would have been to shift the major portion of their list to this range. Since they did not do so, the only reasonable deduction is that the numbers were already occupied by compositions supplied by Tolman.

The peculiar island from 4800 to 4978 has already been mentioned several times. Actually, judging by the dates of deposit, Root & Cady started to fill in the gap from the middle. The first piece was F. W. Root's Fantasie from Offenbach's Orpheus with the PN 4901, deposited on June 12, 1868. Most of the numbers following immediately thereafter were occupied by compositions shifted from earlier ranges. This probably accounts for the numerous gaps in the list. By PN 4929, however, the section was being primarily used for new publications. In spite of the purchases, Root & Cady's own new pieces appeared at such a rate that PN 4978 was reached early in September. Jumping back to 4801, the series was continued with equal dispatch, and PN 4900 was reached in January, 1869. At this point, the gap left by Tolman was filled, and it was necessary to jump over the section of compositions which Tolman had published from 1865 to 1868 and start out into new territory. A few pieces from the Mason & Hamlin purchase were spotted in the few gaps which Tolman had left, but with PN 5436 deposited on the same day as PN 4900, Root & Cady were finally on their own again moving rapidly into the final phase of their existence.

CHAPTER VI

THE END OF THE FIRM, 1868-1871

## THE END OF THE FIRM, 1868-1871

In the Tolman catalog, Messrs. Root & Cady acquired a group of titles more numerous, more varied and more sophisticated than their own publications. Although the personalities of the owners of the two firms undoubtedly influenced their output, the differences between their catalogs probably resulted quite as much from the differences in the cultural climates of Boston and Chicago. Where Henry Tolman and his predecessors found it possible to publish an occasional song by Handel or a sonata by Haydn among the unending series of polkas and ballads, Root & Cady preferred to stick to the known quantities of George F. Root, James R. Murray and Frank Howard. No change in publishing policies is discernable after the purchase of the Boston catalogs, but the variety of the combined catalogs was considered an asset. The Song Messenger Extra for May, 1869, while lamenting the slowness of the music trade since the war, attributed the bulk of Root & Cady's issues -- 1,200,000 copies between April 1, 1868, and April 1, 1869 -- to the size, variety and richness of the catalog, particularly its many standard songs and teaching pieces. "An average of even a hundred or two copies printed of six thousand different pieces makes a large aggregate."

The position of Root & Cady among the music publishers of the United States was indicated by Mr. Cady's election on July 21, 1869, to the presidency of the Board of Music Trade. He had been active as the firm's representative to the Board for several years being elected secretary and treasurer on July 11, 1866, at its meeting in Newport [The Song Messenger of the Northwest 4 (July, 1866) 67]. The 1869 meeting, however, was probably the most important in the history of the Board. Before adjourning to go on a junket to Long Branch, the publishers voted to "make a general catalogue of all the publishers, the work to commence immediately" [Song Messenger, 7 (Aug 1869) 127]. The Complete Catalogue of Sheet Music and Musical Works Published by the Board of Music Trade of the United States of America. 1870, issued in 1871, is the only music trade bibliography issued in this country which can boast of any degree of completeness. Its classified arrangement makes it awkward to use, and the citations it supplies are often inadequate, but the idea behind the catalog would be well worth emulating today.

Cady's fellow officers were Julius Lee (Lee & Walker, Philadelphia), vice president, and Thomas J. Hall (Wm. Hall & Son, New York), secretary and treasurer. At the Niagara Falls meeting, July 20, 1870, they were unanimously re-elected [The Song Messenger, 8 (Sept 1870) 137]; and a third term was voted at Newport in July, 1871. [Ibid 9 (Sept 1871) 138]

With regard to new publications, however, the year 1869 was undistinguished for Root & Cady. The firm was busy pushing its old titles, particularly music books, and new items appeared with less frequency than before. After Songs for the New Life was filed in May, only one other book was issued that year, F. W. Root's Pacific Glee Book, filed August 20.

As the stock of publications grew to many times its former size, Root & Cady were much in need of a complete catalog to help customers who either came to their store or wished to order music by mail. The Song Messenger Extra for May, 1869, informed the public that "The labor of rearranging so many thousand plates ... is already done, and by the time this reaches our readers, we shall have printed that part of 'The Musician's Guide' which gives an alphabetical list of all our publications. This part will be followed by such complete classifications as will make it, when finished, of the greatest value to all persons who wish aid in the selection of music." Not a new catalog, The Musician's Guide originated with Russell & Richardson in 1857-58, the earliest edition found bearing the title:

THE / MUSICIAN'S GUIDE; / A descriptive Catalogue / of / Sheet Music and Musical Works / Containing / Nearly Four Thousand Vocal and Instrumental Compositions / Including the Works of the Most Celebrated Composers. / Price 25 Cents. / Boston: Published by Russell & Richardson, (Successors to Geo. P. Reed & Co., and Nathan Richardson) 291 Washington Street.

Previously Richardson had issued free an "Illustrated Catalogue of Richardson's Musical Exchange, No. 282 Washington Street, Boston, Mass." In turn, Russell & Fuller added a life of Thalberg and "two beautiful pieces of music" to their edition of The Musician's Guide, cutting the price to four cents in stamps "to defray postage expenses," according to the New York Musical Review and Gazette [9 (July 10, 1858) 217]. By 1861, The Musician's Guide, then issued by Russell & Tolman, had grown from 80 to 257 pages, and from 4,000 to 5,000 works. To the life of Thalberg had been added biographies of Bach, Beethoven, Handel, Haydn, and Mozart.

Root & Cady's Musician's Guide, completed in time to be rather fully described in The Song Messenger for November, 1869 [7:176], was often advertised on the covers of editions of sheet music as follows:

> THE MUSICIAN'S GUIDE. / A descriptive catalogue of / sheet music, music books, and the most celebrated composers. / Invaluable to teachers, dealers, and all others interested in the selection of any kind of music, embracing, besides the original publications of / Root & Cady, the following well known catalogues of sheet music: / George P. Reed, Henry Tolman, Nathan Richardson, H. Oakes, Russell & Richardson, Russell & Fuller, Russell & Tolman, Henry Tolman & Co., Mason & Hamlin, Ziegfeld, Gerard & Co., and H. T. Merrill & Co.

The advertisement continued by outlining the arrangement of the catalog at some length. It was divided into six parts: a general alphabetical catalog, a classified catalog, an index to songs with foreign words under the foreign title, a list of all operatic music, vocal or instrumental, arranged by the name of the opera or oratorio, an author catalog with brief biographical and critical notes by W. S. B. Mathews, and a graded course of study for piano prepared by Adolph Baumbach. By and large, the organization of the catalog was taken from the earlier editions of the Guide; as early as the Russell & Richardson edition, it had contained the first four sections in substantially the same form used by Root & Cady.

Unfortunately no edition with the Root & Cady imprint has been found. The Grosvenor Library, Buffalo,[1] however, has a copy with the imprint of S. Brainard's Sons and a title identical with the advertisement already quoted. On pv of the Preface appeared this statement: "... The present edition of "THE MUSICIAN'S GUIDE" contains only about one-half of our publications, (being the catalogue formerly published by ROOT & CADY, Chicago)." Further, the table of contents agreed with that given in Root & Cady's advertisement, except for obvious typographical errors. For all practical purposes, therefore, the Brainard edition may be regarded as identical with Root & Cady's.

A detailed analysis of the Musician's Guide seems unnecessary since the bulk of its contents originated with the Boston firms and were issued only briefly if at all with the Root & Cady imprint. Sufficient for our purposes should be a few statistics indicating its nature and scope. Filling 497 pages, the Guide listed 8,498 titles in the general vocal and instrumental catalogs and 59 books, including three theoretical texts, 45 singing books, and 11 miscellaneous works. The classification of sheet music resembles that used for the Board of Music Trade Catalogue with its irritating overlapping divisions. Under "Ballads, Cavatinas, and Arias," for example, there are listed 1,098 titles as compared with 124 Sonatas, 27 items under "Brass band music," and no orchestral music whatsoever. If Root & Cady blazed no trails in making a catalog, at least they must be credited with a careful revision of preceding editions, bringing all their publications into one volume which was as easy to consult as most publisher's catalogs in those days before the advent of library science. Their successors did not do as well. As late as 1880, Brainard advertised in The Musical World [17 (Feb 1880) 1st prelim leaf] "... We issue six different catalogues as follows ... no. 3. The Musician's Guide. -- a book of over 500 pages ... being the catalogue formerly owned by Root & Cady and H. Tolman & Co. ...."

After the appearance of The Musician's Guide came an expansion of the instrument department headed by William Lewis. He had had a varied career as farmer, carpenter, and grocer, interspersed with appearances as a violinist since his arrival in the United States from England in 1850.[2] Early in the sixties he became associated with Root & Cady as a salesman while continuing his concerts in and around Chicago. He was instrumental in more ways than one in the organization of musical evenings at Root & Cady's warerooms. In May, 1870, The Song Messenger announced [8:80] that he had just returned from a trip to Europe, where he had made arrangements with the manufacturers of instruments, strings, etc., for sales direct to Root & Cady. To provide room for the expanded stock, the firm rented the first floor and basement of No. 70 Washington Street, opposite the main store. The new department contained "full lines of violins, cellos, and double basses of the best German and Italian makes, band instruments, brass and German silver, drums, base and snare; tambourines enough to run forty minstrel troupes and several hundred bands of gipsies; toy drums ... French and German accordeons, a very full line, dulcimers, zithers, flutes, piccolos, flageolets, etc.; guitars ... metronomes ..." and so on and so on, the Chicago Post reported ecstatically [quoted in The Song Messenger, 8 (Aug 1870) 126-7]. Nor

\* \* \*

[1] Now part of the Buffalo and Erie County Public Library
[2] A. T. Andreas, History of Cook Co., Illinois. (Chicago, A. T. Andreas, 1884) p551

was this all. Balconies for sheet music were installed in the main store "after the fashion of some libraries," thereby releasing more floor space for pianos, and in an ingenious move, perhaps better understood at the time, "the Opera House has been tapped, as it were, and a rotunda let down from the sky to the ground floor." In the same issue, The Song Messenger announced [8:121] another forward step in the progress of a great American publisher. The Root & Cady baseball team defeated Lyon & Healy for the second time, 45 to 33.

The fatal year 1871 promised greater success than ever before. In a paper on "Music in the interior," prepared for the second session of the National Musical Congress, W. S. B. Mathews claimed that Root & Cady manufactured and sold a larger amount of sheet music and music books than any New York publisher and that the total sales of music merchandise in Chicago amounted to about $1,500,000 a year [The Song Messenger, 9 (Jan 1871) 10]. An article from the Congregationalist paper, the Advance, (which, incidentally, Mr. Cady had helped to found) declared that Root & Cady's sales were about $400,000 annually, and, for the first half of the current year, they were nearly $100,000 more than ever before in the same period [Reprinted in The Song Messenger, 9 (Aug 1871) 114]. These figures are of great importance in evaluating the firm's failure to survive the fire.

A minor footnote to the history of the Germans in the United States is the attitude toward the Franco-Prussian war illustrated by Root & Cady's publications. Beginning with G. F. Root's The Banner of the Fatherland, dedicated "To the friends of Prussia" and signed G. Friedrich Wurzel, the pro-German effusions continued with James R. Murray's Prussia, Gird Thy Sons for Battle!, an anonymous Viva La Prussia!, and concluded with the amazing Kutschke's War-song (Das Kutschkelied), A Reminiscence of the Great German Peace Festival in Chicago, May 29th, 1871. The opening two lines of the song:

>   Was kraucht dort in dem Busch herum?
>   Ich glaub', es ist Napolium,

are said to go back to 1813-15, but the remainder of the four verse poem, composed by Hermann Alexander Pistorius, was first published on August 16, 1870. The version immediately became the most popular German soldier song of the day. Early in 1871, Wilhelm Ehrenthal published in Leipzig for the benefit of the German wounded a little booklet on the song.[3] It was as elaborate a jest as one could find purporting to trace the song through many a parchment manuscript and Egyptian stele back to the Sanscrit. The originals were reproduced, and German translations and commentaries furnished. At the end of the volume, a section was devoted to translations of the poem into practically every known modern tongue. Apparently, a copy of the book reached Chicago almost immediately since on June 6, 1871, Root & Cady copyrighted a sheet music edition of the song which was clearly inspired by Ehrenthal's volume. The Buddhist [sic] temple in Karnak on the cover was a close copy of Ehrenthal's "Tafel"; the English translation, newly set by a Chicago musician, Otto Lob, was clearly derived from the crude meters given by Ehrenthal on p41; and the other translations, although not always complete, were copied exactly from him. Eight translations were omitted, but the impression made by the remainder -- cuneiform Assyrian, Arabic, Sanscrit, Egyptian hieroglyphics, Low Dutch, Greek, Swedish, Polish, Hebrew, Latin, Danish, Italian, Spanish, French, and Dutch -- all reproduced in their appropriate script, made the publication easily one of the most striking to issue from the presses of Root & Cady. Originally an abridged edition of the song had been printed and distributed to the people from a mobile printing office which was afloat in the monster procession celebrating the German victory. It is beyond the province of this study to discuss the possible implications of Das Kutschkelied for the future expansionist program of the German Reich. Suffice it to say that in 1871 the musical Germans of the Männerchor tradition as represented by Mr. Lob were loyal to the Fatherland in its travail, and the Roots were quite sympathetic. At any rate, no lyric defense of France appeared until, in a spirit of charity toward the defeated, George Root wrote Hear the Cry that Comes across the Sea! which he dedicated to the Producers' French aid organization of Chicago.

As the fall of 1871 set in, the horizon was cloudless. With all the added space that had been acquired, Root & Cady occupied premises "more than twenty-two times larger than those with which they began business thirteen years ago" said the Advance article. In preparation for the fall and winter

\* \* \*

[3] Das Kutschkelied auf der Seelenwanderung. Forschungen über die Quellen des Kutschkeliedes im grauen Alterthume nebst alten Texten und Uebersetzungen in neuere Sprachen. Mit einer Hieroglyphen-Tafel. Herausgegeben zum Besten der Deutschen Invalidenstiftung von Wilhelm Ehrenthal. (Leipzig, F. A. Brockhaus, 1871)

trade, the presses had been at work all summer, and "great piles of books filled the basement of the main building ... They would all be gone in a few weeks, so we did not take out a special insurance upon them, but assumed the risk for that short time ourselves" [G. F. Root, The Story of a Musical Life, p152-3]. The Song Messenger for October advertised inside the front cover a new shipment of music in the celebrated Peters edition including Beethoven's complete sonatas and works by Bach, Mozart, Schubert, Schumann and Weber.

On the night of October 9th, a fire broke out in Chicago spreading rapidly until it was completely out of control. In its eastward course, it consumed the whole of Washington Street to Dearborn including the highly combustible Opera House and its contents. George F. Root described that awful night in his autobiography:

> I lived then in Groveland Park ... about four miles south from our place of business. Between three and four o'clock in the morning of the ninth of October someone waked me and said Jerome Beardslee was at the door in a buggy and wanted to see me ... I got up and tried to light the gas, but there was none. I hurried on my clothes, and went down. "What is the matter, Jerome?" "There's a great fire down town, and it is spreading fearfully. Our store is gone, but I got the books out, and have just brought them home ... I think you'll be in time to see your place go" ...
>
> I was in time to see the costly and elegant opera-house go ... We had built a large brick vault in the cellar of the rear building, but a few months before to make a safe place for the plates of our now very large catalogue ... All our important plates were in the vault, excepting those of the "Song King" and the "Curriculum." They were in use in the printing office, and were destroyed ... When the flames enveloped the beautiful building ... my mind ... ran over a list of the familiar and valuable objects belonging to us that were then being offered up in that fearful holocaust ... In a few minutes all were gone [p153-5].

For days after the fire, the partners anxiously waited to see if the vaults and safes had protected their plates and account books. When, finally, they became cool enough to open, their contents were found intact, although some of the papers were scorched. In this respect Root & Cady was more fortunate than Lyon & Healy whose loss was total including all plates and stock. Church's Musical Visitor for November, 1871 [1:12], reported that for the time being, Lyon & Healy's business was transferred to the parent house, Oliver Ditson & Co. of Boston.

If the fire was a disaster to the community, it was a knock-out blow to the music trade. The extent of the catastrophe was estimated in a Detroit music paper, The Song Journal [1 (Nov 1871) 157]:

> All of the musical firms ... were burnt out, as were the various musical institutes ... As most of the wealthy and cultivated people of Chicago lost their all, until they recover, in some measure, the occupation of many musical instructors will be gone. The effect also upon the various bands of the city cannot but be bad. All the theatres are consumed, with no probability of their being rebuilt until another season has past. Consequently there is no demand for orchestral performers. Many musicians have already left the city, and others are looking about them for situations elsewhere.

Although the future offered little promise under such conditions, Root & Cady was not ready to succumb. Whatever differences there may have been between the partners, none of them were willing to retire from the Chicago scene nor from the music trade despite losses of over $250,000. The days immediately following the fire saw long conferences between the partners as they waited for the vaults to cool. By October 24, they had agreed to dissolve the partnership by mutual consent and to form two firms in its place. The notices of copartnership as given in The Song Messenger for December [9:191] defined the scope of the new organizations.

> The undersigned have this day entered into copartnership under the firm name of ROOT & CADY, to transact a general business in the sale of pianos, organs, imported musical merchandise and music books, of our own publication. We assume liabilities, and receive the assets of the old firm of ROOT & CADY, 612 Michigan Av.
> Chicago, Oct. 24, 1871
>
> E. T. Root<br>C. M. Cady<br>Wm. Lewis

The undersigned have this day entered into copartnership to transact a general business in the sale of sheet music and music books, &c., under the firm name of GEO F. ROOT & SONS.
Chicago, Oct. 24, 1871

Geo. F. Root<br>
Wm. A. Root<br>
Frederic W. Root<br>
Chas. T. Root

Of the men who had been associated with Root & Cady before the fire, some left Chicago for good. James R. Murray, for example, returned to his birthplace, Andover, Massachusetts, where his friends organized a benefit concert for him and found him some pupils [The Song Messenger, 9 (Dec 1871) 179]. Before the end of the year, White, Smith & Perry of Boston had published a "fire" song, Pity the Homeless; or Burnt Out. Words and Music by James R. Murray. "Respectfully Dedicated to Our Friends, Messrs. Root & Cady, Chicago, Ills." George F. Root, his sons, Frederic W. and Charles T., and his brother William, formerly bookkeeper for Root & Cady, withdrew from music publishing, at least temporarily.

Two weeks after the fire, the Chicago Times for October 24 was able to publish a Business Directory giving the new addresses of the burnt out firms [3:8]. Root & Cady were then established at 612 Michigan Avenue in a large house. Somehow, they managed to keep The Song Messenger going although it had to be printed in another city. Nothing if not optimistic, they advertised in the November-December issue of The Chicago Magazine of Fashion, Music and Home Reading [2:362]: "We are now prepared to fill orders for musical merchandise, of every description, nearly as promptly as heretofore. Our sheet music and book catalogue is being reprinted with all possible dispatch, and goods of all kinds in our line are daily arriving in large quantities." These are either brave or foolish words, coming from men who were building a stock from nothing.

In the same issue of the Chicago Magazine of Fashion, etc., Root & Cady announced the publication of three new songs by G. F. Root, From the Ruins Our City Shall Rise, Passing Through the Fire, and Ye Have Done it unto Me. Actually, they were not deposited for copyright until November 25, eight days after Root & Cady had sold its sheet music catalog to S. Brainard's Sons of Cleveland, if we accept the date given on a preliminary leaf in the Grosvenor Library copy of the Musician's Guide. A statement dated November 17, 1871, addressed to the "Musical Public" announced the sale adding that Root & Cady hoped to be able to fill orders for its singing books by the first of December.

In the first months after the reorganization, Root & Cady made some strides toward regaining its former position. The Song Messenger for January, 1872 [10:10], presented apologies from the publisher for its late appearance in the two previous months. That issue was the first printed in Chicago since the fire, and future numbers were promised on or before the first of the month. Apologies were also tendered for the delays in filling orders for the Song King, Song Queen, Triumph, Palm, etc. "Owing to the past difficulties of filling orders, we have hardly dared to advertise our books, or take usual measures in heralding their great success. Our lips will soon be unsealed, when rival publishers, who have very properly profited by our calamity, will learn that we are still in the field as vigorous and jubilant as ever, putting fresh blood into our catalogue in the shape of new books, which will even surpass our previous publications...." Truly surprising was the claim that they sold as many Mason & Hamlin organs in December, 1871 as in December, 1870.

Rival publishers must have noted the full-page advertisement in Brainard's Musical World for March, 1872 [9:47], announcing the newly revised edition of the Musical Curriculum to be ready March 1st and an almost complete list of music books issued by Root & Cady going all the way back to The Silver Lute. The March Song Messenger [10: front inside cover], however, contained a notice dated February 23, 1872, announcing the sale of Root & Cady's book catalog to John Church & Co. of Cincinnati. Beside the published books, the sale included the manuscript of George Root's new book, The Glory, but not The Song Messenger, which remained in Root & Cady's hands. In the playful style so typical of The Song Messenger, Root & Cady told of the sale: "... we can never eradicate the paternal interest we feel in the books just sold. We have watched them through the perils of teething, whooping cough and scarlet fever into the strength of blooming adolescence, and though we have given them away amid the merry jangle of nuptial church bells, they will never cease to be our children. As they honor their parentage by proving themselves prolific of greenbacks and happiness to their possessors we shall be proud of them" [10 (Mar 1872) 41]. The sales to Brainard and John Church realized a sum estimated by

George Root at about $130,000 and by The Song Messenger at $150,000. This plus the insurance money the firm hoped to collect was to provide capital for future business. In April, Geo. F. Root & Sons became joint publishers of The Song Messenger, retaining W. S. B. Mathews as editor, G. F. Root, musical editor; and C. M. Cady, managing editor [10:53]. At the same time, G. F. Root was a regular contributor to Brainard's Musical World, one of The Song Messenger's closest rivals [Brainard's Musical World, 9 (Jan 1872) 6].

In June The Song Messenger proclaimed the recovery of the music trade in Chicago. In view of later events, this eloquence must be viewed as a compound of courageous optimism and bad business judgment.

> It is a curious commentary upon the recuperative powers of Chicago, that, instead of the ruined trade which her enemies predicted immediately after the great fire, in six months from that disaster its leading business houses in all branches of commerce are doing a larger trade than they ever before dared dream of. This is well illustrated in the case of Root & Cady. They lost by the fire a clean quarter of a million dollars. Their creditors did not believe after this loss that they could pay in full; indeed, advised them not to try, but were willing to accept fifty, twenty-five or any other number of cents on the dollar that they thought they could pay comfortably. Root & Cady, however, had too high a sense of honor to do this. They knew better than their creditors the value of their assets, and what they could do with them. They sold their sheet music and book plates for $150,000, which, with their other assets, enables them to pay one hundred cents on the dollar, places their credit on a rock and brings to their command all the capital they desire. With a bold stroke they sacrificed their publishing business, retaining only their popular musical monthly, The Song Messenger, and resolved to put all their energies into the sale of pianos, organs, and imported musical merchandise, and show the world what could be done in these departments.
>
> Eastern manufacturers, recognizing Root & Cady as only a synonym for integrity, pluck, business experience, and sagacity, were not slow to offer them better terms, exclusive and larger territory, and every facility to go in strong ... They have contracted for 1,500 Mason & Hamlin organs, and 850 first class pianos ... Root & Cady are also the largest direct importers of musical merchandise west of New York. They have in stock and on the way brass and German silver instruments enough to fit out one hundred bands, with strings, violins, guitars, accordeons, etc., to match. To make room for such an enormous stock ... they have taken and now occupy the entire four story brick building on the corner of Wabash Avenue and Van Buren Street ... [10:88].

This expansive good humor was to change within a short time to gnawing anxiety as insurance companies defaulted on their policies, business declined, and notes had to be met. No hint of the changing state of affairs was given in The Song Messenger until it suspended publication for three months and by its absence indicated what it did not say. When it reappeared in February, 1873, Root & Cady's name had disappeared from the mast-head. On an inside page was printed a statement by C. M. Cady, giving his account of the events since the fire. To avoid missing any of the overtones which help in assessing the parts played by the partners, the statement is reprinted in full [10:194]:

A CARD

> An intermission of three months in the publication of the SONG MESSENGER calls for an explanation which is as follows: After the great fire of October 9th, 1871, by which Root & Cady lost over $250,000, the firm was dissolved by mutual consent, Geo. F. Root & Sons continuing the sheet music and music book business, and Root & Cady, consisting of E. T. Root, C. M. Cady and Wm. Lewis, continuing the sale of pianos, organs, and imported musical merchandise. Root & Cady took the assets and assumed all the liabilities of the old concern, which they undertook to pay in full. This, we now see, though prompted by the most honorable intentions, was a great mistake, and one for which I, mainly, am responsible. I overestimated the value of our assets and we all overestimated the amount of business that could be done. The blotting out of $200,000,000 of capital by the Chicago fire, not only demoralized, beyond our expectations, the music trade of this city, but disas-

trously affected trade generally throughout the Northwest. Up to June 1st, 1872, however, we were not disheartened. From this time on, the low prices of all agricultural products, the vast sums of money absorbed in rebuilding Chicago, and the steadily increasing stringency of the money market, all added to the burden of our undertaking, until, in the latter part of September, I sunk down under the load, sick. All those who, by a long course of punctilliousness in business, have been educated to such a standard of commercial honor that they fear failure worse than they fear death, can appreciate my situation at this juncture, when, with a pulse below sixty, an inability to sleep more than four hours out of the twenty-four, and threatened with brain fever, as I have since learned from my physicians, I was compelled for more than three months to dismiss from my mind, as far as possible, all thoughts of business. In October, Root & Cady were forced into bankruptcy, from which we are just emerging. It is proper here to state that, as the paper of the new concern was accepted for all ante-fire indebtedness, releasing Mr. Geo. F. Root from all such liabilities, the firm of Geo. F. Root & Sons has in no way been compromised by the failure of Root & Cady. Messrs. E. T. Root and Wm. Lewis, under the firm name of Root & Lewis, continue at 272 State Street, as successors of Root & Cady, in a general music business, including sheet music, music books, pianos, organs, and imported goods. Geo. F. Root & Sons, having, through the Hon. J. Y. Scammon, purchased the bankrupt stock of merchandise, will go on at 283 Wabash Avenue with a general music business, including, also sheet music, music books, pianos, organs, and imported goods, and will hereafter publish the SONG MESSENGER.

Thanks to a good constitution, I have now entirely recovered my health, but have not definitely settled upon any plans of future business.

With many kind remembrances for our old patrons and my old partners, I remain,
Yours truly,
Chicago, Feb. 18, 1873
C. M. Cady

Cady's letter gave a straightforward picture of the combination of circumstances which prevented Root & Cady from weathering the financial storm after the fire. Presumably the rupture between the two firms was complete since he so carefully absolves Geo. F. Root & Sons from any association with the bankruptcy, casually mentioning later that they had purchased all the stock of Root & Cady. Root & Lewis apparently salvaged nothing from the wreckage.

On the other hand, George F. Root's account of this troubled period was very brief and most circumspect. He refrained from expressing his opinion as to a correct course of action while implying that he viewed Cady's plan with strong misgivings. A candid statement of their differences would have done him more honor.

As soon as it could be brought about, our business plans for the future were adjusted. We had lost all our stock, but the plates and copyrights remained, and if I would give up some unencumbered real estate that I had, Mr. Cady and my brother would, with the above and the insurance money they hoped to get, undertake to pay the debts in full and go on with the business. I finally agreed to this proposition, and then two firms were formed [The Story of a Musical Life, p156-7].

After the bankruptcy of Root & Cady,[4] the firm of Root & Lewis continued in business until January 1, 1875, when it was merged with Geo. F. Root & Sons and Chandler & Curtiss to form the Root & Sons Music Co.[5] which was fairly successful for some years.

The check-list of plate numbers for this period starts off from the point where Root & Cady had added most of the plates bought from the Boston firms into their own series. The word "most" is used since

\* \* \*

[4] A search in The National Bankruptcy Register Reports, containing all the important bankruptcy decisions in the United States, 1867-1879. Editor: Willard S. Gibbons. (N. Y., H. Campbell & Co., 1874-1879) disclosed no reference to Root & Cady.

[5] Biographical Sketches of the Leading Men of Chicago. (Chicago, Wilson, Peirce & Co., 1876), p77-8

it seems likely that one more relatively small group from PN 5813-5855 was taken up with Henry Tolman's publications. At least, the blank is broken only by Dudley Buck's rather elaborate cantata, Easter Morning. This is one of the few instances when Tolman's original plate number, 5099, was altered to fit into the Root & Cady series at a different point, PN 5838. Possibly, Root & Cady acquired what they thought would be a sufficient number of copies of a group of larger works and planned to leave them out of their series at first but later realized that they had better include them. Brainard apparently found it desirable to renew the copyright only on this single composition, however, and obviously it is not sufficient to prove a theory.

As the series continued, Root & Cady picked up a scattering of plates from a variety of other publishers, but apparently at no time did they acquire the entire stock of another publisher, unless perhaps they got all of the Molter & Wurlitzer plates, adding them to their series in the region around PNs 6118 to 6167. Even here, the songs of George W. Persley, the pseudonym of George W. Brown, predominate, and pieces by him published either by himself or by T. W. Martin were acquired at the same time. Perhaps Brown was the active agent in the deal selling Root & Cady all of his publications, no matter by whom they were issued, and Molter & Wurlitzer simply threw in a few additional works to round out the transaction. At the same time, Wurlitzer dropped out of the firm at about this period, Molter continuing on his own, and it is possible that Root & Cady acquired everything that the two men had issued previously. In addition to this purchase, a few more Merrill publications were added to the list from PNs 5580-5584; seven or eight pieces were bought from Bach & Kuschbert and Ch. Bach & Co. of Milwaukee and added to the list around PNs 5641-5648; and Robert Goldbeck turned over to Root & Cady an occasional work which had originally appeared with his Conservatory as the publisher. A number of gaps remain in the list around these points since Brainard found few of the purchased plates worth renewing after the expiration of 28 years, and aside from the renewal copies, few of these pieces have been found with the imprint of either Root & Cady or Brainard.

The additional gaps may largely be accounted for by the publication of works which were in the public domain and which therefore could not be deposited for copyright. The Song Messenger lists a goodly number of such titles. Likewise, 26 pieces turned out to have no plate numbers in the deposit copies, but undoubtedly numbers were allowed for them, and in one instance, at least, we know that it was added to the plates at a later date. All sheet music publications registered by the firm, with the single exception of Jolly Jonathan and His Notional Naburs. A Comical Controversy by Pro Phundo Basso [P. P. Bliss], have been found and are duly entered in the list.

It seems likely, however, that a larger percentage of the firm's publications than in previous periods were not deposited even when they bear a printed copyright claim. Up through June of 1870, it was a relatively simple matter for Root & Cady to send a trusted clerk around to the District Court to deposit copies of their publications. The last work so deposited was registered on July 5th, and the last work for any publisher to be inscribed in the record book for Northern Illinois is dated July 7th. Thereafter, publications had to be sent to Washington to be registered in the new central depository where the first work to be recorded bears the date July 9, 1870. Ordinarily, Root & Cady deposited two or three compositions every few days, but the first piece of theirs to appear in the Washington records is dated July 21st. The gaps in the plate number list around this period and for a few months thereafter are more numerous, and it is to be suspected that the firm found it more difficult to send off copies to Washington than to register them right in Chicago. The most notable example of this is the fact that only one of the 13 numbers in Brauer's The Youth's Musical Friend [PNs 5975-5994 (?)] was sent in for registration.

The list begins to collapse shortly after F. W. Root's 50 Piano Pictures began to appear. Clearly, plate numbers were allowed for all 50 at the same time, but since it was customary to issue a series by degrees, there was opportunity to issue a few single works before this series was finished. When the fire came, only ten pieces were completely finished and deposited. Eight more were apparently through the engraving shop and the plates already bore Root & Cady plate numbers. Copies were not yet deposited, however, and registration did not take place until the summer of 1872 after Brainard had bought the sheet music. The remainder of the series were engraved in Brainard's own shop and bear his plate numbers.

The last piece to be registered by Root & Cady is PN 6281, deposited on October 9th. Three freaks appear in the list thereafter between the PNs 7000 and 7003, but they were registered five months earlier. One of these pieces has turned up in two states bearing respectively the PNs 7002 and 6102. Considering the dates of registration, it is obvious that the man who punched out the plate numbers thought that 7000 followed immediately after 6099, and numbered four sets of plates before he realized his mistake. PN 7034 is even further out of line since it bears a claim for 1868 and, in addition, the numbers were stamped with a much smaller punch. Undoubtedly, it has nothing to do with the lower numbers in the 7000s, and hence there is no reason to suppose that the gap from 7004 to 7033 was ever filled.

APPENDIX A

ROOT & CADY PUBLICATIONS

## ROOT & CADY PUBLICATIONS

When the list of plate numbers was published in installments in Notes, searches had been made for missing titles in the libraries of the University of Illinois and the Chicago Historical Society, as well as the Newberry Library, the New York Public Library, the Newark Public Library, the Library of Congress, the American Antiquarian Society, and the Grosvenor Library, the last two through the good offices of Mr. Clarence S. Brigham and Mrs. Margaret M. Mott. The first installment covering the period up to the outbreak of the Civil War also included a "Chronological List of Unlocated Publications," which readers were asked to try and locate. Both libraries and private collectors responded, filling in gaps which otherwise would have remained empty.

In the intervening years additional gaps were filled from time to time, but not until after revision for the present edition was begun were substantial additions made possible, through the generosity of a man and an institution. Mr. W. N. H. Harding, of Chicago, made me welcome in his home and permitted me to examine his extensive collection of pre-fire imprints, while the Music Division of the New York Public Library made available to me newly acquired Root & Cady imprints. For this invaluable assistance I am most grateful.

The Checklist of Plate Numbers is arranged in order of plate number, which is usually, but not always, the order of publication. The symbols used in the list are substantially self-explanatory. When a work was registered for copyright, the filing date is given. When the printed claim of copyright on the music falls in another year, it too is given: otherwise it is omitted as superfluous. When a claim was printed on the music but the logical registration did not follow, the year preceded by the conventional symbol "c" alone is given. And lastly, when the work was not protected by either a printed claim or by registration, the abbreviation "Ncc," standing for "No copyright claim" has been used. "S&Ch" stands for the all but universal "Song & Chorus."

The "Chronological List of Unlocated Publications" which appeared with the first installment of the Checklist did not appear with subsequent installments for a number of reasons. As the volume of publications increased, so did the number of titles listed in advertisements, newspaper announcements and series listings. While the sheer volume of such titles created editorial problems, the frequency with which individual titles turned out to be publications of other firms merely offered for sale by Root & Cady rendered such listings of dubious value. Moreover, listings appearing on sheets of music could only be assigned dates which at best were highly speculative. For these reasons no attempt will be made to list non-copyright works which were advertised but not found. The duplication of plate numbers 613-618 (p102) is discussed on p71.

I. CHECKLIST OF PLATE NUMBERS

## CHECKLIST OF PLATE NUMBERS

1- 5 (or 3690) ROOT, George F., arr. Oh, are ye sleeping, Maggie. Scotch song, as sung by J. G. Lumbard, Esq. Filed Oct. 29, 1859.
Root, George F. Six ballads.

2- 4 (or 3737) No. 1. Only waiting. Filed Oct. 29, 1859.

3- 4 (or 3733) No. 2. Softly she faded. Filed Oct. 29, 1859.

4- 4 (or 3738) No. 3. The forest requiem. Filed Oct. 29, 1859.

5- 4 (or 3761) No. 4. My mother she is sleeping. c1859. Filed Jan. 26, 1861.

6- 4 (or 3760) No. 5. Lilly Brook. c1859. Filed Apr. 13, 1860.

7- 4 (or 3762) No. 6. My home is on the prairie. c1859. Filed Apr. 13, 1860.

8- 5 CADY, Chauncey M. We meet upon the level. c1859.

9- 4 (or C) FLORANCE, George A., arr. by Charles MacEvoy. The pet polka. c1859. Filed Apr. 13, 1860, and Jan. 26, 1861.

10   VAAS, A. J. Briggs House polka. c1860. Filed Apr. 13, 1860, and Jan. 26, 1861.

11   VAAS, A. J. Richmond House polka. c1859. Filed Apr. 13, 1860.

12   VAAS, A. J. Tremont House polka. Filed Apr. 13, 1860.

13   ROOT, George F. Wake! lady wake! (Four part songs with piano forte accompaniment by well known authors. No. 1) Filed Apr. 13, 1860.

14   McEVOY, Charles. The captive bird. c1860.

15   VAAS, A. J. Zouave cadets quickstep. Dedicated to the U. S. Zouave cadets, Governors guard of Illinois. Filed Apr. 13, 1860.

16   [BALFE, Michael William. Norah darling don't believe them.[1]]

17   HUBBARD, James M. List! the evening breeze is stealing. A boat glee. Words by S. E. Coburn. (Four part songs with piano forte accompaniment by well known authors. No. 2) Filed Apr. 13, 1860.

18- 4 VAN RENSSELAER, Eugene. Sister Maggie. Filed Apr. 13, 1860.

19- 4 McEVOY, Charles. Here in this moonlit bower. Words by John O'Reilly, Esq. c1860.

20-21

22  8 McEVOY, Charles. Les zephyrs du matin. Valse brillante. c1860.

23-26

27  5 MARTIN, S. Wesley. Welcome to spring. Quartette. Words by Miss M. F. Warriner. (Four part songs with piano forte accompaniment by well known authors. No. 8) c1860. Filed Jan. 26, 1861.

28-29

30  8 WOLLENHAUPT, H. A. Blanche waltz melodieuse. (His 3 pieces for instruction and recreation for the piano, op. 57, no. 1) c1860.

31  7 HAGEN, Theodore. La gaillarde, morceau de genre, op. 5. c1860. Filed Jan. 26, 1861.

32  8 WOLLENHAUPT, H. A. The rosebud polka rondo. (His 3 pieces ... op. 57, no. 2) c1860. Filed Jan. 26, 1861.

33  8 WOLLENHAUPT, H. A. Marrie polka-mazurka. (His 3 pieces ... op. 57, no. 3) c1860. PN from Brainard ed.

34

35  8 VAAS, A. J. The fire brigade quickstep. c1860.

36

37   ABT, Franz. When the swallows homeward fly. (12 standard songs) Ncc.

38   SCHUBERT, Franz. The secret. English words by Geo. F. Root. (12 standard songs [3]) Filed Jan. 26, 1861.

39  4 CLAEPIUS. Evening. (12 standard songs) Ncc.

40   [HALL, Foley. Ever of thee. (12 standard songs)] The only one of the first six titles in the series not found. It seems to fit here.

41  5 FLOTOW, Friedrich von. Home far away. Arranged from "Depuis ce jour." Arrangement and English words by Geo. F. Root. (12 standard songs) c1860. Filed Sept. 26, 1862.

42-47

48  4 ROOT, Geo. F. Be sure to call as you pass by. Poetry by Chas. Swain, Esq. c1860.

49  4 ROOT, Geo. F. The beautiful maiden just over the way. Song with chorus ad lib. Poetry by Thomas Rogers. c1860.

50

51  6 WAGNER, Richard. Grand march from Tannhauser. Ncc. (Announced, Chicago Tribune, Feb. 23, 1861)

52

\* \* \*

[1] An advertisement in the Tribune for April 2, 1860, lists as "recent and new" titles which have been established as bearing PNs 15, 17, and 18. In addition it gives Michael William Balfe's Norah Darling Don't Believe Them, described as a "beautifully gotten up reprint" with "the most exquisite title page ever published in Chicago. Printed [i.e., lithographed] in seven colors by Mendell of this city." On the grounds of propinquity, this title has been entered tentatively in the table above.

| 53 | 4 | HERTEL, J. W. Michigan schottische. c1860. T-p has map of Michigan and adjacent country, showing locations of the music firms: H. N. Hempsted, Milwaukee, Root & Cady, Chicago, J. W. Hertel, Adrian, Mich., Stein & Bucheister, Detroit, and Doeb & Strengson, Toledo. |
|---|---|---|
| 54 | 4 | VAAS, A. J. Fairy polka redowa. c1860. Filed Sept. 26, 1862. |
| 55 | | |
| 56 | 4 | VAAS, A. J. L'Attacca quickstep. c1860. PN from Brainard ed. |
| 57 | 5 | BRADBURY, William B. The dear ones all at home. S with Ch. Filed Jan. 26, 1861. |
| 58 | | |
| 59 | 4 | VAAS, A. J. Sherman House polka redowa. Filed Jan. 26, 1861. |
| 60 | 4 | SMITH, C. C. Skating polka. Dedicated to the South Side Skating Club. c1861. Filed Sept. 26, 1862. |
| 61-62 | | |
| 63 | 10 | MASON, William. Polka gracieuse pour le piano. Op. 14. c1861. Filed Sept. 26, 1862. |
| 64 | 5 | VAAS, A. J. Major Anderson's march. Respectfully dedicated to the gallant Major Anderson. Ncc. Filed Jan. 26, 1861. |
| 64 | 4 | ROOT, George F. Rock me to sleep mother. As sung by Mrs. Matteson. c1861.[2] |
| 65 | | HUBBARD, James M. 4 songs. c1861. Filed Sept. 26, 1862. |
| 66 | 4 | Mine own. Answer to "Call me pet names." Words by a gentleman of Chicago. As sung by Mr. C. R. Adams. |
| 67 | 4 | Death of the robin. |
| 68 | 4 | Song of the Egyptian girl. |
| 69 | 4 | I never kiss and tell. Ballad. Words by C. Chauncy Burr, Esq. |
| 70 | 4 | ROOT, George F. Kitty Ryder. c1861. Filed Sept. 26, 1862. |
| 71 | 4 | ROOT, George F. Dream on, Lillie. c1861. Filed Sept. 26, 1862. |
| 72 | 4 | ROOT, George F. The first gun is fired! May God protect the right! Filed Apr. 15, 1861. [Deposit copy lacks PN.] |
| 73 | 3 | ROOT, George F. God bless our brave young volunteers. c1861. Filed Sept. 26, 1862. |
| 74 | 2 | ROOT, George F. God bless our brave young volunteers. [Chorus version.] |
| 75 | 2 | ROOT, George F. Forward, boys, forward. c1861. Filed Sept. 26, 1862. [Copy at Univ. of Ill. lacks copyright claim.] |
| 76 | 4 | FRISBIE, Henrie L. The stars and stripes, the flag of the free. c1861. |
| 77 | 3 | SAFFERY, E. C. The union volunteers. c1861. |
| 78 | 4 | ROOT, George F. Mother, oh sing to me of heaven. c1861. Filed Sept. 26, 1862. |
| 79 | 2 | ROOT, George F. Have ye sharpened your swords? c1861. |
| 80 | 3 | ROOT, George F. My heart is like a silent lute. c1861. Filed Sept. 26, 1862. |
| 81 | 5 | VAAS, A. J. Ellsworth requiem march. c1861. Filed Sept. 26, 1862. |
| 82- | 5 | FRISBIE, Henrie L. Thou wilt come never more to the stream; or, Kitty Clyde's grave. (Root & Cady's collection of popular songs, duetts, trios, &c.) Filed Sept. 26, 1862. |
| 83 | | |
| 84 | 3 | HUGHES, William Carter. Camp song of the Chicago Irish brigade. c1861. |
| 85 | 2 | ROOT, George F. Jimmy's wooing. A story in rhyme by Wurzel. c1861. Filed Sept. 26, 1862. |
| 86 | 7 | ROOT, George F. O come you from the Indies? or, Robert's return from the war. A coloquy for two voices. c1861. Filed Sept. 26, 1862. |
| 87 | 5 | BADARZEWSKA, Thekla. Maiden's prayer. Ncc. |
| 88- | 4 | ROOT, George F. My cottage home, dear mother. c1861. Filed Sept. 26, 1862. |
| 89 | | |
| 90- | 4 | CROUCH, Frederick Nicholls. Kathleen Mavourneen. Ncc. |
| 91-98 | | |
| 99 | 5 | WILLIAMS, Henry. Bermuda's fairy isle. Poetry ... by T. M. Y. Chicago, Root & Cady, 95 Clark St., c1854 by Henry Tolman. The address is evidence the piece was published before 1865, long before the purchase of the Boston plates. |

\* \* \*

[2] The Grosvenor Library, Buffalo, has a copy of this song issued by Root & Cady at 95 Clark St., and they are the rightful owners, since the copyright notice gives them as the claimant. The New York Public Library, however, has a copy with the same copyright notice in which the publisher is given as Russell & Patee with Root & Cady reduced to the position of a secondary imprint. Numerous speculative solutions could be offered, but none are currently subject to proof.

| | | |
|---|---|---|
| 100- | 2 | SCOTT, Lady A. A. S. Annie Laurie. (Root & Cady's collection of popular songs, duetts, trios, &c. by various authors) Ncc. |
| 101-109 | | |
| 110 | 7 | EICHBERG, Julius. Genl. Lyon's battle march, composed expressly for and dedicated to the 1st Regt. Iowa Volunteers. Chicago, Root & Cady, 95 Clark St., c1859 by Russell & Tolman. |
| 111-113 | | |
| 114 | 6 | VAAS, A. J. Cincinnati air line railroad galop. c1861. Filed Sept. 26, 1862. |
| 115-117 | | |
| 118 | 4 | KLINGEMANN, C. Delusion. Mazurka characteristique. (His Echoes of the heart. No. 2) c1861. |
| 119-121 | | |
| 122- | 4 | DURFEE, James, Jr. Amateur march. c1856 by Russell & Richardson. R&C PN covers another PN. "Just issued," Chicago Tribune, Oct. 13, 1861, with composer's name given as "Murfee." |
| 123- | 4 | SMITH, Charles C. Tiger polka. c1861. Filed Sept. 26, 1862. |
| 124 | | |
| 125 | 5 | VAAS, A. J. General Fremont's march. c1861. Filed Sept. 26, 1862. |
| 126 | 4 | ROOT, George F. Stand up for Uncle Sam, my boys. c1861. Filed Sept. 26, 1862. |
| 127 | | |
| 128 | 4 | WORK, Henry Clay. Nellie lost and found. c1861. Filed Sept. 26, 1862. |
| 129 | 4 | HAMBAUGH, James S. Stars and stripes schottisch. c1861. Filed Nov. 20, 1861. |
| 130 | 2 | THE JOHN BROWN SONG. (Root & Cady's collection of popular songs, duetts, trios, &c. by various authors) ["Just issued," Chicago Tribune, Dec. 7, 1861.] Ncc. |
| 131 | 5 | OTTO, F. R. The Lafner waltz. c1861. Filed Sept. 26, 1862. |
| 132- | 5 | VAAS, A. J. The skating quadrille. c1861. Filed Sept. 26, 1862. |
| 133- | 4 | ROOT, George F. The vacant chair... (Thanksgiving, 1861). c1861. Filed Sept. 26, 1862. |
| 134 | 3 | WORK, Henry Clay. Our captain's last words. c1861. Filed Sept. 26, 1862. |
| 135 | 4 | PARK, Roswell. The ensign of glory. c1861. |
| 136-137 | | |
| 138 | 4 | MERRILL, Hiram T. Take your gun and go, John. Filed Sept. 26, 1862. |
| 139 | | |
| 140 | 4 | HUBBARD, James M. Silent evening. Filed Sept. 26, 1862. |
| 141 | 4 | VAAS, A. J. The enchantress schottisch. Filed Sept. 26, 1862. |
| 142-177 | | [Not found] |
| 178- | 3 | MERRILL, Hiram T. Song of the Negro boatman. Filed Sept. 26, 1862. |
| 179- | 5 | ZELLNER, Richard. Birds of the forest waltz. Filed Sept. 26, 1862. |
| 180 | 4 | BREYTSPRAAK, Charles. Moment polka. c1862. |
| 181 | 4 | ZELLNER, Richard. Gen. Grant's march. Filed Sept. 26, 1862. |
| 182-184 | | [Cf list of "Copyrighted works not found" at end.] |
| 185 | 5 | LEFÉBURE-WÉLY, L. J. A. L'heure de la prière. (Six popular pieces by Ascher, Blumenthal & Lefébure Wély ... arranged ... by Albert W. Berg. No. 4) Filed Sept. 26, 1862. |
| 186 | | |
| 187 | 5 | VENZANO, Luigi. Venzano valse. (Six popular pieces ... arranged ... by Albert W. Berg. No. 6) Filed Sept. 26, 1862. |
| 188 | 4 | WORK, Henry Clay. Beautiful Rose. (His Songs & ballads. c1861.) Filed Sept. 26, 1862. |
| 189 | 4 | WORK, Henry Clay. The girls at home... (Four part songs with piano forte accompaniment by well-known authors. No. 9) Filed Sept. 26, 1862. |
| 190- | 3 | FREUND, Joseph. Spring style schottisch. Filed Sept. 26, 1862. |
| 191 | 4 | WOOLCOTT, Francis. Happy days of yore. Filed Sept. 26, 1862. |
| 192 | 4 | WORK, Henry Clay. Kingdom coming. Filed Sept. 26, 1862. |
| 193 | 5 | WOOLCOTT, Francis. 9th Missouri quickstep. c1862. |
| 194 | | |
| 195- | 4 | WORK, Henry Clay. Nellie lost and found, arr. for guitar by John Molter. |
| 196 | 4 | WORK, Henry Clay. Kingdom coming, arr. for guitar by John Molter. [Original editions of these two arrangements have not been found, but the plates were reused for a collected edition of songs for the guitar, c1868.] |
| 197-199 | | |
| | | TAYLOR, R. Stewart. Two songs. |
| 200 | 4 | O, wrap the flag around me, boys. Filed Sept. 26, 1862. |
| 201 | 4 | Soldier's dream song. Filed Sept. 26, 1862. |
| 202 | 5 | VAAS, A. J. Northwestern rifles march. Filed Sept. 26, 1862. |
| 203-209 | | |

| | | |
|---|---|---|
| 210- | 4 | WORK, Henry Clay. Uncle Joe's Hail Columbia. Filed Sept. 26, 1862. |
| 211- | 4 | WORK, Henry Clay. Sleep, baby, sleep. c1862. |
| 212- | 4 | COX, J. Sumner. Mother, blame me not for loving. Filed Sept. 26, 1862. |
| 213- | 6 | STAAB, Franz. Coquette mazurka. Filed Sept. 26, 1862. |
| 214- | 14 | STAAB, Franz. Geo. F. Root's Rock me to sleep mother. Transcription de concert pour le piano. Filed Sept. 26, 1862. |
| 215- | 8 | GROBE, Charles. Kingdom coming... by Henry C. Work. With brilliant variations for the piano. Filed Sept. 26, 1862. [No PN on deposit copy.] |
| 216 | | |
| 217 | 4 | SCOTT, R. D. The new skedaddle. S&Ch. Filed Sept. 26, 1862. |
| 218-220 | | |
| 221 | | GLOVER, Stephen Ralph. The song of Blanche Alpen. Words by C. Jeffrys. Ncc. PN 3560 cancelled. |
| 222-223 | | |
| 224 | 4 | ROOT, George F. De day ob liberty's comin'. Filed Sept. 26, 1862. |
| 225- | 4 | ROOT, George F. The battle-cry of freedom. Filed Sept. 26, 1862. |
| 226 | 3 | WORK, Henry Clay. The first love dream. (His Songs & ballads. c1861.) Filed Sept. 26, 1862. |
| 227- | 3 | MERRILL, Hiram T. "Corn is king!" from the Continental Monthly. Chicago, Published by the author at the Academy of Music, no. 164 Clark St. Filed Aug. 7, 1862, by H. T. Merrill. Undoubtedly this piece and Abel's Your Name! (PN 529) were printed in the Root & Cady plant where a workman assigned them Root & Cady plate numbers by mistake. |
| 228-229 | | |
| 230 | 2 | ROOT, George F. Serenade by Jas. Grant Wilson. Set to music by Geo. F. Root. (Four-part songs with piano forte accompaniment by well known authors. [11]) Filed Sept. 26, 1862. Alternative title: Come on this silent night. Serenade. |
| 231-234 | | |
| 235- | 4 | RINK, Louis H. Springfield polka. c1862. |
| 236 | 5 | OESTEN, Theodor. Alpine bells. (12 standard pieces for piano) Ncc. |
| 237- | 5 | RICHARDS, Henry Brinley. Floating on the wind. (12 standard pieces for piano) Ncc. |
| 238 | 6 | LEFÉBURE-WÉLY, L. J. A. Les cloches du monastère. Ncc. |
| 239 | 5 | VALENTINE, T. Aria alla scozzese. Ncc. |
| 240-243 | | |
| 244 | 2 | CHERRY, John William. Shells of ocean. Written by J. W. Lake, Esq. (Standard songs by various authors) Ncc. |
| 245 | | H., D. H. Agawam quickstep. (Choice selections for the piano by various authors) Ncc. PN 245 cancelled and 432 substituted, in the same type face. |
| 246 | | |
| 247 | 4 | ROOT, George F. Father Abraham's reply to the 600,000. Music adapted and partly composed by Geo. F. Root. Filed Sept. 26, 1862. |
| 248 | 4 | ABT, Franz. O ye tears! O ye tears! Words by Dr. Mackay. (12 standard songs) Ncc. |
| 249 | 3 | BREWSTER, O. M. Our comrade has fallen. c1862. Filed as No. 803 on Dec. 13, 1862, and again as No. 929 on Mar. 25, 1863. |
| 250- | 4 | WORK, Henry Clay. Grafted into the army. Filed Dec. 13, 1862. |
| 251- | 4 | RINK, Louis H. Ma belle polka redowa. Filed Dec. 13, 1862. |
| 252 | | |
| 253 | 4 | BIRD, Horace G. Shadow waltz. Filed Dec. 13, 1862. |
| 254 | 4 | S., C. C. Wingfield schottisch. Arranged by C. C. S. Filed Dec. 13, 1862. |
| 255- | 4 | WORK, Henry Clay. We'll go down ourselves. Filed Dec. 13, 1862. |
| 256 | 3 | WORK, Henry Clay. God save the nation! Quartette. Filed Dec. 13, 1862. |
| 257-260 | | |
| 261 | 5 | FAWCETT, George E. The president's emancipation march. c1862. Filed Mar. 25, 1863. |
| 262 | 4 | ROOT, George F. Oh, haste on the battle! c1862. Filed Mar. 25, 1863. |
| 263 | 4 | ROOT, George F. Call 'em names, Jeff. c1862. Filed Mar. 25, 1863. |
| 264 | 3 | RINK, Louis H. Gen. McClernand's grand march. c1862. Filed Mar. 25, 1863. |
| 265- | 4 | WORK, Henry Clay. Little Major. Song or duet. c1862. Filed Mar. 25, 1863. |
| 266 | 4 | FRENCH, D. A. '63 is the jubilee. Filed Mar. 25, 1863. |
| 267 | | |
| 268 | 4 | CRAW, Clara E. Holden guards schottische. Filed Mar. 25, 1863. |
| 269 | 5 | BOWEN, Mrs. F. L. Tread lightly ye comrades; or, The volunteer's grave. Melody suggested by Miss Sadie Crane; arrangement by Mrs. F. L. Bowen. Filed Mar. 25, 1863. |

| | | |
|---|---|---|
| 270 | 4 | GUMBERT, Ferdinand. Eventide. (12 standard songs) Ncc. |
| 271 | 4 | WORK, Henry Clay. Watching for pa. (His Songs & ballads. c1861.) Filed Mar. 25, 1863. |
| 272- | 4 | WORK, Henry Clay. Grandmother told me so. c1861. Filed Mar. 25, 1863. [c1861 on title-page must be misprint, for the song refers to the Emancipation Proclamation.] |
| 273- | 4 | DODGE, Ossian E. Singular dreams. Filed Mar. 25, 1863. |
| 274 | 8 | REIN, Emil. The battle-cry of freecom. With variations for the piano. c1863. |
| 275- | 4 | TAYLOR, R. Stewart. A vesper song for our volunteers' sisters. Filed Mar. 25, 1863. |
| 276- | 4 | TAYLOR, R. Stewart. Jenny Brown and I. Filed Mar. 25, 1863. |
| 277- | 5 | MERRILL, Hiram T. The old house far away. Filed Apr. 11, 1863. |
| 278 | 4 | ROOT, George F. He's comin' again. An old Highland song. Filed Apr. 29, 1863. |
| 279 | | |
| 280- | 5 | PARRY, J. O. The apology. Ncc. |
| 281 | 7 | RIX, B. F., arr. Johnny Schmoker. Filed Apr. 11, 1863. |
| 282 | 7 | ROOT, George F. Who'll save the left. c1863. |
| 283-289 | | |
| 290 | 4 | FOSTER, Stephen C. Mine is the mourning heart. A duet for Soprano and Tenor. c1861 by Daughaday & Hammond. [Originally printed in Clark's School Visitor. Separate publication rights acquired by Root & Cady.] |
| 291 | | |
| 292- | 4 | WORK, Henry Clay. The days when we were young. Filed June 6, 1863. |
| 293- | 4 | WORK, Henry Clay. Song of a thousand years. Filed May 27, 1863. 30 Popular Melodies Arranged for the Piano Forte by Adolph Baumbach. |
| 294 | 3 | No. 1. ROOT, George F. The battle cry of freedom. Filed June 24, 1863. |
| 295 | 4 | No. 2. WORK, Henry C. Kingdom coming. Filed June 24, 1863. |
| 296 | 3 | No. 3. ROOT, George F. The day of liberty's coming. Filed July 9, 1863. |
| 297 | 3 | No. 4. ROOT, George F. The vacant chair. Filed July 11, 1863. |
| 298 | 3 | No. 5. TAYLOR, R. Stewart. Soldier's dream song. Filed July 11, 1863. |
| 299 | 3 | No. 6. FRENCH, D. A. '63 is the jubilee. Filed July 11, 1863. |
| 300 | 3 | No. 7. TAYLOR, R. Stewart. O wrap the flag around me. Filed July 9, 1863. |
| 301 | 3 | No. 8. WORK, Henry C. Little Major. Filed July 9, 1863. |
| 302 | 3 | No. 9. WORK, Henry C. Grafted into the army. Filed July 9, 1863. |
| 303 | 3 | No. 10. WORK, Henry C. Nellie lost and found. Filed July 1, 1863. |
| 304 | 4 | No. 11. WORK, Henry C. Beautiful Rose. Filed July 11, 1863. |
| 305 | 3 | No. 12. ROOT, George F. Dream on, Lillie. Filed Nov. 11, 1863. |
| 306 | 4 | No. 13. WORK, Henry C. First love dream. Filed July 18, 1863. |
| 307 | 3 | No. 14. WORK, Henry C. Home far away. Filed July 18, 1863. |
| 308 | 3 | No. 15. WORK, Henry C. Jenny Brown and I. Filed July 25, 1863. |
| 309 | 3 | No. 16. ROOT, George F. O, are ye sleeping Maggie. Filed July 25, 1863. |
| 310 | 3 | No. 17. ABT, Franz. O! ye tears. Filed Sept. 17, 1863. |
| 311 | 3 | No. 18. WHITE, E. L. Rosemary crown. Filed Sept. 17, 1863. |
| 312 | 3 | No. 19. ROOT, George F. Stand up for Uncle Sam. Filed Sept. 17, 1863. |
| 313 | 4 | No. 20. HUBBARD, James Maurice. Silent evening. Filed Sept. 17, 1863. |
| 314 | 3 | No. 21. ROOT, George F. My cottage home, dear mother. Filed Sept. 17, 1863. |
| 315 | 4 | No. 22. HUBBARD, James Maurice. Song of the Egyptian girl. Filed Sept. 17, 1863. |
| 316 | 3 | No. 23. MERRILL, Hiram T. Take your gun and go, John. Filed Sept. 17, 1863. |
| 317 | 3 | No. 24. BOWEN, Mrs. F. L. Tread lightly ye comrades. Melody by Miss Sadie Crane. Filed Sept. 17, 1863. |
| 318 | 3 | No. 25. SAFFERY, E. C. The union volunteers. Filed Nov. 11, 1863. |
| 319 | 3 | No. 26. TAYLOR, R. Stewart. Vesper song for our volunteer's sisters. Filed Nov. 11, 1863. |
| 320 | 3 | No. 27. WORK, Henry C. Watching for Pa. Filed Nov. 11, 1863. |
| 321 | 3 | No. 28. WORK, Henry C. Song of a thousand years. Filed Dec. 2, 1863. |
| 322 | | |
| 323 | 3 | No. 30. WORK, Henry C. Babylon is fallen. Filed Nov. 11, 1863. |
| 324 | 4 | No. 29. MURRAY, James R. Daisy Deane. Filed Dec. 2, 1863. |
| 325- | 4 | MURRAY, James R. Daisy Deane, by T. F. Winthrop and J. R. Murray. Filed July 15, 1863. |

| | | |
|---|---|---|
| 326 | 2 | GOUGLER, I. W. Soldier's friend, polka quickstep. Filed July 18, 1863. |
| 327 | 6 | LOESCHHORN, Albert. Tarantelle. c1863. |
| 328- | 4 | ROOT, George F. On the field of battle, mother. Filed July 25, 1863. [Other copies with PN 328-3 or 328-4 have title: Just before the battle, mother.] |
| 329- | 4 | WORK, Henry C. Babylon is fallen! Filed July 31, 1863, and again on Sept. 17, 1863. |
| 330 | 5 | ROOT, Fred. W. Come, said Jesus sacred voice. Melody by Abt. Harmonized and arranged by Fred. W. Root. [for mixed quartet and organ] (Selections of sacred music for church and home) Filed Sept. 17, 1863. |
| 331 | 6 | ROOT, George F. Within the sound of the enemy's guns. "In remembrance of Gettysburg." Filed Sept. 17, 1863. |
| 332 | 4 | WORK, Henry C. Kingdom coming, arr. for guitar by George A. Russell. Filed Sept. 17, 1863. |
| 333 | | |
| 334 | 5 | TANNER, T. H. The old brown cot ... as sung by the Barker Family. Filed Sept. 26, and again Oct. 31, 1863. |
| 335 | 5 | HUBBARD, James M. Love, sweet love is everywhere. Filed Oct. 31, 1863. |
| 336- | 4 | WORK, Henry C. Sleeping for the flag. Filed Sept. 26, and again Oct. 31, 1863. |
| 337 | | |
| 338 | 6 | HUBBARD, James M. Angel Mary. Duett and chorus. Filed Oct. 31, 1863. |
| 339- | 5 | ROOT, George F. O, come you from the battle-field? Dialogue duet and chorus. Filed Dec. 2, 1863. |
| 340- | 4 | WORK, Henry C. Little Major, arr. for guitar by G. Borg. (Popular songs arranged for the guitar) Filed Oct. 31, 1863. |
| 341 | 4 | WORK, Henry C. Grafted into the army. Arr. by G. Borg. (Popular songs arranged for the guitar) Filed Oct. 31, 1863. |
| 342- | 4 | MURRAY, James R. Daisy Deane. Arr. by G. Borg. (Popular songs arranged for the guitar) Filed Oct. 31, 1863. |
| 343 | 4 | BALATKA, H. I stood before her portrait. Translated from H. Heine's poems, by Wallis. Filed Oct. 31, 1863. |
| 344 | 4 | ROOT, George F. Will you come to meet me, darling? Song and quartette. Filed Nov. 11, and again Dec. 2, 1863. |
| 345 | 3 | HOLMES, Avanelle L. Will you wed me now I'm lame, love? Arr. by Geo. F. Root. Filed Dec. 2, 1863. |
| 346 | 4 | FRENCH, Laura. Illini polka. Filed Dec. 2, 1863. |
| 347 | | |
| 348 | 3 | THOMAS, John Rogers. Lottie in the lane. (His Six songs) c1864. Filed Dec. 24, 1863. |
| 349 | 4 | DOWLING, Lillia. Oh, he kissed me when he left me. Filed Oct. 31, 1863. |
| 350- | 4 | ROOT, George F. Just before the battle. Arr. by G. Borg. (Popular songs arranged for the guitar) Filed Oct. 31, 1863. |
| 351 | 3 | THOMAS, John Rogers. Maudie Moore. (His Six songs) c1864. Filed Dec. 24, 1863. |
| 352 | 10 | REIN, Emil. The vacant chair, with variations. Filed Dec. 24, 1863. |
| 353- | 4 | WEBSTER, Joseph Philbrick. Sing, softly, love. c1864. Filed Dec. 30, 1863. |
| 354 | 4 | WEBSTER, Joseph Philbrick. She sleeps beneath the elms. c1864. Filed Dec. 30, 1863. |
| 355- | 4 | WORK, Henry Clay. Corporal Schnapps. (Work's Popular Songs. No. 23) Filed Jan. 11, 1864. |
| 356 | 5 | FRISBIE, Henrie L. Sleighing with the girls. Filed Dec. 24, 1863. |
| 357 | 5 | FRISBIE, Henrie L. Oh! bury the brave where they fall. c1863. Filed Jan. 28, 1864. |
| 358- | 4 | WIMMERSTEDT, A. E. Budding of the Tones. Fantasy for piano. Ncc. Filed Jan. 11, 1864. |
| 359 | 4 | WIMMERSTEDT, A. E. Sophia polka. c1863. Filed Jan. 11, 1864. |
| 360 | 6 | WIMMERSTEDT, A. E. Warbling of the birds, for piano. c1863. Filed Jan. 11, 1864. |
| 361 | 8 | WIMMERSTEDT, A. E. Evening bells, nocturne. c1863. Filed Jan. 11, 1864. |
| 362 | 3 | THOMAS, John Rogers. One by one. c1864. Filed Jan. 28, 1864. |
| 363- | 4 | WEBSTER, Joseph Philbrick. I stand on memory's golden shore. Filed Jan. 28, 1864. |
| 364 | 4 | HAYNES, J. E. All hail to Ulysses! Filed Jan. 28, 1864. |
| 365- | 3 | WORK, Henry Clay. Columbia's guardian angels. c1863 [for series title-page] Filed Mar. 5, 1864. |
| 366 | 4 | MINKLER, F. G. Shabona schottisch. Filed Jan. 28, 1864. |
| 367 | 6 | WIMMERSTEDT, A. E. Longing for the shore. Nocturne. c1863. Filed Jan. 28, 1864. |

| | | |
|---|---|---|
| 368 | 4 | WIMMERSTEDT, A. E. Sharpshooter's march. c1864. |
| 369 | 4 | LEWIS, William. March on! march on! A soldier's glee. Filed Mar. 5, 1864. |
| 370 | 5 | TOWNE, Thomas Martin. When will my darling boy return? Filed Mar. 5, 1864. |
| 371- | 5 | WORK, Henry Clay. Song of a thousand years, arr. by Geo. A. Russell. (Popular songs arranged for the guitar) Filed Mar. 5, 1864. |
| 372 | | |
| 373 | 4 | HUBBARD, James Maurice. Little Alice. Filed Mar. 5, 1864. |
| 373 | 4 | THOMAS, John Rogers. I'm dying far from those I love. (His Six songs) Filed Apr. 20, 1864. |
| 374 | 4 | WORK, Henry Clay. Washington and Lincoln. Filed Mar. 5, 1864. |
| 375 | 4 | HICKS, Edmund W. Vicksburg is taken, boys. Filed Mar. 5, 1864. |
| 376 | 4 | ROOT, George F. I'se on de way. Filed Apr. 20, 1864. |
| 377 | 4 | ROOT, George F. Brother, tell me of the battle. Filed Apr. 20, 1864. |
| [377 | 4 | ROOT, George F. Just after the battle. Cf PN 379] |
| 378 | 4 | SILEX. Uncle Sam's funeral. Filed Apr. 20, 1864 |
| 379 | 3 | ROOT, George F. Just after the battle. [LC copy, filed Apr. 20, 1864, has PN 377 4. Apparently, this was a slip, since it was soon corrected on the original plates to 379 4. Later, a stereotyped edition was issued numbered 379-3.] |
| 380 | 4 | VAAS, A. J. St. Paul waltz. Filed Apr. 20, 1864 |
| 381 | 4 | MERZ, Karl. The little drummer boy's march. Filed May 31, 1864. |
| | | GOUNOD, Charles François. Vocal Beauties from the opera Faust. |
| 382 | 6 | No. 1. Le Parlate d'Amor. The Language of love. Filed May 31, 1864. |
| 383 | 5 | No. 2. C'era un Re di Thule. The King of Thule. Filed May 31, 1864. |
| 384 | | [No. 3. Oh Gloria. Glory Immortal.] |
| 385 | 6 | No. 4. Salva dimora casta. All hail! Live innocent and purely. c1864. |
| 386-387 | | |
| 388 | 6 | LEHMAN, William. Des Moines City waltz. Filed May 31, 1864. |
| 389 | 13 | BAUMBACH, Adolph. Czar and Zimmermann. (A. Lortzing.) Pot Pourri. Filed May 31, 1864. |
| 390 | | |
| 391- | 3 | WORK, Henry Clay. Come home, father. Filed May 31, 1864. |
| 392 | 7 | GUMBERT, Ferdinand. Savior breathe an evening blessing. Melody by Gumbert, harmonized and arranged by Horace G. Bird. c1863 (for series) (Selections of sacred music for church & home) Filed July 18, 1864. |
| 393- | 4 | BRAINARD, Julia. Gray distance hid each shining sail. Filed July 18, 1864. |
| 394- | 4 | YATES, Mrs. W. H. Oriole Waltz. Filed July 18, 1864. |
| 395 | 5 | MILES, Frederick William. Central city polka. Filed July 22, 1864. |
| 396 | 4 | BLISS, Philip Paul. Lora Vale, arranged by Geo. F. Root. c1865. Filed July 22, 1864. |
| 397 | 7 | REIN, Emil. Just before the battle, mother ... transcription. Filed July 22, 1864. |
| 398 | 4 | ROOT, George F. Can the soldier forget? Filed Aug. 4, 1864. |
| 399 | 6 | HUBBARD, James Maurice. Bertha Louise. Filed Aug. 24, 1864. |
| 400 | 4 | FRENCH, D. A. Fairy ring. Song and chorus. Filed Aug. 24, 1864. |
| 401 | 4 | DEGENHARD, Charles. April shower, polka redowa. Filed Aug. 24, 1864. |
| 402 | 4 | DEGENHARD, Charles. The coquette waltz. Filed Aug. 24, 1864. |
| 403- | 3 | ROOT, George F. Lay me down and save the flag! Last words of the hero Mulligan. LC copy deposited Aug. 1, 1864, has 403 4. |
| 404 | 3 | THOMAS, John Rogers. Keep a brave heart still. (His Six songs [5]) Filed Sept. 19, 1864. |
| 405 | 3 | THOMAS, John Rogers. The fields of home. (His Six songs [6]) Filed Sept. 19, 1864. |
| 406 | 5 | HUBBARD, James Maurice. Viola schottisch. Filed Sept. 8, 1864. |
| 407 | 16 | BAUMBACH, Adolph. Faust de Ch. Gounod. Pot Pourri. Filed Sept. 19, 1864. |
| 408 | | HAYNES, Edward. We shall miss you dearest brother. Filed Oct. 10, 1864. |
| 409 | 4 | BACH, C. H. The patriot's prayer. Filed Oct. 10, 1864. |
| 410 | 4 | TOWNE, Thomas Martin. Welcome. Song of the 40th Wisconsin volunteers. Filed Oct. 10, 1864. |
| 411- | 3 | WORK, Henry Clay. The picture on the wall. Filed Nov. 23, 1864. |
| 412 | 5 | ROOT, George F. Kiss me mother, kiss your darling. Filed Oct. 10, 1864. |
| 413 | 4 | HAYNES, Edward. Our nation's captain. Filed Oct. 10, 1864. |
| 414 | 3 | STEVENS, George. The Robert Brierly schottisch. Filed Nov. 23, 1864. |

| | | |
|---|---|---|
| 415 | 10 | REIN, Emil. Will you come to meet me darling? ... transcription. Filed Nov. 23, 1864. |
| 416- | 3 | WORK, Henry Clay. Wake Nicodemus. Filed Nov. 23, 1864. |
| 417 | 5 | WALLACE, J. C. We are coming from the cotton fields. Filed Dec. 23, 1864. |
| 418 | 5 | MILLARD, H. Happy Dreams. Filed Dec. 24, 1864. [Plates not numbered in the copyright deposit; but number was added later.] |
| 419 | | |
| 420- | 3 | ROOT, George F. Tramp! tramp! tramp! The prisoners hope. c1864. Filed Jan. 5, 1865. |
| 421 | 4 | ROOT, George F. Just after the battle, arr. for guitar. Filed Dec. 24, 1864. |
| 422 | 7 | PATTIANI, Madame Eliza. May Breeze. Variations brillante ... for the piano. c1864. Filed Jan. 14, 1865. |
| 423 | 4 | COVERT, Bernard. Follow the drum. Filed Jan. 14, 1865. |
| 424- | 2 | WORK, Henry Clay. Marching through Georgia. Filed Jan. 9, 1865. |
| 425 | 4 | SEWARD, Theodore F. Poor mother! Willie's gone. c1864. Filed Jan. 25, 1865. |
| 426 | 4 | WEBSTER, Joseph Philbrick. The wounded boy at Kenesaw. (His Six songs [4]) Filed Jan. 25, 1865. |
| 427 | 5 | WEBSTER, Joseph Philbrick. Brother in the army. (His Six songs [5]) Filed Jan. 25, 1865. |
| 428 | 5 | WEBSTER, Joseph Philbrick. Jenny Wade, the heroine of Gettysberg. (His Six songs [6]) Filed Jan. 23, 1865. |
| 429 | 7 | PATTIANI, Eliza. Soldier's home medley. Filed Feb. 6, 1865. |
| 430 | 4 | PHELPS, Mrs. Minnie André. Star polka. Filed Feb. 11, 1865. |
| 431- | 2 | WORK, Henry Clay. Ring the bell, watchman! Filed Feb. 28, 1865. |
| 432- | 4 | WORK, Henry Clay. Come home, father, arr. by G. A. Russell. (The guitar. [Vocal]) Not registered for copyright. |
| 432 | | H., D. H. Agawam quickstep. (Choice selections for the piano by various authors) Ncc. See PN 245 above. |
| 433 | 4 | HUBBARD, James Maurice. Who comes dar? Filed Mar. 25, 1865. |
| 434 | 6 | MERZ, Karl. The bee song, a quartette for mixed voices. Filed May 20, 1865. |
| 435 | 5 | BLISS, Philip Paul. Good bye Jeff! Filed Mar. 25, 1865. |
| 436 | 5 | ROOT, George F. Comrade, all around is brightness. Filed May 15, 1865. |
| 437 | 5 | REINHART, F. M. Parlor skating schottische. Composed by D. Spencer. ... Arranged for piano by F. M. Reinhart. Filed May 24, 1865. |
| 438 | 4 | MOSES, A. Illinois grand march, arr. for piano by Geo. R. Pfeiffer. Filed May 24, 1865. |
| 439- | 4 | CRANE, W. C. Oil-do-ra-do. Comic song. Filed May 24, 1865. |
| 440 | 20 | GOTTSCHALK, Louis Moreau. Battle cry of freedom, grand caprice de concert. Filed May 15, 1865. |
| 441- | 6 | BRAINARD, Julia. A lullaby. Filed June 28, 1865. |
| 442 | 4 | BROCKWAY. W. H. Nellie Ray. Filed June 5, 1865. |
| 443 | | [Cf list of "Copyrighted works found without plate numbers," at end.] |
| 444 | 5 | MILLER, L. B. The president's grave. Quartette. Filed June 17, 1865. |
| 445 | | |
| 446 | 4 | STEVENS, George. The [Col. Wood's] Museum polka. c1865. [Not filed] |
| 447 | 4 | STEVENS, George. The Masonic March. c1865. [Not filed] |
| 448 | 9 | FRADEL, Charles. La forza del destino (opera di G. Verdi). Transcription elegante. Filed June 17, 1865. |
| 449 | 9 | FRADEL, Charles. Auber's Fra Diavolo transcrit. Filed June 22, 1865. |
| 450 | 8 | GROBE, Charles. Tramp! tramp! tramp! or the prisoner's hope. With brilliant variations. c1865. Some copies lack plate number. Filed July 18, 1865. |
| 451- | 5 | ROOT, Frederic W. Crosby's opera house waltz. Filed July 17, 1865. |
| 452-453 | | |
| 454 | 4 | ROOT, George F. Tramp, tramp, tramp, arr. for guitar by G. N. Brown. Filed July 18, 1865. |
| 455 | 8 | REIN, Emil. Brother tell me of the battle. Transcription. Filed Aug. 14, 1865. |
| 456 | | |
| 457 | 5 | PRATT, Silas G. Matinée Polka. Filed Aug. 14, 1865. |
| 458- | 3 | ROOT, George F. On, on, on, the boys came marching. Iu copy has 458 2. Filed July 19, 1865. |
| 459 | 3 | BLAFE, Michael William. O take me to thy heart again. Song. (Standard songs by various authors) Ncc. |
| 460- | 4 | HALBRON [pseud.] Adalida Polka. Filed Aug. 14, 1865. |
| 461 | 3 | WRIGHTON, W. T. Her bright smile haunts me still. (Standard songs by various composers) Ncc. |

| | | |
|---|---|---|
| 462 | 4 | GLOVER, Stephen Ralph. The valley of Chamouni. Words by F. Enoch. (Standard songs by various authors) Ncc. |
| 463 | | |
| 464 | 4 | SCHUBERT, Camille. Les Postillons valse. Filed Aug. 29, 1865. |
| 465 | 4 | PEARSON, George C. All hail the reign of peace. c1865. |
| 466 | 4 | ROOT, George F. My beau that went to Canada. Filed Sept. 29, 1865. |
| 467 | 4 | WORK, Henry C. Wake Nicodemus, arr. for guitar. (Popular war songs arranged for the guitar by Geo. A. Russell) Filed Aug. 29, 1865. |
| 468 | 4 | ROOT, George F. Brother, tell me of the battle, arr. for guitar. Filed Sept. 13, 1865. |
| | | 20 Popular Melodies. Camps, Tramps and Battle-fields. Arranged as Instrumental Pieces for the Piano-Forte by Geo. F. Root. c1865. |
| 469 | 2 | No. 1. ROOT, George F. Just before the battle. Filed Sept. 29, 1865. |
| 470 | 2 | No. 2. ROOT, George F. Just after the battle. Filed Sept. 29, 1865. |
| 471 | 2 | No. 3. WORK, Henry C. Ring the bell, watchman. Filed Nov. 16, 1865. |
| 472 | 2 | No. 4. HICKS, Edmund W. Vicksburg is taken. Filed Nov. 16, 1865. |
| 472 | 2 | No. 20. WORK, Henry C. 'Tis finished! Filed Dec. 9, 1865. [probably misprint or printer's error for 488] |
| 473 | 2 | No. 5. ROOT, George F. Kiss me mother, kiss your darling. Filed Nov. 16, 1865. |
| 474 | 2 | No. 6. ROOT, George F. Lay me down, and save the flag. c1865, but not filed. |
| 475 | 2 | No. 7. WORK, Henry C. Sleeping for the flag. Filed Nov. 16, 1865. |
| 476 | 2 | No. 8. CHAMBERLIN, E. I wonder why he comes not. Filed Dec. 4, 1865. |
| 477 | 2 | No. 9. ROOT, George F. Tramp! Tramp! Tramp! Filed Sept. 29, 1865. |
| 478 | 2 | No. 10. WORK, Henry C. Marching through Georgia. Filed Dec. 4, 1865. |
| 479 | 2 | No. 11. ROOT, George F. On, on, the boys are marching. Filed Sept. 29, 1865. |
| 480 | 2 | No. 12. ROOT, George F. Comrade, all around is brightness. Filed Dec. 4, 1865. |
| 481 | 2 | No. 13. WORK, Henry C. Wake Nicodemus. Filed Dec. 4, 1865. |
| 482 | 2 | No. 14. ROOT, George F. Brother, tell me of the battle. Filed Dec. 9, 1865. |
| 483 | 2 | No. 15. THOMAS, John R. Maudie Moore. Filed Dec. 9, 1865. |
| 484 | 2 | No. 16. ROOT, George F. How it marches, the flag of the Union. Filed Dec. 4, 1865. |
| 485 | 2 | No. 17. ROOT, George F. Farewell, father, friend and guardian. Filed Dec. 4, 1865. |
| 486 | 2 | No. 18. BLISS, Philip P. Good bye Jeff. Filed Dec. 9, 1865. |
| 487 | 2 | No. 19. ROOT, George F. They have broken up their camps. Filed Dec. 4, 1865. |
| 488 | | |
| 489 | 11 | BURKHART, William. May Queen Quadrille. As danced at Prof. Mirasole's Academy. Filed Sept. 13, 1865. |
| 490 | | |
| 491 | 5 | BLUMENSCHEIN, H. L. Fairy Nora loves me. Filed Sept. 29, 1865. |
| 492 | 3 | ROOT, George F. Good bye old glory. Filed Sept. 29, 1865. |
| 493 | 4 | CHAMBERLIN, E. I wonder why he comes not. Filed Sept. 29, 1865. |
| 493 | 5 | MORGAN, George W. The Chicago mazurka. c1864. Filed Sept. 29, 1865. |
| 494 | 10 | ROOT, George F. North and South, a vocal duet. Filed Sept. 13, 1865. |
| 495 | | |
| 496- | 4 | WORK, Henry C. Kingdom coming, arr. for guitar by John Molter. (The Guitar. [Vocal]) Not registered. |
| 497- | 4 | WORK, Henry Clay. The ship that never return'd. Filed Sept. 29, 1865. |
| 498- | 7 | FRADEL, Charles. Cycloid Polka ... dedicated to Lindeman & Sons. Filed Oct. 10, 1865. |
| 499- | 4 | WHITING, S. K. Father's come home. Sequel to Come home, father. (Root & Cady's vocal quartetts with piano forte accompaniment) Filed Oct. 10, 1865. |
| 500 | 3 | FASSETT, Walter S. Bonnie Venture waltz. Filed Oct. 10, 1865. |
| 501 | 7 | BROWN, T. M. Tramp! tramp! tramp! [by Geo. F. Root] Transcription Brillante. Filed Oct. 10, 1865. |
| 502-511 | | |
| 512 | 4 | ROOT, George F. On, on, on, the boys came marching, arr. for guitar by Geo. A. Russell. Filed Oct. 30, 1865. |
| 513 | 3 | ROOT, George F. Liberty bird. Quartette. Filed Oct. 30, 1865. |
| 514 | 3 | FORMES, Karl. In memory of Abraham Lincoln. (<u>His</u> Three songs without words. No. 1) For piano solo. Filed Nov. 10, 1865. |

| | | |
|---|---|---|
| 515-516 | | |
| 517 | 5 | ROOT, George F. Sing me to sleep, father. Filed Oct. 10, 1865. |
| 518 | 5 | TOWNE, Thomas Martin. Freedom's harvest time. Filed Oct. 30, 1865. |
| 519- | 5 | RICHARDS, Henry Brinley. Warblings at eve. (12 standard pieces for piano) Ncc. |
| 520 | 5 | HANBY, Benjamin R. Angel Nellie; or, Waiting at the old linden tree. Filed Oct. 30, 1865. |
| 521- | 4 | WORK, Henry C. Now, Moses. (Work's Popular Songs. No. 33) Filed Oct. 30, 1865. |
| 522 | 6 | MORGAN, Geo. W. The Hyde Park polka ... dedicated to Mrs. C. M. Cady. Filed Dec. 4, 1865. |
| 523 | 5 | VAAS, A. J. Sleigh ride galop. Filed Nov. 16, 1865. |
| 524- | 4 | VAAS, A. J. San Souci galop. Filed Dec. 4, 1865. |
| 525 | 6 | RICHARDS, Henry Brinley. Her bright smile haunts me still. (W. T. Wrighton) (12 standard pieces for piano) Ncc. |
| 526 | 5 | ANGUERA, Antonio de. La gazetier polka. To James H. Field of the Chicago Evening Journal. Filed Dec. 4, 1865. |
| 527 | | |
| 528 | 6 | OESTEN, Theodor. Love in May. Ncc. |
| 529 | 5 | ABEL, Frederick. Your name! "The honey bee is humming it." Milwaukee, Abel & Sherman; Chicago, Root & Cady. Filed Nov. 24, 1865, by Abel & Sherman. See above PN 227. |
| 530 | 5 | OESTEN, Theodor. Gondellied, op. 56. Ncc. (The pianist's music-drawer; a collection of standard pieces by various authors) |
| 531-533 | | |
| 534 | 4 | BAUMBACH, Adolph. Etta mazurka. Filed Nov. 16, 1865. |
| 535 | | |
| 536 | 5 | ABT, Franz. Love's Delight, (Liebeswonne.) A lyric song as sung by Mr. Oscar Faulhaber. Transposed by Carl Anschutz. Translated by Geo. Howland. Op. 190. Filed Dec. 4, 1865. [The deposit copy came in as published by "Coot & Cady," but this was soon corrected.] |
| 537 | 4 | ROOT, George F. Away on the prairie alone. Filed Dec. 4, 1865. |
| 538- | 9 | MEYERBEER, Giacomo. The celebrated Slumber song from L'Africaine. Filed Dec. 4, 1865. |
| 539 | 5 | BEYER, Ferdinand. Morning star waltz. Ncc. |
| 540 | 4 | ARDITI, Luigi. Il Bacio. (The kiss.) Waltz. Ncc. (The pianist's music-drawer) |
| 541 | 4 | HANBY, Benjamin R. Now den! now den! "The freedman's song." Filed Dec. 9, 1865. |
| 542-543 | | |
| 544 | 4 | CRAMER, Henri. Il desiderio. Ncc. |
| 545 | | |
| 546 | 8 | BLISS, Philip Paul. A grand vocal medley, arranged from Root & Cady's most popular publications. Filed Jan. 12, 1866. |
| 547- | 4 | HANBY, B. R. The revelers' chorus, a temperance song. Filed Jan. 12, 1866. |
| 548 | | |
| 549 | 8 | SMITH, Sydney. Starry Night, op. 36. Ncc. [Found in two series with same music plates: <u>Sydney Smith's Compositions for the piano</u> and <u>The pianist's music-drawer. A collection of standard pieces by various authors.</u>] |
| 550 | 5 | PHELPS, Mrs. Minnie A. Joy bells polka. c1865. Filed Jan. 19, 1866. |
| 551 | 4 | BROCKWAY, W. H. Young Eph's jubilee (answer to Young Eph's lament). Song and dance as performed by Thomas Githings of Kelly & Leon's Minstrels. Filed Feb. 8, 1866. |
| 552 | 5 | ROBJOHN, William James. Christmas chime carol & hymn. A descriptive reverie for the piano. Filed Feb. 8, 1866. |
| 553 | 6 | ROBJOHN, William James. Fountain in the sunlight, idylle for the piano. Filed Feb. 18, 1866. |
| 554 | 6 | ROBJOHN, William James. The miller's song, characteristic etude for the parlor. Filed Mar. 7, 1866. |
| 555 | 5 | ROBJOHN, William James. Golden Dream. A waltz. Filed Feb. 18, 1866. |
| 556- | 3 | ROOT, George F. Glory! glory! or, The little octoroon. Filed Jan. 19, 1866. [First published in the <u>Song Messenger</u>, Extra, 1866.] |
| 557 | 7 | ROBJOHN, William James. Cattle bell at evening. A rural picture for the piano. Filed Feb. 14, 1866. |
| 558 | | |
| 559 | 8 | ROBJOHN, William James. Gala day, a rejoicing. For the piano. Filed Feb. 24, 1866. |
| 560 | 4 | ROBJOHN, William James. Forest temple, a meditation for the piano. Filed Mar. 7, 1866. |

| | | |
|---|---|---|
| 560 | 5 | WALKER, T. R. Lilla is an angel now! [Deposit copy has this number, later corrected to 570 5.] |
| 561 | 4 | ROOT, George F. Glory! glory! or, The little octoroon, arr. for guitar. c1866. |
| 562 | 9 | ROBJOHN, William James. Beneath the loved one's window, a serenade for the piano. Filed Mar. 13, 1866. |
| 563 | 12 | WEHLI, James M. The Rivulet. (Le ruisseau.) c1866. |
| 564 | 6 | WEHLI, James M. The heather bells. Filed Feb. 24, 1866. |
| 565 | 8 | WEHLI, James M. The music of the sea. Meditation. Op. 27. "To Mrs. Belmont of New York." Filed Mar. 17, 1866. |
| 566 | 5 | BAUMBACH, Adolph. Ellsworth Zouave & National Lancers' greeting grand march. Filed Mar. 29, 1866. |
| 567 | 3 | ROOT, George F. Our protective union. Filed Mar. 13, 1866. |
| 568 | 7 | ROBJOHN, William James. Grand instrumental medley from Root & Cady's popular publications. Filed Apr. 20, 1866. |
| 569 | 5 | FRISBIE, Henrie L. Out west, or The down easter's journey. Filed Mar. 9, 1866. |
| 570 | 5 | WALKER, T. R. Lilla is an angel now. Filed Mar. 31, 1866. Cf PN 560 |
| 571 | 10 | [WIGGINS (BETHUNE), Thomas.] The battle of Manassas for the piano by Blind Tom. Filed Apr. 13, 1866. |
| 572- | 4 | WORK, Henry C. Lillie of the snow-storm, or "Please, Father, let us in!" S&Ch. Filed Apr. 13, and again Sept. 26, 1866. |
| 573 | 4 | BOWE, Emma. Lake shore mazurka. Filed June 25, 1866. |
| 574 | 4 | MITCHELL, Clara C. Charlie schottische. Filed June 25, 1866. |
| 575 | 4 | DARLING, Miss Hattie. His voice still speaks to me. Song, sequel to Her bright smile haunts me still. Filed July 21, 1866. |
| 576 | | |
| 577 | 5 | FERRIL, Fred. Sophia waltz. Composed by Fred. Ferril. Arranged for piano by J. A. Hahn. Filed Aug. 6, 1866. |
| 578 | 10 | HOFFMAN, Edward. Shooting star galop di bravura. Filed Aug. 29, 1866. |
| 579 | | |
| 580- | 4 | VOSSELLER, E. Sweet buried friend of mine! S&Ch. Words by Libby Locke. Filed Sept. 5, 1866. |
| 581 | 4 | ROOT, George F. Foes and friends. Filed Sept. 5, 1866. |
| 582 | 5 | PRATT, Silas G. 2 Musical thoughts for the piano. No. 2. The smile. Polka gracieuse. Filed Sept. 5, 1866. |
| 583 | 6 | No. 1. The sigh. Nocturne sentimentale. Filed Sept. 5, 1866. |
| 584 | | |
| 585- | 5 | KIMMELL, Abram. In the valley of the west. S&Ch. Filed Sept. 21, 1866. |
| 586 | 6 | SCOTT, Mrs. Clara H. Grand Girard mazurka. (3 Parlor concert pieces for the piano) Filed Nov. 21, 1866. |
| 587 | 4 | SCOTT, Mrs. Clara H. Lillie schottische. (3 Parlor concert pieces for the piano) Filed Nov. 21, 1866. |
| 588 | 9 | MOELLING, Theodore. Gems from Crispino e la Comare, arranged for piano. Op. 73. Filed Apr. 20, 1866. |
| 589 | 6 | SCOTT, Mrs. Clara H. Dearborn waltz. (3 Parlor concert pieces for the piano) Filed Nov. 21, 1866. |
| 590- | 4 | TOWNE, Thomas Martin. Pining for the old fireside. Filed Sept. 21, 1866. |
| 591- | 4 | WORK, Henry C. Who shall rule this American nation? "To the Hon. Lyman Trumball of Chicago." Filed Sept. 25, 1866. |
| 592- | 5 | TOWNE, Thomas Martin. Touch not the fair cup, though it sparkles; or, The drunkard's wife to her husband. S&Ch. Words by Josephine Furman. Filed Oct. 10, 1866. |
| 593- | 4 | WORK, Henry C. When the Evening Star went down. S&Ch, relating to the loss of the ocean steamer, "Evening Star," on the morning of October 3, 1866. Filed Nov. 13, 1866. |
| 594 | 3 | WORK, Henry Clay. Dad's a millionaire! S&Ch. Filed Mar. 5, 1867. |
| 595- | 4 | Fireman's marching song, a walk around. By "Quails." Dedicated to the St. Paul firemen. [Announced in the Song Messenger, June, 1866.] |
| 596 | 5 | KINNEY, Miss Virginia S. Fairy footsteps waltz. Filed Mar. 31, 1866. |
| 597- | 5 | SPINNING, Edgar G. At the golden gate, a ballad. Filed Apr. 9, 1866. |
| 598 | | |
| 599 | 6 | MOELLING, Theodore. Souvenir de L'Africaine. Valse pour le piano. Op. 71. Filed Apr. 7, 1866. |
| 600 | 5 | ROOT, George F. Songs of the Free Masons. (1. The Masons' home; 2. The Masons' holiday; 3. The Masons' dirge) Filed May 25, 1866. |

| | | |
|---|---|---|
| 601 | 5 | [WIGGINS (BETHUNE), Thomas.] Daylight. A musical expression for the piano by Blind Tom. Filed Mar. 31, 1866. |
| 602- | 4 | SEWARD, Theodore F. Is your heart still the same to me, my darling? S&Ch. Filed Mar. 31, 1866. |
| 603 | 7 | ROBJOHN, William James. Soft breezes in the solemn night. Nocturne. Filed May 25, 1866. |
| 604 | 4 | [WIGGINS (BETHUNE), Thomas.] Water in the moonlight. A piano piece by Blind Tom. Filed Apr. 21, 1866. |
| 605 | 4 | BLISS, P. P. Mr. Lordly & I, or The difference. Parody on "Mrs. Lofty & I." Filed May 7, 1866. |
| 605 | | HUBBARD, Charles P. Come where the morning is breaking. Duett with chorus. Filed Aug. 26, 1865, by Merrill & Brennan. PN from Brainard ed. |
| 606 | 5 | FRISBIE, Henrie L. The songs we sang upon the old camp ground. Filed June 4, 1866. |
| 607 | 4 | PEPLOW, J. Luna Polka [for piano] as played by the Philharmonic Orchestra at their Matinees. Filed Apr. 9, 1866. |
| 608 | 4 | VOSSELLER, E. "Betsy Jane" Polka. ("Betsy Jane and I are 1." A. Ward.) "To Artemus Ward." May 14, 1866. |
| 609 | | |
| 610- | 4 | WORK, Henry C. Andy Veto. Filed Apr. 13, 1866. |
| 611 | 4 | HANBY, Benjamin R. In a horn, a song for the times, adapted and arranged by B. R. H. Filed May 14, 1866. |
| 612 | 4 | [WIGGINS (BETHUNE), Thomas.] Specimens of Blind Tom's vocal compositions. The man who got the cinder in his eye. Filed May 14, 1866. |
| 613 | 4 | HOWARD, Frank. Lottie's all the world to me. Filed May 7, 1866. |
| 614 | 14 | BACH, Charles H. The musical album march. A potpourri. Filed June 18, 1866. |
| 615 | 5 | HANBY, Benjamin R. Crowding awfully. A temperance song and chorus as sung by the Hutchinsons. Filed June 4, 1866. |
| 616- | 5 | SMITH, James Sargent. Con anima polka. Filed June 11, 1866. |
| 617 | | |
| 618- | 4 | ROOT, George F. Mabel! S&Ch. Filed June 18, 1866. |
| 613- | 4 | DICAL, R. A. Dinna ye hear the s'Logan? Dedicated to Gen. John A. Logan. Filed Sept. 26, 1866. |
| 614- | 3 | WORK, Henry C. Come back to the farm. S&Ch. Filed Mar. 16, 1867. |
| 615- | 4 | ROOT, George F. Columbia's call. S&Ch. [First printed in Song Messenger, "Extra," April 1867.] Filed Apr. 10, 1867. |
| | | Brilliant Duets arranged by Theo. Moelling for the Piano-Forte. Op. 90. |
| 616 | 14 | No. 1. GODFREY, D. Mabel waltzes. Filed Oct. 19, 1866. |
| 617 | 6 | No. 2. RICHARDS, Brinley. Floating on the wind. Filed Oct. 8, 1866. |
| 618 | 6 | No. 3. VAAS, A. J. Cincinnati air line railroad galop. Filed Oct. 19, 1866. |
| 619 | 6 | No. 4. PEPLOW, J. Luna polka. Filed Oct. 8, 1866. |
| 620 | 8 | No. 5. OESTEN, Theodore. Alpine bells. Filed Oct. 27, 1866. |
| 621 | 6 | No. 6. STEVENS, George. Robert Brierly schottisch. Filed Oct. 27, 1866. |
| 622 | 13 | HOFFMAN, Edward. Come home, father; song. Transcription. Filed Oct. 29, 1866. |
| 623 | 10 | MOELLING, Theodore. Daisy Deane, transcription for the piano. Op. 94. Filed Nov. 9, 1866. |
| 624 | | |
| 625 | 7 | MOELLING, Theodore. Ristori grande valse pour le piano. Op. 96. Filed Nov. 13, 1866. |
| | | MOELLING, Theodore. Dulcet strains from the opera. Composed for the piano. Op. 88. |
| 626 | 4 | No. 1. TROVATORE [by] VERDI. Filed Dec. 7, 1866. |
| 627 | 4 | No. 2. MARTHA [by] FLOTOW. Filed Dec. 7, 1866. |
| 628 | 4 | No. 3. SOMNAMBULA [by] BELLINI. Filed Dec. 10, 1866. |
| 629 | 4 | No. 4. DINORAH [by] MEYERBEER. Filed Dec. 10, 1866. |
| 630 | 4 | No. 5. TRAVIATA [by] VERDI. Filed Dec. 7, 1866. |
| 631 | | No. 6. DON GIOVANNI [by] MOZART. Filed Dec. 7, 1866. |
| 632- | 4 | SPAULDING, John F. I love the charming autumn! Ballad ... sung by Georgie Dean Spaulding ... of the renowned "Spaulding Brothers' Swiss Bell Ringers." Filed Nov. 22, 1866. |
| 633 | | |
| 634 | 4 | BAKER, John C. Dream on, my soul! Filed Dec. 5, 1866. |
| 635 | 8 | GROBE, Charles G. Come home, father. With brilliant variations. Filed Dec. 22, 1866. |
| | | BAILEY, Ephraim H. 3 vocal pieces. |
| 636 | 5 | Long ago. Words by O. S. Ingham. Filed Dec. 22, 1866. |

| | | |
|---|---|---|
| 637 | 5 | Did the loved one return? Words by Capt. Wm. S. Trask. Filed Dec. 21, 1866. |
| 638 | 5 | Absent Mary. Words by Capt. Wm. S. Trask. Filed Dec. 21, 1866. |
| 639 | 5 | PRATT, Silas G. Griffith Gaunt schottische. Filed Dec. 10, 1866. |
| 640 | 4 | BARNARD, Mrs. Charlotte A. [Claribel] Five o'clock in the morning. Ncc. |
| 641-651 | | [Probably includes the series begun with PN 640; "Parepa's Songs and Ballads." Nine titles of public domain songs, mostly by "Claribel," are listed in the Song Messenger for December, 1866. Also, 3 arrangements from Mozart's Don Juan for cabinet organ, piano and violin with cello ad lib.] |
| 643 | 5 | GANZ, Wilhelm. Sing, birdie, sing. (Songs and ballads of Mlle. Parepa. 4) Ncc. PN cancelled and 2734 substituted. |
| 652 | 7 | KIDDER, W. C. O, ye tears! (F. Abt.) Transcription brillante. c1866. Filed Jan. 18, 1867. |
| 653 | 4 | CALKINS, J. Morton. Hallie Lee! Ballad for one or two voices. c1866. Filed Jan. 23, 1867. |
| 654 | 6 | HAYWOOD, George. When my ship comes in! Arr. by Geo. F. Root. (Root & Cady's new vocal quartettes) Filed Feb. 5, 1867. |
| 655 | 5 | SNELLING, George. Father, come down with the stamps. [Comic song.] Filed Feb. 9, 1867. |
| 656 | 5 | ROOT, George F. Away! away! the track is white. A new sleighing quartette & chorus. (Root & Cady's new vocal quartettes) Filed Feb. 12, and again Feb. 15, 1867. |
| 657 | 5 | ROOT, George F. Home again returning. Quartette with solos for each voice. (Root & Cady's new vocal quartettes) Filed Mar. 5, and again Apr. 5, 1867. |
| 657 | 5 | TOWNE, Thomas Martin. There's music in my heart, love! (Root & Cady's new vocal quartettes) c1867. |
| 658 | 4 | TOWNE, Thomas Martin. Oh, Louie is my fair one! S&Ch. Filed Feb. 12, 1867. |
| 659 | 3 | STEVENS, George. The Barry schottische ... respectfully dedicated to Mrs. Thos. Barry. Filed Feb. 9, 1867. |
| 660 | 5 | STEVENS, George. Huguenot captain polka. "To Frank Aiken, Esq." Filed Feb. 21, 1867. |
| 661 | 4 | ROOT, George F. Yes, we will be true to each other. S&Ch. Words by Paulina. Filed Feb. 14, 1867. |
| 662 | 4 | ROOT, George F. I ask no more. S&Ch. Words by J. Wm. Van Namee, Esq. Filed Feb. 14, 1867. |
| 663 | | |
| 664 | 6 | ROOT, Frederic W. The broken band! Quartette & chorus. Words by Eben E. Rexford. (Root & Cady's new vocal quartettes) Filed Mar. 25, 1867. |
| 665 | 8 | ROOT, Frederic W. Touch the keys softly. Quartette. Words by Mrs. M. B. C. Slade. (Root & Cady's new vocal quartettes) Filed Mar. 30, 1867. |
| 666 | | ROOT, Frederic W. D. C. mazurka, dedicated to the ladies of the D. C. Society. Filed Apr. 25, 1867. |
| 667 | | |
| 668 | 4 | MURRAY, James R. Baby's gone to sleep. S&Ch. Words by W. D. Smith, Jr. Filed Mar. 28, 1867. |
| 669 | | |
| 670 | 4 | BLUMENTHAL, Jacob. Les deux anges. Arr. by Baumbach. c1867. (Les deux debutantes! A collection of easy duets for cabinet organ & piano. [1]) Filed Mar. 25, 1868. |
| 671 | 5 | STEVENS, George. Carrickfergus schottische. Filed Apr. 5, 1867. |
| 672 | 4 | ROOT, Frederic W. Let me go! Song. Filed Apr. 20, 1867. |
| 673 | 4 | ROOT, George F. Jenny Lyle. S&Ch. Words by L. H. Dowling. Filed Apr. 23, 1867. |
| 674 | 4 | HENNIG, W. A. Parting song. Words by Miss Augusta P. Rhodes. Filed May 8, 1867. |
| 675 | | |
| 676 | 4 | Sally Ann's away! Comic S&Ch. Words by Spoons, Music by Keep Shady. Filed Apr. 25, 1867. |
| 677 | 5 | HOWARD, Frank. Lend a kind helping hand to the poor. S&Ch. Filed Apr. 20, 1867. |
| 678 | 4 | BAKER, W. C. Let us forget the past. S&Ch. Filed Apr. 20, 1867. |
| 678 | 4 | TITCOMB, C. G. Julie polka. Filed by F. Ziegfeld, Feb. 13, 1866. |
| 679 | 7 | HUTCHINSON, John Wallace. Lashed to the mast, a patriotic song. Sung by the Hutchinson Family (Tribe of John) at all their concerts throughout the Union. Words by F. H. Stauffer. Arr. by M. F. H. Smith. Filed May 3, 1867. |
| 680 | 4 | HEATH, Wilbur F. There is no one like a mother. S&Ch. c1866 by Ziegfeld, Gerard & Co., but not filed. |

| | | |
|---|---|---|
| 680 | | REED, J. W. The coming of day. Song. See PN 718. |
| 681 | 3 | ROTHGERBER, Leonora. Ruck waltz. Filed May 7, 1867. |
| 682 | 8 | WIMMERSTEDT, A. E. Rain on the calm lake, for piano. Op. 32. Filed Oct. 18, 1864, by A. Reed. Deposit copy lacks PN; PN taken from Brainard ed. |
| 683 | 6 | HARRISON, James. Floating on the lake. Solo. Words by Miss Amanda T. Jones. ... c1865 by Ziegfeld & Willson, but not filed. PN taken from Brainard ed. |
| 684-685 | | |
| 686 | 5 | WIMMERSTEDT, A. E. General Sherman's grand Atlanta march. Filed by A. Reed on Oct. 18, 1864. PN taken from Brainard ed. |
| 687 | 4 | ZIEGFELD, Florenz. My angel spirit bride, a song. Words by P. Fishe Reed. c1864 by A. Reed. |
| 688 | | |
| 689 | 4 | MURRAY, James R. They tell me thou art sleeping. S&Ch. Words by Thomas F. Winthrop. Filed May 18, 1867. |
| 690 | 3 | J., H. W. Put up the bars. Ballad. Music composed by H. W. J. Filed May 14, 1867. |
| 691 | 3 | MILLER, C. C. O, soft sleep the hills! Ballad. Filed May 18, 1867. |
| 692 | 4 | HOWARD, Frank. Since the day I signed the pledge. S&Ch. Filed June 3, 1867. |
| 693 | 4 | HEATH, Wilbur F. We are traveling on together. S&Ch. Filed June 3, 1867. |
| 694 | 4 | MURRAY, James R. I'm thinking of our youth, Tom! S&Ch. "To Thomas Winthrop, Esq." Filed July 1, 1867. |
| 695 | 4 | NEWCOMB, C. R. Kitty More. S&Ch. Words by L. J. Newcomb. Filed July 1, 1867. |
| 696 | 11 | SCHINDLER, M. L. Annie Laurie with brilliant variations. c1866 by Miss M. L. Schindler. PN from Brainard ed. where it is cancelled and 341 substituted. |
| 697 | 4 | HEWITT, W. Grand waltz for the guitar. Filed Apr. 16, 1866, by Ziegfeld, Gerard & Co. PN from Brainard ed. |
| 698-700 | | |
| 701 | 4 | HAHN, Jacob H. Rippling rill polka. Filed Aug. 8, 1865, by Ziegfeld & Willson. |
| 702-703 | | |
| 704 | 6 | LOB, Otto. Pic nic waltz. Filed Oct. 19, 1865, by Florence Ziegfeld. |
| 705 | 6 | HARRISON, James. Linden bowers, or Emma May. S&Ch. As sung by Kelly & Leon's Concert Troupe. Written by P. Fische Reed, Esq. c1865 by Alanson Reed, but not filed. |
| 706 | 4 | TOWNE, Thomas Martin. Shaking of hands. S&Ch. Filed June 17, 1867. |
| 707- | 4 | BLISS, Philip Paul. Room for one more. S&Ch. Filed June 10, 1867. |
| 708 | 6 | HARRISON, James. I'm queen of the night. Words by Marshall S. Pike, Esq. Filed May 6, 1865, by Ziegfeld & Willson. Z&W ed. uses title instead of PN, which is taken from Brainard ed. |
| 709-710 | | |
| 711 | 10 | HAVENS, Charles Arthur. La Volta. Caprice, pour le piano. c1865 by Ziegfeld & Willson, but not registered. |
| 712-714 | | |
| 715 | 4 | WIMMERSTEDT, A. E. Olivet College march. Op. 45. "To the profs and friends of Olivet College, Mich." Filed July 12, 1867. |
| 716-717 | | |
| 718 | 5 | REED, J. W. The coming of day. Song. Chicago, Root & Cady, 67 Washington St., c1864 by A. Reed, Ill. Listed in "New publications. Vocal." *Song Messenger*, July, 1867. PN cancelled and 680 substituted. |
| 719-721 | | |
| 722 | 5 | BACH, Christian H. Funeral march to the memory of Abraham Lincoln. c1865 by Ziegfeld & Willson, but not filed. |
| 723-724 | | |
| 725 | 6 | SPIER, Lion. Thinking of home polka. Filed May 6, 1865, by Ziegfeld & Willson. PN from Brainard ed. |
| 726- | 4 | FREIBERG, Fred, arr. Skating waltz, played by Dean's Union Light Guard Band, at the Skating Rink. Filed Sept. 4, 1866, by Ziegfeld, Gerard & Co. |
| 727 | | |
| 728 | 4 | FAWCETTE, George W. Summer night schottisch. Filed Oct. 19, 1865, by F. Ziegfeld. PN from R&C ed. which has also 2717. |
| 729 | 5 | PRATT, Silas Gamaliel. Shakesperian grand march. "Most respectfully dedicated to Edwin Booth, Esq." Filed June 22, 1867. |
| 730 | 4 | HARRISON, James. We're waiting for father! Words by Olynthus. Filed May 3, 1867. Deposit copy lacks PN. |
| 731 | | |

| 732 | 4 | ROGERS, William T. The midnight winds, duett & chorus. Words by Clarence May. Filed July 1, 1867. |
| 733 | 5 | TOWNE, Thomas Martin. I'm always your lovin' Katreen; or, Katrina's story. Written by Mrs. Maud L. Brainard. Filed July 19, 1867. |
| 734 | 6 | ROOT, Frederic W. Tribute of affection. A transcription of Geo. F. Root's beautiful melody, "Kiss me mother, kiss your darling." Filed July 26, 1867. |
| 735- | 6 | BRAINARD, Julia. The Sabbath morning. German words by Eichendorff. c1867. Filed Jan. 16, 1868. |
| 736 | 6 | MOELLING, Theodore. Columbia's call! Melodie by Geo. F. Root. Transcribed & varied for the piano. Filed July 26, 1867. |
| 737- | 10 | GOLDBECK, Robert. Auld lang syne, grand morceau de concert pour piano. "To Mr. Geo. F. Root." Filed July 22, 1867. |
| 738- | 10 | GOLDBECK, Robert. Caprice de concert d'apres une polka de Schulhoff par Robert Goldbeck. Filed July 13, 1867. |
| 739- | 12 | GOLDBECK, Robert. Sogni d'amore, morceau de concert pour piano. Filed July 22, 1867. |
| 740 | 10 | MOELLING, Theodore. Myrtle wreath. Caprice composed for the piano ... op. 105. Filed Aug. 10, 1867. |
| 741 | 4 | BAKER, W. C. Poor broken heart. Ballad. Filed July 6, 1867. |
| 742 | 4 | ROOT, Frederic W. Poor Carlotta! (The last words of Maximilian) S&Ch. Words by Paulina. Filed July 12, 1867. |
| 743-745 | | |
| 746 | 4 | ZIEGFELD, Florenz. Turner march, respectfully dedicated to the Turners of Jever. Filed Aug. 8, 1865, by Ziegfeld & Willson. PN from Brainard ed. |
| 747 | 4 | ROOT, Frederic W. D. C. Mazurka. ... rearranged & simplified. Filed July 26, 1867. |
| 748 | | |
| 749 | 5 | ROOT, Frederic W. Home run galop. To the Atlantic Club of Chicago, the boys who make 'em. Filed July 22, 1867. |
| 750 | 4 | ROOT, Frederic W. Faces to memory dear. S&Ch. Words by John C. Shea. Filed Aug. 3, 1867. |
| 751 | 4 | SCHUMANN, Robert A. In the woods! German words by Eichendorff. Filed Aug. 13, 1867. |
| 752 | 5 | MURRAY, James R. What shall I ask for thee! S&Ch. Words by Mrs. R. B. Edson. Filed Sept. 2, 1867. |
| 753 | 5 | BOUDEMAN, Dallas. Come while the world lies dreaming. S&Ch. Words & music by Dallas Boudeman. Filed Aug. 27, 1867. |
| 754 | | |
| 755 | 4 | BLISS, Philip Paul. The photograph, or Not at all like me! Duet for husband & wife. Words and music by P. P. Bliss. Filed Sept. 2, 1867. |
| 756 | 4 | [BLISS, Philip Paul.] The tragical tail of poor Thomas Maltese! A catastrophic dirge. Composed and sung by Pro Phundo Basso. Filed Sept. 2, 1867. |
| 757 | 5 | ROBJOHN, William James. Impatience. [S&Ch.] Filed Sept. 27, 1867. |
| 758 | 5 | TOWNE, Thomas Martin. The old church choir. S&Ch. Words by Mrs. L. Hawley. Filed Sept. 20, 1867. |
| 759 | 11 | HOFFMAN, Edward. Night before Petersburgh. Burlesque military fantasia. [Utilizes Dixie, Star Spangled Banner, and Taps.] Filed Oct. 2, 1867. |
| 760 | 4 | BAKER, W. C. Laura Anna. S&Ch. Filed Sept. 25, 1867. |
| 761- | 4 | GORHAM, A. Templeton. Let me dream of home and loved ones. S&Ch. c1867. Not registered. |
| 762 | 7 | ADAMS, O. D. O, worship the Lord! S&Ch. Subject from R. Schumann. Arr. by O. D. Adams. (Selections of sacred music for church & home) Filed Oct. 8, 1867. |
| 763 | 7 | HEYER, Charles. Softly now the light of day. Quartette. (Selections of sacred music for church & home) Filed Oct. 5, 1867. |
| 764- | 5 | ZAULIG, Fred W. Flowers of beauty schottische. Hommage à sa majestée l'Imperatrice Charlotte. c1867. |
| 765 | 3 | MORGAN, George W. The Stevens march. Composed and dedicated to his friend Geo. Stevens, Esq. Filed Dec. 9, 1867. |
| 766 | 4 | GIRAC, Max E. The founder of Notre Dame. S&Ch. Respectfully dedicated to Very Rev. Father Sorin, S.S.C. Provincial of the Order of the Holy Cross in the United States and founder of Notre Dame University, Indiana. Words by A. J. Stace, A. M., music by Max Girac, LL.D. Filed Oct. 12, 1867. |
| 767 | 3 | ROOT, George F. Octoroon schottische. Arr. for guitar by Geo. W. Brown. (Arrangements for guitar. Vocal & instrumental) Ncc. |

| | | |
|---|---|---|
| 767 | 5 | WEBSTER, Joseph Philbrick. All rights for all! A song for the times. Words by E. B. Dewing, Esq. "To that newspaper which has been most signal in the advocacy of 'All rights for all,' the New York Tribune, this song is respectfully dedicated." Filed Jan. 30, 1868. |
| 768 | 4 | ROOT, George F. Honor to Sheridan. S&Ch. Words by Paulina. Ncc. Listed in "New publications. Vocal." Song Messenger, November, 1867. PN from Brainard ed. |
| 769 | 4 | ROOT, Frederic W. Treasures, Ballad. "To T. Martin Towne." Filed Oct. 31, 1867. |
| 770 | 5 | ROOT, George F. Yes, we will be true to each other. Words by "Paulina." Arr. for guitar by Geo. W. Brown. (Popular songs arranged for the guitar) c1863 [for series] |
| 771 | 4 | ROOT, George F. I ask no more. Arr. for guitar by Geo. W. Brown. (Arrangements for guitar, vocal and instrumental) c1867. |
| 772 | 5 | VAAS, A. J. Beads man polka, by La Morte. Arr. for the piano forte ... by A. J. Vass. Filed Nov. 7, 1867. |
| 773 | | |
| 774 | 4 | ROOT, George F. Mabel ... Arr. for guitar by G. W. Brown. (Arrangements for guitar, vocal & instrumental) c1867. |
| 775 | 4 | STEVENS, George. The Barry schottische ... Arr. for guitar by G. W. Brown. (Arrangements for guitar, vocal & instrumental) c1867. |
| 776 | 12 | VAAS, A. J. Sleigh-ride galop. (Vaas.) Arr. by F. W. Root. (Les deux debutantes! A collection of easy duets for cabinet organ & piano) c1867. Filed Jan. 10, 1868. |
| 777 | | LISZT, Franz. Grand galop chromatique, pour le piano. PN from Brainard ed. [Plates look like Boston product] |
| 778 | 3 | VAAS, A. J. Templar march ... Composed & dedicated to the Sir Knights of the Apollo Commandery No. 1. Knights Templar, Chicago, Ill. ... As performed by the Great Western Light Guard Band. Filed Nov. 26, 1867. |
| 779 | 5- | [VERDI, Giuseppe.] Miserere. (Il Trovatore) ... Arr. by A. Baumbach. (Les deux debutantes! A collection of easy duets for cabinet organ & piano) Filed Dec. 21, 1867. |
| 780 | 4 | |
| 781 | 5- | MOZART, Wolfgang Amadeus. Vedrai carino. (From Mozart's "Don Giovanni.") [Arr. by] A. Baumbach. (Les deux debutantes! A collection of easy duets for cabinet organ & piano) c1867 [for series?] Filed Jan. 16, 1868. |
| 782 | 4 | |
| 783 | 3 | MOELLING, Theodore. Santa Lucia for piano & cabinet organ. Arr. by Theodore Moelling. (Les deux debutantes ...) c1867 [for series?] Filed Mar. 25, 1868. |
| 784 | | |
| 785 | 5 | PRATT, Silas Gamaliel. Ola, fantasie romanesque. Filed Dec. 13, 1867. |
| 786 | | |
| 787 | 5 | TOWNE, Thomas Martin. Let woman vote! S&Ch. Words by Mrs. E. S. Kellogg. "Respectfully inscribed to Mrs. L. Maria Child." c1867. Filed Jan. 14, 1868. |
| 788 | 5 | WEBSTER, Joseph Philbrick. Bessie Jayne. Words by Luke Collin. (His Songs of the present time. Melodies of beauty, ideas of progress, words of sense. First series) Filed Mar. 25, 1868. |
| 789 | 5 | WEBSTER, Joseph Philbrick. Lost Lomie Laine. Words by Luke Collin. (His Songs of the present time ...) Filed Mar. 25, 1868. |
| 790 | 5 | WEBSTER, Joseph Philbrick. Woman is going to vote. Words by Luke Collin. (His Songs of the present time ...) Filed Apr. 22, 1868. |
| 791 | 6 | SWEET, O. P. Passing away. As sung by the popular baritone, C. S. Fredericks of Arlington's Minstrels. S&Ch. Filed Dec. 12, 1867. PN cancelled and 2079 substituted. PN from Brainard ed. |
| 792 | 4 | ROOT, George F. Only four. S&Ch. "Dedicated to Mrs. Emily Huntington Miller, author of the words." Filed Feb. 3, 1868. |
| 793-795 | | |
| 796 | 6 | WEBSTER, Joseph Philbrick. Northmen, awake. Quartette and chorus. Words by S. Fillmore Bennett. (His Songs of the present time ...) Filed Apr. 22, 1868. |
| 797 | | |
| 798 | 4 | WEBSTER, Joseph Philbrick. The cottage in the wood. Words by Luke Collin. (His Songs of the present time ...) Filed Mar. 16, 1868. |

| | | |
|---|---|---|
| 799- | 6 | WEBSTER, Joseph Philbrick. The spring at the foot of the hill. S&Ch. Words by Luke Collin. (<u>His</u> Songs of the present time ...) c1868. |
| | | LEFÉBURE-WÉLY, Louis James Alfred. Fireside harmonies; six pieces composed expressly for the Mason & Hamlin cabinet organ. Filed Jan. 2, 1868. |
| 800 | 4 | No. 2. Berceuse. |
| 801 | 6 | No. 6. Marche. |
| 802 | 4 | No. 4. Romance sans paroles. |
| 803 | 6 | No. 3. Pastorale. |
| 804 | 4 | No. 1. Prière. |
| 805 | 4 | No. 5. Rêverie. |
| 806 | 5 | ROOT, Frederic W. Sailing into dreamland. c1867. Lithographed title-page, "Design taken by permission from an oil painting by Selden J. Woodman, Esq." Filed Jan. 9, 1868. |
| 807-808 | | |
| 809 | 4 | ROOT, Frederic W. Undine's song, O, come, O, come with me! Words by J. R. Murray, Esq.; music arranged by F. W. Root. Filed Jan. 13, 1868. |
| 810 | 8 | SCHLOTTER, Franz. Airs from Undine. No. 1. Merrily we trip it. No. 2. Beneath the deep. No. 3. Come, O come with me. No. 4. I'll love you as long as fishes have tails. No. 5. Fly not, ladies. Arranged for piano by Franz Schlotter. Filed Jan. 30, 1868. |
| 811 | | |
| 812 | 5 | GOLDBECK, Robert. Marche de Faust pour piano. c1864 by R. Goldbeck. |
| 813 | | |
| 814- | 10 | WEBSTER, Joseph Philbrick. Cupid and Mammon. Duet. Words by C. C. Haskins. (<u>His</u> Songs of the present time ...) Filed Feb. 21, 1868. |
| 815 | 8 | ROOT, Frederic W. Romeo and Juliet. Opera by Gounod. Transcription. Filed Feb. 21, 1868. |
| 816 | | |
| 817 | 5 | SMART, Henry. Poor Jack Brown, an old sea ballad sung by Mr. Geo. C. Pearson. Words by Frederick Enoch. Ncc. |
| 818 | 3 | WEBSTER, Joseph Philbrick. My Margaret. Words by Luke Collin. (<u>His</u> Songs of the present time ...) Filed Mar. 25, 1868. |
| 819- | 5 | WORK, Henry Clay. Song of the Redman. c1868. |
| 820 | | |
| 821 | 4 | WEBSTER, Joseph Philbrick. The past we can never recall, Jamie. Response to "When you & I were young, Maggie." Words by Luke Collin. (His Songs of the present time ...) Filed Mar. 16, 1868. |
| 822 | 3 | TOWNE, Thomas Martin. The little boot black. S&Ch. Words and music by T. Martin Towne. Filed Apr. 27, 1868. |
| 823 | 4 | SEAVERNS, C. L. Where go you, pretty Maggie? Ballad. Words by T. B. Aldrich. Filed Mar. 12, 1868. |
| 824 | 5 | VON ROCHOW, Alfred. The girl for me! Song. Filed Mar. 25, 1868. |
| 825 | 4 | VON ROCHOW, Alfred. Song of the cuckoo (Das Kuckuck Lied.) Put into English by "Paulina." Music arranged and performed with immense applause by Alfred Von Rochow. Filed Apr. 20, 1868. |
| 825 | | GOLDBECK, Robert. Faust caprice de concert. c1864 by author in New York. PN from Brainard ed. |
| 826 | 4 | WEBSTER, Joseph Philbrick. Cousin John. Words by S. Fillmore Bennett. (Gems of western song. 12) Filed Nov. 14, 1868. |
| 827 | 4 | BLISS, Philip Paul. If papa were only ready! Ballad. Words and music by P. P. Bliss. Filed Apr. 4, 1868. |
| 828 | 3 | WEBSTER, Joseph Philbrick. Summer's sweets shall bloom again. Words by L. J. Bates. (<u>His</u> Songs of the present time ...) Filed June 3, 1868. |
| 828 | | EICHBERG, Julius. Fraternity march, dedicated to the worshipful master-wardens and brethren of Gate of the Temple Lodge of Free and Accepted Masons. Composed for Mason and Hamlin's cabinet organ. c1866 by Mason & Hamlin. PN from Brainard ed. |
| 829 | 4 | WEBSTER, Joseph Philbrick. For President, Ulysses Grant. A smoking his cigar. S&Ch. Words by Ason O'Fagun. Filed May 24, 1868. |
| 830 | 4 | WEBSTER, Joseph Philbrick. Hurrah for General Grant! Dedicated to the convention that nominated Gen. Grant for the presidency at Crosby's Opera House, May 20th, 1868. S&Ch. Words by Luke Collin. [Lithographed title-page showing interior of the opera house during the convention.] Filed May 20, 1868. |
| 831 | 4 | VON ROCHOW, Alfred. Out of the tavern! (Grad aus dem Wirthshaus.) Words by Von Muehler. "To the Harmony Club of Rochester, N.Y." Filed May 28, 1868. |
| 832 | 4 | LACHNER, Franz. Lachner's serenade. (Ständchen.) Arr. by Alfred Von Rochow. Filed May 5, 1868. |

| | | |
|---|---|---|
| 833 | 3 | WEBSTER, Joseph Philbrick. When I lie dreaming. Words by L. J. Bates. (His Songs of the present time ...) Filed June 20, 1868. |
| 834 | 5 | ROOT, George F. Old friends and true friends ... Words by E. Scrantom, Esq. (Gems of western song. 2) Filed July 21, 1868. |
| 835 | 6 | MURRAY, James R. Angels guard her dreams tonight! Quartette serenade. Words by Bertha J. Scrantom. Filed June 6, 1868. |
| 836 | 11 | BAKER, W. C. It is an age of progress! Quartette written and composed by W. C. Baker. "To the noble reformers of our country. Rallying song." Filed May 2, 1868. |
| 837 | 5 | ADAMS, O. D. My mother bids me bind my hair. A canzonet. c1868 by O. D. and H. C. Adams in Minnesota. |
| 838 | 3 | LOCKWOOD, C. T. Tommy's return. Filed May 13, 1868. |
| 839 | 8 | ROOT, Frederic W. Belle Helene. (Opera by J. Offenbach) Brilliant transcription. Filed May 28, 1868. |
| 880 | | STRAUB, S. W. Gird on! gird on! or, The temperance band. Filed Apr. 20, 1868. PN from Brainard ed. |
| 896 | | HÜNTEN, Franz. La rose, variations brillantes sur une air allemand. Ncc. |
| 922 | | JOHNSON, L. H. Hurrah polka. Filed Apr. 13, 1865, by Ziegfeld & Willson. LC had Brainard ed. with this number. |
| 983 | | STRACK, Louis. Variations brillantes, sur l'air favorite Musette de Nina (Bring flowers) composée et arrangée pour le piano avec introduction ... c1849 by G. P. Reed & Co.; c1888 by L. Strack. PN from Brainard ed. |
| 1025 | | Silver Lake waltz. Arr. for the piano. (Gems of the ball room; a collection of popular dance music, for the piano) Ncc. Caption title includes Boston crossed out, imprint obliterated. PN cancelled and 1248 substituted. |
| 1060 | | MERZ, Karl. I'd mourn the hopes that leave me. Words by Thos. Moore. c1867 by H. T. Merrill & Co. PN from Brainard ed. |
| 1121 | | MERRILL, Hiram T. Be a man, a beautiful S&Ch. c1865 by Merrill & Brennan. PN from Brainard ed. |
| 1127 | | MERRILL, Hiram T. Anyhow. This song may be sung by one or two voices. Words by R. Tompkins, Esq. c1864 by H. T. Merrill, but not registered. PN from Brainard ed. |
| 1143 | | HUBBARD, Charles P. Ida waltz. Filed by Merrill & Brennan, Mar. 2, 1866. PN from Brainard ed. |
| 1145 | | ROOT, George F. If Maggie were my own! S&Ch. Words by Lieut. L. H. M. Byers. Filed Jan. 18, 1868. PN lacking on deposit copy, taken from Brainard ed. |
| 1182 | | MURRAY, James R. Kind smiles for all. S&Ch. Filed Feb. 12, 1868. PN from Brainard ed. |
| 1196 | | BACH, Charles H. Look out upon the stars. Serenade. For soprano or tenor. Filed by Ziegfeld & Willson, May 6, 1865. PN from Brainard ed. |
| 1248 | | Silver Lake waltz. See PN 1025. |
| 1492 | | WIMMERSTEDT, A. E. Moonlight vespers. Nocturne, evening meditation composed for the piano. Filed May 31, 1867, by Merrill & Brennan. PN from Brainard ed. |
| 1511 | | MATHEWS, William Smythe Babcock. Nightfall at home. Nocturne. Filed Apr. 18, 1868. Deposit copy has N in place of PN. PN from Brainard ed. |
| 1758 | | GOLDBECK, Robert. Nabucodonosor. (His L'opéra dans le salon. Une serie de fantaisies brillante pour le piano. IV) PN from Brainard ed.; deposit copy has N. Filed Mar. 16, 1868. |
| 2011 | | HUBBARD, Charles P. Pond lilly schottisch. Filed by Merrill & Brennan, Mar. 2, 1866. PN from Brainard ed. |
| 2062 | | ARDITI, Luigi. Ecstasy. (L'estasi.) Valse brillante. Words by Claude Vincent. (Songs and ballads of Mlle. Parepa. 5) Ncc. |
| 2075 | | BERGMANN, Carl. Ocean House polka redowa. (A choice collection of waltzes & polkas as performed by the Germania Musical Society. No. 11) c1852 by G. P. Reed. |
| 2079 | | SWEET, O. P. Passing away. See PN 791. |
| 2320 | | STAAB, Franz. Light guard schottisch. (A new collection of standard and popular dance music. 66) Filed July 17, 1868. Plates and PN obviously from Boston firm; series included 107 titles, all from Boston. It is doubtful whether R&C had any legal right to claim copyright. By filing one title, R&C could print copyright claim on the title-page for the whole series. |

| | | | |
|---|---|---|---|
| 2419 | GOLDBECK, Robert. Rigoletto. (His L'opera dans le salon. Une serie de fantaisies brillante pour le piano. V) PN from Brainard ed.; deposit copy has R. Filed Mar. 25, 1868. | 3621 | ROOT, George F. To whom shall we give thanks, song recitando or quartette. Words by Mrs. Levi Wade. c1871 by R&C; c1872 by S. Brainard's sons. |
| 2421 | HELLER, Stephen. 30 progressive studies. 2d book. Op. 46. (His 25 etudes. No. 2) Ncc. | 3678 | ROOT, George F. Dreaming, ever dreaming. Ballad. (Gems of western song. 9) c1868 for series. PN from Brainard ed. |
| 2452 | HAHN, Madame C. The soldier's last request. Filed May 6, 1865, by Ziegfeld & Willson. | 3759 | BAUMBACH, Adolph. Shells of ocean with brilliant variations for the piano. c1859 by Russell & Tolman. |
| 2690 | VAAS, A. J. Sleigh ride galop. Filed Nov. 16, 1865. | 4152 | BLESSNER, Gustave. Grand polonaise. Duo concertant for Mason & Hamlin's cabinet organ & piano forte. Filed Nov. 22, 1865, by Mason & Hamlin. Deposit copy has no PN; PN from Brainard ed. |
| 2734 | GANZ, Wilhelm. Sing, birdie, sing. See PN 643. |
| 2741 | SPEIER, Wilhelm. The trumpeter. Poetry by Kopisch, translated by H. Ware, Esq. Copyright claim obliterated. |
| 2848 | PHELPS, Mrs. Minnie A. The sparkling schottische. Filed by Merrill & Brennan, May 26, 1865. PN from Brainard reprint. | 4160 | BLESSNER, Gustave. Commencement march for four hands with accompaniment for Mason & Hamlin's cabinet organ. c1865 by Mason & Hamlin. PN from Brainard ed. |
| 2951 | COOTE, Charles. Corn flower valse. (The pianists musical library. No. 29) Ncc. | 4249 | RICHARDS, Brinley. Warbling at eve, romance. (His compositions for the piano forte. 1) Ncc. BAUMBACH, Adolph. Golden memories. Filed Sept. 8, 1868, if not otherwise specified. |
| 2966 | LACHNER, J. Thou everywhere. (Überall du.) Song for mezzo soprano or baritone. English version by Chas. J. Sprague. (Gems of German song, with English and German words. 135) c1863 by H. Tolman & Co. |
| | | 4801 | No. 1. La fille du regiment. |
| | | 4802 | No. 2. Martha, Flotow. |
| 2967 | KÜCKEN, Friedrich Wilhelm. Fly, birdling, through the verdant wood. (Gems of German song with English and German words. 139) c1861 by Russell & Tolman? | 4803 | No. 3. Hark! the vesper hymn is stealing. |
| | 4804 | No. 4. Drinking song from Lucrezie Borgia. [Donizetti.] |
| 3113 | LEFÉBURE-WÉLY James Alfred. Les cloches du monastère. Ncc. | 4805 | No. 5. The blue bells of Scotland. |
| | 4806 | No. 6. Linda di Chamounix. Donizetti. |
| 3160 | ASCHER, Joseph. La cascade de roses, op. 80. (Compositions pour piano par J. Ascher, Th. Oesten) Ncc. | 4807 | No. 7. The heart bowed down. (Bohemian girl) [Balfe.] |
| | 4808 | No. 8. Donna e mobile. Rigoletto. [Verdi.] |
| 3221 | ASCHER, Joseph. Victoire. Galop militaire. Ncc. | 4809 | No. 9. Prison duet from Trovatore. [Verdi.] |
| 3350 | ROOT, George F. Home's harmony. Quartette. (His Collection of vocal quartettes. No. 3) c1861 by Russell & Tolman? | 4810 | No. 10. Home, sweet home. Filed Sept. 21, 1868. |
| | 4811 | No. 11. Masquerade, Ernani. Verdi. Filed Sept. 22, 1868. |
| 3582 | THORNTON. The little gem; or Darling Jenny Lee. Filed by Merrill & Brennan, Mar. 16, 1868. PN from Brainard ed. | 4812 | No. 12. Auld lang syne. Filed Sept. 22, 1868. |
| | 4813 | No. 13. Lucia di Lammermoor. Donizetti. Filed Sept. 22, 1868. |
| 3583 | HAYWOOD, George. When my ship comes in! Written and composed by Geo. Haywood; arr. by Geo. F. Root. (Root & Cady's new vocal quartettes) c1867 [for series?] | 4814 | No. 14. Roberto il Diavolo. Meyerbeer. Filed Sept. 21, 1868. |
| | 4815 | No. 15. Le petit tambour. Filed Sept. 15, 1868. |

| | |
|---|---|
| 4816 | No. 16. Sounds from home, by Gung'l. Filed Sept. 15, 1868. |
| 4817 | No. 17. Romeo and Juliet by Gounod. Filed Sept. 23, 1868. |
| 4818 | No. 18. Fra Diavolo. Auber. Filed Sept. 21, 1868. |
| 4819 | No. 19. Then you'll remember me. Balfe. Filed Sept. 24, and Sept. 28, 1868. |
| 4820 | No. 20. Don Giovanni. Filed Sept. 28, 1868. |
| 4821 | No. 21. La grande duchesse. Offenbach. Filed Sept. 25, 1868. |
| 4822 | No. 22. La Barbe Bleue. Offenbach. Filed Sept. 28, 1868. |
| 4823-4825 | |
| 4826 | HARRIS, Charles. Sounds from Mexico. (The guitar. Instrumental. 2) Filed Sept. 21, 1868. |
| 4827 | HUBBARD, James Maurice. The ruler in peace and the leader in war. S&Ch. Respectfully inscribed to my comrades at the siege of Vicksburg. Filed Sept. 12, 1868. |
| 4828 | HOWARD, Frank. Down by the brook at the end of the lane. Words & music by Frank Howard. (Gems of western song. 8) Filed Nov. 3, 1868. |
| 4829 | HOWARD, Frank. Why not? Ballad. Filed Oct. 3, 1868. |
| 4830 | GORHAM, A. Templeton. Bonnie Marguerita. S&Ch. Filed Sept. 28, 1868. |
| 4831 | DODGE, Ossian E. Ho! westward ho! (Choice quartets. 12) Filed Oct. 31, 1868. |
| 4832 | RUELL, . There is no heart. Song. Filed Oct.3, 1868. |
| 4833 | WEBSTER, Joseph Philbrick. Come to me memories olden! S&Ch. Words by S. Fillmore Bennett. Filed Oct. 3, 1868. |
| 4834 | LOCKWOOD, C. T. Still I love thee! S&Ch. Words and music by C. T. Lockwood. Filed Oct. 6, 1868. |
| 4835 | MURRAY, James R. I wait for thy coming, my darling! S&Ch. Words by Dexter Smith. Filed Oct. 19, 1868. |
| 4836 | MACY, J. C. Good bye Johnnie, or Mother's request. S&Ch. Words and music by J. C. Macy. Filed Oct. 14, 1868. |
| 4837 | LOCKWOOD, C. T. Little stub toe polka. "Respectfully dedicated to little Jake." Filed Oct. 20, 1868. |
| 4838 | TOWNE, Thomas Martin. Gather 'round the table. A song of home. Words by Mrs. E. S. Kellogg. Filed Oct. 31, 1868. |
| 4839 | HOWARD, Frank. Often in dreams I'm roaming. S&Ch. Words and music by Frank Howard. Filed Oct. 24, 1868. |
| 4840 | WEBSTER, Joseph Philbrick. What might have been! S&Ch. Words by S. Fillmore Bennett. Filed Oct. 24, 1868. |
| 4841 | DODGE, Ossian W. Keep the ball a-rolling! S&Ch. Written & composed by Ossian E. Dodge. "Dedicated to the 'Little Giant of Minnesota,' Hon. Ignatius Donnelly." Filed Oct. 12, 1868. |
| 4842 | LOCKWOOD, C. T. Days that are gone! S&Ch. Filed Oct. 27, 1868. |
| 4843 | LOCKWOOD, C. T. My Madeline! S&Ch. Words by H. M. Look. Filed Oct. 24, 1868. |
| 4844 | |
| 4845 | BLISS, Philip Paul. Pro Phundo Basso. Comic song, with solo, duetts & quartet. Words & music by P. P. Bliss. Filed Oct. 24, 1868. |
| 4846 | HOWARD, Frank. The way it's done. Words & music by Frank Howard. Filed Oct. 24, 1868. |
| 4847 | WEBSTER, Joseph Philbrick. Sister May. S&Ch. Words by S. Fillmore Bennett. Filed Nov. 14, 1868. |
| 4848 | WEBSTER, Joseph Philbrick. My Lily. S&Ch. Words by S. Fillmore Bennett. Filed Nov. 14, 1868. |
| 4849 | HARRIS, Charles. Polka grotesque. (The guitar. Instrumental. 15) Filed Nov. 25, 1868. |
| 4850 | HARRIS, Charles. Impromptu brilliante. (The guitar. Instrumental. 14) Filed Nov. 25, 1868. |
| 4851 | WEBSTER, Joseph Philbrick. Old friends. S&Ch. Words by S. Fillmore Bennett. c1868. Filed Jan. 8, 1869. |
| 4852 | HOWARD, Frank. The short girl dressed in green. Written for and sung by William Delahanty, words and music by Frank Howard. Filed Nov. 18, 1868. |
| 4853 | PHELPS, E. B. Coralline mazurka brillante for piano. Filed Nov. 17, 1868. |
| 4854 | LOCKWOOD, C. T. Sparkle, schottische. Filed Nov. 14, 1868. |
| 4855 | KAPPES, J. H. Evening prayer, or Savior breathe an evening blessing. (Selections of sacred music for church & home) Filed Nov. 20, 1868. |

4856  MURRAY, James R. How sweet the thought. Song, words by Dexter Smith, Esq. Filed Nov. 18, 1868.

4857  WEBSTER, Joseph Philbrick. Cousin John. Words by S. Fillmore Bennett. (Gems of western song. 12) Cf 826 4

4858  HOWARD, Frank. Oh, Sorosis! S&Ch. Filed Nov. 7, 1868, without PN. PN from Brainard ed.

4859  COX, John S. The crossing sweeper, beautiful S&Ch. Poetry by C. W. Filed Dec. 7, 1868.

4860  SHATTUCK, C. F. The light auburn curl, ballad. Words by A. G. Chase. "To her who presented the author with the curl." Filed Nov. 28, 1868.

4861  MURRAY, James R. Mona's reverie. Filed Dec. 4, 1868.

4862  COX, John S. Only a waiting maid. S&Ch. Filed Dec. 9, 1868.

4863  HUBBARD, James Maurice. Sabbath morn. A sacred hymn. Words by D. Blakely. "Written for and respectfully dedicated to Plymouth Church & Society, Chicago." Filed Nov. 21, 1868.

4864  BAUMBACH, Adolph. Valse a la mode. (Fashionable waltz.) Composee pour le piano. "To the young ladies of the C. P. Club." Filed Nov. 24, 1868.

4865  HOFFMAN, Edward. The nation's hero grand march. "Dedicated by permission to Hon. Ulysses S. Grant, elected President of the U. S., Nov. 3, 1868." Filed Dec. 7, 1868.

4866  LOCKWOOD, C. T. Silver whistle. Composed for piano. Filed Nov. 28, 1868.

4867  ADAMS, O. D. My mother bids me bind my hair. A canzonet. c1868 by O. D. and H. C. Adams. PN from Brainard ed. Cf 837 5

4868  MACY, J. C. Joanna dear, my Jo. Ballad. Words and music by J. C. Macy. Filed Dec. 4, 1868.

4869  COX, John S. My thoughts are far away. Ballad, words by Fred Lawton. Filed Dec. 3, 1868.

4870  HARRISON, James. Dillon schottische for the piano forte ... As performed by G. Stevens' Orchestra at Woods Museum. "To John Dillon, Esq., Chicago." Filed Dec. 19, 1868.

4871  WEBSTER, Joseph Philbrick. Oh! lady fair, I dream of thee. S&Ch. Words by S. Fillmore Bennett. Filed Dec. 7, 1868.

4872  HOWARD, Frank. Mind your own bread and butter. Serio-comic S&Ch. Words and music by Frank Howard. Filed Dec. 8, 1868.

4873  CLARK, Ernst. Tommy Dodd! As sung in "After dark" by Mr. John S. Marble at Wood's Museum. Written and composed by Ernst Clark. Filed Dec. 8, 1868.

4874  HOWARD, Frank. 'Twas after twelve when you came home. S&Ch. Words and music by Frank Howard. Filed Dec. 18, 1868.

4875  MURRAY, James R. Ever with me. S&Ch. Words by T. L. H. Filed Dec. 18, 1868.

4876  HEYER, Charles. Safely through another week. (Selections of sacred music for church & home) Another copy: (His Sacred music. Quartettes. [6]) Filed Dec. 28, 1868.

4877  WEBSTER, Joseph Philbrick. Floraline Shore, ballad. Words by E. B. Dewing. Filed Dec. 19, 1868.

4878  DOANE, W. Howard. Shadows of the past! Duett. Filed Dec. 18, 1868.

4879  MURRAY, James R. When Sue and I went skating. S&Ch. Words by E. E. Rexford. c1868. Filed Jan. 9, 1869.

4880

4881  VON ROCHOW, Alfred. Popping corn. (Gems of western song. 13) c1868. Filed Jan. 2, 1869.

4882  HOWARD, Frank. It's not poor mother's fault. S&Ch. Words and music by Frank Howard. Filed Dec. 26, 1868.

4883  BAKER, W. C. O linger no longer. c1868. Filed Jan. 2, 1869.

4884  MURRAY, James R. Christmas cheer. S&Ch. Words by Mrs. M. L. Rayne. Filed Dec. 19, 1868.

4885  HOWARD, Frank. She has such winning ways. S&Ch. Words & music by Frank Howard. Filed Dec. 28, 1868.

4886  KRUGER, Edward H. Golden ringlets. S&Ch. Words by Amelia. Filed Mar. 6, 1869.

4887  MASON, William. Amitié pour amitié, morceau de salon pour piano ... Second edition. Revised, corrected and fingered expressly for the publisher by the author. Arranged for four hands by K. Klauser. [Title-page from N. Richardson ed. for two hands and bears his copyright claim for 1854. At one stage had PN 7308.] Filed Dec. 28, 1868.

4888 TAYLOR, Virgil Corydon. Te Deum laudamus. We praise Thee, No. 3, in F for morning service. Written for the author's choir, St. Paul's Church, Des Moines, c1868. Filed Jan. 2, 1869.

4889 HEYER, Charles. Now from labor and from care. (His Sacred music. Quartettes. [4]) Filed Jan. 19, 1869.

4890 HEYER, Charles. The Lord is my shepherd. (His Sacred music. Quartettes. [3]) Filed Jan. 23, 1869.

4891 HEYER, Charles. Bow down Thine ear. (His Sacred music. Quartettes. [5]) Filed Jan. 22, 1869.

4892 HEYER, Charles. Rock of ages. (His Sacred music. Quartettes. [2]) Filed Jan. 21, 1869.

4893 WEBSTER, Joseph Philbrick. Little Hattie Harvey, Christmas and New Year's song, words by E. B. Dewing. Filed Dec. 30, 1868.

4894

4895 HEYER, Charles. Cast thy burden on the Lord. (His Sacred music. Quartettes. [7]) Filed Feb. 4, 1869.

4896 MURRAY, James R. Bright eyes waltz. c1868. Filed Jan. 18, 1869.

4897 MERZ, Karl. Miriam's song of triumph. "Sound the loud timbrel." Words by Thomas Moore, chorus & solos with piano accompaniment. Filed Jan. 22, 1869.

4898 LEE, A. [The man on the] Flying trapeze. (Songs and ballads from over the sea. 3) Ncc.

4899 MacLAGEN, T. Captain Jinks. (Songs and ballads from over the sea. 2) Ncc.

4900 HOWARD, Frank. The little stone cot in the dell. S&Ch. Words and music by Frank Howard. Filed Jan. 15, 1869.

4901 ROOT, Frederic W. Orpheus. Opera by Offenbach. Fantasie for piano. Filed June 12, 1868.

4902 [PRATT, Silas Gamaliel.] White fawn schottische, by V. B. Aubert. "To Mlle. Bonfanti" [whose likeness is lithographed on cover]. Filed July 9, 1868.

4903-4904

4905 VAAS, A. J. St. Paul waltz. Arr. for the piano. c1864. Cf 380 4

4906 TOWNE, Thomas Martin. The little boot black. PN from Brainard ed. Cf PN 822

4907-4911

4912 MERRILL, Hiram T. First bud waltz. Filed Aug. 13, 1864, by H. T. Merrill. PN from Brainard ed.

4913 ROOT, Frederic W. Touch the keys softly. Quartette. c1867. Cf 665 8

4914

4915 WORK, Henry C. Nellie lost and found. [Compositions of Henry C. Work, series c1866] Cf 128 4

4917 SCOTT, Mrs. Clara H. Snowflakes. PN from Brainard ed. Deposit copy has S.F. Filed Apr. 27, 1868.

4922 BAUMBACH, Adolph. First dreams. Nocturne. Filed June 12, 1868.

4923 First finger waltz. Composed by a little joker. Filed June 19, 1868.

4924 BLISS, Philip Paul. Lora Vale. PN from Brainard ed. Cf PN 396

4925

4926 LOCKWOOD, C. T. Blushing rose polka. c1867 by C. T. Lockwood. PN from Brainard ed.

4927-4928

4929 [PRATT, Silas Gamaliel.] White fawn march, by V. B. Aubert. Filed June 17, 1868.

4930 SCHINDLER, M. L. In those bright eyes. (Gems of western song. 5) Filed July 23, 1868.

4931 FRANKS, W. The little wanderer's song. (Gems of western song. 4) Filed July 24, 1868.

4932 ROOT, George F. Old friends and true friends. Words by E. Scrantom, Esq. (Gems of western song. 2) Filed July 21, 1868. Cf 834 5

4933 WEBSTER, Joseph Philbrick. When I lie dreaming. Words by L. J. Bates. (His Songs of the present time ...) Filed June 20, 1868. Cf 833 3

4934

4935 LOCKWOOD, C. T. Gathering home. S&Ch. c1868. Listed in the Song Messenger, July, 1868.

4936 MERRILL, Hiram T. The first blossom waltz. c1864 by H. T. Merrill. PN from Brainard ed.

4937 HOWARD, Frank. The old church bells. S&Ch. Deposit copy has title in lower margin; PN added later. Filed Apr. 24, 1868.

4938

4939 CALDWELL, Susie B. Name me in thy prayer. Song. Filed June 3, 1868, without PN.

4940 GROBE, Charles. Tramp! tramp! tramp! or the prisoner's hope, with brilliant variations. c1865. PN from Brainard ed. Cf 450 8

4941-4942

4943 MERZ, Karl. The little drummer boy's march. For the piano forte. c1864. Cf 381 4

4943 MURRAY, James R. Little sunshine. A song. Filed Apr. 28, 1868, with L. S. in place of PN.

4944-4946

4947 LINWOOD, E. That little room up stairs. S&Ch. Words by Elmer Ruán Coates. Filed June 26, 1868.

4948 HOFFMAN, Edward. The dell of roses, mazurka elegante. Filed June 26, 1868.

4949 LOCKWOOD, C. T. Feather waltz. Filed June 29, 1868.

4950 [PRATT, Silas Gamaliel.] A night of love. Une nuit d'amour. Nocturne for the piano by V. B. Aubert. Filed June 24, 1868.

4951 LOCKWOOD, C. T. Pebble polka. Filed June 24, 1868.

4952 LOCKWOOD, C. T. Shun the broad road ... Words by H. M. L. c1868 by C. T. Lockwood. Originally published by Lockwood & Hoyt, Pontiac, Mich. PN from Brainard ed.

4953 LOCKWOOD, C. T. The little ones at home! Words by E. F. D. Filed July 7, 1868.

4954 A very bad cold. Quartette. (Choice quartets. 3) Filed July 17, 1868.

4955 LOCKWOOD, C. T. Walk! walk! walk! S&Ch. Words by H. M. L. c1867 by Lockwood & Hoyt, Pontiac, Mich. PN from Brainard ed. Listed as "New music," Song Messenger Extra, August, 1868. Filed Dec. 18, 1867.

4956 DUER; Mrs. E. A. Parkhurst. Beautiful hands. S&Ch. Words by Ellen M. H. Gates ... Music by Mrs. Duer, formerly Mrs. E. A. Parkhurst. Filed July 10, 1868.

4957 LOCKWOOD, C. T. Ella Bell. S&Ch. Words by Sallie Hoffman. Filed July 17, 1868.

4958 KINKEL, Johanna. The knight's farewell. (Ritters Abschied.) Quartette for male voices. As performed with great success by the Maenner Gesang Verein "Arion" of New York City, at the 16th Saengerfest of the N. A. Saengerbund ... English version by Martin Meyer. "Dedicated to the 'Arion' of New York City." Filed July 15, 1868. SARONI, Hermann S. Idyls of the prairie. Recitations for the piano.

4959 Sunrise. Filed July 25, 1868.

4960 Mid-day. Filed Aug. 1, 1868.
4961 Sunset. Filed July 25, 1868.

4962 WORK, Henry Clay. Agnes by the river. Poetry by Mary J. McDermit. (Gems of western song. 1) Filed Aug. 21, 1868.

4963 ROOT, Frederic W. Repose! ... A sketch from James R. Murray's theme, "Baby's gone to sleep." For piano. Filed July 25, 1868.

4964 ANGUERA, Antonio de. Crystal showers. Filed Aug. 4, 1868.

4965 MURRAY, James R. Beautiful spirit of song. S&Ch. Words by Mattie Winfield Torrey. Filed Aug. 6, 1868.

4966 LONG, James W. The artillery galop, introducing the popular Army air of Benny Havens, by James W. Long. (Brvt. Major, U.S.A.) "To the Artillery Corps, U.S.A." Filed Aug. 6, 1868.

4967 BRIDEWELL, W. W. Nasby's lament over the New York nominations. Filed Aug. 21, 1868.

4968 TOWNE, Thomas Martin. The angel choir, quartette. Poetry by Mrs. S. B. Herrick. (Choice quartets. 1) Filed Aug. 21, 1868.

4969 MURRAY, James R. Brothers of the mystic tie. Words by Capt. Samuel Whiting. (Choice quartets. 2) Filed Aug. 21, 1868.

4970 MURRAY, James R. The tanner and the blue! A campaign S&Ch. Words by James Summerfield. "To the 1st Ward Tanner Club, of Chicago & all Tanner Clubs throughout the Union." Filed Aug. 14, 1868.

4971 MARYATT, Pendleton. The mountains of life, or My soul shall know thine in that beautiful land. S&Ch. Words by Andrew Sherwood. "To the memory of Wm. B. Bradbury." Filed Aug. 24, 1868.

4972 GORHAM, A. Templeton. Is there room among the angels. Words by T. D. C. Miller, M. D. (Gems of western song. 6) Filed Sept. 8, 1868.

4973 MURRAY, James R. When mother fell asleep. (Gems of western song. 3) Filed Sept. 4, 1868.

4974 HILL, Will. Minnesota, the lily of the west. Quartette composed by Will Hill, Rushford, Minn. (Choice quartets. 4) Filed Sept. 4, 1868.

| | | | |
|---|---|---|---|
| 4975 | MOZART, Wolfgang Amadeus. Mozart's Fantasie C moll. New [sic] herausgegeben mit Vortragsbezeichnung und Fingersatz von F. Ziegfeld. Filed Sept. 2, 1868. | 5226 | BENDEL, Franz. Nocturne, op. 92. (Piano. 8) Ncc. |
| 4976 | P., S. G. [PRATT, Silas Gamaliel?] Life's dream is o'er! Romanza for tenor & contralto, as sung by Mrs. Cassie Mattison & J. R. Nilsen. Arranged from Ascher's "Alice" by S. G. P. Filed Sept. 3, 1868. | 5319 | BLESSNER, Gustave. Atlanta (grand victory march). (A collection of transcriptions for the Mason & Hamlin cabinet organ) c1865 by Mason & Hamlin. PN from Brainard ed. deposited for renewal by G. Blessner, 1893. |
| 4977 | BLISS, Philip Paul. When grandmama is gone. Words & music by P. P. Bliss. (Gems of western song. 7) Filed Sept. 8, 1868. | 5422 | STRAUSS, Johann. Donau Walzer. (On the Danube.) (Favorite waltzes by popular authors. 1) Ncc. |
| 4978 | HARRIS, Charles. Silver star waltz. (The guitar. Instrumental. 1) Filed Sept. 21, 1868. | 5436 | SARONI, Hermann S. Winter flowers. Song. Filed Jan. 16, 1869. |
| 4982 | MAYER, Ferdinand, arr. The maiden's prayer. Words by "Mary." c[date illegible] by H. Tolman. | 5437 | HOWARD, Frank. The prettiest girl in town. S&Ch. Words and music by Frank Howard. Filed Feb. 6, 1869. |
| 5050 | BLESSNER, Gustave. Camp schottische. (His A collection of transcriptions for the Mason & Hamlin cabinet organ) Filed Dec. 13, 1865, by Mason & Hamlin. PN from Brainard ed. | 5438 | HOWARD, Frank. Golden leaves of autumn. S&Ch. Words and music by Frank Howard. c1868. Filed Jan. 9, 1869. |
| 5089 | BLESSNER, Gustave. Homeward. (A collection of transcriptions for the Mason & Hamlin cabinet organ) c1865 by Mason & Hamlin. PN from Brainard ed. | 5439 | ROOT, George F. Kiss me mother, kiss your darling! Arr. for guitar by W. O. Hayden. Words by Letta C. Lord. (The Guitar. (Vocal) 70) c1868 [for series?] Filed Feb. 2, 1869. |
| 5100 | CHOPIN, Frederic. Impromptu, op. 29. (24 classical compositions for piano by eminent European composers. No. 1) c1866 by H. Tolman. | 5440 | BLISS, Philip Paul. 'Tis the heart makes the home. Trio for soprano, tenor & bass. Words and music by P. P. Bliss. Filed Jan. 22, 1869. |
| 5105 | [BARNARD, Mrs. Charlotte.] Five o'clock in the morning. As sung with immense success by Mlle. Parepa. Words and music by Claribel. Ncc. | 5441 | WEBSTER, Joseph Philbrick. The land o' the leal. S&Ch. [Words by Lady Catherine Nairne] Filed Jan. 22, 1869. |
| 5140 | DEMAR, John, arr. When ye gang awa, Jamie. (Hunting tower) Scotch song. Ncc. | 5442 | BLISS, Philip Paul. Watcher Gray, or (The owl in the ruin). Words furnished by Z. S. Hills to whom the song is respectfully inscribed. Filed Feb. 19, 1869. |
| 5158 | [BARNARD, Mrs. Charlotte.] Take back the heart. Song by Claribel. Ncc. | 5443 | HOWARD, Frank. Songs that we never forget. S&Ch. Words and music by Frank Howard. Filed Feb. 4, 1869. |
| 5173 | EICHBERG, Julius. Pilgrim's night-march. Originally issued in <u>Collection of Pieces composed for Cabinet Organ</u> No. 6, c1866 by Mason & Hamlin, no PN; reissued by Brainard with PN added in <u>12 Morceaux for the Mason and Hamlin Cabinet Organ</u>. No. 7) | 5444 | HOWARD, Frank. The velocipede. S&Ch. Words and music by Frank Howard. ("Velocipedia") c1868 [for series?] Filed Jan. 22, 1869. |
| 5190 | BLESSNER, Gustave. Grand polonaise. (<u>His</u> A collection of transcriptions for the Mason & Hamlin cabinet organ) Filed Dec. 13, 1865, by Mason & Hamlin. PN from Brainard ed. | 5445 | HOWARD, Frank. List to me. Serenade, words and music by Frank Howard. Filed Feb. 19, 1869. |
| | | 5446-5490 | |
| 5207 | DOLORES. The brook. Words by Tennyson. Ncc. | 5491 | MURRAY, James R. Guests of the heart. Song. Filed Feb. 4, 1869. |
| | | 5492 | KIMBALL, Horace E. Velocipede polka. ("Velocipedia") Filed Jan. 26, 1869. |

5493  HOWARD, Frank. Velocipede waltz. ("Velocipedia") Filed Jan. 27, 1869.
5494  HOWARD, Frank. Making love while on the ice. S&Ch. Words & music by Frank Howard. c1869.
5495  HOWARD, Frank. Kitty McKay. Ballad. Words & music by Frank Howard. Filed Mar. 26, 1869.
5496  WEBSTER, Joseph Philbrick. Dawning of the better day. Words by L. J. Bates. (Choice quartets. 13) Filed Apr. 14, 1869.
5497  TOWNE, Thomas Martin. The voice that I love. S&Ch. Words by Mrs. E. S. Kellogg. Filed Feb. 6, 1869.
5498-  4  MURRAY, James R. Gone to heaven. S&Ch. Words and music by James R. Murray. A companion piece to "Baby's gone to sleep" ... "To my friend, Charles T. Root." Filed Jan. 15, 1869. PN from J. Church ed.; R&C deposit copy has title only.
5499
5500  PERRING, J. Ernest. Waiting for angels to come. Ballad. c1868 by Smith & Perring in the Eastern District of N. Y. PN from Brainard ed. Listed as "New music" in Song Messenger Extra, March, 1869.
5501
5502  HOWARD, Frank. I'm such a nice young man. S&Ch. Filed Feb. 8, 1869.
5503  KNORTZ, Carl. I can not forget. Song. Filed Mar. 17, 1869.
5504  LOCKWOOD, C. T. And he's got the money too. Words & music by C. T. Lockwood. Filed Feb. 4, 1869.
5505  HOWARD, Frank. When the birds come in spring. S&Ch. Filed Feb. 17, 1869.
5506-5509
5510  GOLDBECK, Robert. Belles de Chicago. Or, Les plaisirs de la valse, valse elegante pour le piano. "To the young ladies of Chicago." c1869 by R. Goldbeck. Listed in Song Messenger Extra, February, 1869. PN from Brainard ed.
5511-5512
5513  HOWARD, Frank. Philander Brown, the ill-used young man. (His Songs) PN from Brainard ed. Ncc.
5514  ADAMS, O. D. Try, John! try, John! S&Ch. Filed Feb. 23, 1869.
5515  GORHAM, A. Templeton. Baby goes alone. (His Home melodies ... 5) Filed Feb. 23, 1869.
5516
5517  HUTCHINSON, John Wallace. Vote it right along! ... S&Ch. Words & music composed by John W. Hutchinson ... and sung by the Hutchinson family at their concerts. Arr. by Mrs. E. H. Jackson. "Dedicated to the Universal Suffrage and Equal Rights Association of Illinois." Filed Feb. 12, 1869.
5518  GORHAM, A. Templeton. Kiss me when I come home. ... (His Home melodies, a collection of choice songs and choruses. 7) Filed Feb. 26, 1869.
5519-5520
5521  HUTCHINSON, John Wallace. A hundred years hence, a very desirable song for the conservatives who pray for a procrastination of the milennial day. Words by Fannie Gage, [that long, tried, and earnest advocate of human progress, and the rights of the family of man, Aunt Fannie Gage]. Arr. by James R. Murray. Filed Mar. 10, 1869.
5522
5523  GORHAM, A. Templeton. If I only knew it came from Paris ... (His Home melodies ... 4). Filed Apr. 6, 1869.
5524  GOLDBECK, Robert. The million dollar waltz. Filed Apr. 22, 1869.
5525  LOCKWOOD, C. T. Shower waltz. Filed Mar. 5, 1869.
5526  HOWARD, Frank. This beautiful world that we live in. S&Ch. Filed Mar. 20, 1869.
5527  BOGUE, Elias. L'Etoile galop. Filed Mar. 10, 1869.
5528
5529  SHATTUCK, C. F. Not for thy beauty. Ballad. Words by A. G. Chase. Filed Mar. 17, 1869.
5530  HOWARD, Frank. I'm in love. S&Ch. Filed Mar. 23, 1869.
5531  HOWARD, Frank. There's a void in our household. S&Ch. Filed Mar. 25, 1869.
5532  HOWARD, Frank. Go ask my wife. S&Ch. Filed Mar. 20, 1869.
5533  BISHOP, Thomas Brigham. Love among the roses. Words by W. H. Delehanty, and sung by Delehanty and Hengler. "To Billy Emerson." Filed Apr. 22, 1869.

5534 HARRISON, James. Sibylla valse. "To Charles C. Smith of N. Y." Filed Mar. 23, 1869.

5535 HOWARD, Frank. Grandma. S&Ch. Filed June 3, 1869.

5536 ABT, Franz. The German youth. (Der deutsche Knabe) ... op. 61, no. 6. (Songs and ballads from over the sea. 5) Filed Apr. 12, 1869.

5537 BENSON, P. The singing skewl. Song & coreas. By P. Benson Sr. Whitch the Sr. it stans for singger. "Respectubly dedikated to F. W. Root, his airs & assines forever." Filed Mar. 23, 1869.

5538 HACKELTON, M. W. When you told me the tale of your love. S&Ch. Words & music by Mrs. M. W. Hackelton. Filed Apr. 22, 1869.

5539

5540 GORHAM, A. T. Tripping through the barley. (His Home melodies, a collection of choice songs and choruses. 8) "To James R. Murray, Esq." c1869.

5541 ROOT, Frederic W. I'm married! Song. Words from the Scotch. Filed Apr. 12, 1869.

5542 HOWARD, Frank. There's no such beau as mine. S&Ch. Filed Apr. 17, 1869.

5543 HOWARD, Frank. Who's to blame? S&Ch. Filed Apr. 17, 1869.

5544 HOWARD, Frank. Heigh ho! I'm in want of a beau! S&Ch. Filed May 4, 1869.

5545 HOWARD, Frank. Old sayings. S&Ch. Filed Apr. 30, 1869.

5546 WEBSTER, Joseph Philbrick. Nora MacRae. Song. Words by Luke Collin. Filed May 15, 1869.

5547 VON ROCHOW, Alfred. Queen of hearts. Or, Playing for a wife. Ballad, words by Miss Lizzie H. Garrison. Filed Apr. 19, 1869.

5548 ROOT, Frederic W. Bells of Sabbath morning; pastoral sketch for piano. Filed Apr. 19, 1869.

5549 PHELPS, E. B. Studio polka. "To my artist friend, John Phillips, Esq." Filed May 3, 1869.

5550-5551

5552 HOFFMAN, Edward. O, take me to thy heart again. Transcription [from Balfe]. Filed Apr. 23, 1869.

5553 KNAEBEL, S. The musical garland; a collection of choice pieces for the piano. [Cf also PNs 5573-74]

5554 [5] Smith schottische. Filed May 12, 1869.

5555 [6] Welcome schottische. Filed May 12, 1869.

5556 [8] Social waltz. Filed May 7, 1869.

5557 [7] Banquet polka. Filed May 20, 1869.

5558 [3] Young American galopade. Caption title: "Young America" galop. Filed May 14, 1869.

5559 [4] Monticello waltz. Filed May 12, 1869.

5560

5561 MURRAY, James R. Treasures of the past. A new S&Ch. Filed May 28, 1869.

5562 HOWARD, Frank. My heart is far over the sea. S&Ch. Filed May 20, 1869.

5563 HOWARD, Frank. Little shoes and stockings. S&Ch. Filed May 27, 1869.

5564 ROOT, George F. Somewhere! ... Assisted in the preparation of the words by Mrs. M. B. C. Slade. "To the readers of 'Gates ajar.'" Filed Apr. 30, 1869.

5565 WEBSTER, Joseph Philbrick. Little dimpled hands; S&Ch. Words by Miss Sara Maria Wells. Filed June 1, 1869.

5566

5567 HOWARD, Frank. Shadows on the stream. S&Ch. Filed May 7, 1869.

5568 HOWARD, Frank. Childhood songs. S&Ch. "To E. T. Root, Esq." Filed May 15, 1869.

5569 HOWARD, Frank. Come home, mother. A song for the times. Filed May 5, 1869.

5570 SEAVERNS, C. L. O, summer moon! Song. Words by Robert Buchanan. c1869.

5571 WEBSTER, Joseph Philbrick. Darling Ella; S&Ch. Words by Luke Collin. Filed May 20, 1869.

5572 HOWARD, Frank. Among the angels. (Answer to "Little barefoot.") S&Ch. Filed May 22, 1869.

5573 KNAEBEL, S. Sally Port polka. (His The musical garland ... [2]) Filed May 15, 1869.

5574 KNAEBEL, S. Sleigh bells mazurka. (His The musical garland ... [1]) Filed May 15, 1869.

5575 CLARK, James G. The unseen city. Sacred quartette. Poetry by Emma Tuttle. Composed & arranged by James G. Clark. Filed June 1, 1869.

5576 HACKELTON, M. W. Willie's coming home. Song. Words and music by M. W. Hackelton. Filed May 21, 1869.

5577 HOWARD, Frank. Young man of the period. (His 12 new songs. 1) Filed May 21, 1869.

5578 CLARK, James G. The promised land tomorrow; trio. Poetry by Gerald Massey. "To Theodore Tilton & Frederick Douglass." Filed May 14, 1869.

5579

5580 HOWARD, Frank. I met her at the mat-inee. Words and music by Frank Howard. c1868 by H. T. Merrill. PN from Brainard ed.

5581 MERRILL, H. T. The little angel: a sequel to Little barefoot. S&Ch. Filed by H. T. Merrill on Oct. 7, 1868. PN from Brainard renewal copy.

5582 MERRILL, H. T. The old hickory cane. S&Ch. Filed by H. T. Merrill on Oct. 7, 1868. PN from Brainard renewal copy.

5583

5584 MERRILL, H. T. My mother's song. A very beautiful S&Ch. Filed by H. T. Merrill on Mar. 16, 1868. PN from Brainard renewal copy.

5585 LOCKWOOD, C. T. Shun the broad road. Words by H. M. L. Song ... Arr. for guitar by W. L. Hayden. (The guitar. (Vocal) 71) c1868 [for series?] Filed June 11, 1869.

5586 HOWARD, Frank. Little bother. (His 12 new songs. 3) Filed June 4, 1869.

5587 HOWARD, Frank. Profit and loss. (His Popular songs) c1868 by H. T. Merrill. Filed June 5, 1869, by R&C.

5588 HOWARD, Frank. Maggie Blair. (His 12 new songs. 7) c1869.

5589 HOWARD, Frank. Young girl of the period. (His 12 new songs. 2) Filed May 25, 1869.

5590 HOWARD, Frank. Why don't he write. (His 12 new songs. 8) Filed May 25, 1869.

5591 HOWARD, Frank. Keep straight ahead. (His 12 new songs. 4) Filed May 28, 1869.

5592

5593 HOWARD, Frank. He'll soon propose. (His 12 new songs. 5) Filed May 28, 1869.

5594 HOWARD, Frank. Minnie Munroe. (His Popular songs) c1868 by H. T. Merrill. Filed June 10, 1869, by R&C.

5595 BISHOP, Thomas Brigham. Some day when I am far away. A new and exquisite song, as sung by Mr. Geo. Grey. Filed June 26, 1869.

5596 BISHOP, Thomas Brigham. Gentle naiad. A new song. Filed May 27, 1869.

5597 HOWARD, Frank. Cruel, cruel men. (His 12 new songs. 6) Filed June 1, 1869.

5598 SANDERSON, W. H. Up in a balloon. (Songs and ballads from over the sea. [8]) c1869.

5599 HOWARD, Frank. Millie Clair. (His Popular songs) c1868 by H. T. Merrill. Filed June 4, 1869, by R&C.

5600 HOWARD, Frank. My landlady's pretty little daughter. (His 12 new songs. 10) Filed June 2, 1869.

5601 WEBSTER, Joseph Philbrick. Under the beautiful stars. A beautiful duett for soprano & alto. Words by Luke Collin. Filed June 24, 1869.

5602 HOWARD, Frank. The time for love. (His Popular songs) c1868 by H. T. Merrill. Filed June 4, 1869, by R&C.

5603 HOWARD, Frank. I know a lovely maiden. (His 12 new songs. 11) Filed June 4, 1869.

5604-5606

5607 MURRAY, James R. The land of the loving. S&Ch. Filed June 10, 1869.

5608 HOWARD, Frank. My native hills. S&Ch. Filed June 10, 1869.

5609 HOWARD, Frank. O'Googerty's wedding. Irish song & dance as sung by Wm. H. Crane, Comedian. Filed June 19, 1869.

5610 HOWARD, Frank. Where are the dear friends of childhood? c1868 by H. T. Merrill. Filed by R&C, June 10, 1869. No ed. with Merrill imprint has been found.

5611

5612 HOWARD, Frank. There's always a welcome for thee. (His Popular songs) c1868 by H. T. Merrill. Filed June 11, 1869, by R&C.

5613

5614 DELOS. If you love me, say so! S&Ch. Filed June 28, 1869.

117

5615 HOWARD, Frank. I feel I'm growing old, dear wife. (His 12 new songs. 12) Filed June 12, 1869.

5616 HACKELTON, M. W. The golden morn. S&Ch. Words & music by M. W. Hackelton. Filed Nov. 3, 1869. PN probably error for 5716.

5616 DELOS. Oh! sing with the birds. Words & music by Delos. (His Prairie melodies; 12 new songs and choruses. 1) Filed June 29, 1869.

5617 WEBSTER, Joseph Philbrick. Come to me, dearest! S&Ch. Words by Edwin Bruce. Filed June 29, 1869.

5618 BLISS, Philip Paul. The tin wedding. S&Ch. Words & music by P. P. Bliss. Filed July 2, 1869.

5619 WEBSTER, Joseph Philbrick. The Union Pacific; S&Ch. Words by E. B. Dewing. "To the directors of the U.P.R.R." Filed June 24, 1869.

5620 HEYER, Charles. Saviour when in dust, to Thee. (His Sacred music. Quartettes [8]) Filed July 3, 1869.

5621

5622 DELOS. I'm happy tonight. (His Prairie melodies; 12 new S&Ch. 4) Filed July 3, 1869.

5623 DELOS. Some people think only of money. Ballad. (His Prairie melodies; 12 new S&Ch. 3) Filed July 3, 1869.

5624 HACKLETON, M. W. Ever in dreams, song. Filed July 28, 1869.

5625 LOCKWOOD, C. T. Starry waves. S&Ch. Filed July 20, 1869.

5626 VON ROCHOW, Alfred. Jerome Jenkins. Comic song as sung and performed by Billy Emerson. Filed July 30, 1869.

5627 BERNARD, John S. Ixion medley, dedicated to the city of brotherly love by the Chicago exiles. Sung with great success at Crosby's Opera House, Chicago, by Mrs. J. A. Oates. Arrangement of music by John S. Bernard. Filed June 24, 1869.

5628 HACKELTON, M. W. Old folk's love song. S&Ch. Filed Aug. 17, 1869.

5629-5633

5634 WEBSTER, J. P. When I am gone. Duett. Filed July 28, 1869.

5635 WEBSTER, J. P. The sweet times were the old. S&Ch. Filed July 30, 1869.

5636 KIMBALL, Horace E. Would I? Comic ballad. Filed July 28, 1869.

5637 LOCKWOOD, C. T. Call me when breakfast is ready! Song. Filed July 20, 1869.

5638 HOWARD, Frank. I'll tell you why. Song. Answer to "Wont you tell me why, Robin." Filed July 31, 1869.

5639 MAYO, Oscar. The Phi gamma delta march. For the Delta deuteron chapter of the North-Western university. Filed July 17, 1869.

5640 KIMBALL, Horace E. I've got a baby. S&Ch. Filed July 10, 1869.

5641 KUSCHBERT, Emanuel. Josephine waltz. Filed Dec. 9, 1867, by Ch. Bach & Co.; filed July 3, 1869, by R&C.

5642 KUSCHBERT, Emanuel. Hans and Hanne polka. Filed Dec. 9, 1867, by Ch. Bach & E. Kuschbert; filed July 3, 1869, by R&C.

5643

5644 BACH, Charles H. Home greeting. (Gruss au [!] die Heimath.) Song. Filed Dec. 9, 1867, by Ch. Bach & Co.; deposit copy has "Gruss an die Heimath"; filed July 6, 1869, by R&C, using same plates but "an" has been changed to "au."

5645-5648

5649 MORRISON, John. When the roses bud and blossom. S&Ch. Filed Aug. 18, 1869.

5650 HARRISON, James. La Grenadille, passion flower, waltzes ... op. 25. Chicago, Published by the author; filed by J. Harrison July 23, 1869.

5651

5652 WEBSTER, J. P. "What then!" S&Ch. Filed Aug. 18, 1869.

5653 DELOS. When we've nothing else to do. (His Prairie melodies; 12 new S&Ch. [5]) Filed Aug. 12, 1869.

5654

5655 ROTHGERBER, Leonora. My mother's farewell kiss. [S&Ch.] Filed Aug. 10, 1869.

5656-5659

5660 WEBSTER, J. P. There's a darling girl I know. "To all the darling girls, everywhere." Filed Aug. 28, 1869.

5661 EDWARDS, M. E. Little Elma's waltz. A beautiful piece for young pianists. Filed Aug. 5, 1869.

5662 VAAS, A. J. Prairie queen quadrilles. c1869. Not filed.

5663 LOCKWOOD, C. T. Rosy hours. [Song] Filed Aug. 26, 1869.

5664 HOWARD, Frank. Meet me just at twilight. (His 12 new songs. 9) c1869. PN from Brainard ed.

5665
5666 MURRAY, James R. Sweets to the sweetest. Song or S&Ch. Filed Aug. 28, 1869.
5667 HOWARD, Frank. Little barefoot. Arr. for guitar by Charles Harris. (12 choice songs for the guitar. 1) Filed Sept. 2, 1869.
5668 WEBSTER, J. P. Some sweet day. Filed Aug. 28, 1869.
5669 LOCKWOOD, C. T. Gathering home. Song. Arr. for guitar by W. L. Hayden. (12 choice songs for the guitar. 2) Filed Sept. 8, 1869.
5670 ROOT, George F. Somewhere! Song. Arr. for guitar by W. L. Hayden. (12 choice songs for the guitar. 3) Filed Sept. 8, 1869.
5671 MURRAY, James R. What shall I ask for thee. Song. Arr. for guitar by W. L. Hayden. (12 choice songs for the guitar. 4) Filed Sept. 2, 1869.
5672 HOWARD, Frank. Songs that we never forget. Song. Arr. for guitar by W. L. Hayden. (12 choice songs for the guitar. 5) Filed Sept. 8, 1869.
5673 WEBSTER, J. P. The past we can never recall, Jamie. Response to "When you & I were young, Maggie." Song. Arr. for guitar by W. L. Hayden. (12 choice songs for the guitar. 6) Filed Sept. 8, 1869.
5674 EDWARDS, M. E. Drifting leaflets. Reverie for the piano. Filed Sept. 6, 1869.
5675 GORHAM, A. Templeton. Sweet Ethelinda. S&Ch. Filed Aug. 28, 1869.
5676 GORHAM, A. Templeton. Where the firelight gleams at home. S&Ch. Filed Sept. 6, 1869.
5677 GORHAM, A. Templeton. Summer bloom waltz. Filed Aug. 17, 1869.
5678 BLISS, P. P. Lora Vale. Song. Arr. for guitar by Charles Harris. (12 choice songs for the guitar. 7) Filed Sept. 2, 1869.
5679 DELOS. Such is fashion. (His Prairie melodies; 12 new S&Ch. 6) Filed Sept. 20, 1869.
5680 WEBSTER, J. P. Call me darling, darling call me. S&Ch. Filed Sept. 6, 1869.
5681 VAAS, A. J. Ladies' favorite polka. From the operetta of Seven girls and no man. Arr. for piano by A. J. Vaas. Filed Sept. 20, 1869.
5682 WEBSTER, J. P. In dreams of my childhood; or, Memories' graves. S&Ch. Filed Sept. 21, 1869.
5683 VAAS, A. J. Concert polka mazurka. Filed Sept. 14, 1869.

Root & Cady's Juvenile Series. First pieces. Carefully marked and fingered. Ed. by Jules Benedict.

5684 No. 1. Le chant du depart. French national air. Filed Oct. 4, 1869.
5685 No. 2. DONIZETTI, Gaetano. Air from Favorita. Filed Oct. 4, 1869.
5686 No. 3. CHOPIN, F. F. Funeral march. Filed Oct. 2, 1869.
5687 No. 4. HEROLD, L. J. F. Air from Le pré aux clercs. Filed Sept. 30, 1869.
5688 No. 5. ROSSINI, G. A. The tyrolienne from William Tell. Filed Oct. 4, 1869.
5689 No. 6. Bohemian air. Filed Oct. 4, 1869.
5690 No. 7. WEBER, K. M. von. Invitation to the waltz. Filed Sept. 30, 1869.
5691 No. 8. DONIZETTI, Gaetano. The serenade from Don Pasquale. Filed Oct. 6, 1869.
5692 JACKSON, Mrs. Libbie Higgins. My barefoot boy. S&Ch. (Her Songs of affection. No. 5; Nos. 1-4 had been published for the composer by De Motte Bros.) Published for author by R&C. Filed Sept. 20, 1869, by C. P. Jackson.
5693 BLISS, P. P. He's gone! quartette. "To the memory of Wm. B. Bradbury." Filed Sept. 30, 1869.
5694
5695 BLISS, P. P. John Chinaman. S&Ch. Filed Oct. 22, 1869. [Song welcoming Chinese to the U.S.]
5696 JACKSON, Mrs. Libbie Higgins. Thy spirit will ever be near. Dedicated to my much loved brother, A. J. Higgins, M. D., lately deceased. (Her Songs of affection. 6) Published for the author by R&C. Filed Oct. 14, 1869, by C. P. Jackson.
5697
5698 BROWN, Frank E. Sadly to-night I am dreaming. Song for alto or baritone. Filed Oct. 30, 1869.
5699 BLISS, P. P. Willie's wooing. S&Ch. Filed Oct. 13, 1869.

Musical Bon-Bons. Five little pieces arr. for very little fingers, by H. E. Kimball. Op. 6.

5700  No. 1?
5700  No. 2. ZAULIG, Fred W. Flowers of beauty schottische. Filed Oct. 16, 1869.
5702  No. 3. BISHOP, T. B. Love among the roses. Filed Oct. 19, 1869?
5703  No. 4. BUCKLEY. Leaf by leaf the roses fall. c1869. Not registered.
5704  No. 5. OESTEN, Theodor. Love in May. c1869. Not registered.
5705  LOCKWOOD, C. T. We'll have to mortgage the farm. Filed Oct. 16, 1869.
5706  MURRAY, James R. The sweetness of thy smile. S&Ch. Filed Nov. 3, 1869.

HOFFMAN, Edward. Bridal flowers for the piano.

5707  No. 1. Camelia (polka) c1869. Not filed.
5708  No. 2. Orange blossom (mazurka). c1869. Not filed.
5709  No. 3. Fuchsia (galop) Filed Nov. 5, 1869.
5710  No. 4. Rose waltz. Filed Nov. 8, 1869.
5711  REYNOLDS, John. Sweet Molly Matilda Jane. Song and refrain. S&Ch. Filed Nov. 3, 1869.
5712  DELOS. Under the arbor. (His Prairie melodies; 12 new S&Ch. 7) Filed Nov. 4, 1869.
5713  HOWARD, Frank. Only a part, S&Ch. Filed Oct. 30, 1869.
5714  STAAB, Louis. Belles of Chicago, polka brillante. Filed Oct. 16, 1869.
5715  STAAB, Louis. Flower of the West. Mazurka elegante. Filed Oct. 26, 1869.
5716  Cf HACKELTON, M. W., PN 5616
5717  HOWARD, Frank. Girls, don't fool with cupid. Ballad. Filed Oct. 30, 1869.
5718  BUTTERFIELD, James A. Jamie's awa'. Scotch ballad. Filed Nov. 4, 1869.
5719  ROSS, L. L. Jennie's gone home; or, The angels took Jennie away. S&Ch. Filed Oct. 30, 1869.
5720  PENFIELD, Smith N. Souvenir de Paris. Rondino pour le piano. Op. 11. Filed Nov. 11, 1869.
5721  PENFIELD, Smith N. Invitation to the galop. For the piano. Filed Nov. 16, 1869.
5722-5723  GRUND, F. W. Grund's etudes. Op. 24. With notes by Robert Schumann. Edited by S. N. Penfield. Filed Jan. 19, 1870.
5724-5726
5727  WORK, Henry C. No letters from home! S&Ch. Filed Nov. 17, 1869.
5728  LEFOY. Idol of my heart. Ballad. Words from an unpublished MS. of Lord Byron. Filed Nov. 9, 1869.
5729
5730  LOCKWOOD, C. T. Bessie's trust. S&Ch. Filed Nov. 24, 1869.

[PRATT, S. G.] 2 nocturnes, composed by V. B. Aubert.

5731  The midnight stars, op. 100. Filed Nov. 27, 1869.
5732  The midnight zephyrs, op. 101. Filed Dec. 2, 1869.
5733  BLISS, P. P. For you! duet. Filed Dec. 2, 1869.
5734  ZAULIG, Fred W. Flowers of beauty schottische. Arr. for four hands by Horace E. Kimball. Filed Dec. 2, 1869.
5735
5736  WEBSTER, J. P. Our own. Filed Dec. 4, 1869.
5737-5738
5739  CHING FOO. Tin-ni-min-ni-winkum-ka, or the Chinaman's farewell. S&Ch. Filed Nov. 26, 1869.
5740  WEBSTER, J. P. Hope on the unseen shore. c1869. Not filed.

PENFIELD, Smith N. A poem of life. Four characteristic pieces in the form of a sonata, for the piano. Op. 10.

5741  No. 1. Parnassus. Allegro moderato. Filed Feb. 18, 1870.
5742  No. 2. The vale of romance. Adagio. Filed Feb. 19, 1870.
5743  No. 3. The cascade of pleasure. Scherzo and trio. Filed Feb. 19, 1870.
5744  No. 4. The stream of time. Rondo brillante. Filed Feb. 19, 1870.
5745  WORK, Henry C. The buckskin bag of gold. c1869. Not filed.
5746  HARRISON, James. Te Deum. (We praise Thee, O God) [Op. 28] (Harrison's Church Music. No. 2) Filed Dec. 9, 1869.
5747  MURRAY, James R. Mother's waiting for her children. S&Ch. Filed Dec. 9, 1869.
5748  DEANE, Lyman W. Fisherman, fisherman, over the sea. Song. Filed Dec. 28, 1869.
5749  WOODMAN, J. C. The antique ring. Song. c1869. Filed Jan. 5, 1870.
5750  KING, Frank H. The happy daughters. S&Ch. Filed Dec. 31, 1869.

5751 DELOS. The pride of the dell. (His Prairie melodies; 12 new S&Ch. 8) c1869. Filed Jan. 3, 1870.

5752

5753 ROWLEY, C. E. Zimenia. S&Ch. c1869. Filed Jan. 5, 1870.

5754 STAAB, Louis. Love among the roses, caprice de concert. Filed Jan. 19, 1870.

5755 ROOT, George F. Marching home! Song for tenor voice. c1869. Filed Jan. 4, 1870.

5756

5757 LEHMAN, Albert. Dew pearls waltz. Op. 14. Filed Jan. 22, 1870.

5758 ROOT, George F. Poverty flat. Or, "Her letter." Words selected and arr. from a poem in the "Overland monthly" [by Bret Harte]. Filed Jan. 11, 1870.

5759 BLISS, P. P. What shall the harvest be. S&Ch. Filed Feb. 7, 1870.

5760 WEBSTER, J. P. The harp of Katie Bell. S&Ch. Filed Feb. 7, 1870.

5761

5762 GOLDBECK, Robert. Adoration polka. For piano. Filed Feb. 12, 1870.

5763 BAKER, W. C. Would you could meet me to-night. Serenade. S&Ch. As sung by the Tremaine brothers and Pierson. Filed Jan. 28, 1870.

5764 HARTWELL, Mrs. S. Sunlight to the soul. S&Ch. Published by R&C for the author. Filed Jan. 28, 1870, by the author.

5765 WEBSTER, J. P. She shines in honor like a star. S&Ch. Filed Feb. 25, 1870.

5766

5767 HOWARD, Frank. The girl with the auburn tress! Song & dance. As sung by Cooper & Fields of Skiff & Wheeler's minstrels. Filed Feb. 25, 1870.

5768 GOERDELER, R. ·umop əpısdn Galop. Op. 85. Filed Feb. 23, 1870.

5769 PRATT, S. G. Gone! Impromptu. Filed Feb. 22, 1870.

5770

5771 WEBSTER, J. P. Darling blue eyed Mell. S&Ch. Filed Mar. 3, 1870.

5772 GOLDBECK, Robert. Traumgewebe. (Dream visions) Nocturne pour piano. Filed Mar. 9, 1870.

5773 MAYO, Oscar A. Fairy bridal polka. Composed for piano. Filed Mar. 21, 1870.

5774 BLISS, P. P. Remembered. S&Ch. Subject from Bonar. Filed Mar. 3, 1870.

5775 WORK, Henry C. Crossing the grand Sierras. "Continental railroad chorus." Filed Mar. 11, 1870.

5776 Chase among the roses. Music by Irma. Filed Mar. 15, 1870.

5777 HOWARD, Frank. "It." S&Ch. Filed Mar. 12, 1870.

5778

5779 CADY, C. M. Fond heart, oh, think of me. A parting song & duett. Filed Mar. 5, 1870.

5780 ROOT, E. T. Those wildering eyes of thine! Filed Mar. 14, 1870.

5781 BISHOP, T. Brigham. Love among the roses. Arr. for guitar by Charles Harris. (12 choice songs for the guitar. 8) Filed Apr. 4, 1870.

5782 HACKELTON, M. W. Come where the south wind wanders. Song. Filed Apr. 4, 1870.

5783

5784 STAAB, Louis. Damenwahl. (Ladies' choice) polka. Filed Mar. 31, 1870.

5785 VAAS, A. J. Vaas' own trois temps polka mazurka. Filed Mar. 15, 1870.

5786 LEE, Alfred. Par excellence, the idol of the day [a Lingard song]. (Songs and ballads from over the sea. 10) Ncc.

5787 LOCKWOOD, C. T. Give the boy a chance. S&Ch. Filed Mar. 26, 1870.

5788 MÜLLER, Edward. Sodowa march. Published by R&C for the author. Filed Mar. 26, 1870, by the author.

5789 LOCKWOOD, C. T. Father will settle the bill. Filed Apr. 2, 1870.

5790 HOWARD, Frank. When the clover was in bloom. Filed Apr. 4, 1870.

5791 WEBSTER, J. P. How sweetly she's sleeping, a duet. Filed Apr. 4, 1870.

5792 HOWARD, Frank. Making love by moonlight. S&Ch. Filed Apr. 6, 1870.

5793 [BROWN, George W.] Allie. A beautiful S&Ch. ... by George W. Persley. Filed Apr. 18, 1870.

5794 VAAS, A. J. St. Paul waltz. Arr. for the guitar by Charles Harris. (The guitar. Instrumental. 16) c1868 [for series] Filed Apr. 9, 1870.

5795 HOWARD, Frank. Down brakes. S&Ch. Filed Apr. 9, 1870.

5796 HACKELTON, M. W. At the beautiful gate. S&Ch. Filed Apr. 7, 1870.

5797-5799
5800 WEBSTER, J. B. Beautiful angels. S&Ch. "To my little household angels, Lizzie, Kate and Jennie." Filed Apr. 9, 1870.
5801 WEBSTER, J. P. Kiss me good night. Song. Filed Apr. 9, 1870.
5802 DELOS. Never borrow trouble. (His Prairie melodies; 12 new S&Ch. 9) c1869 [for series] Filed Apr. 18, 1870.
5803 MURRAY, James R. There's sunshine after rain. S&Ch. Filed Apr. 18, 1870. [Deposit copies have no PN.]
5804 WEBSTER, J. P. Medora. S&Ch. Filed Apr. 23, 1870.
5805 WEBSTER, J. P. Lizzie, the lass of the brown wavy hair. Filed May 14, 1870.
5806 MAYER, Henry. La belle brunette. Valse. Filed Apr. 30, 1870.
5807 GIMBEL, Charles, Jr. Love's flirtation. Polka brillante. Filed Apr. 28, 1870.
5808 WEBSTER, J. P. Open the gates. S&Ch. Filed Apr. 18, 1870.
5809
5810 SUTTON, P. M. A terrible war with nobody hurt. A song for the times. Accompaniments by Miss Lulu Upson. Filed May 12, 1870.
5811 STEVENS, George. Εκατών (Hecaton) waltzes ... dedicated to the Hecaton Club. Filed Apr. 22, 1870. [Issued later by S. Brainard's sons as The Pythian waltzes, c1875.]
5812 HOWARD, Frank. If you'll promise not to tell. S&Ch. Filed May 4, 1870.
5813-5837
5838 BUCK, Dudley, Jr. Easter morning. Cantata for solo voices and chorus [with piano accompaniment] op. 21. c1865 by Henry Tolman & Co., original PN 5099. Note on p2: The full orchestral parts to this work may be obtained on application to the publisher. Also, an arrangement of the same, by the author, for nine instruments.
5839-5855
MAYER, Henry. Soir et matin. (Evening and morning.) Deux fantaisies mignonnes sur des themes originaux pour le piano.
5856 Soir (Evening). Filed May 14, 1870.
5857 Matin (Morning). Filed May 23, 1870.
5858 MAYER, Henry. La joyeuse polka. Filed May 14, 1870.
5859 MURRAY, James R. Heart to heart and soul to soul. Song. Filed Apr. 30, 1870.
5860 WEBSTER, J. P. I don't sing 'cause I can't. Song. Filed May 23, 1870.
5861 CADY, C. M. All in the golden prime of May. Filed Apr. 9, 1870, and May 9, 1870. Issued also in octavo ed.; no PN.
5862 MURRAY, James R. A tear for the comrade that's gone. Quartet & Chorus for Decoration Day. Filed Apr. 28, 1870.
5863 ROOT, E. T. Precious to thee. Filed May 9, 1870.
5864 BOOTT, F. How to put the question. Song. Filed May 21, 1870.
5865 MAYER, Henry. Emita redowa. Filed June 3, 1870.
5866
5867 DEAN, Frederick. My love and I. Song. Filed May 21, 1870.
5868 WEBSTER, J. P. The days that are no more. Quartet. Filed May 21, 1870.
5869 MULLER, Edward. Marie quadrilles. Published by R&C for the author. Filed May 23, 1870, by the author.
5870 SULLIVAN, Sir Arthus Seymour. O hush thee, my babie. Quartet. Words by Sir Walter Scott. Ncc.
5871 DEAN, Frederick. When thou'rt lonely think of me. Ballad. Filed May 31, 1870.
5872 DEAN, Frederick. Emmeline. Mazurka de salon. Filed June 8, 1870.
5873 GOERDELER, R. Pray for me! Pensee sentimental. Filed May 31, 1870.
5874 HAVENS, A. W. The land that is fairer than day. S&Ch. Answer to "The sweet by and by." Filed May 21, 1870.
5875 STILLMAN, J. M. Beautiful starlight. Quartet. Filed June 8, 1870.
5876 BLISS, P. P. Brave battery boys, in honor of Bishop, Seborn, Ferris ... [and others]. Written for and sung at the dedication of the monument erected at Rose Hill Cemetery by the Bridges Battery Association, May 30th, 1870. Filed May 21, 1870.
5877 HARRIS, Charles. Imitation of the banjo. [For guitar.] Filed June 8, 1870.
5878 VON ROCHOW, Alfred. Croquet, ballad. Filed June 9, 1870.
5879 WEBSTER, J. P. Johnny is a farmer boy. S&Ch. Filed June 15, 1870.

5880 DEAN, Frederick. Forget me not. Duet for treble voices. Filed June 15, 1870.

5881 GOERDELER, R. The one horse galop. [Op. 98.] Filed June 22, 1870.

5882 PAPE, Willie. Recollections of a music box. Morceau caractéristique pour le piano. Filed June 24, 1870.

5883 PAPE, Willie. Irish diamonds. A fantasie on the popular melodies, "Believe me if all those endearing young charms" and "Garry Owen." Composed by Willie Pape, pianist to the Royal family of England. Filed June 25, 1870.

5884 PAPE, Willie. Highland gems for the piano forte; containing "Ye banks and braes o' bonnie Doon" and "Bonnie Dundee." Filed June 25, 1870.

5885 GOLDBECK, Robert. Dreams of heaven. Duett. (D'apres une mélodie de Schubert) (His Three duetts. No. 1) Filed July 20, 1870.

5886 GOLDBECK, Robert. Willow song [for soprano and tenor] (His Three duetts. No. 2) Filed July 20, 1870.

5887
5888 LOCKWOOD, C. T. "Look me in the eye Johnny." Filed June 18, 1870.

5889 GOLDBECK, Robert. Where'er the heart to true heart beats. Duett for soprano and alto. From Goldbeck's cantata, The pioneer. (His Three duetts. No. 3) Filed July 20, 1870.

5890 HOWARD, Frank. Underfoot. S&Ch. Filed June 25, 1870.

5891 HARRISON, James. Eleanore waltzes. Filed July 20, 1870.

5892 P., E. S. The leaves around me falling. Tenor solo and quartet. Arr. from Luttwitz, by E. S. P. Filed June 24, 1870.

5893 HOWARD, Frank. The fortune daisy, a beautiful ballad. Filed July 20, 1870.

5894
GOLDBECK, Robert. Eight songs.
5895 No. 1. A love song. Tenor or soprano. Filed July 20, 1870.
5896 No. 2. Soprano song from Goldbeck's cantata, The pioneer. Words by H. C. Watson. Filed July 25, 1870.
5897 No. 3. The day is cold. Words by Longfellow. Filed July 27, 1870.
5898 No. 4. O moonlight deep and tender. Words by James R. Lowell. Filed July 25, 1870.
5899 No. 5. Break, break, break. Baritone or mezzo soprano. Words by Tennyson. Filed July 20, 1870.
5900 [No. 6. Torrent song. Not filed.]
5901 No. 7. The nun. Soprano or tenor. Filed July 20, 1870.
5902 [No. 8. Willow song. Not filed.]

5903 GIMBEL, Charles, Jr. Sans souci, marche triumphal. Filed July 25, 1870.

5904
THOMAS, Carrie. Two sacred songs. Published by R&C for the author. Filed July 7, 1870, by the author.
5905 No. 1. My faith looks up to Thee.
5906 No. 2. I heard the voice of Jesus say.

5907 GOERDELER, R. Lily queen waltz, op. 99. Filed July 20, 1870.

HOFFMAN, Edward. The four sisters for piano. [Two copies of each number are on file at LC. Apparently, they were sent in for registration, but the recording clerk failed to enter two of them.]
5908 No. 1. Adelina (polka). c1870. Not filed.
5909 No. 2. Isabella (waltz). Filed Aug. 1, 1870.
5910 No. 3. Carlotta (galop). c1870. Not filed.
5911 No. 4. Henrietta (mazurka). Filed July 27, 1870.
5912
5913 MURRAY, James R. The old kitchen floor. S&Ch. Words furnished by D. L. Moody, Esq. to whom the song is respectfully inscribed. Filed July 25, 1870.

5914
5915 HOFFMAN, Edward. Grand Fantasia, Whippoorwill, composed by Edward Hoffman and played by him with even more success than his world wide popular Fantasia, The mocking bird. Filed Oct. 6, 1869, by the composer in the Dist. Court for southern New York. PN from Brainard renewal copy.

5916 HARRISON, James. Dear little barefeet, I've counted your toes! Words from "The little corporal." Filed July 25, 1870.

5917 MARTIN, S. Wesley. Annie Snow. S&Ch. Filed Aug. 9, 1870.

5918 MARTIN, S. Wesley. Daughter of the Isles. S&Ch. Filed Aug. 8, 1870.

5919
5920 GOLDBECK, Robert. Where'er the heart to true heart beats. Popular song. "Also published as a duet." Cf PN 5889. Filed Aug. 8, 1870.
5921 WEBSTER, J. P. O Father take my hand. Sacred S&Ch. Filed Aug. 1, 1870.
5922
5923 WEBSTER, J. P. Together. Song. Filed Aug. 12, 1870.
5924
5925 HOWARD, Frank. It's true, 'twas in the papers. S&Ch. Filed Aug. 1, 1870.
5926 MURRAY, James R. I love to think of thee. Filed Aug. 9, 1870.
5927
5928 WEBSTER, J. P. Ervie Morie. S&Ch. Filed Aug. 12, 1870.
5929 GORHAM, A. Templeton. Papa, help me across. S&Ch. Filed Aug. 12, 1870.
5930
5931 WEBSTER, J. P. Bonnie Annie Lee; or, I'm hame again. S&Ch. Filed Aug. 15, 1870.
5932 WEBSTER, J. P. Good luck. S&Ch. Filed Aug. 15, 1870.
5933 SCHLEIFFARTH, George. Riverside polka, as performed by the Great Western light guard band. Arr. for orch. by A. J. Vaas. Filed Aug. 1, 1870.
5934 BLACKMER, E. T. Wait, my little one, wait. S&Ch. Filed Aug. 26, 1870.
5935 NAYLOR, Fred B. O'er my little brother's grave. As sung by the Duprez and Benedict's minstrels. Filed Aug. 26, 1870.
5936
5937 NAYLOR, Fred B. Angel Nettie Bane. As sung by Duprez & Benedict's minstrels. Filed Aug. 15, 1870.
5938 SMITH, John. Base ball. S&Ch. "To the Root & Cady B. B. C." Filed Aug. 1, 1870.
5939 Trust me Cathleen. S&Ch. Words by Mrs. M. A. Kidder. Music by Max. Filed Aug. 26, 1870.
5940 WEBSTER, J. P. Marie. Song. Filed Aug. 15, 1870.
5941 GORHAM, A. Templeton. Yes, dearest, I'll love thee. S&Ch. Filed Aug. 15, 1870.
5942 NAYLOR, Fred B. Where little baby rests. S&Ch. Filed Aug. 26, 1870.

5943 STAAB, Louis. Promesse. Reverie pour le piano. Filed Sept. 7, 1870.
5944 [ROOT, George F.] The banner of the fatherland. S&Ch. By G. Friedrich Wurzel. "To the friends of Prussia." Filed Aug. 4, 1870.
5945 HAVENS, A. W. Fatherless. S&Ch. Filed Aug. 15, 1870.
5946-5947
5948 PEASE, Alfred H. 'Tis lone on the waters. Barcarolle. Words by Mrs. Hemans. Filed Aug. 26, 1870.
5949 HOWARD, Frank. The bonnie bright eyes of somebody. S&Ch. Filed Aug. 26, 1870.
5950
5951 MURRAY, James R. Prussia, gird thy sons for battle! S&Ch. Words by C. Ernst Fahnestock. German translation by C. H. Pfeiffer. Filed Sept. 1, 1870.
5952 [LOCKWOOD, C. T. Father will settle the bill. Arr. for guitar by Charles Harris. (12 choice songs for the guitar. 9) c1869 [for series] Filed Sept. 1, 1870.
5953 HOWARD, Frank. There! I told you so. S&Ch. Filed Sept. 7, 1870.
5954 WEBSTER, J. P. I am weary and faint in the battle of life! S&Ch. Filed Sept. 23, 1870.
5955-5956
5957 PAPE, Willie. No. 2. Irish diamonds. For the pianoforte. "The harp that once thro' Tara's halls" & "Rory O'More." Op. 32. Filed Sept. 21, 1870.
5958 LEIDNER, John. Piano forte march of the 23rd Regiment, U. S. Infantry. Composed by John Leidner, chief musician, 23rd Infantry. Published for the author by R&C. Filed Sept. 30, 1870.
5959
5960 AMSDEN, M. Why doesn't he speak? Ballade. Filed Sept. 16, 1870.
5961 DELOS. Trumps, song. Filed Sept. 16, 1870.
5962 HOWARD, Frank. Sing to me dear sister. S&Ch as sung by J. J. Kelly, Esq. Filed Sept. 16, 1870.
5963 WEBSTER, J. P. Tomorrow! Duet. Filed Sept. 16, 1870.
5964 Viva la Prussia! S&Ch. Filed Sept. 5, 1870.
5965-5967
5968 LEYBACH, Ignace Xavier Joseph. La sonnambula. (His Pianoforte compositions) Ncc. PN from Brainard ed.

| | |
|---|---|
| 5969 | HOWARD, Frank. Patiently waiting. S&Ch. Filed Sept. 23, 1870. |
| 5970 | WEBSTER, J. P. The master's gold year. Quartette & chorus. Filed Sept. 23, 1870. |
| 5971 | HOWARD, Frank. Grandfather darling. S&Ch. Filed Oct. 4, 1870. |
| 5972 | ROOT, Frederic W. Beyond. A descriptive song for contralto or base. Filed Sept. 26, 1870. |
| 5973 | |
| 5974 | MASSETT, Stephen. Then and now. Song. Filed Oct. 4, 1870. |
| 5975-5984 | |
| 5985 | BRAUER, Fr. Melody, Russian air. [His The youth's musical friend. (Musicalischer Jugendfreund.) A collection of melodies arranged progressively for beginners on the piano forte. No. 4] Filed Dec. 2, 1870. [There are 13 nos. in group, only one of which was filed.] |
| 5986-5994 | |
| 5995 | HOWARD, Frank. Little pet schottische. c1870. PN from Brainard renewal copy. |
| 5996 | TOWNER, Charles. The golden dream-land, ballad. Filed Oct. 7, 1870. |
| 5997 | |
| 5998 | GOLDBECK, Robert. The conservatory waltz for the piano. Filed Oct. 8, 1870. |
| 5999 | [BLISS, P. P.] Bonapo, a medley. By Pro Phundo Basso. Filed Oct. 21, 1870. |
| 6000 | |
| 6001 | STRAUSS, Johann. Wein, Weib und Gesang ... For piano, op. 333 (Favorite waltzes by popular authors. 8) Ncc. |
| 6002-6003 | |
| 6004 | HOWARD, Frank. Sit thee down beside me Nannie. S&Ch. Filed Nov. 3, 1870. |
| 6005 | HOWARD, Frank. I'll leave it all to you. S&Ch. c1870. |
| 6006 | ROOT, Frederic W. Deux nocturnes pour le pianoforte "Le soir ramène le silence." No. 1. Filed Oct. 26, 1870. |
| 6007 | |
| 6008 | PAPE, Willie. The brook. Improvisation for the piano upon Dolores' popular song. Filed Nov. 4, 1870. |
| 6009 | |
| 6010 | BAKER, Arthur. Grandmother's cot. S&Ch. Filed Nov. 3, 1870. |
| 6010 | WEBSTER, J. P. Kitty McCree O'Tossell. S&Ch. Filed Nov. 12, 1870. |
| 6011 | BLAMPHIN, C. Little Maggie May. Arr. for the guitar by Charles Harris. (12 choice songs for the guitar. 10) c1869 [for series] Filed Nov. 3, 1870. |
| 6012 | GANZ, Wilhelm. Qui vive! Grand galop concert pour piano. Op. 12. Solo. Ncc. |
| 6013 | |
| 6014 | WEBSTER, J. P. On the banks of the Pearl. S&Ch. Filed Nov. 21, 1870. |
| 6015 | MURRAY, James R. Mother's room. S&Ch. Filed Nov. 12, 1870. |
| 6016 | HOWARD, Frank. Where are you going? S&Ch. Filed Nov. 21, 1870. |
| 6017 | MURRAY, James R. It is better farther on. S&Ch. c1870. PN from Brainard ed. |
| 6018 | ROOT, Frederic W. The opera season, a series of sparkling fantasias, upon the celebrated operas by Offenbach. With fingering and expression carefully marked. Arr. by F. W. Root. |
| 6019 | No. 1. La belle Hélène. Filed Dec. 29, 1870. |
| 6020 | No. 2. Barbe Bleue. Filed Dec. 27, 1870. |
| 6021 | No. 3. La Périchole. Filed Dec. 22, 1870. |
| 6022 | No. 4. Lischen et Fritzchen. Filed Dec. 29, 1870. |
| 6023 | No. 5. Vert-vert. Filed Dec. 29, 1870. |
| 6024 | No. 6. La princesse de Trébizonde. Filed Dec. 24, 1870. |
| 6025 | No. 7. Tromb-al-ca-zar. Filed Dec. 24, 1870. |
| 6026 | No. 8. Robinson Crusoe. Filed Dec. 24, 1870. |
| 6027 | No. 9. La grande duchesse. Filed Dec. 29, 1870. |
| 6028 | No. 10. Orphée aux enfers. Filed Dec. 29, 1870. |
| 6029 | No. 11. Apothecaire et perruquier. (Overture) Filed Dec. 29, 1870. |
| 6030 | No. 12. Geneviève de Brabant. Filed Dec. 29, 1870. |
| 6031 | No. 13. Monsieur et Madame Denis. Filed Dec. 24, 1870. |
| 6032 | No. 14. Le château à Toto. Filed Dec. 22, 1870. |
| 6033 | No. 15. Le pont des soupirs. Filed Dec. 29, 1870. |
| 6034 | No. 16. Les Bavards. Filed Dec. 27, 1870. |

| | | | |
|---|---|---|---|
| 6035 | SULLIVAN, Sir Arthur S. Birds in the night, a lullaby. "Sung by Miss Annie Louise Cary." Ncc. | 6056 | GEARY, Gustavus. Our blue eyed darling. S&Ch. Filed Jan. 27, 1871. |
| 6036 | RINK, Louis H. Excuse me! schottische. Filed Nov. 28, 1870. | 6057 | GEARY, Gustavus. Behind the jessamine. Ballad. Dedicated by permission to Mlle. Christine Nilsson. Filed Jan. 24, 1871. |
| 6037 | HAVENS, A. W. Take me from my little bed. Companion to "Put me in my little bed." Filed Dec. 5, 1870. | 6058 | SISSON, C. T. Sisson's polka. Filed Jan. 17, 1871. |
| 6038 | WEBSTER, J. P. Our turn is coming. S&Ch. Filed Dec. 2, 1870. | 6059 | |
| 6039 | | 6060 | MOZART, Wolfgang Amadeus. The Lord my pasture shall prepare. Duett for soprano and bass from Mozart's "Magic flute" [Bei Männern]. Arr. by Philo A. Otis. (Selections of sacred music for church & home) c1868? |
| 6040 | MURRAY, James R. The latest polka for piano. Filed Dec. 2, 1870. | | |
| 6041 | PALMER, H. R. Have courage my boy to say no. S&Ch. Filed Dec. 10, 1870. | | |
| 6042 | SCULL, S. F. Come again sweet holiday. Song. Filed Jan. 12, 1871. | 6061 | SISSON, C. T. Chicago schottische. Composed for the piano. Filed Jan. 27, 1871. |
| 6043 | PEASE, Alfred H. Absence, as sung by Miss Adelaide Phillips. Song for contralto, baritone or bass. Filed Dec. 24, 1870. | 6062 | WEBSTER, J. P. When I courted Mary Ann. Song. Filed Feb. 6, 1871. |
| | | 6063 | HOWARD, Frank. Little pet schottische. Arr. by F. W. Root. (Hand in hand; a graded collection of duets for the piano forte; prepared by F. W. Root. First pieces) Filed Mar. 1, 1871. |
| 6044 | HOBSON, M., arr. Pulling hard against the stream. (Songs and ballads from over the sea. [11]) Ncc. | | |
| 6045 | | | |
| 6046 | MURRAY, James R. The irresistible schottische for piano. Filed Dec. 22, 1870. | 6064 | WEBSTER, J. P. Oh, say to my spirit, thy bride will I be. S&Ch. Filed Feb. 10, 1871. |
| 6047 | HOWARD, Frank. What is the use of our being unhappy? S&Ch. Filed Jan. 12, 1871. | 6065 | HOWARD, Frank. Our folks schottische. Filed Feb. 10, 1871. |
| 6048 | [BROWN, George W.] Somebody's waiting down in the dell. Composed by George W. Persley. Arr. for guitar by Chas. Harris. (12 choice songs for the guitar. 11) c1869 [for series] Filed Jan. 14, 1871. | 6066 | |
| | | 6067 | MERRILL, Hiram T. The first bud waltz. (Hand in hand; a graded collection of duets, for the piano forte; prepared by F. W. Root) Filed Mar. 6, 1871. |
| 6049 | MAYO, Oscar. Fancy free polka characteristique. Filed Jan. 23, 1871. | | MAYO, Oscar. Opus 5; eight orchestral beauties transcribed for the pianoforte. (See also: 6074-76; 6080) |
| 6050 | TOWNER, Charles. The "Heathen Chinee." S&Ch. Words by "Bret Harte." Filed Dec. 15, 1870. | 6068 | No. 6. Mozart's minuet. Filed Feb. 27, 1871. |
| 6051 | STILLMAN, J. M. Songs of summer. Quartette. c1870. Filed Jan. 17, 1871. | 6069 | No. 5. Scene from <u>Robert le Diable</u>. (Meyerbeer) Filed Feb. 27, 1871. |
| 6052 | BURKHART, William. La mode. "Trois temps" as danced at Prof. Sullivan's academy. c1870. Filed Jan. 17, 1871. | 6070 | No. 2. Serenade from <u>Don Juan</u>. Filed Feb. 27, 1871. |
| | | 6071 | No. 8. William Tell march (Rossini). Filed Feb. 27, 1871. |
| 6053 | GEARY, Gustavus. O set my heart at rest. Song, as sung by Mlle. Christine Nilsson. Filed Dec. 31, 1870. | 6072 | GOERDELER, R. Sweet robin waltz. Filed Feb. 20, 1871. |
| | | 6073 | MURRAY, James R. Make home beautiful. S&Ch. Filed Feb. 10, 1871. |
| 6054 | METCALFE, J. A. La pluie de météores. Shower of meteors. Mazurka caprice pour le piano. Filed Jan. 17, 1871. | 6074 | MAYO, Oscar. Les jeunes beautees from the <u>Huguenots</u>. (Meyerbeer) (<u>His</u> Op. 5, no. 3) Filed Mar. 1, 1871. |
| 6055 | | | |

6075 MAYO, Oscar. Wedding march from the Huguenots. (Meyerbeer) (His Op. 5, no. 3) Filed Mar. 1, 1871.

6076 MAYO, Oscar. Mara march from the opera Mara. (His Op. 5, no. 4) Filed Feb. 27, 1871.

6077 MURRAY, James R. The irresistible schottische. (Hand in hand; a graded collection of duets for the pianoforte; prepared by F. W. Root.) Filed Mar. 6, 1871.

6078 BERGMANN, Carl. The Mary polka redowa. (Hand in hand; a graded collection of duets for the pianoforte; prepared by F. W. Root.) Filed Feb. 27, 1871.

6079

6080 MAYO, Oscar. At sunrise. (From La muette de Portici by Auber) Transcribed by Oscar Mayo. (His Op. 5, no. 7) Filed Mar. 1, 1871.

6081 ROOT, Frederic W. The fly-away waltz. Filed Feb. 27, 1871.

6082 WEBSTER, J. P. Touches of little hands. Words by Alice Cary. Filed Mar. 11, 1871.

6083 BARNARD, Mrs. Charlotte (Alington) Janet's choice [by] Claribel [pseud.] (Songs and ballads from over the sea. 12) Ncc.

6084 WEBSTER, J. P. I stand beside a lonely grave. S&Ch. Filed Mar. 16, 1871.

6085 HAVENS, A. W. Curiosity galop. Filed Mar. 11, 1871.

6086

6087 [SCHLEIFFARTH, George.] Hanky-panky polka, composed by Geo. Maywood. Filed Mar. 11, 1871.

6088 GORHAM, A. Templeton. Katie waiting at the door. S&Ch. Filed Mar. 21, 1871.

6089 ROOT, Frederic W. Bells of Sabbath morning. (Hand in hand; a graded collection of duets for the pianoforte. More difficult.) Filed Mar. 24, 1871.

6090 WEBSTER, J. P. The dear sweet bells of memory. Filed Apr. 3, 1871.

6091 WEBSTER, J. P. Always of thee. Ballad. Filed Apr. 3, 1871.

6092 [SCHLEIFFARTH, George.] Susie had a mocking bird, song & dance ... by Geo. Maywood. (His 2 beautiful songs) Filed Apr. 6, 1871.

6093 SMITH, J. F. O. The day is ended. Sacred quartette suitable for closing service, or for social singing. Filed Apr. 28, 1871.

6094

6095 HUBBARD, J. M. Bird of the mountain, with violin obligato. Performed by Vieuxtemps, sung by Mlle. Christine Nilsson, at whose request it was composed. Filed May 1, 1871.

6096

6097 ROOT, George F. That little church around the corner. Arr. for the guitar by Charles Harris. (12 choice songs for the guitar. 12) c1869 [for series] Filed Apr. 20, 1871.

6098

6099 MAYO, Oscar. El Kohinoor polka for the pianoforte. Filed May 1, 1871.

6100 Cf PN 7000, and text, p84

6101 WELLS, C. L. Rippling wave schottische for the pianoforte. Filed May 31, 1871.

6102 GEARY, Gustavus. The trumpet of glory. Song. Filed May 10, 1871.

6103

6104 WEBSTER, J. P. The olive of love. S&Ch. Filed July 17, 1871.

6105

6106 BLISS, P. P. Baby's sweet sleep. S&Ch. Filed May 18, 1871.

6107 WELLS, C. L. Dash away galop for the piano. Filed June 6, 1871.

6108 REED, Charles A. Out on the shore. Filed June 10, 1871.

6109

6110 MAYO, Oscar. Castanet waltz (Creole). Op. 7, for the piano. Filed May 31, 1871.

6111

6112 GOLDBECK, Robert. Flashes from the west. (Eclairs occidentals) Concert piece for the piano. "Dedicated to the high grade pupils of the Chicago conservatory of music from the 10th grade upwards." Filed June 3, 1871.

6113

6114 MORRIS, Robert. The children in the grave yard. Words and music by Robert Morris, LL.D., harmonized by H. R. Palmer. Filed June 10, 1871.

6115 ROOT, George F. Farewell beloved friends, farewell. (Choice quartets. 14) c1868 [for series] Filed June 10, 1871.

6116 HOWARD, Frank. Where the woodland birdlings warble. Song. Filed July 5, 1871.

6117  BLISS, P. P. The temperance ship. S&Ch. Filed July 5, 1871.

6118-6120

6121  HARRIS, C. Crown of Roses waltz. (Aeolian Strains. A collection of beautiful instrumental pieces for the guitar. No. 2) Filed by Molter & Wurlitzer on Apr. 27, 1869. PN from Brainard renewal copy.

6122  HARRIS, C. Sparkling Dew Polka. (Aeolian Strains ... No. 1) Filed by Molter & Wurlitzer on Mar. 29, 1869. PN from Brainard renewal copy.

6123-6127

6128  [BROWN, George W.] Softly fall the silvery moonbeams. Words by Frank Howard. Composed by George W. Persley. (His Wreath of vocal beauties with piano forte accompaniment) Filed Dec. 6, 1870, by Molter & Wurlitzer. Deposit copy lacks PN, which is from Brainard ed.

6129  [BROWN, George W. When we sleep beneath the daises [sic]. S&Ch. Composed by George W. Persley. Filed Dec. 18, 1869, by Geo. W. Brown. PN from Brainard ed.

6130

6131  [BROWN, George W.] O bring my darling back to me. A beautiful S&Ch. Composed by George W. Persley. Filed Aug. 5, 1869, by Molter & Wurlitzer. PN from Brainard ed.

6132

6133  [BROWN, George W.] Darling little Eva Ray ... sung by J. F. Dunnie, of Emerson & Manning's minstrels. Composed by George W. Persley. Filed by Geo. W. Brown, Sept. 24, 1869. PN from Brainard ed.

6134-6139

6140  LOB, Otto. The papillion. (His Six songs with English and German words, op. 42, no. 5) Filed by Molter & Wurlitzer, Mar. 13, 1869. PN from Brainard ed.

6141-6148

6149  [BROWN, George W.] Little Robin tell Kitty I'm coming. S&Ch. Music by George W. Persley. Filed Dec. 6, 1870, by Molter & Wurlitzer. PN from Brainard ed.

6150-6154

6155  LOB, Otto. The lonely tear. (His Six songs with English & German words. No. 6) Filed Apr. 27, 1869, by Molter & Wurlitzer. PN from Brainard ed.

6156  LOB, Otto. Thou art my own. (His Six songs with English & German words. No. 1) Filed by Molter & Wurlitzer on Dec. 22, 1868. PN from Brainard ed.

6157  LOB, Otto. Repose. Geh' zur ruh'. Words by Marg. Pilgram Diehl. (His Six songs with English and German words, op. 42, no. 2) c1868 by Molter & Wurlitzer. Filed Jan. 18, 1869. PN from Brainard ed.

6158-6166

6167  MOLTER, John. Softly fall the silvery monbeams [sic] [by Geo. W. Brown]. (His Brilliant transcriptions of favorite ballads. No. 2) Filed Dec. 6, 1870, by Molter & Wurlitzer. PN from Brainard ed.

6168

6169  LOB, Otto. Kutschke's war-song (Das Kutschkelied.) A reminiscence of the great German peace festival in Chicago, May 29th, 1871. Filed June 6, 1871. [Words in English, German, and, on p4-[5], in cuneiform Assyrian, Arabic, Sanscrit, Egyptian hieroglyphics, Low Dutch, Greek, Swedish, Polish, Hebrew, Latin, Danish, Italian, Spanish, French, and Dutch.]

6170  BLISS, P. P. Bessie Lee (the Highland lassie). Scotch ballad. Filed July 17, 1871.

6171  TOWNE, T. M. Lake Forest mazurka. Filed July 5, 1871.

6172-6173

6174  MALLANDAINE, J. E. Faces I see in my dreams. Ballad. Filed July 10, 1871.

6175  GABRIEL, Virginia. Only. Song and duet ... as sung by Miss Annie Goodall and Mr. Charles Wyndham, in the comedy of "Home." Filed July 10, 1871.

6176  ROOT, Frederic W. The crimson glow of sunset fades. Barcarolle for two voices with accompaniment for four hands. Filed July 19, 1871.

6177  STREETER, Frederic V. Sister in heaven. S&Ch. Filed July 31, 1871.

6178  JUCH, Justin. On land and sea. Filed July 22, 1871.

6179  GORHAM, A. Templeton. Send the little ones happy to bed. A song for the fireside. Filed July 22, 1871.

6180  WEBSTER, J. P. Only love me. S&Ch. Filed July 22, 1871.

6181  ROOT, George F. Free as air quickstep for piano or cabinet organ. Filed Aug. 3, 1871.

6182  BLISS, P. P. Loving little Lou. S&Ch. Filed July 27, 1871.

6183  PENFIELD, Smith N. The sunny south, reverie for the piano. Filed Aug. 4, 1871.

6184  MURRAY, James R. Carl Pretzel waltz for the piano. Filed July 31, 1871.

6185  [SCHLEIFFARTH, George.] Belle of Lincoln Park; song & dance. As sung with the greatest success in: "The field of the cloth of gold." Composed by Geo. Maywood. (His 2 beautiful songs) Filed July 31, 1871.

6186-6187

6188  GOLDBECK, Robert. Harmonized progressive finger exercises for the piano. v.3. Cf PN 6195

6189-6192

6193  GOLDBECK, Robert. Blue Beard. (His Young pianist's repertory, six fantaisies for the piano. 3) c1871 by R. Goldbeck. Other titles in the series, not found, include 1. La grand duchesse. 2. La belle Helene. 4. Lucia. 5. Lucrezie Borgia. 6. Traviata.

6194

6195-6196  GOLDBECK, Robert. Harmonized progressive finger exercises for the piano. v.1-2. [The title is entered once without indication of the volume number on Dec. 28, 1868, giving R. Goldbeck as claimant. Only v.1 in this state is extant at LC, and probably it was the only one filed. Brainard, nonetheless, renewed all three, and the PNs come from this series.]

6197-6199

6200  WELLS, C. L. Evening chimes. Reverie. (Popular pieces for the piano-forte) Filed Aug. 7, 1871.

6201-6202  The little carnival, a collection of popular compositions by Strauss and others, made easy. Fingered and arranged for the piano by F. W. Root.

6203  STRAUSS, Johann. On the beautiful blue Danube waltz. Filed Aug. 12, 1871.

6204  STRAUSS, Johann. Wine, wife & song waltz. Filed Aug. 11, 1871.

6205  BLISS, P. P. Sweetly, softly, quartette. Filed Aug. 16, 1871.

6206  GODFREY, Daniel. The Mabel waltzes. (The little carnival ... arr. by F. W. Root) Filed Aug. 16, 1871.

6207  KETTERER, Eugene. Gaetana mazurka. (The leisure hour. Instrumental) Ncc.

6208  MURRAY, James R. When the dear ones gather at home. S&Ch. Filed Aug. 21, 1871.

6209  HYDE, B. Excursion schottische. For piano. Filed Aug. 16, 1871.

6210  GARDNER, Miss H. Little flirt waltz. Filed Aug. 18, 1871.

6211  DOTZLER, Charles. Wyndham polka ... respectfully dedicated to Charles Wyndham. Filed Aug. 21, 1871.

6212  PROCTOR, H. Irwin. Riverside mazurka. Filed Sept. 7, 1871.

6213  ROOT, G. F. The whole story, ballad with chorus ad. lib. Filed Sept. 6, 1871.

6214  HOAG, A. B. I dream of the beautiful past. S&Ch. Filed Sept. 13, 1871.

6215  HOLST, Ed. I cannot forget thee; in the key of E flat. Filed Sept. 2, 1871.

6216  MELFI, Signor Peppino. The pagoda waltz. Filed Sept. 6, 1871.

6217-6218

6219  OFFENBACH, Jacques. From the bosom of the waters (Soprano & tenor) (Le salon; a collection of vocal duets & trios) Filed Sept. 11, 1871.

6220  HOLST, Ed. I cannot forget thee; in the key of A flat. Filed Sept. 23, 1871.

6221  KNAPP, A. B. The Annie Huger galop; for piano. Filed Sept. 21, 1871.

6222  DOTZLER, Charles. The Fitzpatrick polka, composed & respectfully dedicated to J. H. Fitzpatrick, stage manager at Hooley's Opera House. The orchestral parts may be had of the publishers. Filed Sept. 25, 1871.

6223  WEBSTER, J. P. Why not I. S&Ch. Filed Oct. 3, 1871.

6224  GEARY, Gustavus. Fly love to me. (Soprano & tenor) (Le salon; a collection of vocal duets & trios) Filed Oct. 3, 1871.

6225-6226  Piano pictures; fifty first pieces for the piano-forte. Edited by F. W. Root.

6227  No. 33. ROOT, F. W. Lightly rocking. Filed Sept. 26, 1871.

| | |
|---|---|
| 6228 | No. 26. ROOT, F. W. The old clock in the corner. Filed Sept. 30, 1871. |
| 6229 | No. 40. MURRAY, James R. The merry sleigh-ride. Filed Sept. 25, 1871. |
| 6230 | No. 46. HOWARD, Frank. The rustic lassie polka. Filed Oct. 7, 1871. |
| 6231 | No. 20. ROOT, G. F. Sparkling wavelets. Filed Oct. 7, 1871. |
| 6232 | No. 18. ROOT, G. F. Mill wheel polka. Filed Sept. 30, 1871. |
| 6233 | No. 22. ROOT, G. F. Off for a holiday. Filed Sept. 30, 1871. |
| 6234 | No. 35. ROOT, F. W. The boat ride. Filed Sept. 30, 1871. |
| 6235-6236 | |
| 6237 | No. 9. ROOT, G. F. Mary of the glen waltz. Filed Sept. 30, 1871. |
| 6238 | No. 45. MURRAY, James R. Over the dancing waves. Filed Sept. 30, 1871. |
| 6239-6257 | |
| 6258 | No. 23. MILLER, C. C. The bee march. c1872 by S. Brainard's sons. |
| 6259 | |
| 6260 | No. 27. ROOT, F. W. A voice from the ocean. c1872 by S. Brainard's sons. |
| 6261 | No. 29. ROOT, F. W. Five finger waltz. c1872 by S. Brainard sons. |
| 6262-6264 | |
| 6265 | No. 34. ROOT, F. W. The pony ride. c1872 by S. Brainard's sons. |
| 6266 | |
| 6267 | No. 37. ROOT, F. W. Wandering in the greenwood. c1872 by S. Brainard's sons. |
| 6268-6271 | |
| 6272 | No. 44. MURRAY, James R. Song of the fairies. c1872 by S. Brainard's sons. |
| 6273 | No. 47. HOWARD, Frank. The sugar plum waltz. c1872 by S. Brainard's sons. |
| 6274 | No. 50. MATHEWS, W. S. B. Linden waltz. c1872 by S. Brainard's sons. |
| 6275-6276 | |
| 6277 | GEARY, Gustavus. Swinging in the trees. S&Ch. c1871. |
| 6278 | |
| 6279 | CADY, C. M. We are the boys that fear no noise. Nautical ditty, arr. by C. M. Cady. "Dedicated to H. M. Brainard, I. J. Hall, J. L. Peters, & W. F. Smith. In commemoration of the famous voyage of the five doughty music publishers in an open boat from Newport to Martha's Vineyard, July 21st & 22nd, 1871. Time 26 hours." Filed Oct. 7, 1871. |
| 6280 | |
| 6281 | ROOT, F. W. Silvery ripples waltz for the piano-forte. Filed Oct. 9, 1871. |
| 7000 | LEHMAN, W. H. Terrace hill waltz for the piano. Filed May 12, 1871. |
| 7001 | Cf PN 6101, and text, p84 |
| 7002 | GEARY, Gustavus. The trumpet of glory. Song. Filed May 10, 1871. Cf PN 6102 |
| 7003 | [HAVENS, A. W.] Take me from my little bed. Arr. for guitar by Charles Harris. (Guitar. Vocal 2) c1867 [for series] Filed May 18, 1871. |
| 7004-7033 | [?] |
| 7034 | MORGAN, George W. Emilie waltz. c1868 by H. W. Chant. |

II. CHRONOLOGICAL LIST OF COPYRIGHTED WORKS
FOUND WITHOUT PLATE NUMBERS

# CHRONOLOGICAL LIST OF COPYRIGHTED WORKS FOUND WITHOUT PLATE NUMBERS

ROOT, George F. Farewell father, friend and guardian. [At head:] We mourn the Nation's dead. Abraham Lincoln, President, assassinated in Washington, April 14, 1865. Filed Apr. 25, 1865.

HAWLEY, H. H. How it marches! The flag of the Union, arranged by Geo. F. Root. Filed May 20, 1865.

ROOT, George F. Starved in prison. Filed May 20, 1865.

ROOT, George F. They have broken up their camps. Filed June 23, 1865.

WORK, Henry C. 'Tis finished! or, Sing hallelujah! Filed June 23, 1865.

WORK, Henry C. Poor Kitty Popcorn; or, The Soldier's pet. Filed Jan. 5, 1866.

|   |   |
|---|---|
| 48 | CELLI, Adelina Murio. La clochette de l'esperance schottisch. Pour le piano par Mme. Adelina Murio Celli. Published for the author by Root & Cady, c1866 by the author. PN not typical R&C type. Filed Mar. 3, 1866. |
|  | "Engaged." S&Ch. Composed by "Frederick." Chicago, published by Root & Cady, 67 Washington St.; Street & Pearson, 101 Washington St.; c1866 by Street & Pearson. Inside front cover: advertisement of Street, Pearson & Co., publishers, booksellers and stationers, Chicago, Ill., April, 1866. |
|  | WRIGHT, William C. L'agréable reverie, romance originale avec variations pour le piano forte. Filed Aug. 29, 1866. |
|  | BOUDEMAN, Dallas. We'll have to get the style. Comic S&Ch. c1867. |
|  | HARRISON, James. We're waiting for father! S&Ch. Words by Olynthus. Filed May 3, 1867. |
| title | CONCORDIUS. Uncle Sam. S&Ch. Words by Mary Kinnear Grute. Music by Concordius. Pubd. for the author by R&C, c1867 by Mary K. Grute. Filed by R&C, July 22, 1867. |
| title | HARRISON, James. The latch string at the door. S&Ch as sung by J. R. Rickey. Words by January Searle. Filed Aug. 3, 1867. |
|  | ROOT, George F. Hymn. -- Because He loved me so. Words by Emily Huntington Miller. Single leaf, excerpted from hymn book. Filed Oct. 15, 1867. |
|  | SWEET, O. P. Passing away. As sung by the popular bariton C. S. Fredericks of Arlington's Minstrels, Chicago, Ill. S&Ch. Filed Dec. 12, 1867. |
| U.P.B. | [PRATT, Silas Gamaliel.] Undine polka brillante, by V. B. Aubert. Filed Dec. 28, 1867. |
| U.V.G. | [PRATT, Silas Gamaliel.] Undine... Valse brillante. By V. B. Aubert. Filed Dec. 31, 1867. |
|  | BRAND, T. H. Sounds from the old camp ground. To the members of the Grant Soldiers & Sailors Club. Madison, Wis. ... and to the Grant Clubs in general. Words and music by T. H. Brand, Principal of the Madison Vocal Academy. Choruses selected from Root and Cady's Army Songs. Published for the author by Root & Cady, c1868 by T. H. Brand. [Chorus includes Battle cry of freedom, Tramp, tramp, tramp and John Brown's body.] |
|  | ROOT, George F. If Maggie were my own! S&Ch. Words by Lieut. S. H. M. Byers. Filed Jan. 18, 1868. |
| S | Sara Neighed! For four male voices, being the air that should have been sung in the celebrated balcony scene of the new opera of Romeo and Juliet. Music by G. Whoknows. Filed Feb. 2, 1868. R&C deposit copy has letter only. Brainard has 2738. |
| title | MURRAY, James R. Kind smiles for all. S&Ch. Filed Feb. 12, 1868. Brainard ed. has 1182. |
|  | MURRAY, James R. Loving thee ever. S&Ch. Filed Mar. 7, 1868. |
|  | GOLDBECK, Robert. L'Opéra dans le salon. Une serie de fantaisies brillante pour le piano. |
| U | I. Un ballo in maschera. Filed Mar. 16, 1868. |
| E | III. Ernani. Filed Mar. 16, 1868. |
| N | IV. Nabucodonosor. Filed Mar. 16, 1868. See PN 1758 |
| A | II. Aroldo. Filed Mar. 24, 1868. |
| R | V. Rigoletto. Filed Mar. 25, 1868. See PN 2419 |
| F. C. | SCOTT, Mrs. Clara H. Floating clouds. "Respectfully dedicated to Pres. Geo. F. Magoun, D.D., of Iowa College." Filed Mar. 24, 1868. |

| | | |
|---|---|---|
| N | | MATHEWS, William Smythe Babcock. Nightfall at home. Nocturne. Words & music by W. S. B. Mathews. Filed Apr. 18, 1868. |
| title | | STRAUB, S. W. Gird on! gird on! or, The temperance band. S&Ch. Words by Maria Straub. "Dedicated to the friends of temperance everywhere." Filed Apr. 20, 1868. |
| M | | ANGUERA, Antonio de. My loved one's grave. Ballad. Filed Apr. 23, 1868. |
| S.F. | | SCOTT, Mrs. Clara H. Snow-flakes. Filed Apr. 27, 1868. See PN 4917 |
| L.S. | | MURRAY, James R. Little sunshine. A song. Filed Apr. 28, 1868. |
| R | | [PRATT, Silas Gamaliel.] Rêve d'artist. (The artist's dream.) Reverie pour piano, composée par V. B. Aubert. Filed May 5, 1868. |
| | | ROOT, George F. We'll fight it out here on the old Union line. S&Ch. Words by Rev. John Hogarth Lozier. (Late Chaplain, 37 Indiana Infantry.) "Sung at the Republican National Convention by Chaplain Lozier, Chaplain McCabe and Maj. H. G. Lumbard." Filed May 21, 1868. |
| rally | | HERRICK, George D. Rally for the leader. S&Ch. Words by D. McNaughton. "To Col. Geo. G. Briggs, Prest. of Grant Club, Grand Rapids, Mich." Filed May 21, 1868. |
| title | | LOCKWOOD, C. T. Don't stay late to-night. S&Ch. "To husbands who keep late hours." Filed May 24, 1868. |
| Maggie | | TOWNE, Thomas Martin. Poor little blind Maggie! S&Ch. Filed May 28, 1868. |
| | | CALDWELL, Susie B. Name me in thy prayer. Song. Words and music by Miss Susie B. Caldwell. Filed June 3, 1868. |
| Alice | | STEVENS, George. The Alice polka, composed and dedicated to Alice Holland, by George Stevens, leader of orchestra at Col. Woods Museum. Filed June 6, 1868. |
| | | LOCKWOOD, C. T. Feather polka. Filed June 9, 1868. |
| title | | WEBSTER, Joseph Philbrick. Old Glory and U. S. Grant. Words by L. J. Bates. (His Songs of the present time ...) "During the war some of our boys used to call the flag 'OLD GLORY.'" Filed June 17, 1868. |
| | | REEVES, F. Moonlight on the billow. Words by G. W. Birdseye. c1867 by Henry Tolman & Co. (Beauties of English song.) R&C filed this apparently so that they could claim copyright on the whole series. Filed Sept. 10 and 12, 1868. |
| | | HOWARD, Frank. Oh, Sorosis! S&Ch. Filed Nov. 7, 1868. |
| title | | LOCKWOOD, C. T. Shall I ever see my boy! A quartet. Words by John Southard. Filed Nov. 30, 1868. |
| | | MORGAN, George W. May march. For organ with pedal obligato, by Geo. W. Morgan. Organist of St. Anne R. C. church, N.Y. "To my friend H. W. Chant." Filed by H. W. Chant, Dec. 15, 1868. |
| | | GOSS, Samuel T. Ella schottische; a pretty piece for little fingers. Filed Aug. 11, 1869. |
| | | MURRAY, James R. Angels beckon me! S&Ch. Words by Mrs. M. E. Guilford. Published for Mrs. M. E. Guilford by R&C. Filed by Mrs. Guilford on Feb. 9, 1869. |
| | | GORHAM, A. Templeton. Too genteel you know! S&Ch. Filed July 3, 1869. |
| | | HOWARD, Frank. Meet me just at twilight. (His 12 new songs. 9) Filed June 10, 1869. |
| title | | MURRAY, James R. Gone to heaven. Filed Jan. 15, 1869. |
| | | SANDERSON, W. H. Up in a balloon. (Songs and ballads from over the sea. [8]) Filed May 10, 1869. |
| | | WOODBURY, M. Amsden. Still thy tumult, wild, wild waves! Song. Filed by M. A. Woodbury, Sept. 20, 1869. |
| | | MURRAY, James R. There's sunshine after rain. S&Ch. Copies filed Apr. 18, 1870, have no PN, but later PN 5803 was added. |
| | | MAYER, Henry. Jeunesse (youth) polka; composed for the piano. Filed Apr. 23, 1870. |
| | | BLISS, P. P. Hold the fort! S&Ch. "To Major D. W. Whittle." Filed Dec. 10, 1870. |
| | | MURRAY, James R. Merry Christmas. Quartet and chorus. 8vo. Filed Dec. 13, 1870. |
| | | ROOT, George F. That little church around the corner. S&Ch. Filed Feb. 6, 1871. |
| | | ROOT, George F. Hear the cry that comes across the sea! Rallying S&Ch. "To the Producers' French aid organization, Chicago. AMERICANS! France is exhausted by this terrible war ... let us now share with her from our abundance ..." Filed Feb. 27, 1871. |
| | | THAYER, J. H. The Nilsson waltz. Published by R&C for the author. Filed Apr. 20, 1871, by the author. |
| | | MURRAY, James R. Baby blue-eyes. (Who took her on the other side?) S&Ch. Filed May 6, 1871. |

JOHNSON, Mrs. H. Mills. Memories of home. Published for the author by R&C. Filed July 10, 1871.

WELLER, S. M. Our angel child. S&Ch. Published by R&C for the author. Filed July 17, 1871, by the author.

HART, Henry. Idlewild mazurka for the piano. Published by R&C for the author. Filed July 22, 1871, by the author.

MURRAY, James R. One I love, two I love; or, Counting seeds. S&Ch. Words by Hope Ardor. Filed Aug. 4, 1871.

ROOT, George F. The boy at the fountain, as a song recitando, or as a quartette. Filed Aug. 4, 1871.

P., E. F. Come to me, gentle sleep. Words by Mrs. Hemans. Music by E. F. P. Published by R&C for the author. Filed Aug. 18, 1871.

HART, Henry. My thoughts are of thee. Published by R&C for the author. Filed Aug. 25, 1871.

HOWARD, Frank. Quit that, as sung by all the minstrels. Published by R&C for the author; Cincinnati, John Church, Jr.; New York, W. A. Pond; [etc., etc.] Filed Sept. 7, 1871, by Abbie L. Spalding.

| | |
|---|---|
| title | ROOT, George F. From the ruins our city shall rise. Filed Nov. 25, 1871. |
| title | ROOT, George F. Passing through the fire. Filed Nov. 25, 1871. |
| title | ROOT, George F. Ye have done it unto me. "Inscribed to all who have helped us while we've been 'Passing through the fire.'" Filed Nov. 25, 1871. |

ROOT, F. W. Kitty Vane and I. S&Ch. Cleveland, S. Brainard. Filed Dec. 18, 1871.

## III. COPYRIGHTED WORKS NOT FOUND

## COPYRIGHTED WORKS NOT FOUND

Filed Sept. 26, 1862

CHOICE SELECTIONS for the Catholic Church from Haydn, Mendelssohn and Weber. Latin words adapted by Prof. E. Girac, Director of Music at the Church of the Holy Name, Chicago.

    O Vos Omnes [Copyright no. 747]
    Panis Angelicus fit panis hominum [Copyright no. 748]
    Tantum Ergo [Copyright no. 749]
    O lux beati Trinitas [Copyright no. 750]
    O quam suavis est [Copyright no. 751]
    Ave Maris Stella [Copyright no. 752]

SIX POPULAR PIECES by Ascher, Blumenthal and Lefébure-Wély. Arranged, simplified and fingered expressly for teaching purposes by Albert W. Berg.

    1. Gouttes d'Eau (Tremolo) [Copyright no. 772]
    2. Les Deux Anges (varied) [Copyright no. 773]
    3. Chant National des Croates [Copyright no. 774]
    5. March de la Reine [Copyright no. 776]
    [Cf also PNs 185 and 187]

Filed Nov. 16, 1865

FORMES, Karl. The Polish refugee. (His Three songs without words. No. 2)
FORMES, Karl. Addio. Madrid, 1851. (His Three songs without words. No. 3)

Filed Feb. 27, 1871

LOCKWOOD, C. T. Gathering home. (Hand in hand; a graded collection of duets. For the pianoforte; prepared by F. W. Root)

Filed Aug. 7, 1871

[BLISS, Philip Paul.] Jolly Jonathan and his notional naburs. A comical controversy by Pro Phundo Basso.

## IV. MUSIC BOOKS

MUSIC BOOKS

The date on which each work was deposited for copyright is given below each entry to the left; to the right is the number of sales (where a figure is available) as given in The Song Messenger "Extra" for April, 1867.

ROOT & CADY'S ECLECTIC PIANO FORTE INSTRUCTOR. Scales, exercises, and graded pieces. Price, $1.50.
 Advertised, Chicago Tribune, Sept. 9, 1861 [1:6]
 Not registered for copyright.        Not found

ARMY REGULATIONS FOR THE DRUM, FIFE AND BUGLE. Being a complete manual for these instruments, giving all the calls for camp and field duty. To which is added suitable music for each instrument. By William Nevins, Drum Major of Gen. McClellan's Body Guard. Arranged by A. J. Vaas, leader of Vaas & Dean's Light Guard Band. Price, 50 cents.
 Announced, Chicago Tribune, Sept. 16, 1861 [4:1]
 Not registered for copyright.        Not found

THE SILVER LUTE: A new singing book for schools and academies. Containing musical notation, progressive song-lessons, exercise and occupation songs, hymns, tunes and chants, and pieces for concerts and exhibitions. By Geo. F. Root, author of "Academy Vocalist," "Flower Queen," "Silver Chime," and other musical works. Chicago: Published by Root & Cady, 95 Clark Street; New York: Mason Brothers; Philadelphia: Lee & Walker; Boston: H. Tolman & Co.; Cleveland: S. Brainard & Co.; 1862. On verso of title-page: Tribune, Print., 51 Clark St., Chicago. Lyman, Zeese & Co., Stereotypers, 47 Clark St. Small oblong format, 192 pages.
 Filed Sept. 26, 1862.   Together with the Enlarged Edition, nearly 200,000 copies

THE BUGLE CALL. Edited by Geo. F. Root. Small oblong format, 60 pages.
 Filed Apr. 29, 1863.        50,000 copies sold

TEACHERS SONGS. A collection of music for teachers' meetings, conventions and associations. By Charles Ansorge, teacher of music in the Chicago High School, and Geo. F. Root.
 Filed Mar. 5, 1864.   Rarely publicized; no figure on sales available

MUSICAL CURRICULUM: For solid and symmetrical acquirement in piano-forte playing, singing, and harmony; containing copious and carefully progressive exercises, pieces, songs, technics, solfeggios, and etudes, in all the keys ... [Root apparently considered this his most important contribution, and The Song Messenger ran pages of testimonials without end. The volume was of such large format, containing 240 pages, that later it was broken down into four parts, which could be purchased separately.]
 Filed Dec. 24, 1864.        23,050 copies

THE CABINET ORGAN COMPANION: A collection of exercises, pieces and songs for the Cabinet organ together with some instructions in the principles of music, and directions for playing the instrument. By Geo. F. Root. [A small oblong booklet of 77 pages; sold for $.75.]
 Filed June 28, 1865.

THE CORONET: A collection of music for singing schools, musical conventions and choirs; consisting of a course for elementary instruction and training, a large number of part songs, solos, duets, quartets, glees and choruses, and a smaller number of tunes, anthems and chants. Composed and arranged by Geo. F. Root. [Larger than most Root & Cady books, it resembles the standard oblong hymn book of the period, and contains 304 pages.]
 Filed Sept. 1, 1865.        33,000 copies

ROOT'S GUIDE FOR THE PIANO FORTE. [Same music as The Cabinet Organ Companion, except that "the directions for playing the instrument" have been appropriately modified.]
 Filed Nov. 3, 1865.

THE SNOW-BIRD; a collection of music for sabbath and day schools, juvenile singing classes and the social circle, being the Winter number of "Our Song Birds," a juvenile Musical Quarterly. By Geo. F. Root and B. R. Hanby. [Hanby is credited after his death with originating the idea of the series and with doing most of the work on it. The books were appropriately small, containing only 62 pages.]
  Filed Dec. 9, 1865.                   100,000 copies

THE MUSICAL FOUNTAIN. By Geo. F. Root. [The earlier edition is in paper covers with no inside title-page. In advertisements it is described as: A little collection of temperance music for public and social meetings and the home circle, to which is appended the odes of the Good Templars, with some new music. Small format; 62pp.]
  Filed Mar. 13, 1866.

THE ROBIN. [April number of Our Song Birds, cf above.]
  Filed Mar. 20, 1866.

THE RED BIRD. [The Summer number of Our Song Birds.]
  Filed June 20, 1866.

THE DOVE. [The Fall number of Our Song Birds.]
  Filed Sept. 26, 1866.

CHAPEL GEMS for Sunday Schools, selected from "Our Song Birds for 1866. By Geo. F. Root and B. R. Hanby.
  Filed Oct. 4, 1866.                15,000 copies

Enlarged Edition. THE SILVER LUTE: A new singing book for schools and academies ... By Geo. F. Root. [The title-page in the deposit copy has the date 1865, whereas the orange board covers are dated 1866. Same format as the earlier edition, but the number of pages have been increased from 192 to 215. The sales figure below must cover both editions.]
  Filed Oct. 4, 1866.              Nearly 200,000 copies

THE FOREST CHOIR: A collection of vocal music for young people; embracing "Our Song Birds' Singing School," music for concert, school and home, and songs, hymns, anthems and chants for worship. By Geo. F. Root. [Small format with 254 pages.]
  Filed Jan. 23, 1867.                 8,000 copies

THE BLUE BIRD. April number of Our Song Birds.
  Filed Mar. 30, 1867.

THE MUSICAL FOUNTAIN, ENLARGED; a collection of temperance music, for public and social meetings and the home circle. To which is appended the odes of the Good Templars. By Geo. F. Root.
  Filed June 26, 1867 (Copyright no. 2644) and July 1, 1867 (Copyright no. 2645).

THE LINNET, a collection of music for day and Sunday Schools, Juvenile singing classes and the social circle, being the Fall Number of "Our Song Birds," a Juvenile Musical Semi-Annual. By F. W. Root and J. R. Murray. (Apparently the only issue to be prepared after Hanby's death. Note that it had been changed from a quarterly to a semiannual.)
  Filed Oct. 5, 1867.

AN AID TO CONGREGATIONAL SINGING; being introductory to a book of church, convention and singing school music. (Now in press.) By Geo. F. Root. This pamphlet, also, contains specimen pages from the Forest Choir, Musical Fountain (Temperance) and Chapel Gems.
  Filed Feb. 1, 1868.

THE FUNDAMENTAL TECHNICS OF PIANO PLAYING. Adapted to the use of conservatories and private teaching, containing independence of each single finger, together with exercises for five fingers. Diatonic scales, major and minor. Also the chromatic scales; three and four tone arpeggios; the trill. Adopted by the Conservatory of Music, Chicago, Ill. By Robert Goldbeck.
  Filed Feb. 3, 1868.                 Not found

TESTAMENT HYMNS, No. 2, or Object Singing Lessons.
    Filed Apr. 25, 1868. (Cf below.)

THE GRANT SONGSTER, for the campaign of 1868. (R&C's only political songster.)
    Filed May ?4, 1868. [A second, enlarged edition was advertised a few weeks later.]

THE TRIUMPH; a collection of music containing an introductory course for congregational singing, theory of music and teacher's manual, elementary, intermediate and advanced courses, for singing schools and musical convention, and tunes, hymns, anthems and chants, for choirs. Edited by Geo. F. Root. (50,000 copies had been sold by 1868 and the rate of sale had reached 1,500 a day. Cf Chicago Tribune, December 19, 1868 [4:3], G. F. Root estimated the sale for the first year at 90,000 with a profit to Root & Cady of $30,000.)
    Filed June 29, 1868.

THE THOROUGH BASE SCHOOL, an easy and progressive course; for acquiring a practical knowledge of rudimental harmony: especially adapted to the wants of those desirous of learning to play or write church music, accompaniments, songs, choruses, etc. Written for the piano-forte or organ. By W. Ludden.
    Filed Oct. 10, 1868.

LILY-BELL, THE CULPRIT FAY. An operetta for ladies' voices. Designed for concerts, school exhibitions, etc. Words and m ic by Herman S. Saroni.
    Filed Nov. 21, 1868.

GRADED SONGS FOR DAY SCHOOLS, Nos. 1-3 by O. Blackman. (Mr. Blackman, the music teacher in the Chicago public schools, prepared this series for his own classes. In 1866, he had issued GRADED SONGS FOR CHICAGO SCHOOLS, a 24-page booklet with no publisher indicated. GRADED SONGS FOR PUBLIC SCHOOLS, Nos. 1-2. By O. Blackman and Geo. B. Loomis bore the imprint, Chicago, Root & Cady, c1867, and ran to 22 and 38 pages respectively. No. 3 has not been examined. GRADED SONGS FOR DAY SCHOOLS. No. 4. By O. Blackman. Chicago, Root & Cady, 1869, is a book of 128 pages. No. 5 has not been examined. To complete the tale, GRADED SONGS. No. 6. For high schools, seminaries, musical conventions, and choral societies. By O. Blackman. c1870. 95p.) Nos. 1-3 not registered for copyright. Listed as given above in the Song Messenger, November, 1868, p176.

SACRED LYRICS; a collection of hymns and tunes: with selections for chanting. For social and public worship. Edited and compiled by W. Ludden.
    Filed Dec. 31, 1868.

SCHOOL LYRICS; a collection of hymns and tunes; with selections for reading or chanting, and adapted to the opening and closing exercises of schools and seminaries; to which is appended a complete rudimental course in musical notation. Edited and compiled by W. Ludden.
    Filed Dec. 31, 1868.

HEART HYMNS FOR THE NEW LIFE. From a forthcoming hymn and tune book designed for public and social worship. Edited by Darius E. Jones, editor of Temple Melodies.
    Filed Feb. 15, 1869.

TESTAMENT HYMNS, Nos. 1-3, or Object Singing Lessons.
    Filed Mar. 18, 1869.                              No copies found

THE SILVER CLARION; for public schools, seminaries and vocal classes. Containing a new, practical, and progressive course of elementary instruction together with a large number of beautiful songs for class practice, concerts, exhibitions, etc., arranged for two, three, and four voices, with hymns, tunes and chants. By D. Shryock, author of Shryock's mammoth music charts.
    Filed Apr. 3, 1869.

SONGS FOR THE NEW LIFE. Designed for the public, social and private Christian uses. By Rev. Darius E. Jones.
    Filed May 26, 1869.                              No copies found

PACIFIC GLEE BOOK. A collection of secular music consisting of part songs, solos and choruses, glees and operatic arrangements. Edited by Frederic W. Root and James R. Murray. [304p, oblong.]
    Filed Aug. 20, 1869.

SPECIMEN PAGES FOR THE PRIZE for our Sunday School. By Geo. F. Root. To be completed and issued April 15th, Chicago.
    Filed Feb. 28 and Mar. 15, 1870.

THE PRIZE, a collection of songs, hymns, chants, anthems and concert pieces, for the Sunday School, by Geo. F. Root. [192p, oblong.]
    Filed Apr. 20, 1870.

PALMER'S NORMAL COLLECTION OF SACRED MUSIC consisting of anthems, choruses, opening and closing pieces. Also pieces adapted to dedication, ordination, installation, Christmas, temperance, festival, national, anniversary, missionary, funeral occasions, etc., etc. ... By H. R. Palmer ... [272p, oblong.]
    Filed Mar. 7, 1870.

YOUNG MEN'S CHRISTIAN ASSOCIATION HYMNS, No. 3.
    Filed Apr. 9, 1870. Nos. 1-2 not filed. None of these have been found.

NEW AND POPULAR SELECTIONS for the Triennial and Pilgrim Memorial conventions commencing at Farwell Hall, Chicago, April 25th, 1870.
    Filed Apr. 27, 1870.                                                       Not found

THE PALM, by C. M. Wyman [on cover; after several preliminary leaves:] The Palm. A collection of Sacred Music, for choirs, singing schools and conventions. [400p, oblong.]
    Filed July 5, 1870.

CHRISTIAN HYMN AND TUNE BOOK. For use in churches, and for social and family devotions. By A[mos] S[utton] Hayden. [8vo, 272p]
    Filed Aug. 9 and Sept. 8, 1870.

GRADED SONGS. No. 6. For high schools, seminaries, musical conventions, and choral societies. By O. Blackman.
    Filed Oct. 4, 1870.   Cf p145

THE CHARM: A collection of Sunday School Music. By P. P. Bliss. [160p; small oblong.]
    Filed Apr. 28, 1871.

THE CROWN OF SUNDAY SCHOOL SONGS: consisting principally of the works of Geo. F. Root and P. P. Bliss. Edited by L. H. Dowling. c1871. [160p] Single copy, 35 cts., $30 per hundred.
    Not filed.

THE GLORY by G. F. Root was announced in 1871, but the fire delayed its publication. The manuscript was included in the sale of Root & Cady's book catalog to the John Church Co., and the book was eventually issued by that firm.

APPENDIX B

COMPOSER INDEX TO SHEET MUSIC PUBLICATIONS

COMPOSER INDEX TO SHEET MUSIC PUBLICATIONS

ABEL, Frederick, conductor of the Milwaukee Musical Society, 1860-66.
   Your name! "The honey bee is humming it." 529
ABT, Franz, 1819-1885.
   The German youth. 5536
   Love's delight. 536
   Now the swallow are returning. 36
   O ye tears! O ye tears. 248
   When the swallows homeward fly. 37, 457
ADAMS, O. D., d. 1869.
   O, worship the Lord! 762
   My mother bids me bind my hair. 837, 4867
   Try, John! Try, John! 5514
AMSDEN, M. [WOODBURY, M. Amsden?]
   Why doesn't he speak? 5960
ANGUERA, Antonio de, Chicago pianist, composer and piano salesman.
   Crystal showers. 4964
   La gazetier polka. 526
   My loved one's grave. p134
ARDITI, Luigi, 1822-1903.
   Il bacio. 540
   Ecstasy. 2062
ASCHER, Joseph, 1829-1869.
   La cascade de roses. 3160
   Victoire. Galop militaire. 3221
AUBERT, V. B., pseud. See PRATT, Silas Gamaliel.
BACH, Christoph, b. 1835.
   Funeral march. 722
   Home greeting. 5644
   Look out upon the stars. 1196
   The musical album march. 614
   The patriot's prayer. 409
BADARZEWSKA, Thekla, 1838-1862.
   Maiden's prayer. 87
BAILEY, Ephraim H.
   Absent Mary. 638
   Did the loved one return? 637
   Long ago. 636
BAKER, Arthur.
   Grandmother's cot. 6010
BAKER, John C., b. 1822.
   Dream on, my soul! 634
BAKER, W. C.
   It is an age of progress! 836
   Laura Anna. 760
   Let us forget the past. 678
   O linger no longer. 4883
   Poor broken heart. 741
   Would you could meet me to-night. 5763
BALATKA, Hans, 1827-1899.
   I stood before her portrait. 343

BALFE, Michael William, 1808-1870.
   [Norah darling don't believe them.] 16
   O take me to thy heart again. 459
   Then you'll remember me. 243
BARNARD, Mrs. Charlotte Alington, 1830-1869.
   Five o'clock in the morning. 640, 5105
   Janet's choice. 6083
   Take back the heart. 5158
BASSO, Pro Phundo, pseud. See BLISS, Philip Paul.
BAUMBACH, Adolph, ca1830-1880.
   Czar and Zimmermann. Pot pourri. (arr.) 389
   Ellsworth Zouave & National lancers' greeting grand march. 566
   Etta mazurka. 534
   Faust pot pourri. (arr.) 407
   First dreams nocturne. 4922
   Golden memories. (arr.) 4801-22
   Shells of ocean with brilliant variations. 3759
   30 popular melodies arr. for the piano forte. 294-321, 323-4
   Valse a la mode. 4864
BENDEL, Franz, 1833-1874.
   Nocturne, op. 92. 5226
BENEDICT, Sir Julius, 1804-1885.
   Root & Cady's juvenile series. (ed.) 5684-91
BENSON, P., pseud. See MILLER, Charles C.
BERGMANN, Karl, 1821-1876.
   The Mary polka redowa. 6078
   Ocean House polka redowa. 2075
BERNARD, John S.
   Ixion medley. (arr.) 5627
BETHUNE, Thomas Greene, 1849-1908.
   The battle of Manassas. 571
   Daylight. 601
   The man who got the cinder in his eye. 612
   Water in the moonlight. 604
BEYER, Ferdinand, 1803-1863.
   Morning star waltz. 539
BIRD, Horace G., 1829 or 30-1897.
   Shadow waltz. 253
BISHOP, Thomas Brigham, 1835-1905.
   Gentle naiad. 5596
   Love among the roses. 5533 (guitar) 5781
   Some day when I am far away. 5595
BLACKMER, E. T., onetime (1876) musical director of the San Diego, Cal., Philharmonic Society.
   Wait, my little one, wait. 5934
BLAMPHIN, Charles.
   Little Maggie May. (guitar) 6011

BLANDIN, J. W.
    Minnehaha polka. 1652
BLESSNER, Gustave, 1808-1888.
    Atlanta (grand victory march). 5319
    Camp schottisch. 5050
    Commencement march. 4160
    Grand polonaise. 4152, 5190
    Homeward. 5089
BLIND TOM. See BETHUNE, Thomas Greene.
BLISS, Philip Paul, 1838-1876.
    Baby's sweet sleep. 6106
    Bessie Lee. 6170
    Bonapo, a medley. 5999
    Brave battery boys. 5876
    The difference. See Mr. Lordly & I.
    For you! 5733
    Good bye Jeff! 435
    A grand vocal medley. 546
    He's gone! 5693
    Hold the fort! p134
    If papa were only ready! 827
    John Chinaman. 5695
    Jolly Jonathan and his notional naburs. p139
    Lora Vale. 396, 4924 (guitar) 5678
    Loving little Lou. 6182
    Mr. Lordly & I, or The difference. 605
    Not at all like me! See The photograph.
    The owl in the ruin. See Watcher Gray.
    The photograph, or Not at all like me! 755
    Pro Phundo Basso. 4845
    Remembered. 5774
    Room for one more. 707
    Sweetly, softly. 6205
    The temperance ship. 6117
    The tin wedding. 5618
    'Tis the heart makes the home. 5440
    The tragical tail of poor Thomas Maltese. 756
    Watcher Gray, or (The owl in the ruin). 5442
    What shall the harvest be. 5759
    When grandmama is gone. 4977
    Willie's wooing. 5699
BLUMENSCHEIN, H. L.
    Fairy Nora loves me. 491
BLUMENTHAL, Jacques, 1829-1908.
    Les deux anges. 670
BOGUE, Elias, onetime (1873) vocal teacher at Ferry Hall, Lake Forest, Ill.
    L'etoile galop. 5527
BOOTT, Francis, 1813-1904.
    How to put the question. 5864
BOUDEMAN, Dallas.
    Come while the world lies dreaming. 753
    We'll have to get the style. p133
BOWE, Emma.
    Lake shore mazurka. 573
BOWEN, Mrs. F. L.
    Tread lightly ye comrades; or, The volunteer's grave. 269

BRADBURY, William Batchelder, 1816-1868.
    The dear ones all at home. 57
BRAINARD, Julia.
    Gray distance hid each shining sail. 393
    A lullaby. 441
    The Sabbath morning. 735
BRAND, T. H., principal of the Madison (Wis.) Vocal Academy, 1869-70.
    Sounds from the old camp ground. p133
BRAUER, Fr.
    The youth's musical friend. 5985
BREWSTER, O. M.
    Our comrade has fallen. 249
BREYTSPRAAK, Charles.
    Moment polka. 180
BRIDEWELL, W. W.
    Nasby's lament over the New York nominations. 4967
BROCKWAY, William H., 1834 or 35-1888.
    Nellie Ray. 442
    Young Eph's jubilee. 551
BROWN, Frank.
    Sadly to-night I am dreaming. 5698
BROWN, George W., 1840-1894.
    Allie. 5793
    Darling little Eva Ray. 6133
    Little Robin tell Kitty I'm coming. 6149
    O bring my darling back to me. 6131
    Softly fall the silvery moonbeams. 6128
    Somebody's waiting down in the dell. 6048
    When we sleep beneath the daisies. 6129
BROWN, T. M., Missouri pianist, teacher, and composer.
    Tramp! tramp! tramp! Transcription brillante. 501
BUCK, Dudley, 1839-1909.
    Easter morning. 5838
BURKHART, William.
    May queen quadrille. 489
    La mode. "Trois temps." 6052
BUTTERFIELD, James Austin, 1837-1891.
    Jamie's awa'. 5718
C. C. S. See S., C. C.
CADY, Chauncey Marvin, 1824-1889.
    All in the golden prime of May. 5861
    Fond heart, oh, think of me. 5779
    We are the boys that fear no noise. 6279
    We meet upon the level. 8
CALDWELL, Susie B.
    Name me in thy prayer. 4939  p134
CALKINS, J. Morton.
    Hallie Lee. 653
CELLI, Adelina Murio. See MURIO-CELLI, Adelina.
CHAMBERLIN, E.
    I wonder why he comes not! 493
CHERRY, John William, 1824-1889.
    Shells of ocean. 244

CHING FOO.
  Tin-ni-min-wi-win-kum-ka, or The Chinaman's farewell. 5739
CHOPIN, Fryderyk Franciszek, 1810-1849.
  Impromptu, op. 29. 5100
CLAEPIUS, Wilhelm Hermann, 1801-1868.
  Evening 39
CLARIBEL, pseud. See BARNARD, Mrs. Charlotte Alington.
CLARK, Ernst.
  Tommy Dodd. 4873
CLARK, James Gowdy, 1830-1897.
  The promised land tomorrow. 5578
  The unseen city. 5575
CONCORDIUS, pseud.
  Uncle Sam. p133
COOTE, Charles, 1807-1879.
  Corn flower valse. 2951
COVERT, Bernard, singer and composer of The Sword of Bunker Hill.
  Follow the drum. 423
COX, John Sumner, 1831 or 32-1902.
  The crossing sweeper. 4859
  Mother, blame me not for loving. 212
  My thoughts are far away. 4869
  Only a waiting maid. 4862
CRAMER, Henri, 1818-1877.
  Il desiderio. 544
  Last idea. 3527
CRANE, W. C.
  Oil-do-ra-do. 439
CRAW, Clara E
  Holden guards schottische. 268
CROUCH, Frederick William Nicholls, 1808-1896.
  Kathleen Mavourneen. 90
D. H. H. See H., D. H.
DARLING, Hattie
  His voice still speaks to me! 575
DEAN, Frederick.
  Emmeline. Mazurka de salon. 5872
  Forget me not. 5880
  My love and I. 5867
  When thou'rt lonely think of me. 5871
DEANE, Lyman W.
  Fisherman, fisherman, over the sea. 5478
DEGENHARD, Charles, d. 1867.
  April shower, polka redowa. 401
  The coquette waltz. 402
DELOS [pseud. of SPALDING, Delos Gardner?]
  If you love me, say so! 5614
  I'm happy to night. 5622
  Never borrow trouble. 5802
  Oh! sing with the birds. 5616
  The pride of the dell. 5751
  Some people think only of money. 5623
  Such is fashion. 5679

DELOS (Continued)
  Trumps. 5961
  Under the arbor. 5712
  When we've nothing else to do. 5653
DEMAR, John, arr.
  When ye gang awa, Jamie. 5140
DICAL, R. A.
  Dinna ye hear the s'Logan? 613
DOANE, William Howard, 1832-1915.
  Shadows of the past. 4878
DODGE, Ossian Euclid, 1820-1876.
  Ho! westward ho! 4831
  Keep the ball a-rolling. 4841
  Singular dreams. 273
DOLORES.
  The brook. 5207
DOTZLER, Charles.
  The Fitzpatrick polka. 6222
  Wyndham polka. 6211
DOWLING, Lillia.
  Oh! he kissed me when he left me. 349
DUER, Mrs. E. A. Parkhurst.
  Beautiful hands. 4956
DURFEE, James, Jr.
  Amateur march. 122
E. F. P. See P., E. F.
E. S. P. See P., E. S.
EDWARDS, M. E.
  Drifting leaflets. 5674
  Little Elma's waltz. 5661
EICHBERG, Julius, 1824-1893.
  Fraternity march. 828
  Gen. Lyon's battle march. 110
  Pilgrim's night -- march. 5173
ELPEUX, Adelina Murio-Celli d'. See MURIO-CELLI, Adelina.
FASSETT, Walter S.
  Bonnie venture waltz. 500
FAWCETT, George E.
  The president's emancipation march. 261
  Summer night schottisch. 728
FERRILL, Fred.
  Sophia waltz. 577
FLORANCE, George A.
  The pet polka. 9
FLOTOW, Friedrich von, 1812-1883.
  Home far away. 41
FOO, Ching. See CHING FOO.
FORMES, Karl Johann, 1816-1889.
  Addio Madrid. p139
  In memory of Abraham Lincoln. 514
  The Polish refugee. p139
FOSTER, Stephen Collins, 1826-1864.
  Mine is the mourning heart. 290
FRADEL, Karl, 1821-1886.
  Auber's Fra Diavolo transcript. 449
  Cycloid polka. 498
  La forza del destino. Transcription elegante. 448

FRANKS, W.
    The little wanderer's song. 4931
"FREDERICK," pseud.
    Engaged. p133
FREIBERG, Fred.
    Skating waltz. 726
FRENCH, D. A.
    Fairy ring. 400
    '63 is the jubilee. 266
FRENCH, Laura.
    Illini polka. 346
FREUND, Joseph.
    Spring style schottisch. 190
FRISBIE, Henrie L.
    The down easter's journey. See Out West.
    Kitty Clyde's grave. See Thou wilt come never more to the stream.
    Oh! bury the brave where they fall. 357
    Out west; or, The down easter's journey. 569
    Sleighing with the girls. 356
    The songs we sang upon the old camp ground. 606
    The stars and stripes, the flag of the free. 76
    Thou wilt come never more to the stream; or, Kitty Clyde's grave. 82
GABRIEL, Mary Ann Virginia, 1825-1877.
    Only. 6175
GANZ, Wilhelm, 1833-1914.
    Qui vive! grand galop concert. 6012
    Sing, birdie, sing. 643, 2734
GARDNER, Miss H.
    Little flirt waltz. 6210
GEARY, Gustavus, d. 1877.
    Behind the jessamine. 6057
    Fly love to me. 6224
    O set my heart at rest. 6053
    Our blue eyed darling. 6056
    Swinging in the trees. 6277
    The trumpet of glory. 6102, 7002
GIMBEL, Charles, Jr.
    Love's flirtation. Polka brillante. 5807
    Sans souci, marche triumphal. 5903
GIRAC, Max Emilius, ca.1789-1869.
    The founder of Notre Dame. 766
GLOVER, Stephen, 1812-1870.
    The song of Blanche Alpen. 221
    The valley of Chamouni. 462
GOERDELER, Richard.
    Lily queen waltz. 5907
    The one horse galop. 5881
    Pray for me! Pensee sentimental. 5873
    Sweet robin waltz. 6072
    Upside down galop. 5768
GOLDBECK, Robert, 1839-1908.
        Piano
    Adoration polka. 5762
    Auld lang syne, grand morceau de concert. 737

GOLDBECK, Robert, 1839-1908. (Continued)
    Belles de Chicago. Valse elegante; or, Les Plaisirs de la valse. 5510
    Blue Beard. 6193
    Caprice de concert d'après une polka de Schulhoff. 738
    The conservatory waltz. 5998
    Faust caprice de concert. 825
    Flashes from the west. 6112
    Harmonized progressive finger exercises for the piano. 6195-96, 6188
    Marche de Faust. 812
    The million dollar waltz. 5524
    L'opera dan le salon. Une serie de fantaisies brillante pour le piano. I-IV 1758, 2419 p133
    Les plaisirs de la valse. See Belles de Chicago.
    Sogni d'amore, morceau de concert. 739
    Traumgewebe. Nocturne. 5772
        Vocal
    Break, break, break. 5899
    The day is cold. 5897
    Dreams of heaven. 5885
    A love song. 5895
    The nun. 5901
    O moonlight deep and tender. 5898
    Soprano song from Goldbeck's cantata -- The pioneer. 5896
    [Torrent song.] 5900
    Where'er the heart to true heart beats. Duett. 5889 Song. 5920
    Willow song. Duett. 5886 [Song] 5902
GORHAM, A. Templeton.
    Baby goes alone. 5515
    Bonnie Marguerita. 4830
    If I only knew it came from Paris. 5523
    Is there room among the angels. 4972
    Katie waiting at the door. 6088
    Kiss me when I come home. 5518
    Let me dream of home and loved ones. 761
    Papa, help me across. 5929
    Send the little ones happy to bed. 6179
    Summer bloom waltz. 5677
    Sweet Ethelinda. 5675
    Too genteel you know. p134
    Tripping through the barley. 5540
    Where the firelight gleams at home. 5676
    Yes, dearest, I'll love thee. 5941
GOSS, Samuel T.
    Ella schottische. p134
GOTTSCHALK, Louis Moreau, 1829-1869.
    Battle cry of freedom, grand caprice de concert. 440
GOUGLER, I. W.
    Soldier's friend, polka quickstep. 326
GOUNOD, Charles Francois, 1818-1893.
    Vocal beauties of Faust. 382-5

GROBE, Charles G., 1817-
    Come home, father. With brilliant variations. 635
    Kingdom coming. With brilliant variations. 215
    Tramp! tramp! tramp! with brilliant variations. 450, 4940

GRUND, Friedrich Wilhelm, 1791-1874.
    Grund's etudes, ed. by S. N. Penfield. 5722-23

GUMBERT, Ferdinand, 1818-1896.
    Eventide. 270
    Savior breathe an evening blessing. 392

H., D. H.
    Agawam quickstep. 245

H. W. J. See J., H. W.

HACKELTON, Mrs. Maria W.
    At the beautiful gate. 5796
    Come where the south wind wanders. 5782
    Ever in dreams. 5624
    The golden morn. 5616
    Old folk's love song. 5628
    When you told me the tale of your love. 5538
    Willie's coming home. 5576

HAGEN, Theodor, 1823-1871.
    La gaillarde morceau de genre. 31

HAHN, Madam C.
    The soldier's last request. 2452

HAHN, Jacob H., 1847-1902.
    Rippling rill polka. 701

HALBRON, pseud.
    Adalida polka. 460

HALL, Foley.
    Ever of thee. 40

HAMBAUGH, James S.
    Stars and stripes schottisch. 129

HANBY, Benjamin Russell, 1833-1867.
    Angel Nellie; or, Waiting at the old linden tree. 520
    Crowding awfully. 615
    The freedman's song. See Now den! now den!
    In a horn. 611
    Now den! now den! 541
    The revelers' chorus. 547
    Waiting at the old linden tree. See Angel Nellie.

HARRIS, Charles, teacher of and composer for the guitar.
    Crown of roses waltz. 6121
    Imitation of the banjo. 5877
    Impromptu brilliante. 4850
    Polka grotesque. 4849
    Silver star waltz. 4978
    Sounds from Mexico. 4826
    Sparkling dew polka. 6122

HARRISON, James, d. 1878.
    Dear little barefeet, I've counted your toes! 5916
    Dillon schottische. 4870

HARRISON, James, d. 1878. (Continued)
    Eleanore waltzes. 5891
    Emma May. See Linden bowers.
    Floating on the lake. 683
    La Grenadille, passion flower, waltzes. 5650
    I'm queen of the night. 708
    The latch string at the door. p133
    Linden bowers, or Emma May. 705
    Sibylla valse. 5534
    Te Deum. 5746
    We're waiting for father! 730, p133

HART, Henry.
    Idlewild mazurka. p135
    My thoughts are of thee. p135

HARTWELL, Mrs. S.
    Sunlight to the soul. 5764

HAUSE, Carl.
    O moonlight deep and tender. 155

HAVENS, A. W.
    Curiosity galop. 6085
    Fatherless. 5945
    The land that is fairer than day. 5874
    Take me from my little bed. 6037
    (guitar) 7003

HAVENS, Charles Arthur, 1842-
    La volta, caprice. 711

HAWLEY, Horace H., 1817-
    How it marches! the flag of the union. p133

HAYNES, Edward
    Our nation's captain. 413
    We shall miss you dearest brother. 408

HAYNES, J. E.
    All hail to Ulysses! 364

HAYWOOD, George.
    When my ship comes in! 654, 3583

HEATH, Wilbur F., 1843-1915.
    There is no one like a mother. 680
    We are traveling on together. 693

HELLER, Stephen, 1814-1888.
    30 progressive studies. 2421

HENNIG, W A.
    Parting song. 674

HERRICK, George D.
    Rally for the leader! p134

HERTEL, J. W.
    Michigan schottische. 53

HEWITT, W.
    Grand waltz for guitar. 697

HEYER, Charles Otto, 1832-1897.
    Bow down Thine ear. 4891
    Cast thy burden on the Lord. 4895
    The Lord is my shepherd. 4890
    Now from labor and from care. 4889
    Rock of ages. 4892
    Safely through another week. 4876
    Saviour when in dust, to Thee. 5620
    Softly now the light of day. 763

HEYER, Karl Otto.
　See HEYER, Charles Otto.
HICKS, Edmund W.
　Vicksburg is taken boys!　375
HIGGINS, Libbie.
　See JACKSON, Mrs. Libbie Higgins.
HILL, Will
　Minnesota, the lily of the west.　4974
HOAG, A. B.
　I dream of the beautiful past.　6214
HOBSON, M., arr.
　Pulling hard against the stream.　6044
HOFFMAN, Edward.
　Adelina (polka).　5908
　Bridal flowers for the piano.　5707-10
　Camelia (polka).　5707
　Carlotta (galop).　5910
　Come home father. Transcription.　622
　The dell of roses, mazurka elegante.　4948
　The four sisters for piano.　5908-11
　Fuchsia (galop).　5709
　Grand fantasia, Whippoorwill.　5915
　Henrietta (mazurka).　5911
　Isabella (waltz).　5909
　The nation's hero grand march.　4865
　Night before Petersburgh. Burlesque military fantasia.　759
　O, take me to thy heart again. Transcription. 5552
　Orange blossom (mazurka).　5708
　Rose waltz.　5710
　Shooting star galop di bravura.　578
　Whippoorwill. See Grand fantasia, Whippoorwill.
HOLMES, Avanelle L.
　Will you wed me now I'm lame, love?　345
HOLST, Eduard, 1843-1899.
　I cannot forget thee.　in A flat　6220
　　　　　　　　　　　in E flat　6215
HOWARD, Frank, pseud. (Real name: SPALDING, Delos Gardner, 1833-1884)
　Among the angels.　5572
　The bonnie bright eyes of somebody.　5949
　Childhood songs.　5568
　Come home, mother.　5569
　Cruel, cruel men.　5597
　Down brakes.　5795
　Down by the brook at the end of the lane. 4828
　The fortune daisy.　5893
　The girl with the auburn tress!　5767
　Girls, don't fool with cupid.　5717
　Go ask my wife.　5532
　Golden leaves of autumn.　5438
　Grandfather darling.　5971
　Grandma.　5535
　Heigh ho! I'm in want of a beau!　5544
　He'll soon propose.　5593
　I feel I'm growing old, dear wife.　5615

HOWARD, Frank, pseud. (Continued)
　I know a lovely maiden.　5603
　I met her at the mat-inee.　5580
　If you'll promise not to tell.　5812
　I'll leave it all to you.　6005
　I'll tell you why.　5638
　I'm in love.　5530
　I'm such a nice young man.　5502
　"It."　5777
　It's not poor mother's fault.　4882
　It's true, 'twas in the papers.　5925
　Keep straight ahead.　5591
　Kitty McKay.　5495
　Lend a kind helping hand to the poor.　677
　List to me.　5445
　Little barefoot. (guitar)　5667
　Little bother.　5586
　Little pet schottische.　5995
　Little shoes and stockings.　5563
　The little stone cot in the dell.　4900
　Lottie's all the world to me.　613
　Maggie Blair.　5588
　Making love by moonlight.　5792
　Making love while on the ice.　5494
　Marching home.　5755
　Meet me just at twilight.　5664　p134
　Millie Clair.　5599
　Mind your own bread and butter.　4872
　Minnie Munroe.　5594
　My heart is far over the sea.　5562
　My landlady's pretty little daughter.　5600
　My native hills.　5608
　Oh, Sorosis!　4858　p134
　Often in dreams I'm roaming.　4839
　O'Googerty's wedding.　5609
　The old church bells.　4937
　Old sayings.　5545
　Only a part.　5713
　Our folks schottische.　6065
　Patiently waiting　5969
　Philander Brown, the ill-used young man. 5513
　The prettiest girl in town.　5437
　Profit and loss.　5687
　Quit that.　p135
　The rustic lassie polka.　6230
　Shadows on the stream.　5567
　She has such winning ways.　4885
　The short girl dressed in green.　4852
　Since the day I signed the pledge.　692
　Sing to me dear sister.　5962
　Sit thee down beside me Nannie.　6004
　Songs that we never forget.　5443
　　(guitar)　5672
　The sugar plum waltz.　6273
　There! I told you so.　5953
　There's a void in our household.　5531
　There's always a welcome for thee.　5612

HOWARD, Frank, pseud. (Continued)
    There's no such beau as mine. 5542
    This beautiful world that we live in. 5526
    The time for love. 5602
    'Twas after twelve when you came home. 4874
    Underfoot. 5890
    The velocipede. 5444
    Velocipede waltz. 5493
    The way it's done. 4846
    What is the use of our being unhappy? 6047
    When the birds come in spring. 5505
    When the clover was in bloom. 5790
    Where are the dear friends of childhood. 5610
    Where are you going. 6016
    Where the woodland birdlings warble. 6116
    Who's to blame? 5543
    Why don't he write? 5590
    Why not. 4829
    Young girl of the period. 5589
    Young man of the period. 5577
HUBBARD, Charles P.
    Come where the morning is breaking. 605
    Ida waltz. 1143
    Pond lilly schottisch. 2011
HUBBARD, James Maurice, 1821 or 22-1900.
    Angel Mary. 338
    Bertha Louise. 399
    Bird of the mountain. 6095
    Bright Kalamazoo. 419
    Death of the robin. 67
    I never kiss & tell. 69
    List! The evening breeze is stealing. 17
    Little Alice. 373
    Love, sweet love is everywhere. 335
    Mine own. 66
    The ruler in peace and the leader in war. 4827
    Sabbath morn. 4863
    Silent evening. 140
    Song of the Egyptian girl. 68
    Viola schottisch. 406
    Who comes dar? 433
HÜNTEN, Franz, 1793-1878.
    La rose. 896
HUGHES, William Carter.
    Camp song of the Chicago Irish brigade. 84
HUTCHINSON, Asa Burnham, 1823-1884.
    Tender tones memory bells. 5278
HUTCHINSON, John Wallace, 1821-1908.
    A hundred years hence. 5521
    Lashed to the mast. 679
    Vote it right along! 5517
HYDE, B.
    Excursion schottische. 6209
IRMA, pseud.
    Chase among the roses. 5776
J., H. W.
    Put up the bars. 690

JACKSON, Mrs. Libbie Higgins.
    My barefoot boy. 5692
    Thy spirit will ever be near. 5696
JOHNSON, Mrs. H. Mills.
    Memories of home. p135
JOHNSON, L. H.
    Hurrah polka. 922
JUCH, Justin.
    On land and sea. 6178
KAPPES, J. Henry, 1824-1915.
    Evening prayer; or, Savior breathe an evening blessing. 4855
KEEP SHADY, pseud.
    Sally Ann's away! 676
KETTERER, Eugene, 1831-1870.
    Gaetana mazurka. 6207
KIDDER, W. C., teacher of music at Cornell College, Mount Vernon, Ia., 1878-79.
    O, ye tears! Transcription brillante. 652
KIMBALL, Horace E.
    I've got a baby. 5640
    Musical bon-bons. Five little pieces arr. for very little fingers. 5700-04
    Velocipede polka. 5492
    Would I? 5636
KIMMELL, Abram.
    In the valley of the west. 585
KING, Frank H., 1844 or 45-1900.
    The happy daughters. 5750
KINKEL, Johanna Mockel, 1810-1858.
    The knight's farewell. 4958
KINNEY, Virginia S.
    Fairy footsteps waltz. 596
KLINGEMANN, C.
    Delusion. Mazurka characteristique. 118
KNAEBEL, Simon.
    Banquet polka. 5557
    Monticello waltz. 5559
    The musical garland. 5554-59, 5573-74
    Sally port polka. 5573
    Sleigh bells mazurka. 5574
    Smith schottische. 5554
    Social waltz. 5556
    Welcome schottische. 5555
    Young American galopade. 5558
KNAPP, A. B.
    The Annie Huger galop. 6221
KNORTZ, Carl.
    I can not forget. 5503
KRUGER, Edward H.
    Golden ringlets. 4886
KÜCKEN, Friedrich Wilhelm, 1810-1882.
    Fly, birdling, through the verdant wood. 2967
KUSCHBERT, Emanuel, b. 1832.
    Hans and Hanne polka. 5642
    Josephine waltz. 5641
LACHNER, Franz, 1803-1890.
    Lachner's serenade. 832

LACHNER, Ignaz, 1807-1895.
    Überall du. 2966
LAMOTTE, Antoine, 1819-1912.
    Beads man polka. 772
LANNER, Joseph Franz Karl, 1801-1843.
    Faust grand march. 386
LEE, Alfred.
    [The man on the] flying trapeze. 4898
    Par excellence. 5786
LEFÉBURE-WÉLY, Louis James Alfred, 1817-1870.
    Berceuse. 800
    Les cloches dû monastère. 238, 3113
    Fireside harmonies. 800-805
    L'heure de la priere. 185
    Marche. 801
    Pastorale. 803
    Prière. 804
    Rêverie. 805
    Romance sans paroles. 802
LEFOY
    Idol of my heart. 5728
LEHMAN, Albert.
    Dew pearls waltz. 5757
LEHMAN, W. H.
    Terrace hill waltz. 7000
LEHMAN, William.
    Des Moines city waltz. 388
LEIDNER, John.
    Piano forte march of the 23rd Regiment, U. S. Infantry. 5958
LEWIS, William, 1837-1902.
    March on! march on! 369
LEYBACH, Ignace Xavier Joseph, 1817-1891.
    La sonnambula. 5968
LINWOOD, E.
    That little room up stairs. 4947
LISZT, Franz, 1811-1886.
    Grand galop chromatique. 777
A LITTLE JOKER, pseud.
    First finger waltz. 4923
LOB, Otto.
    Kutschke's war-song. 6169
    The lonely tear. 6155
    The papillion. 6140
    Pic nic waltz. 704
    Repose. 6157
    Thou art my own. 6156
LOCKWOOD, C. T., 1834 or 35-1870.
    And he's got the money too. 5504
    Bessie's trust. 5730
    Blushing rose polka. 4926
    Call me when breakfast is ready! 5637
    Days that are gone! 4842
    Don't stay late to-night. p134
    Ella Bell. 4957
    Father will settle the bill. 5789 (guitar) 5952
    Feather polka. p134

LOCKWOOD, C. T., 1834 or 35-1870. (Continued)
    Feather waltz. 4949
    Gathering home. 4935 (guitar) 5669
    Give the boy a chance. 5787
    The little ones at home! 4953
    Little stub toe polka. 4837
    "Look me in the eye Johnny." 5888
    My Madeline! 4843
    Pebble polka. 4951
    Rosy hours. 5663
    Shall I ever see my boy! p134
    Shower waltz. 5525
    Shun the broad road. 4952 (guitar) 5585
    Silver whistle. 4866
    Sparkle, schottische. 4854
    Starry waves. 5625
    Still I love thee. 4834
    Tommy's return. 838
    Walk! walk! walk! 4955
    We'll have to mortgage the farm. 5705
LOESCHHORN, Albert, 1819-1905.
    Tarantelle. 327
LONG, James W.
    The artillery galop. 4966
McEVOY, Charles.
    The captive bird. 14
    Here in this moonlit bower. 19
    Les zephyrs du matin; or, Zephyrs of morning waltz. 22
MacLAGEN, T.
    Captain Jinks. 4899
MACY, James Cartwright, 1845-1918.
    Good bye Johnnie; or, Mother's request. 4836
    Joanna dear, my Jo. 4868
MALLANDAINE, J. E.
    Faces I see in my dreams. 6174
MARSH, Mrs. Mary Ann. See GABRIEL, Mary Ann Virginia.
MARTIN, S. Wesley, 1839-
    Annie Snow. 5917
    Daughter of the Isles. 5918
    Softly dream, sweet love. 24
    Welcome to spring. 27
MARYATT, Pendleton.
    The mountains of life; or, My soul shall know thine in that beautiful land. 4971
MASON, William, 1829-1908.
    Amitié pour amitié, morceau de salon. 4887
    Polka gracieuse. 63
MASSETT, Stephen C., 1820-1898.
    Then and now. 5974
MATHEWS, William Smythe Babcock, 1837-1912.
    Linden waltz. 6274
    Nightfall at home, nocturne. 1511 p134
MAX, pseud.
    Trust me Cathleen. 5939

MAYER, Ferdinand.
    The maiden's prayer. 4982
MAYER, Henry.
    La belle brunette valse. 5806
    Emita redowa. 5865
    Jeunesse (youth) polka. p134
    La joyeuse polka. 5858
    Matin (Morning). 5857
    Soir (Evening) 5856
MAYO, Oscar, ca.1836-
    Castanet waltz (Creole). 6110
    Fairy bridal polka. 5773
    Fancy free polka characteristique. 6049
    El Kohinoor polka. 6099
    Op. 5, eight orchestral beauties transcribed. 6068-71, 6074-76, 6080
    The Phi gamma delta march. 5639
MAYWOOD, George, pseud. See SCHLEIFFARTH, George.
MELFI, Peppino.
    The pagoda waltz. 6216
MENDELSSOHN-BARTHOLDY, Felix, 1809-1847.
    The wedding march. 1405
MERRILL, Hiram T., Chicago teacher and music publisher.
    Anyhow. 1127
    Be a man. 1121
    "Corn is king!" 227
    The first blossom waltz. 4936
    First bud waltz. 4912
    The little angel. 5581
    My mother's song. 5584
    The old hickory cane. 5582
    The old house far away. 277
    Song of the Negro boatman. 178
    Take your gun and go, John. 138
MERZ, Karl, 1836-1890.
    The bee song. 434
    I'd mourn the hopes that leave me. 1060
    The little drummer boy's march. 381, 4943
    Miriam's song of triumph. 4897
METCALFE, J. A.
    La pluie de meteores... Mazurka caprice. 6054
MEYERBEER, Giacomo, 1791-1864.
    Slumber song from L'Africaine. 538
MILES, Frederick William.
    Central city polka. 395
MILLARD, Harrison, 1830-1895.
    Happy dreams. 418
MILLER, Charles C., 1831-1920.
    The bee march. 6258
    O, soft sleep the hills! 691
    The singin skewl. 5537
MILLER, L. B., music dealer and choir leader of Galesburg, Ill.
    The president's grave. 444
MINKLER, F. G.
    Shabona schottisch. 366

MITCHELL, Clara C.
    Charlie schottische. 574
MOELLING, Theodore, ca.1822-1894.
    Brilliant duets for the piano forte. Op. 90 (arr.) 616-21
    Columbia's call! transcribed & varied. 736
    Daisy Deane. Transcription. 623
    Dulcet strains from the opera for piano. Op. 88. 626-31
    Gems from Crispino e la Comare, arr. for piano. 588
    Myrtle wreath. Caprice. 740
    Ristori grande valse. 625
    Santa Lucia for piano & cabinet organ. (Arr.) 783
    Souvenir de L'Africaine. Valse. 599
MOLTER, John, Chicago teacher and music publisher.
    Softly fall the silvery moonbeams. [Transcription] 6167
MORGAN, George Washbourne, 1822-1892.
    The Chicago mazurka. 493
    Emilie waltz. 7034
    The Hyde Park polka. 522
    May march. p134
    The Stevens march. 765
MORRIS, Robert, LL.D.
    The children in the grave yard. 6114
MORRISON, John.
    When the roses bud and blossom. 5649
MOSES, A.
    Illinois grand march. 438
MOZART, Wolfgang Amadeus, 1756-1791.
    Fantasie C moll. 4975
    The Lord my pasture shall prepare. 6060
    Vedrai carino. 781-2
MÜLLER, Edward.
    Marie quadrilles. 5869
    Sodowa march. 5788
MURIO-CELLI, Adelina, 1843 or 44-1900.
    La clochette de l'esperance schottisch. p133
MURRAY, James Ramsey, 1841-1905.
        Piano
    Bright eyes waltz. 4896
    Carl Pretzel waltz. 6184
    The irresistible schottische. 6046
    The latest polka. 6040
    The merry sleigh-ride. 6229
    Mona's reverie. 4861
    Over the dancing waves. 6238
    Song of the fairies. 6272
        Vocal
    Angels beckon me! p134
    Angels guard her dreams tonight! 835
    Baby blue-eyes. p134
    Baby's gone to sleep. 668
    Beautiful spirit of song. 4965
    Brothers of the mystic tie. 4969

MURRAY, James Ramsey, 1841-1905. (Continued)
    Christmas cheer. 4884
    Daisy Deane. 325 (guitar) 342
    Ever with me. 4875
    Gone to heaven. 5498 p134
    Guests of the heart. 5491
    Heart to heart and soul to soul. 5859
    How sweet the thought. 4856
    I love to think of thee. 5926
    I wait for thy coming, my darling. 4835
    I'm thinking of our youth, Tom! 694
    It is better farther on. 6017
    Kind smiles for all. 1182 p133
    Little sunshine. 4943 p134
    Loving thee ever. p133
    Make home beautiful. 6073
    Merry Christmas. p134
    Mother's room. 6015
    Mother's waiting for her children. 5747
    The old kitchen floor. 5913
    One I love, two I love. p135
    Prussia, gird thy sons for battle! 5951
    The sweetness of thy smile. 5706
    Sweets to the sweetest. 5666
    The tanner and the blue! 4970
    A tear for the comrade that's gone. 5862
    There's sunshine after rain. 5803 p134
    They tell me thou art sleeping. 689
    Treasures of the past. 5561
    What shall I ask for thee. 752 (guitar) 5671
    When mother fell asleep. 4973
    When Sue and I went skating. 4879
    When the dear ones gather at home. 6208

NAYLOR, Fred B.
    Angel Nettie Bane. 5937
    O'er my little brother's grave. 5935
    Where little baby rests. 5942

NEWCOMB, C. R.
    Kitty More. 695

OESTEN, Theodor, 1813-1870.
    Alpine bells. 236
    Gondellied. 530
    Love in May. 528

OFFENBACH, Jacques, 1819-1880.
    From the bosom of the waters. 6219
    The opera season ... fantasias ... arr. by F. W. Root. 6019-34

OTTO, F. R.
    The Lafner waltz. 131

P., E. F.
    Come to me, gentle sleep. p135

P., E. S.
    The leaves around me falling. 5892

P., S. G. [PRATT, Silas Gamaliel?]
    Life's dream is o'er! 4976

PALMER, Horatio Richmond, 1834-1907.
    Have courage my boy to say no. 6041

PAPE, William Barnesmore, 1840-1901.
    The brook, Improvisation. 6008
    Highland gems for the piano forte. 5884
    Irish diamonds. 5883
    No. 2, Irish diamonds. 5957
    Recollections of a music box. 5882

PARK, Roswell, 1807-1869.
    The ensign of glory. 135

PARRY, John Orlando, 1810-1879.
    The apology; or, You know. 280

PARKHURST, Mrs. E. A. See DUER, Mrs. E. A. Parkhurst.

PATTIANI, Eliza.
    May breeze. Variations brillante. 422
    Soldier's home medley. 429

PEARSON, George C.
    All hail the reign of peace. 465

PEASE, Alfred Humphries, 1838-1882.
    Absence. 6043
    'Tis lone on the waters. 5948

PENFIELD, Smith Newell, 1837-1920.
    The cascade of pleasure. 5743
    Invitation to the galop. 5721
    Parnassus. 5741
    A poem of life. Four pieces in the form of a sonata. 5741-44
    Souvenir de Paris. Rondino. 5720
    The stream of time. 5744
    The sunny south, reverie. 6183
    The vale of romance. 5742

PEPLOW, J.
    Luna polka. 607    arr. as duet. 619

PERRING, J. Ernest, one-time teacher of singing at the Cincinnati College of Music.
    Waiting for angels to come. 5500

PERSLEY, George W., pseud. See BROWN, George W.

PHELPS, Edward B.
    Coralline mazurka brillante. 4853
    Studio polka. 5549

PHELPS, Mrs. Minnie Andre
    Joy bells polka. 550
    The sparkling schottische. 2848
    Star polka. 430

PRATT, Silas Gamaliel, 1846-1916.
    Gone! impromptu. 5769
    Griffith Gaunt schottische. 639
    The matinée polka. 457
    The midnight stars. 5731
    The midnight zephyrs. 5732
    Musical thoughts for the piano. 582-3
    A night of love. Nocturne. 4950
    Ola, fantasie romanesque. 785
    Reve d'artist. p134
    Shakesperian grand march. 729
    The sigh. Nocturne. 583
    The smile. Polka gracieuse. 582
    Undine polka brillante. p133

PRATT, Silas Gamaliel, 1846-1916. (Continued)
    Undine valse brillante. p133
    White fawn march. 4929
    White fawn schottische. 4902
PRO Phundo Basso, pseud. See BLISS, Philip Paul.
PROCTOR, H. Irwin, Chicago teacher.
    Riverside mazurka. 6212
"QUAILS," pseud.
    Fireman's marching song. 595
REED, Charles A.
    Out on the shore. 6108
REED, J. W.
    The coming of day. 680, 718
REEVES, F.
    Moonlight on the billow. p134
REIN, Emil.
    The battle-cry of freedom. With variations. 274
    Brother, tell me of the battle. Transcription. 455
    Just before the battle, mother, transcription. 397
    The vacant chair with variations. 352
    Will you come to meet me darling? Transcription. 415
REINHART, F. M.
    Parlor skating schottische. (arr.) 437
REYNOLDS, John.
    Sweet Molly Matilda Jane. 5711
RICHARDS, Brinley, 1817-1885.
    Floating on the wind. 237
    Her bright smile haunts me still. 525
    Warblings at eve. 519, 4249
RICHTER, Ernst Friedrich Eduard, 1808-1879.
    Parting. 5426
RINK, Louis H., d.1871.
    Excuse me! schottisch. 6036
    Gen. McClernand's grand march. 264
    Ma belle polka redowa. 251
    Springfield polka. 235
RIX, B. F.
    Johnny Schmoker. (arr.) 281
ROBJOHN, William James, 1843-1920.
    Beneath the loved one's window, a serenade. 562
    Cattle bell at evening. 557
    Christmas chime carol & hymn. 552
    Forest temple. 560
    Fountain in the sunlight. 553
    Gala day, a rejoicing. 559
    Golden dream, a waltz. 555
    Grand instrumental medley. 568
    Impatience. 757
    The miller's song, characteristic etude. 554
    Soft breezes in the solemn night, nocturne. 603
ROGERS, William T.
    The midnight winds. 732
ROOT, Ebenezer Towner, 1822-1896.
    Precious to thee. 5863
    Those wildering eyes of thine! 5780

ROOT, Frederick Woodman, 1846-1916.
    Piano
    Belle Helene. Brilliant transcription. 839
    Bells of Sabbath morning. 5548
    The boat ride. 6234
    Crosby's opera house waltz. 451
    D. C. mazurka. 666 Simplified. 747
    Five finger waltz. 6261
    The fly-away waltz. 6081
    Hand in hand: a graded collection of duets. (arr.) 6063, 6067, 6077-78, 6089
    Home run galop. 749
    Lightly rocking. 6227
    The little carnival. (arr.) 6203-04, 6206
    Nocturne no. 1. 6006
    The old clock in the corner. 6228
    The opera season, a series of sparkling fantasias, upon the ... operas by Offenbach. 6019-6134
    Orpheus fantasie. 4901
    Piano pictures. 6227-74
    The pony ride. 6265
    Repose! 4963
    Romeo and Juliet transcription. 815
    Sailing into dreamland. 806
    Silvery ripples waltz. 6281
    Tribute of affection. A transcription of "Kiss me mother, kiss you darling." 734
    A voice from the ocean. 6260
    Wandering in the greenwood. 6267
    Voice
    Beyond. 5972
    The broken band. 664
    Come, said Jesus sacred voice. (arr.) 330
    The crimson glow of sunset fades. 6176
    Faces to memory dear. 750
    I'm married! 5541
    Kitty Vane and I. p135
    Let me go! 672
    O, come, O, come with me. See Undine's song.
    Poor Carlotta! 742
    Touch the keys softly. 665, 4913
    Treasures. 769
    Undine's song, O, come, O, come with me. (arr.) 809
ROOT, George Frederick, 1820-1895.
    Away! away! the track is white. 656
    Away on the prairie alone. 537
    The banner of the fatherland. 5944
    The battle-cry of freedom. 225
    Be sure to call as you pass by. 48
    The beautiful maiden just over the way. 49
    Because He loved me so. See Hymn.
    The boy at the fountain. p135
    Brother, tell me of the battle. 377 (guitar) 468
    Call 'em names, Jeff. 263

ROOT, George Frederick, 1820-1895. (Continued)
- Can the soldier forget? 398
- Camps, tramps, and battlefields. Arr. for piano forte. 469-87
- Columbia's call. 615
- Come on this silent night. 230
- Comrade, all around is brightness. 436
- De day ob liberty's comin'. 224
- Dream on, Lillie. 71
- Dreaming, ever dreaming. 3678
- Farewell beloved friends, farewell. 6115
- Farewell father, friend and guardian. p133
- Father Abraham's reply to the 600,000. 247
- The first gun is fired! May God protect the right! 72
- Foes and friends. 581
- The forest requiem. 4
- Forward, boys, forward. 75
- Free as air quickstep. 6181
- From the ruins our city shall rise. p135
- Glory! glory! or, The little octoroon. 556 (guitar) 561
- God bless our brave young volunteers. 73 (Chorus version) 74
- Good bye old glory. 492
- Have ye sharpened your swords? 79
- Her letter. See Poverty flat.
- He's comin' again. 278
- Hear the cry that comes across the sea. p134
- Home again returning. 657
- Home's harmony. 3350
- Honor to Sheridan. 768
- Hymn. -- Because He loved me so. p133
- I ask no more. 662 (guitar) 771
- If Maggie were my own! 1145, p133
- I'se on de way. 376
- Jenny Lyle. 673
- Jimmy's wooing. 85
- Just after the battle. 379 (guitar) 421
- Just before the battle, mother. 328 (guitar) 350
- Kiss me mother, kiss your darling. 412 (guitar) 5439
- Kitty Ryder. 70
- Lay me down and save the flag. 403
- The liberty bird. 513
- Lilly Brook. 6
- The little octoroon. See Glory! glory!
- Mabel. 618 (guitar) 774
- Marching home! 5755
- Mary of the glen waltz. 6237
- The Masons' dirge. 600
- The Masons' holiday. 600
- The Masons' home. 600
- Mill wheel polka. 6232
- Mother, oh sing to me of heaven. 78
- My beau that went to Canada. 466
- My cottage home dear mother. 88

ROOT, George Frederick, 1820-95. (Continued)
- My heart is like a silent lute. 80
- My home is on the prairie. 7
- My mother she is sleeping. 5
- North and South. 494
- Oh, are ye sleeping Maggie. 1
- O come you from the battle-field? 339
- O come you from the Indies? or, Robert's return from the war. 86
- Oh, haste on the battle! 262
- Octoroon schottische. (guitar) 767
- Off for a holiday. 6233
- Old friends and true friends. 834, 4932
- On, on, on, the boys came marching. 458 (guitar) 512
- On the field of battle, mother. 328
- Only four. 792
- Only waiting. 2
- Our protective union. 567
- Passing through the fire. p135
- Poverty flat; or, Her letter. 5758
- The prisoner's hope. See Tramp! tramp! tramp!
- Robert's return from the war. See O come you from the Indies?
- Rock me to sleep mother. 64
- Serenade. See Come on this silent night.
- Sing me to sleep father. 517
- Six ballads. 2-7
- Softly she faded. 3
- Somewhere. 5564 (guitar) 5670
- Songs of the Free Masons. 600
- Sparkling wavelets. 6231
- Stand up for Uncle Sam, my boys. 126
- Starved in prison. p133
- That little church around the corner. p134 (guitar) 6097
- They have broken up their camps. p133
- To whom shall we give thanks. 3621
- Tramp! tramp! tramp! or, The prisoner's hope. 420 (guitar) 454
- 20 popular melodies. See Camps, tramps and battlefields.
- The vacant chair. 133
- Wake! lady wake! 13
- We'll fight it out here on the old Union line. p134
- The whole story. 6213
- Who'll save the left. 282
- Will you come to meet me darling? 344
- Within the sound of the enemy's guns. 331
- Ye have done it unto me. p135
- Yes, we will be true to each other. 661 (guitar) 770

ROSS, L. L.
- Jennie's gone home; or, The angels took Jennie away. 5719

ROTHGERBER, Leonora.
    My mother's farewell kiss. 5655
    Ruck waltz. 681
ROWLEY, C. E.
    Zimenia. 5753
RUELL
    There is no heart. 4832
RUSSELL, George A.
    Kingdom coming arr. with brilliant variations for guitar. 332
S., C. C. [SMITH, Charles C.?]
    Wingfield schottisch. (arr.) 254
S. G. P. See P., S. G.
SAFFERY, E. C.
    The union volunteers. 77
SANDERSON, W. H.
    Up in a balloon. 5598, p134
SARONI, Herrman S.
    Idyls of the prairie. 4959-61
    Mid-day. 4960
    Sunrise. 4959
    Sunset. 4961
    Winter flowers. 5436
SCHINDLER, Miss M. L.
    Annie Laurie with brilliant variations. 696
    In those bright eyes. 4930
SCHLEIFFARTH, George, 1849-
    Belle of Lincoln park. 6185
    Hanky-panky polka. 6087
    Riverside polka. 5933
    Susie had a mocking bird. 6092
SCHLOTTER, Franz.
    Airs from Undine (arr.). 810
SCHUBERT, Camille, pseud.
    Les postillons valse. 464
SCHUBERT, Franz Peter, 1797-1828.
    The secret. 38
SCHUMANN, Robert Alexander, 1810-1856.
    In the woods. 751
SCOTT, Lady Alicia Anne Spottiswoode, 1810-1900.
    Annie Laurie. 100
SCOTT, Mrs. Clara H. Jones, 1841-1897.
    Floating clouds. 740, p133
    Dearborn waltz. 589
    Grand Girard mazurka. 586
    Lillie schottische. 587
    Snow-flakes. 4917, p134
    3 parlor concert pieces for the piano. 586-7, 589
SCOTT, R. D.
    The new skedaddle. 217
SCULL, Benjamin F., d. 1869.
    Come again sweet holiday. 6042
SEAVERNS, C. L.
    O, summer moon! 5570
    Where go you, pretty Maggie? 823

SEWARD, Theodore Frelinghuysen, 1835-1902.
    Is your heart still the same to me, my darling? 602
    Poor mother! Willie's gone. 425
SHADY, Keep, pseud. See KEEP SHADY, pseud.
SHATTUCK, Charles F., 1835 or 36-1901.
    The light auburn curl. 4860
    Not for thy beauty. 5529
SILEX, pseud.
    Uncle Sam's funeral. 378
SISSON, Charles T., agent for Root & Cady; in 1871 settled in Austin, Tex.
    Chicago schottische. 6061
    Sisson's polka. 6058
SMART, Henry, 1813-1879.
    Poor Jack Brown. 817
SMITH, Charles C., 1835 or 36-1901.
    Skating polka. 60
    Tiger polka. 123
SMITH, J. F. O.
    The day is ended. 6093
SMITH, James Sargent.
    Con anima polka. 616
SMITH, John.
    Base ball. 5938
SMITH, Sydney, 1839-1889.
    Starry night. 549
SNELLING, George.
    Father, come down with the stamps. 655
SPAULDING, John F.
    I love the charming autumn! 632
SPENCER, D.
    Parlor skating schottische. 437
SPEYER, Wilhelm, 1790-1878.
    The trumpeter. 2741
SPIER, Lion.
    Thinking of home polka. 725
SPINNING, Edgar G.
    At the golden gate. 597
STAAB, Franz, Chicago composer of salon pieces for the piano.
    Coquette mazurka. 213
    Rock me to sleep mother. Transcription de concert. 214
    Light guard schottisch. 2320
STAAB, Louis, d. 1899.
    Belles of Chicago, polka brillante. 5714
    Flower of the West. Mazurka elegante. 5715
    Damenwahl polka. 5784
    Love among the roses, caprice de concert. 5754
    Promesse. Reverie. 5943
STEVENS, George, Chicago conductor.
    The Alice polka. p134
    The Barry schottische. 659 (guitar) 775
    Carrickfergus schottische. 671
    Εκατον (Hecaton) waltzes. 5811

STEVENS, George, Chicago conductor. (Continued)
    Huguenot captain polka. 660
    The Masonic march. 447
    The Museum polka. 446
    The Robert Brierly schottisch. 414

STILLMAN, J. M.
    Beautiful starlight. 5875
    Songs of summer. 6051

STRACK, Louis.
    Variations brillantes. 983

STRAUB, Solomon W., 1842-1899.
    Gird on! gird on! or, The temperance band. 880, p134

STRAUSS, Johann, 1825-1899.
    Donau Walzer. 5422
    Wein, Weib und Gesang. 6001

STREETER, Frederic V.
    Sister in heaven. 6177

SULLIVAN, Sir Arthur Seymour, 1842-1900.
    Birds in the night. 6035
    O hush thee, my babie. 5870

SUTTON, P. M.
    A terrible war with nobody hurt. 5810

SWEET, O. P.
    Passing away. 791, 2079, p133

TANNER, T. H.
    The old brown cot. 334

TAYLOR, B. S.
    A very bad cold. 4954

TAYLOR, R. Stewart.
    Jenny Brown and I. 276
    O, wrap the flag around me, boys. 200
    Soldier's dream song. 201
    A vesper song for our volunteers' sisters. 275

TAYLOR, Virgil Corydon, 1817-1891.
    Te Deum laudamus. 4888

THAYER, J. H.
    The Nilsson waltz. p134

THOMAS, Carrie.
    I heard the voice of Jesus say. 5906
    My faith looks up to Thee. 5905

THOMAS, John Rogers, 1829-1896.
    The fields of home. 405
    I'm dying far from those I love. 373
    Keep a brave heart still. 404
    Lottie in the lane. 348
    Maudie Moore. 351
    One by one. 362

THORNTON
    The little gem. 3582

TITCOMB, C. G., teacher and music dealer, Janesville, Wis.
    Julie polka. 678

TOPLIFF, Robert, 1793-1868.
    Ruth and Naomi. 2540

TOWNE, Thomas Martin, 1835-1911 or 12.
    The angel choir. 4968
    The drunkard's wife to her husband. See Touch not the fair cup, though it sparkles.

TOWNE, Thomas Martin, 1835-1911 or 12. (Continued)
    Freedom's harvest time. 518
    Gather 'round the table. 4838
    I'm always your lovin' Katreen; or, Katrina's story. 733
    Lake Forest mazurka. 6171
    Let woman vote! 787
    The little boot black. 822, 4906
    Oh, Louie is my fair one. 658
    The old church choir. 758
    Pining for the old fireside. 590
    Poor little blind Maggie! p134
    Shaking of hands. 706
    There's music in my heart, love! 657
    Touch not the fair cup, though it sparkles; or, The drunkard's wife to her husband. 592
    The voice that I love. 5497
    Welcome. Song of the 40th Wisconsin volunteers. 410
    When will my darling boy return? 370

TOWNER, Charles [ROOT, Charles Towner?]
    The golden dreamland. 5996
    The "Heathen Chinee." 6050

VAAS, Augustus J., ca.1815-
    L'attacca quickstep. 56
    Beads man polka. (arr.) 772
    Briggs house polka. 10
    Cincinnati air line R.R. galop. 114
    Concert polka mazurka. 5683
    Ellsworth requiem march. 81
    The enchantress schottisch. 141
    Etta mazurka. 534
    Fairy polka redowa. 54
    The fire brigade quickstep. 35
    General Fremont's march. 125
    Ladies' favorite polka. (arr.) 5681
    Major Anderson's march. 64
    Northwestern rifles march. 202
    Prairie queen quadrilles. 5662
    Richmond house polka. 11
    Sans souci galop. 524
    St. Paul waltz. 380, 4905 (guitar) 5794
    Sherman house polka redowa. 59
    The skating quadrille. 132
    Sleigh ride galop. 523, 2690 (arr. for cabinet organ & piano) 776
    Templar march. 778
    Tremont house polka. 12
    Vaas' own trois temps polka mazurka. 5785
    Zouave cadets quickstep. 15

VALENTINE, Thomas, 1790-1878.
    Aria alla scozzese. 239

VAN RENSSELAER, Eugene.
    Sister Maggie. 18

VENZANO, Luigi, 1814-1878.
    Venzano valse. 187
VERDI, Giuseppe, 1813-1901.
    Miserere. 779-80
VON ROCHOW, Alfred.
    Croquet. 5878
    The girl for me! 824
    Grad aus dem Wirthshaus. See Out of the tavern!
    Jerome Jenkins. 5626
    Out of the tavern! 831
    Popping corn. 4881
    Queen of hearts; or, Playing for a wife. 5547
    Song of the cuckoo! 825
VOSSELLER, E.
    Betsy Jane polka. 608
    Sweet buried friend of mine! 580
WAGNER, Richard, 1813-1883.
    Grand march from Tannhauser. 51
WALKER, T. R.
    Lilla is an angel now. 560, 570
WALLACE, J. C.
    We are coming from the cotton fields. 417
WEBSTER, Joseph Philbrick, 1819-1875.
    All rights for all! 767
    Always of thee. 6091
    Beautiful angels. 5800
    Bessie Jayne. 788
    Bonnie Annie Lee; or, I'm hame again. 5931
    Brother in the army. 427
    Call me darling, darling call me. 5680
    Come to me, dearest! 5617
    Come to me memories olden! 4833
    The cottage in the wood. 798
    Cousin John. 826, 4857
    Cupid and Mammon. 814
    Darling blue eyed Mell. 5771
    Darling Ella. 5571
    Dawning of the better day. 5496
    The days that are no more. 5868
    The dear sweet bells of memory. 6090
    Ervie Morie. 5928
    Floraline Shore. 4877
    For president, Ulysses Grant, a smoking his cigar. 829
    Good luck. 5932
    The harp of Katie Bell. 5760
    Hope on the unseen shore. 5740
    How sweetly she's sleeping. 5791
    Hurrah for General Grant! 830
    I am weary and faint in the battle of life! 5954
    I don't sing 'cause I can't. 5860
    I stand beside a lonely grave. 6084
    I stand on memory's golden shore. 363
    I'm hame again. See Bonnie Annie Lee.
    In dreams of my childhood. 5682
    Jenny Wade, the heroine of Gettysberg. 428

WEBSTER, Joseph Philbrick, 1819-1875. (Continued)
    Johnny is a farmer boy. 5879
    Kiss me good night. 5801
    Kitty McCree O'Tossell. 6010
    The land o' the leal. 5441
    Little dimpled hands. 5565
    Little Hattie Harvey. 4893
    Lizzie, the lass of the brown wavy hair. 5805
    Lost Lomie Laine. 789
    Marie. 5940
    The master's gold year. 5970
    Medora. 5804
    My Lily. 4848
    My Margaret. 818
    Nora MacRae. 5546
    Northmen, awake. 796
    O Father take my hand. 5921
    Oh! lady fair, I dream of thee. 4871
    Oh, say to my spirit, thy bride will I be. 6064
    Old friends. 4851
    Old glory and U. S. Grant. p134
    The olive of love. 6104
    On the banks of the Pearl. 6014
    Only love me. 6180
    Open the gates. 5808
    Our own. 5736
    Our turn is coming. 6038
    The past we can never recall, Jamie. 821 (guitar) 5673
    She sleeps beneath the elms. 354
    She shines in honor like a star. 5765
    Sing softly, love. 353
    Sister May. 4847
    Some sweet day. 5668
    The spring at the foot of the hill. 799
    Summer's sweets shall bloom again. 828
    The sweet times were the old. 5635
    There's a darling girl I know. 5660
    Together. 5923
    Tomorrow. 5963
    Touches of little hands. 6082
    Under the beautiful stars. 5601
    The Union Pacific. 5619
    What might have been! 4840
    "What then!" 5652
    When I am gone. 5634
    When I courted Mary Ann. 6062
    When I lie dreaming. 833, 4933
    Why not I. 6223
    Woman is going to vote. 790
    The wounded boy at Kenesaw. 426
WEHLI, James M.
    Heather bells. 564
    The music of the sea, meditation. 565
    The rivulet. 563
WELLER, S. M.
    Our angel child. p135

WELLS, C. L.
    Dash away galop. 6107
    Evening chimes. Reverie. 6200
    Rippling wave schottische. 6101

WHITING, S. K.
    Father's come home. 499

WHOKNOWS, G., pseud.
    Sara neighed! p133

WIGGINS, Thomas. See BETHUNE, Thomas Greene, 1849-1908.

WILLIAMS, Henry.
    Bermuda's fairy isle. 99

WIMMERSTEDT, A. E., pianist, Jacksonville, Ill.
    Budding of the tones. 358
    Evening bells, nocturne. 361
    General Sherman's grand Atlanta march. 686
    Longing for the shore. 367
    Moonlight vespers. Nocturne. 1492
    Olivet college march. 715
    Rain on the calm lake. 682
    Sharp-shooters march. 368
    Sophia polka. 359
    Warbling of the birds. 360

WINNEMORE, A. F.
    The gum tree canoe. 109

WOLLENHAUPT, Heinrich Adolf, 1827-1863.
    Blanche waltz. 30
    Marrie polka-mazurka. 33
    The rosebud polka rondo. 32

WOODBURY, M. Amsden.
    Still thy tumult, wild, wild waves. p134

WOODMAN, Jonathan Call, 1813-1894.
    The antique ring. 5749

WOOLCOTT, Francis.
    Happy days of yore. 121
    9th Missouri quickstep. 193

WORK, Henry Clay, 1832-1884.
    Agnes by the river. 4962
    Andy Veto. 610
    Babylon is fallen! 329
    Beautiful Rose. 188
    The buckskin bag of gold. 5745
    Columbia's guardian angels. 365
    Come back to the farm. 614
    Come home, father. 391 (guitar) 432
    Corporal Schnapps. 355
    Crossing the grand Sierras. 5775
    Dad's a millionaire! 594
    The days when we were young. 292
    The first love dream. 226
    The girls at home. 189
    God save the nation! 256

WORK, Henry Clay, 1832-1884. (Continued)
    Grafted into the army. 250 (guitar) 341
    Grandmother told me so. 272
    Kingdom coming. 192 (guitar) 196, 332, 496
    Lillie of the snowstorm; or, "Please, Father, let us in!" 572
    Little Major. 265 (guitar) 340
    Marching through Georgia. 424
    Nellie lost and found. 128, 4915 (guitar) 195
    No letters from home! 5727
    Now, Moses. 521
    Our captain's last words. 134
    The picture on the wall. 411
    "Please, Father, let us in!" See Lillie of the snowstorm.
    Poor Kitty Popcorn; or, The soldier's pet. p133
    Ring the bell, watchman! 431
    The ship that never return'd. 497
    Sing hallelujah! See 'Tis finished!
    Sleep, baby, sleep. 211
    Sleeping for the flag. 336
    The soldier's pet. See Poor Kitty Popcorn.
    Song of a thousand years. 293 (guitar) 371
    Song of the redman. 819
    'Tis finished! or, Sing hallelujah! p133
    Uncle Joe's Hail Columbia. 210
    Wake Nicodemus. 416 (guitar) 467
    Washington and Lincoln. 374
    Watching for pa. 271
    We'll go down ourselves. 255
    When the Evening Star went down. 593
    Who shall rule this American nation? 591

WRIGHT, William C.
    L'agréable reverie. p133

WRIGHTON, W. T.
    Her bright smile haunts me still. 461

WURZEL, G. Friedrich, pseud. See ROOT, George Frederick.

YATES, Mrs. W. H.
    Oriole waltz. 394

ZAULIG, Fred W.
    Flowers of beauty schottische. 764 (4 hands) 5734

ZELLNER, Richard.
    Birds of the forest waltz. 179
    Gen. Grant's march. 181

ZIEGFELD, Florenz, 1841-1923.
    My angel spirit bride. 687
    Turner march. 746

APPENDIX C

SUBJECT INDEX TO PUBLICATIONS OF EXTRA-MUSICAL INTEREST

SUBJECT INDEX TO PUBLICATIONS OF EXTRA-MUSICAL INTEREST

Popular music, so called, is an invaluable record of cultural history. An event, a movement, a catastrophe, a man, a fad -- all of these have been chronicled by the composer and the poet and pictured by the artist who decorated the cover. During the nineteenth century, the lithographs on sheet music were in many cases its greatest attraction, overshadowing the music far too frequently for the comfort of the music lover. The passing years have only added to their charm and brought them recognition as a graphic historical record. Many pieces issued without illustrated covers, however, have nevertheless associations with the past that attract the librarian, the historian, and the collector. To bring together in a subject list the scattered items of extra-musical interest in Root & Cady's catalog is the purpose of this <u>Appendix</u>.

Such vast subjects of perennial appeal as Love, Filial Devotion, Death and the Grave have been omitted, as has teaching material. Those pieces that survived the winnowing process have been grouped under the following headings:

> Civil war music -- Instrumental and Vocal
> Music associated with Abraham Lincoln and Ulysses S. Grant
> Songs of reconstruction
> Songs of reform and utopia
> "Votes for women!"
> Temperance songs
> Miscellaneous political and topical songs
> Transportation
> Sports
> Comic songs and musical jokes
> Songs of literary interest
> Portraits
> Masons and Templars
> Colleges and universities
> Firemen
> Chicago and the Northwest
> Miscellaneous Illustrated Covers

The variety of subjects demonstrates the breadth of interests touched in Root & Cady's publications. No claim can be made, however, that they were at all exceptional in this respect. American popular songs, then as now, may have been deficient musically, but they have never lacked for local color or topical interest.

The arrangement of the list is alphabetically by title within each subject group. The name of the composer and the plate number are given to facilitate reference to the Plate Number List with its more complete descriptions.

Pieces which were issued without plate numbers or which have not been located are followed by page references. Pieces with illustrated covers of interest, whether lithographed, wood-cut or engraved, are preceded by an asterisk.

CIVIL WAR MUSIC

Unquestionably the most important group of titles includes the pieces, vocal and instrumental, associated with the Civil War. Root & Cady were foremost among the publishers of the North for the volume and excellence of their war songs, which are not only a record of a vital chapter of American history, but a living part of our national traditions. Pictorially the outstanding pieces are the <u>Ellsworth Zouave and National Lancers' greeting grand march</u> and the <u>Zouave cadets quickstep</u>, both handsome colored lithographs of Zouaves in their gaudy uniforms.

## INSTRUMENTAL

| | | |
|---|---|---|
| The artillery galop. | James W. Long | 4966 |
| Atlanta (grand victory march). | Gustave Blessner | 5319 |
| Battle cry of freedom, grand caprice de concert. | L. M. Gottschalk | 440 |
| The battle-cry of freedom, with variations. | Emil Rein | 274 |
| The battle of Manassas. | [Thomas G. Bethune] | 571 |
| Brother, tell me of the battle, transcription. | Emil Rein | 455 |
| Columbia's call! Transcribed & varied. | Theodore Moelling | 736 |
| *Ellsworth requiem march. | A. J. Vaas | 81 |
| *Ellsworth Zouaves and National lancers' greeting grand march. | Adolph Baumbach | 566 |
| General Fremont's march. | A. J. Vaas | 125 |
| Gen. Grant's march. | Richard Zellner | 181 |
| Genl. Lyon's battle march. | Julius Eichberg | 110 |
| Gen. McClernand's grand march. | Louis H. Rink | 264 |
| General Sherman's grand Atlanta march. | A. E. Wimmerstedt | 686 |
| Holden guards schottische. | Clara E. Craw | 268 |
| Just before the battle, mother, transcription. | Emil Rein | 397 |
| Kingdom coming arr. with variations for guitar. | George A. Russell | 332 |
| Kingdom coming with variations for piano. | Charles Grobe | 215 |
| The little drummer boy's march. | Karl Merz | 381 |
| Major Anderson's march. | A. J. Vaas | 64 |
| Night before Petersburgh, burlesque military fantasia. | Edward Hoffman | 759 |
| 9th Missouri quickstep. | Francis Woolcott | 193 |
| Northwestern rifles march. | A. J. Vaas | 202 |
| The president's emancipation march. | George E. Fawcett | 261 |
| Soldier's friend, polka quickstep. | I. W. Gougler | 326 |
| Soldier's home medley. | Eliza Pattiani | 429 |
| Stars and stripes schottisch. | James S. Hambaugh | 129 |
| Tramp! tramp! tramp! transcription. | T. M. Brown | 501 |
| Tramp! tramp! tramp! with variations. | Charles Grobe | 450 |
| The vacant chair with variations. | Emil Rein | 352 |
| *Zouave cadets quickstep. | A. J. Vaas | 15 |

## VOCAL

| | | |
|---|---|---|
| All hail the reign of peace. | George C. Pearson | 465 |
| All hail to Ulysses! | J. E. Haynes | 364 |
| Babylon is fallen! | Henry Clay Work | 329 |
| The battle-cry of freedom. | George F. Root | 225 |
| Brave battery boys. | Philip Paul Bliss | 5876 |
| Brother in the army. | J. P. Webster | 427 |
| Brother, tell me of the battle. | George F. Root | 377 |
| Call 'em names, Jeff. | George F. Root | 263 |
| *Camp song of the Chicago Irish brigade. | Wm. Carter Hughes | 84 |
| Can the soldier forget? | George F. Root | 398 |
| Columbia's call. | George F. Root | 615 |
| Columbia's guardian angels. | Henry Clay Work | 365 |
| Comrade, all around is brightness. | George F. Root | 436 |
| "Corn is king!" | Hiram T. Merrill | 227 |
| Corporal Schnapps. | Henry Clay Work | 355 |
| De day ob liberty's comin'. | George F. Root | 224 |
| Did the loved one return? | Ephraim H. Bailey | 637 |
| The ensign of glory. | Roswell Park | 135 |
| Father Abraham's reply to the 600,000. | George F. Root | 247 |

| Title | Composer | Page |
|---|---|---|
| The first gun is fired! May God protect the right! | George F. Root | 72 |
| Follow the drum. | Bernard Covert | 423 |
| Forward, boys, forward. | George F. Root | 75 |
| The girls at home. | Henry Clay Work | 189 |
| Glory! glory! or, The little octoroon. | George F. Root | 556 |
| God bless our brave young volunteers. | George F. Root | 73, 74 |
| God save the nation! | Henry Clay Work | 256 |
| Good bye Jeff! | Philip Paul Bliss | 435 |
| Good bye old glory. | George F. Root | 492 |
| *Grafted into the army. | Henry Clay Work | 250 |
| *Grandmother told me so. | Henry Clay Work | 272 |
| Have ye sharpened your swords? | George F. Root | 79 |
| Honor to Sheridan. | George F. Root | 768 |
| How it marches! the flag of the Union. | Horace H. Hawley | p133 |
| I wonder why he comes not! | E. Chamberlin | 493 |
| I'm dying far from those I love. | John Rogers Thomas | 373 |
| I'se on de way. | George F. Root | 376 |
| Jenny Wade, the heroine of Gettysburg. | J. P. Webster | 428 |
| The John Brown song. |  | 130 |
| Just after the battle. | George F. Root | 379 |
| Just before the battle, mother. | George F. Root | 328 |
| Keep a brave heart still. | John Rogers Thomas | 404 |
| Kingdom coming. | Henry Clay Work | 192 |
| Kiss me mother, kiss your darling. | George F. Root | 412 |
| Lashed to the mast. | John W. Hutchinson | 679 |
| "Lay me down and save the flag!" | George F. Root | 403 |
| The liberty bird. | George F. Root | 513 |
| Little Major. | Henry Clay Work | 265 |
| The little octoroon. See Glory! glory! |  |  |
| March on! march on! | William Lewis | 369 |
| Marching through Georgia. | Henry Clay Work | 424 |
| My beau that went to Canada. | George F. Root | 466 |
| The new skedaddle. | R. D. Scott | 217 |
| North and South. | George F. Root | 494 |
| Oh! bury the brave where they fall. | Henrie L. Frisbie | 357 |
| O, come you from the battle-field? | George F. Root | 339 |
| Oh, haste on the battle! | George F. Root | 262 |
| O wrap the flag around me boys. | R. Stewart Taylor | 200 |
| On, on, on, the boys came marching. | George F. Root | 458 |
| On the field of battle, mother. | George F. Root | 328 |
| Our captain's last words. | Henry Clay Work | 134 |
| Our comrade has fallen. | O. M. Brewster | 249 |
| Our nation's captain. | Edward Haynes | 413 |
| The patriot's prayer. | Christoph Bach | 409 |
| *Poor Kitty Popcorn; or, The soldier's pet. | Henry Clay Work | p133 |
| Poor mother! Willie's gone. | Theodore F. Seward | 425 |
| The prisoner's hope. See Tramp! tramp! tramp! |  |  |
| Ring the bell, watchman! | Henry Clay Work | 431 |
| Sing hallelujah! See 'Tis finished! |  |  |
| '63 is the jubilee. | D. A. French | 266 |
| Sleeping for the flag. | Henry Clay Work | 336 |
| Soldier's dream song. | R. Stewart Taylor | 201 |
| The soldier's last request. | Mme. C. Hahn | 2452 |
| The soldier's pet. See Poor Kitty Popcorn. |  |  |
| Song of a thousand years. | Henry Clay Work | 293 |
| Song of the Negro boatman. | Hiram T. Merrill | 178 |
| The songs we sang upon the old camp ground. | Henrie L. Frisbie | 606 |
| Stand up for Uncle Sam my boys. | George F. Root | 126 |

| | | |
|---|---|---|
| The stars and stripes, the flag of the free. | Henrie L. Frisbie | 76 |
| Starved in prison. | George F. Root | p133 |
| Take your gun and go, John. | Hiram T. Merrill | 138 |
| A tear for the comrade that's gone. | James R. Murray | 5862 |
| They have broken up their camps. | George F. Root | p133 |
| 'Tis finished! or, Sing hallelujah! | Henry Clay Work | p133 |
| Tramp! tramp! tramp! or, The prisoner's hope. | George F. Root | 420 |
| Tread lightly ye comrades; or, The volunteer's grave. | Mrs. F. L. Bowen | 269 |
| Uncle Joe's hail Columbia. | Henry Clay Work | 210 |
| Uncle Sam. | Concordius | p133 |
| Uncle Sam's funeral. | Silex | 378 |
| The union volunteers. | E. C. Saffery | 77 |
| The vacant chair. | George F. Root | 133 |
| A vesper song for our volunteers' sisters. | R. Stewart Taylor | 275 |
| Vicksburg is taken boys! | Edmund W. Hicks | 375 |
| The volunteer's grave. See Tread lightly ye comrades. | | |
| *Wake Nicodemus. | Henry Clay Work | 416 |
| Washington and Lincoln. | Henry Clay Work | 374 |
| We are coming from the cotton fields. | J. C. Wallace | 417 |
| We shall miss you dearest brother. | Edward Haynes | 408 |
| Welcome. Song of the 40th Wisconsin volunteers. | T. Martin Towne | 410 |
| *We'll go down ourselves. | Henry Clay Work | 255 |
| When will my darling boy return? | T. Martin Towne | 370 |
| Who comes dar? | J. M. Hubbard | 433 |
| Who'll save the left. | George F. Root | 282 |
| Will you wed me now I'm lame love? | Avanelle L. Holmes | 345 |
| Within the sound of the enemy's guns. | George F. Root | 331 |
| The wounded boy at Kenesaw. | J. P. Webster | 426 |
| Young Eph's jubilee. | Wm. H. Brockway | 551 |

## MUSIC ASSOCIATED WITH ABRAHAM LINCOLN AND ULYSSES S. GRANT

Two groups of pieces, closely related to the war songs, but with a special appeal of their own, are those associated with President Lincoln and General, later President, Grant. Strangely enough, Root & Cady published no political songs specifically for the campaigns of 1860 and 1864. The war songs served the purpose, apparently. But in 1868, the war over, campaign songs streamed from the presses. Of all the Grant items, only two were not composed for the campaign -- <u>All hail to Ulysses!</u> and <u>Gen. Grant's march</u>. Especially notable is the cover of <u>Hurrah for General Grant</u>, with its view of the interior of Crosby's Opera House during the convention which nominated Grant for the presidency.

### ABRAHAM LINCOLN

| | | |
|---|---|---|
| Farewell father, friend and guardian. | George F. Root | p133 |
| Father Abraham's reply to the 600,000. | George F. Root | 247 |
| Funeral march to the memory of Abraham Lincoln. | Christoph Bach | 722 |
| In memory of Abraham Lincoln. | Karl Formes | 514 |
| Our nation's captain. | Edward Haynes | 413 |
| The president's emancipation march. | George E. Fawcett | 261 |
| The president's grave. | L. B. Miller | 444 |

## ULYSSES S. GRANT

| | | |
|---|---|---|
| All hail to Ulysses! | J. E. Haynes | 364 |
| For president, Ulysses Grant, a-smoking his cigar. | J. P. Webster | 829 |
| Gen. Grant's march. | Richard Zellner | 181 |
| *Hurrah for General Grant. | J. P. Webster | 830 |
| Keep the ball a-rolling. | Ossian E. Dodge | 4841 |
| The nation's hero grand march. | Edward Hoffman | 4865 |
| Old glory and U. S. Grant. | J. P. Webster | p134 |
| Rally for the leader! | George D. Herrick | p134 |
| The ruler in peace and the leader in war. | J. M. Hubbard | 4827 |
| Sounds from the old camp ground. | T. H. Brand | p133 |
| The tanner and the blue! | James R. Murray | 4970 |
| We'll fight it out here on the old Union line. | George F. Root | p134 |

## SONGS OF RECONSTRUCTION

In an attempt to continue the successful style of the war songs, these songs were written about the political and social issues of the reconstruction period. Although they never achieved the wide popularity of their predecessors, they are a reflection of the troubled post-war period and the attitude of certain musicians of the North toward its problems.

| | | |
|---|---|---|
| Andy Veto. | Henry Clay Work | 610 |
| Dinna ye hear the s'Logan? | R. A. Dical | 613 |
| Foes and friends. | George F. Root | 581 |
| Freedom's harvest time. | T. Martin Towne | 518 |
| In a horn. | B. R. Hanby | 611 |
| Northmen, awake. | J. P. Webster | 796 |
| Now den! now den! | B. R. Hanby | 541 |
| Who shall rule this American nation? | Henry Clay Work | 591 |

## SONGS OF REFORM AND UTOPIA

Like the Hutchinson family, many mid-nineteenth century American musicians were actively concerned with the various social movements of their time. Songs like these were apparently intended as an adjunct of the drive for universal and wholesale reform, while others dealing with more specific measures were designed to be of practical assistance in furthering the chosen ideal.

| | | |
|---|---|---|
| All rights for all! | J. P. Webster | 767 |
| Dawning of the better day. | J. P. Webster | 5496 |
| A hundred years hence. | John W. Hutchinson | 5521 |
| It is an age of progress! | W. C. Baker | 836 |
| Our protective union. | George F. Root | 567 |
| The promised land to morrow. | James G. Clark | 5578 |

## "VOTES FOR WOMEN!"

Root & Cady's contribution to the suffrage controversy included three pro-suffrage songs and two heavy parodies by Frank Howard, who apparently lacked the reforming zeal of some of his contemporaries. It is a little surprising that one firm should have issued so many songs on this subject -- all before 1871.

| | | |
|---|---|---|
| Come home mother. | Frank Howard | 5569 |
| Let woman vote! | T. Martin Towne | 787 |
| Oh, Sorosis! | Frank Howard | 4858, p134 |
| Vote it right along! | John W. Hutchinson | 5517 |
| Woman is going to vote. | J. P. Webster | 790 |

## TEMPERANCE SONGS

During the nineteenth century, temperance was not only a personal virtue, but a social ideal, which together with education, suffrage, free soil, a religious revival, and so on, would lead to a true democracy throughout the world. The number of temperance songs published by Root & Cady, not only as sheet music, but in various singing books, indicates the great popularity of the movement, particularly in church circles. Come home, father was unquestionably the most successful of the songs, but by no means the worst.

| | | |
|---|---|---|
| Come home, father. | Henry Clay Work | 391 |
| Crowding awfully. | B. R. Hanby | 615 |
| Father's come home. | S. K. Whiting | 499 |
| Gird on! gird on! or, The temperance band. | Solomon W. Straub | 880, p134 |
| The happy daughters. | Frank H. King | 5750 |
| It's not poor mother's fault. | Frank Howard | 4882 |
| Lillie of the snowstorm; or, "Please, Father, let us in!" | Henry Clay Work | 572 |
| The revelers' chorus. | B. R. Hanby | 547 |
| Since the day I signed the pledge. | Frank Howard | 692 |
| The temperance ship. | Philip Paul Bliss | 6117 |
| Touch not the fair cup, though it sparkles; or, The drunkard's wife to her husband. | T. Martin Towne | 592 |
| Try, John! try, John! | O. D. Adams | 5514 |

## MISCELLANEOUS POLITICAL AND TOPICAL SONGS

Among the subjects chosen for topical songs of more than ordinary interest were the execution of Maximilian, Emperor of Mexico, the immigration of the Chinese to the United States, oil, the Franco-Prussian war, and the Chicago fire of 1871. The Kutschke's war song [cf p79], with its words translated into fifteen languages, is undoubtedly one of the most striking publications of this press.

| | | |
|---|---|---|
| *John Chinaman. | Philip Paul Bliss | 5695 |
| Nasby's lament over the New York nominations. | W. W. Bridewell | 4967 |
| Oil-do-ra-do. | W. C. Crane | 439 |
| Poor Carlotta! (The last words of Maximilian) | Frederick W. Root | 742 |
| *Tin-ni-min-ni-win-kum-ka, or, The Chinaman's farewell. | Ching Foo | 5739 |

## FRANCO-PRUSSIAN WAR

| | | |
|---|---|---|
| The banner of the fatherland. | [George F. Root] | 5944 |
| Hear the cry that comes across the sea. | George F. Root | p134 |
| *Kutschke's war-song. | Otto Lob | 6169 |
| Prussia, gird thy sons for battle! | James R. Murray | 5951 |
| Viva la Prussia! | | 5964 |

## CHICAGO FIRE

| | | |
|---|---|---|
| From the ruins our city shall rise. | George F. Root | p135 |
| Passing through the fire. | George F. Root | p135 |
| Ye have done it unto me. | George F. Root | p135 |

## TRANSPORTATION

Of all the subjects listed in this Appendix, transportation alone has been adequately treated, in Transportation in American Popular Songs, issued by the Grosvenor Library, Buffalo. The possibilities yet to be explored are indicated by the fact that, of the titles listed here, only three are included in that bibliography, and, of the three, only one was listed in the Root & Cady edition. The subdivisions used in the Grosvenor list are repeated here, making this a sort of supplement in miniature.

### AVIATION-BALLOONS

| | | |
|---|---|---|
| Up in a balloon. | W. H. Sanderson | 5598 |

### BICYCLES

| | | |
|---|---|---|
| *Velocipede polka. | Horace E. Kimball | 5492 |
| *The velocipede song. | Frank Howard | 5444 |
| *Velocipede waltz. | Frank Howard | 6593 |

### CARRIAGES

| | | |
|---|---|---|
| *The one horse galop. | Richard Goerdeler | 5881 |

### RAILROADS

| | | |
|---|---|---|
| Cincinnati air line R. R. galop. | A. J. Vaas | 114 |
| *Crossing the grand Sierras. | Henry Clay Work | 5775 |
| The Union Pacific. | J. P. Webster | 5619 |

### SHIPS -- IMAGINARY SHIPS

| | | |
|---|---|---|
| *Sailing into dreamland. | Frederick W. Root | 806 |
| When my ship comes in! | George Haywood | 654, 3583 |

### SHIPS -- SAILING VESSELS

| | | |
|---|---|---|
| The ship that never return'd. | Henry Clay Work | 497 |

### SHIPS -- STEAMSHIPS

| | | |
|---|---|---|
| When the Evening Star went down. | Henry Clay Work | 593 |

### SLEIGHS

| | | |
|---|---|---|
| Away, away, the track is white. | George F. Root | 656 |
| Sleigh bells mazurka. | Simon Knaebel | 5574 |
| Sleigh ride galop. | A. J. Vaas | 523, 2690 |
| Sleighing with the girls. | Henrie L. Frisbie | 356 |

## SPORTS

Baseball, croquet, skating, boat racing, and swinging (if it can be called a sport) were referred to in Root & Cady's publications. To save space, they will be listed in one alphabet, since the titles are self-explanatory, except The Annie Huger galop, which has on its cover pictures of the champion crew with crossed flags above and crossed oars beneath.

| | | |
|---|---|---|
| *The Annie Huger galop. | A. B. Knapp | 6221 |
| Base ball. | John Smith | 5938 |
| Croquet. | Alfred von Rochow | 5878 |
| *Home run galop. | Frederick W. Root | 749 |
| Making love while on the ice. | Frank Howard | 5494 |
| *Skating polka. | Charles C. Smith | 60 |
| *The skating quadrille. | A. J. Vaas | 132 |
| *Skating waltz. | Fred Freiberg | 726 |
| *Swinging in the trees. | Gustavus Geary | 6277 |
| *When Sue and I went skating. | James R. Murray | 4879 |

## COMIC SONGS AND JOKES

The playful type of humor, peculiar to Root & Cady publications, is perhaps too self-consciously "cute" for contemporary tastes, but in its day some people thought it funny. P. Benson (Charles C. Miller), like Artemus Ward, depended largely on mistakes in grammar and pseudo-phonetic spelling for his effects, while Pro Phundo Basso (Philip Paul Bliss) specialized in whimsy. Not all the comic songs (so-called) issued by Root & Cady are listed here, but only those which seem a part of this tradition.

| | | |
|---|---|---|
| Bonapo, a medley. | [Philip Paul Bliss] | 5999 |
| First finger waltz. | A Little Joker | 4923 |
| Pro Phundo Basso. | Philip Paul Bliss | 4845 |
| Sally Ann's away! | Keep Shady | 676 |
| Sara neighed! | G. Whoknows | p133 |
| The singin' skewl. | [Charles C. Miller] | 5537 |
| The tragical tail of poor Thomas Maltese! | [Philip Paul Bliss] | 756 |

## SONGS OF LITERARY INTEREST

Here are listed settings by American musicians of poems by authors of some distinction. As interpretations by minor composers of well-known poems and as separate editions of the poems, these items are interesting. Arrangement is alphabetically by the name of the author of the words.

Beaconsfield, Benjamin Disraeli, 1st earl of, 1804-1881.
    My heart is like a silent lute.     George F. Root     80
Byron, George Gordon Noel Byron, 6th baron, 1788-1824.
    Idol of my heart.     Lefoy     5728
Eichendorff, Joseph Karl Benedikt, freiherr von, 1788-1857.
    The Sabbath morning.     Julia Brainard     735
Harte, Bret, 1836-1902.
    *The "Heathen Chinee."     Charles Towner     6050
    Poverty flat. Or, "Her letter."     George F. Root     5758
Heine, Heinrich, 1797-1856.
    I stood before her portrait.     Hans Balatka     343
Longfellow, Henry Wadsworth, 1807-1882.
    The day is cold.     Robert Goldbeck     5897
Lowell, James Russell, 1819-1891.
    O moonlight deep and tender.     Robert Goldbeck     5898
Moore, Thomas, 1779-1852.
    I'd mourn the hopes that leave me.     Karl Merz     1060
    Miriam's song of triumph. "Sound the loud timbrel."     Karl Merz     4897
Tennyson, Alfred Tennyson, baron, 1809-1892.
    Break, break, break.     Robert Goldbeck     5899

## PORTRAITS

The lithographed portraits on nineteenth century sheet music covers inevitably attract collectors. Although anyone in the public eye was likely to have music dedicated to him with his portrait on the cover, Root & Cady seem to have honored in this way only actors and musicians, except possibly the unidentified Mr. H. W. Chant. Of the portraits listed below, only a few are included in the excellent Catalogue of dramatic portraits in the Theatre collection of the Harvard college library (Cambridge, Harvard University press, 1930-34) -- those of Frank Aiken, Alice Holland, Mrs. Oates, and Mlle. Ristori. Many of the dates and identifying phrases for the subjects of the portraits were found in the Harvard Catalogue.

| | | |
|---|---|---|
| Aiken, Frank Eugene, 1840-1910.  actor-manager | | |
| *The Robert Brierly schottisch. (2 versions) | George Stevens | 414 |
| *Huguenot captain polka. | George Stevens | 660 |
| Barry, Mrs. Thomas.  actress | | |
| *The Barry schottische. | George Stevens | 659 |
| Bliss, Philip Paul, 1838-1876. | | |
| *The tin wedding. | Philip P. Bliss | 5618 |
| Bonfanti, Marie, d. 1921, aged 70.  dancer | | |
| *White fawn march. | [Silas G. Pratt] | 4929 |
| *White fawn schottische. | [Silas G. Pratt] | 4902 |
| Booth, Edwin, 1833-1893. | | |
| *Shakesperian grand march. | Silas G. Pratt | 729 |
| Chant, H. W. | | |
| *May march. | George W. Morgan | p134 |
| Dillon, John, 1831-1913. (Real name: John Daily Marum)  actor | | |
| *Dillon schottische. | James Harrison | 4870 |
| Goodall, Annie.  actress | | |
| *Only. | Virginia Gabriel | 6175 |
| Holland, Alice.  actress | | |
| *The Alice polka. | George Stevens | p134 |
| McManus, C. A.  actor | | |
| *Carrickfergus schottische. | George Stevens | 671 |
| Murray, James Ramsey, 1841-1905. | | |
| *Carl Pretzel waltz. | James R. Murray | 6184 |
| Nilsson, Christine, condesa de Casa Miranda, 1843-1921. | | |
| *The Nilsson waltz. | J. H. Thayer | p134 |
| Oates, Alice (Merritt), 1849-1887. "Mrs. James A. Oates."  dramatic singer and manageress | | |
| *Ixion medley. | John S. Bernard | 5627 |
| Ristori, Adelaide, 1822-1906.  actress | | |
| *Ristori grande valse. | Theodore Moelling | 625 |
| Stevens, George.  Chicago conductor | | |
| *The Stevens march. | George W. Morgan | 765 |
| Wyndham, Charles, 1837-1919.  actor, manager and dramatic author | | |
| *Only. | Virginia Gabriel | 6175 |

## MASONS AND TEMPLARS

Excepting the <u>Templar march</u>, notable for its handsome colored lithograph, these are all Masonic in content or inspiration.

| | | |
|---|---|---|
| Fraternity march. | Julius Eichberg | 828 |
| The Masonic march. | George Stevens | 447 |
| *Songs of the Free Masons. | George F. Root | 600 |
| *Templar march. | A. J. Vaas | 778 |
| We meet upon the level. | C. M. Cady | 8 |

## COLLEGES AND UNIVERSITIES

Like other institutions, the schools of the Northwest inspired local composers. Needless to say, these pieces are not performed at alumni gatherings.

| | | |
|---|---|---|
| *The founder of Notre Dame. | Max E. Girac | 766 |
| Olivet college march. | A. E. Wimmerstedt | 715 |
| The Phi gamma delta march. | Oscar Mayo | 5630 |

## FIREMEN

Although Root & Cady paid no tribute to the police, the postmen, or the sanitation department, two pieces published by the firm were inspired by that popular public servant, the noble fire fighter.

| | | |
|---|---|---|
| The fire brigade quickstep. | A. J. Vaas | 35 |
| Fireman's marching song. | "Quails" | 595 |

## CHICAGO AND THE NORTHWEST

Local and regional pride has always been strong in the United States, inspiring many compositions dedicated to the home town or even one of its hotels. Of this emotion and inspiration, Chicago had her full share. Outstanding among the Chicago items is <u>Crosby's opera house waltz</u>, decorated with a fine lithograph of the Opera House and Root & Cady's store.

### CHICAGO

| | | |
|---|---|---|
| Belle of Lincoln park. | [George Schleiffarth] | 6185 |
| Belles de Chicago; or, Les plaisirs de la valse. | Robert Goldbeck | 5510 |
| Belles of Chicago, polka brillante. | Louis Staab | 5714 |
| *Briggs house polka. | A. J. Vaas | 10 |
| The Chicago mazurka. | George W. Morgan | 493 |
| Chicago schottische. | C. T. Sisson | 6061 |
| *Crosby's opera house waltz. | Frederick W. Root | 451 |
| The Hyde Park polka. | George W. Morgan | 522 |
| *Richmond house polka. | A. J. Vaas | 11 |
| Sherman house polka redowa. | A. J. Vaas | 59 |
| *Tremont house polka. | A. J. Vaas | 12 |

### THE NORTHWEST

| | | |
|---|---|---|
| Bright Kalamazoo. | J. M. Hubbard | 419 |
| Des Moines city waltz. | William Lehman | 388 |
| Flashes from the west. | Robert Goldbeck | 6112 |
| Ho! westward ho! | Ossian E. Dodge | 4831 |
| Illini polka. | Laura French | 346 |
| Illinois grand march. | A. Moses | 438 |
| *Michigan schottische. | J. W. Hertel | 53 |
| Minnesota, the lily of the west. | Will Hill | 4974 |
| Out west, or The down easter's journey. | Henrie L. Frisbie | 569 |
| *Song of the redman. | Henry Clay Work | 819 |
| Springfield polka. | Louis H. Rink | 235 |

## MISCELLANEOUS ILLUSTRATED COVERS

| | | |
|---|---|---|
| *Bridal flowers for the piano. | Edward Hoffman | 5707-5710 |
| *The crossing sweeper. | John S. Cox | 4859 |
| *Cycloid polka. | Charles Fradel | 498 |
| *Dear little barefeet, I've counted your toes! | James Harrison | 5916 |
| *The fly-away waltz. | Frederick W. Root | 6081 |
| *The four sisters for piano. | Edward Hoffman | 5908-5911 |
| *La Grenadille, passion flower waltzes. | James Harrison | 5650 |
| *I'm such a nice young man. | Frank Howard | 5502 |
| *"It." | Frank Howard | 5777 |
| *The little boot black. | T. Martin Towne | 822, 4906 |
| *Little sunshine. | James R. Murray | p134 |
| *Name me in thy prayer. | Susie B. Caldwell | p134 |
| *The old kitchen floor. | James R. Murray | 5913 |
| *The prettiest girl in town. | Frank Howard | 5437 |
| *Shun the broad road. | C. T. Lockwood | 4952 |
| *Studio polka. | E. B. Phelps | 5549 |
| *Undine polka and valse. | Silas G. Pratt | p133 |
| *We are the boys that fear no noise. | C. M. Cady | 6279 |
| *We'll have to mortgage the farm. | C. T. Lockwood | 5705 |

APPENDIX D

DIRECTORY OF THE MUSIC TRADE IN CHICAGO BEFORE 1871

# DIRECTORY OF THE MUSIC TRADE IN CHICAGO BEFORE 1871

This <u>Directory</u> has been planned to help identify and date publications, instruments, lithographs and engravings of Chicago manufacture. Listed here are all significant names that were associated with the music trade in Chicago before the fire of 1871, just as they were listed in the city directories of that period - music printers, publishers and dealers, instrument manufacturers and dealers, and those lithographers and engravers whose names have been found on music publications. The names are arranged in one alphabet, with listings for each name given chronologically. The form of entry was in part modelled on that used by Virginia Larkin Redway in her <u>Music Directory of Early New York City</u> (New York, The New York Public Library, 1941). The dates opposite the entries are for the years covered by the individual directories. A vain attempt was made to mold consistent entries from directory listings which were at times inconsistent, incomplete, or obviously misprinted. Immigrants Americanized their names, partnerships changed, and sons took their fathers' places, but city directories gave neither cross references nor explanatory footnotes. At length the conclusion was unavoidable that this list could not be more dependable than the directories themselves were, although explicatory notes could be (and have been) given wherever possible.

To avoid the possibility of confusing two people with similar names, no assumptions have been made, no matter how common sense protested. Reason and economy demanded, however, that entries for succeeding years which differed slightly in wording but not in meaning be consolidated, and that home addresses for some minor figures be omitted. Those men whose connection with the music trade was fleeting have had their other lines of business indicated for a year or two, but not followed in detail. The available Chicago city directories from 1843 (the earliest issued) to 1875 were searched, but for only a few prominent names are listings given beyond 1872. A list of "Directories Consulted" is appended. Commonly the directories of that period included all changes in address through May 1st. Those compiled by John Gager for 1856 and 1857 added to the customary facts each man's former home and length of residence in Chicago. For the years in which two rival directories were issued with sometimes conflicting information - 1855-56, 1859 and 1864-67 - the most likely listing has been chosen, with explanatory notes where desirable, but without identifying the source of each individual address. Those entries marked with an asterisk were found either in the classified business directory section, or in an advertisement, rather than in the main alphabet of the directory. With these exceptions, the listings included in this <u>Directory</u> are a fairly exact reproduction of those given in contemporary city directories. No attempt has been made to duplicate the eccentricities of punctuation found, and a few abbreviations have been standardized to avoid ambiguity. (A list of the abbreviations used appears at the end of this Introduction.) The supplementary notes, drawn from contemporary newspapers or periodicals, or authoritative local histories, supply such factual information as the exact dates of formation, dissolution, and change of address for those firms for which they could be found.

Some of the names listed in the classified sections of the city directories as dealers in music and musical instruments were identified in the alphabetical sections as furniture dealers, gift shops, and the like. It seemed pointless to give detailed directory listings for such firms as Jacob Beiersdorf, manufacturer and dealer in furniture and upholstery, etc.; Auguste Fredin, cabinetmaker and upholsterer; Joseph Galle, cabinetmaker; Gerstenberg & Westerman, fancy goods; Charles Kauffeld, Berlin woolen and embroidery goods; Thomas W. Martin, books and stationery; J. W. Middleton & Co., stationers, lithographers and blank book mnfrs.; and Henry K. Walker, furniture, &c. Jevne & Almini, sign and ornamental painters, occasionally did some lithographing in the middle sixties. All these firms had at one time or another some minor part in the music trade, but their major interests lay elsewhere.

## ABBREVIATIONS USED

| | | | |
|---|---|---|---|
| agt. | agent | lith. | lithographer, lithographic |
| asst. | assistant | manfs., manufs. | manufacturers |
| av. | avenue | mdse. | merchandise |
| b., bds. | boards | mer. | merchant |
| bet., bt. | between | mkr., mr. | maker |
| bkpr. | bookkeeper | mnfg. | manufacturing |
| bldg. | building | mnfr. | manufacturer |
| blk. | block | n., nr. | near |
| bros. | brothers | ne. | northeast |
| c., cor. | corner | n. s. | north side |
| clk. | clerk | nw. | northwest |
| com. mer. | commission merchant | Pk. | Park |
| ct. | court | pl. | place |
| Dem. | Democratic | proprs., props. | proprietors |
| dlrs. | dealers | r., res. | residence, resident |
| e. | east | ret. | retail |
| e. s. | east side | sec. | secretary |
| Eng. | England | s. s. | south side |
| Ex. | Exchange | st. | street |
| gen. agt. | general agent | sw. | southwest |
| h. | home, house | whol. | wholesale |
| Jeff. | Jefferson | wks. | works |
| | | y. | year |

| | | |
|---|---|---|
| BACON, Charles E. (George A. Prince & Co.) | r. Buffalo, N. Y. | 1869-1870 |
| BAKER, William D., engraver [or wood engraver] | 65 S. Clark | 1858-1860 |
| | Randolph n. e. cor. Clark | 1861 |
| | 65 Clark | 1862-1863 |
| | n. e. cor. Clark and Randolph | 1864 |
| BAKER, William D., engraver and lithographer | 63 Clark | 1865 |
| BAKER, William D., wood engraver | Clark ne. cor. Randolph | 1866-1867 |
| BAKER, William D., designer and engraver on wood | Randolph ne. cor. Clark, r. 478 W. Lake | 1868 |
| BAKER, William D., gen. engraver | 63 Clark, cor. Randolph, r. 478 Lake | 1869-1870 |
| BAKER, William D., wood engraver | 73 Clark, r. 478 W. Lake | 1871 |
| BAKER, W. D. Mrs. (Baker & Co.) | r. 238 Warren av. | 1872 |
| BAKER & CO. (Mrs. W. D. Baker and S. W. Fallis) designers and engravers on wood | 50 W. Randolph | 1872 |
| BARNET, James, printer | h. Carroll bt. Jefferson and Clinton[1] | 1853-1854 |
| BARNET, James, printer, R. Fergus | | 1855 |
| BARNET, James, printer | S. Halsted st. bt. Madison and Monroe Scotland 4 y. | 1856-1857 |
| | 189 Lake, h. 98 S. Halsted | 1858 |
| BARNET, James, book and job printer | 189 Lake, h. Newberry c. Mitchell | 1859-1860 |
| BARNET, James, printer | | 1861-1863 |
| BARNET, James, book, job and music printer | 191 Lake, up stairs | 1864-1865 |
| BARNET, James, book and job printer | 191 Lake, 3d floor | 1866 |
| BARNET, James, printer | r. 158 Newberry | 1867 |
| | basement 52 and 54 LaSalle, h. same | 1868 |
| BARNET, James (Barnet & Hanna) | r. 158 Newberry av. | 1869-1870 |
| BARNET, James (Barnet & Son) | r. 160 Newberry av. | 1871[2] |
| BARNET, James, printer and publisher | r. 160 Newberry av. | 1872 |
| BARNET, James A. (Barnet & ---) | bds. 158 Newberry | 1867 |
| BARNET, James A., printer | bds. 158 Newberry | 1868 |
| BARNET, James A., printer | | not in 1869-1870 |
| BARNET, James A. (Barnet & Son) | r. 160 Newberry av. | 1871 |
| BARNET, James A., printer | r. 160 Newberry av. | 1872 |
| BARNET & --- (James Barnet and James A. Barnet) printers | 40 State | 1867 |
| BARNET & HANNA (James Barnet and John B. Hanna) book and job printers | 192 Lake | 1869 |
| | 142 Lake | 1870 |
| BARNET & SON, job printers | 186 Lake | 1871 |
| BAUER, Hermann T., cooper | h. n.s. Hickory, e. Green Bay | 1860 |
| BAUER, Herrmann T., drum mkr. | h. 17 Hickory | 1861 |
| BAUER, Herrmann T. | | not in 1862 |
| BAUER, Hermann, salesman | bds. 17 Hickory | 1863 |
| BAUER, Herrmann, salesman, J. Bauer | boards 17 Oak nr. Greenbay rd. | 1864 |
| BAUER, Herman (Julius Bauer & Co.) | h. 221 Oak | 1865-1867 |
| | r. 140 Erie | 1868 |
| | r. 542 N. Clark | 1869-1870 |
| BAUER, Herman (Julius Bauer & Co.) | | not in 1871 |
| BAUER, Hermann, manager, Julius Bauer & Co. | r. 657 N. Halsted | 1872 |
| BAUER, John R., clerk, Julius Bauer | bds. room 23, Larmon blk. | 1862 |

\* \* \*

[1] In "Names too late for Regular Insertion."
[2] Not listed in Edwards' Chicago Directory ... up to Dec. 12, 1871. Fire ed. (Chicago, R. Edwards, 1871)

| | | |
|---|---|---|
| BAUER, John K. [sic], bookkeeper | bds. 17 Hickory | 1863 |
| BAUER, John, bookkeeper, Julius Bauer & Co. | bds. 17 Oak nr. Greenbay | 1864 |
| BAUER, John R. (Julius Bauer & Co.) | r. New York | 1865-1870 |
| BAUER, John R. (Julius Bauer & Co.) | | not in 1871 |
| BAUER, John, clk., Julius Bauer & Co. | bds. 199 Rush | 1872 |
| BAUER, Julius, musical instruments | 99 S. Clark, h. Hickory bet. Green Bay road and the lake | 1859 |
| BAUER, Julius, music store | 99 S. Clark, h. Hickory e. of Green Bay | 1860 |
| BAUER, Julius, music dealer | 99 Clark, h. 17 Hickory | 1861-1862 |
| BAUER, Julius, musical instruments | 99 Clark; varieties, 104 N. Clark; bds. 17 Hickory | 1863 |
| BAUER, Julius (Julius Bauer & Co.) | h. 17 Oak nr. Greenbay Road | 1864 |
| | h. 221 Oak | 1865-1870 |
| | r. 270 Michigan av. | 1871-1872 |
| *BAUER, Julius & Co. [music & musical instruments] | 99 Clark | 1864 |
| BAUER, Julius & Co. (Julius, Herman and John R. Bauer) dealers in pianos, manfs. and importers of musical merchandise | 69 Washington, Crosby's Opera House | 1865 |
| BAUER, Julius & Co. (Julius, Herman and John R. Bauer) manufacturers and importers of musical instruments, pianos and organs | Crosby's Opera House, 69 Washington | 1866 |
| BAUER, Julius & Co. (Julius and Herman Bauer) importers and dealers in musical merchandise, pianos, organs, etc. | 69 Washington | 1867 |
| BAUER, J. & Co. (Julius, John R. and Herman Bauer) mnfrs. and importers of music and musical instruments | 69 Washington | 1868 |
| BAUER, J. & Co. (Julius, Herman and John R. Bauer) musical instruments, mnfrs. and importers | 69 Washington | 1869-1870 |
| BAUER, J. & Co., music and musical instruments | 69 Washington [3] | 1871 |
| BAUER, Julius & Co. (Julius Bauer and ---) pianos, organs, etc. | 390 to 396 Wabash av. | 1872 |
| BAUER, William | h. 17 Oak nr. Greenbay | 1864 |
| BAUER, William, musical instrument maker | 221 Oak | 1865 |
| BELL, Jo. W., music store | 72 Lake, h. 15 N. Carpenter, office, 77 S. Clark [4] | 1858 |
| BELL, Jo. W., lawyer | 87 S. Dearborn, h. 411 W. Madison | 1859 |
| BENSON, E. A., clerk | b. E. Bayley's | 1849 |
| BENSON, E. A. | | not in 1851 |
| BENSON, Eli A., Apollo Music Store | 61 Clarke, b. Sherman house | 1852 |
| BENSON, E. A., music store | 61 Clark, bds. cor. LaSalle and Washington | 1853 |
| BENSON, E. A., music store | | not in 1854-1863 |
| BENSON, Eli A., music and musical instruments | 105 Randolph, r. Wabash av., cor. Adams | 1864 |
| BENSON, Eli A., music store and stationery | 105 Randolph, r. 126 LaSalle | 1865 |
| BENSON, Eli A., music mer. | r. 126 LaSalle | 1866 |

\* \* \*

\* Entry found in classified business directory section or advertisement.

[3] Post-fire address: 270 and 614 Michigan Ave. - The Weekly Trade Circular, 1 (Jan. 18, 1872) 13

[4] D. B. Cooke & Co.'s Directory of Chicago for ... 1858 lists in "Names too late for insertion": Bell, Jo. W., music store, 100 Randolph, h. 15 N. Carpenter.

| | | |
|---|---|---|
| BENSON, E. A., importer and dealer in musical instruments and merchandise | 115 Randolph, r. 208 Wabash av.[5] | 1867 |
| BLACK, G. N. (Nelke, Black & Co.) | r. 511 Washington av. | 1871 |
| BLACK, George M. [sic] | 165 W. Washington, r. 511 Washington | 1872 |
| BRABANT, Herbert (B. & Co.) | h. 175 State | 1854 |
| BRABANT & CO., music and fancy goods [6] | 70 Lake | 1854 |
| *BRABANT & CO. [piano fortes] | 90 LaSalle | 1855 |
| *BRABANT & CO. [piano forte manufacturer] | 90 LaSalle | 1856 |
| BRAINARD H. M., of B & Mould | h. Clarke b. Mad[ison] and Mon[roe] sts. | 1847 |
| | h. Lake b. Mich. and Wab[ash] avs. | 1848-1849 |
| BRAINARD & MOULD, music and confectionery | 196 Lake st., Ex Buildings | 1847-1848 |
| BRAINARD & MOULD, Music Store | 196 Lake | 1849 |
| | 98 Lake [7] | 1851 |
| BRENNAN, John H., with H. T. Merrill | 113 Randolph | 1863 |
| BRENNAN, John H. (Merrill & Brennan) | r. 91 Washington | 1864 |
| | r. Hubbard ne. c. Paulina | 1865 |
| BRENNAN, John H., pianos | 91 Washington, r. Hubbard ne. cor. Paulina | 1866 |
| BRENNAN, John H., piano forte mnfr. | 232 Washington, h. same | 1867-1869 |
| | r. Van Buren, se. cor. Hermitage Ave. [8] | 1870 |
| BUEHLER, Edward, German and French book seller | 126 Clark, h. Bryan Hall bldg. | 1865 |
| *BUEHLER, Edward [Music books, German and French] | 111 Monroe | 1866 |
| BUEHLER, Edward, German and French book and print store | 111 Monroe, r. same | 1867 |
| BUEHLER, Edward, dealer in German and French music, and circulating library | 111 Monroe, r. same | 1868 |
| BUEHLER, Edward, books and stationery | 111 Monroe, r. same | 1869-1870 |
| BUEHLER, Edward, bookseller | 117 Monroe | 1871 |
| | 371 Wabash av. | 1872 |
| BULLARD, Joel (J. Estey & Co.) | r. 225 Ohio | 1865 |
| BULLARD, Joel, architect | r. 225 Ohio | 1866 |
| BURDETT, Frederick J., organ tuner | r. 101 Huron | 1867 |
| BURDETT, Fred. J., tuner, R. Burdett & Co. | r. 67 Oak | 1868 |
| BURDETT, Fred. J., tuner | | not in 1869-1870 |
| BURDETT, Fred J., organmkr. | r. 113 Chicago av. | 1871 |
| BURDETT, Riley (J. Estey & Co.) | r. Brattleboro, Vt. | 1865 |
| BURDETT, Riley (R. Burdett & Co.) | bds. 115 Chicago av. | 1866 |
| | r. 101 Huron | 1867 |
| | r. 284 Ohio | 1868 |
| | r. 384 N. LaSalle | 1869-1870 |
| | r. 71 Maple | 1871 |
| BURDETT, R. & Co. (Riley Burdett and ---) cottage organs and melodeon manufacturers | 77, 79 and 81 Sedgwick | 1866 |
| BURDETT, Riley & Co. (Riley Burdett and ---) organ mnfrs. | 77, 79 and 81 Sedgwick | 1867 |
| BURDETT, R. & Co. (Riley Burdett and S. M. Waite) organ mnfrs. | 77, 79 and 81 Sedgwick | 1868 |
| BURDETT, R. & Co. (Riley Burdett and Silas M. Waite) Burdett organ mnfrs. | 77, 79 and 81 Sedgwick | 1869-1870 |

\* \* \*

[5] A rolling stone, Benson, "... proud of his roving disposition, related with satisfaction that in the course of 28 years, in which he has been in business, he has had 14 music stores, dividing his fortune and time between Chicago, Memphis and St. Louis ..." - The Music Trade Review, 9 (July 12, 1879) 21.

[6] First advertisement found - The Daily Democratic Press, June 28, 1854, p [2], col. 8.

[7] Also listed at the same address: Chicago Music Store, E. C. Mould.

[8] An alternate listing gives the same home address with: Brennan, John H., saloon, 31 W. Randolph.

| | | |
|---|---|---|
| BURDETT, R. & Co., organ mnfrs. | 77, 79 and 81 Sedgwick | 1871 |
| CADY, Chauncey M., editor, Musical Review | 84 Randolph, h. 246 State | 1858 |
| CADY, Chauncey M. (Root & Cady) | bds. 44 S. Peoria | 1859 |
| | h. Madison cor. Röby | 1860 |
| | h. Fulton 1 door w. of Sheldon | 1861 |
| | h. 258 W. Randolph | 1862 |
| | h. 158 W. Randolph | 1863 |
| | h. 258 W. Randolph | 1864 |
| | h. Hyde Park | 1865-1870 |
| | r. Lake av. nr. 47th st. | 1871 |
| | r. Kenwood | 1872 |
| CADY, Chauncey M. | | not in 1873 |
| CADY, Chauncy M., vice-pres., Chicago Post & Mail Co. | r. Kenwood | 1874 |
| CAMP, J. M. [sic] dealer in organs | Reed's Temple of Music, 47 and 49 Dearborn | 1868 |
| CAMP, I. N. (H. L. Story & Co.) | r. 409 W. Randolph | 1869-1871 |
| CAMP, I. N. (Story & Camp) | r. 549 W. Monroe | 1872 |
| CARLIN, Frederick, melodeonmnfr. | r. 130 Larrabee | 1871 |
| CARLEN, Frederick, jr. (Carlen & Son) | r. 102 Archer av. | 1869-1870 |
| CARLEN, F. (of Cox & C) | W. Lake st. | 1857 |
| CARLIN, [sic] Fredolin, melodeon mkr., tuner and repairer of piano fortes | W. Lake n. Robey | 1858 |
| CARLEN, Fredolin | | not in 1859 |
| CARLIN, Fredolin, melodeons | 209 W. Randolph, h. same | 1860 |
| | 254 Wells, h. same | 1861 |
| CARLEN, Fredolin, melodeon mnfr. | 254 Wells, h. same | 1862 |
| *CARLEN, F. [Music & musical instruments] | 254 Wells | 1863 |
| CARLIN, Fredolin, melodians [sic] | r. 254 Wells | 1864 |
| CARLEN, Fredolin | | not in 1865-1868 |
| CARLEN, Fridolin (Carlen & Son) | r. 102 Archer av | 1869-1870 |
| CARLEN & SON (Fridolin and Frederick Carlen) organ builders | 102 Archer av. | 1869-1870 |
| CARQUEVILLE, Edward (Charles Shober & Co.) | | 1872 |
| CASE, A. B., foreman, press room, Democratic Press | h. 148 Madison | 1853 |
| CASE, A. B., printer, Democratic Press office | h. 172 Buffalo | 1854-1855 |
| CASE, A. B. | 149 Buffalo st. N.Y. 4 y. | 1856 |
| CASE, A. B. | | not in 1857-1861 |
| CASE, Abijah B., printer, Root & Cady[9] | bds. 134 Franklin | 1862 |
| CASE, Abijah B., music printer | h. 156 Quincy | 1863 |
| CASE, Abijah B., music printer, Root & Cady | h. 156 Quincy | 1864 |
| CASE, Abijah B., foreman, Root & Cady's music printing rooms | h. 156 Quincy | 1865 |
| CASE, A. B., music printer | room 18, 77 Dearborn, r. 156 Quincy | 1866-1867 |
| CASE, Abijah B., printer | r. 156 Quincy | 1868 |
| CASE, Abijah B., music printer | 182 Clark, r. 156 Quincy | 1869-1870 |
| CASE, A. B., printer | 168 Clark | 1871 |
| CASE, A. B., music and job printer | 24 and 26 N. Jefferson | 1871F |
| CASE, A. B. (A. B. Case & Son) | r. 79 W. Adams | 1872 |
| CASE, A. B. & Son (A. B. and L. T. Case) job printers | 79 W. Adams | 1872 |
| *CASPER, Winfield G. [piano forte dealer] | 151 Clark | 1854 |
| CASPER, Winfield G. | | not in 1855-1858 |
| CASPER, Winfield, grocer | ss. Hubbard, bet. Paulina and Reuben, h. same | 1859 |

\* \* \*

[9] In "Names too late for Regular Insertion."

| | | |
|---|---|---|
| CASPER, Winfield G., piano tuner & repairer | h. W. Hubbard bet. N. Reuben and N. Paulina | 1860 |
| CASPER, William D., [sic] music instruments | h. Hubbard nr. Paulina | 1861 |
| CASPER, William G. [sic] musician | h. ss. Hubbard bet. N. Paulina and Reuben | 1862 |
| CASPER, W. G., piano tuner | h. Hubbard, bet. N. Reuben and Paulina | 1863 |
| CASPER, Winfield G., pianos and melodeons | 153 Clark, bds. 146 Monroe | 1864 |
| | 153 Clark, r. same [10] | 1865 |
| CASPER, W. G., piano-forte dealer | 155 S. Clark, r. 170 E. Madison [10] | 1866 |
| CASPER, William G., pianos and melodeons | 170 Madison, r. same | 1867 |
| CASPER, Winfield G., pianos and melodeons | 155 Clark, r. same | 1868 |
| CASPER, Winfield G., piano dealer | room 7, 155 Clark, r. same | 1869-1870 |
| CASPER, W. G., pianos, melodeons and organs | 155 Clark, r. 419 Butterfield | 1871 |
| CHALKER, Sumner, salesman | 174 Lake | 1863-1864 |
| CHALKER, Sumner, pianos, melodeons, etc. | 96 Randolph, bds. 296 $\frac{1}{2}$ State | 1865 |
| CHALKER, Samuel [sic] piano stool manufacturer | 96 Randolph | 1866 |
| CHANDLER, Francis S., printer | bds. cor. Randolph and Canal | 1865 |
| CHANDLER, Francis S., music plate engraver | 114 Randolph, bds. Lincoln House | 1866-1867 |
| CHANDLER, Francis S. | | not in 1868-1869 |
| CHANDLER, F., printer, Church, Goodman & Donnelly | r. 224 W. Monroe | 1870 |
| CHANDLER, F. S., music plate engraver | room 48, 124 Washington, r. room 6, 124 Washington | 1871 |
| *CHANT, H. W. [music teacher] | 206 Edina | 1855 |
| | 40 LaSalle | 1856 |
| CHANT, Henry Wm., agent for Boardman & Gray | 89 LaSalle st. Eng. 1 y. | 1857 |
| CHANT, Henry W., organist | h. W. Lake c. Ann | 1858 |
| | h. 366 W. Lake | 1859-1860 |
| CHANT, Henry W., organbuilder | h. 366 W. Lake | 1861 |
| CHANT, Henry W., clerk, Jones, Perdue & Small [stationers] | h. 366 W. Lake | 1862 |
| CHANT, Henry W. | 122 Lake, h. 366 W. Lake cor. Ann | 1863 |
| CHANT, Henry W., organ builder | h. 366 W. Lake | 1864 |
| CHANT, Henry W. (Pilcher & Chant) | r. 366 W. Lake | 1865 |
| CHANT, Henry W., music teacher and piano tuner | r. 366 W. Lake | 1866 |
| CHANT, H. W., organ builder | 130 N. May, r. same | 1867 |
| | 128 N. May, r. 130 N. May | 1868-1870 |
| | r. 346 Fulton | 1871 |
| CHANT, H. W., tuner, A. Reed & Sons | r. Hinsdale | 1872 |
| CHICAGO LITHOGRAPHING CO. (Otto Knirsch, Louis Kurz, Edward Carqueville and Jevner [sic] & Almini) | 152 & 154 S. Clark | 1866 |
| CHICAGO LITHOGRAPHING COMPANY | 152 and 154 Clark | 1867 |
| CHICAGO LITHOGRAPHING CO., Wm. Floto, gen. business manager; Louis Kurz, supt., art dept.; Edward Carqueville, supt., engraving dept. | 152 and 154 Clark | 1868-1870 |
| CHICAGO LITHOGRAPHING CO., Floto, Kurz & Co. | 150, 152 and 154 Clark | 1871 |
| CHICAGO LITHOGRAPHING CO., Charles Shober & Co., proprs. | 71 and 73 W. Washington | 1872 |
| *CHICAGO MUSIC STORE, E. C. Mould. Dealer in music, musical instruments, music books, etc., piano fortes and patent melodeons [11] | 98 Lake Street | 1851 |
| COCKROFT, Joseph, Printer at Journal Office | h. Kinzie bt. Union and Halsted | 1851 |
| COCKROFT, Joseph, Printer & Stereotyper, Daily Journal | h. Michigan bt. Dearborn & Wolcott | 1852 |

\* \* \*

[10] John C. W. Bailey's directories for 1865-66 give the address: 147 Clark.
[11] Also listed at the same address: Brainard & Mould.

| | | |
|---|---|---|
| COCKROFT, Joseph, printer and stereotyper | 73 Lake, h. cor. Mich. and Wolcott | 1853 |
| COCKROFT, Joseph, printer, W. W. Danenhower [12] | 117 Lake | 1854 |
| COCKROFT, Joseph, printer | | not in 1855-1859 |
| COCKROFT, [sic] Joseph, printer and electrotyper | 32 W. Randolph, h. same | 1860 |
| COCKROFT, Joseph, printer | | not in 1861 |
| COCKROFT, Joseph, printer | h. ss. Elm, bet. Clark and LaSalle | 1862 |
| | h. Lincoln cor. Fulton | 1863 |
| COLE, George T. (H. C. Schomacker & Co.) | r. 159 Clark | 1869-1870 |
| CONDE, S. B. & Co. [pianos and music] [13] | 277 W. Randolph | 1858 |
| COX & CARLEN [musical instruments] | 119 Wells | 1856 |
| COX & CARLEN, musical inst. repairers | 119 Wells st. 3rd story 1 y. | 1857 |
| DAVIE, Charles H. (Davie & Co.) | | 1868 |
| DAVIE, Charles H., liquordealer | r. 608 Wabash av. | 1869-1870 |
| DAVIE, Charles H. (Davie, Jackson & Co.) | r. 128 Throop | 1871 |
| DAVIE, Charles H., bkpr. auditor's dept., P. P. Car Co. | r. 448 W. Van Buren | 1872 |
| DAVIE & CO. (Charles H. Davie and ---) wines and liquors | 84 LaSalle | 1868 |
| DAVIE, Jackson & Co., organ builders, and patentees of Magic Flute Organ | 47 and 49 W. Lake | 1871 |
| DAVIS, W. J. [musical instruments] [14] | 89 LaSalle | 1856-1857 |
| DAVIS, William J., music | 72 Lake, h. N. May n. W. Kinzie | 1858 |
| DAVIS, William J., music | | not in 1859 |
| DAVIS, William J., clerk, Newell Snow | h. 98 LaSalle | 1860 |
| De MOTTE, A. Huyler (De Motte Bros.) | | 1868 |
| De MOTTE, A. H., with De Motte Brothers | r. 9 N. Carpenter | 1869 |
| De MOTTE, Edgar M. (De Motte Brothers) | bds. 472 W. Randolph | 1869 |
| De MOTTE, Thomas G. (De Motte Bros.) | r. W. Washington ne. cor. Paulina | 1868 |
| | r. 462 W. Washington | 1869 |
| De MOTTE BROS. (A. Huyler and Thomas G. De Motte) music and musical instruments [15] | 91 Washington | 1868 |
| De MOTTE BROTHERS (Thomas G. and Edgar M. De Motte) music and musical instruments | 91 Washington | 1869 |
| DIEFFENBACHER, Wm. F. (Robert Teufel & Co.) | | 1867 |
| DYE, ---, Vocal and Instrumental Music Teacher | h. 126 LaSalle | 1849 |
| DYE, Nathan, music teacher | b. T. S. Stevens' | 1851 |
| | b. Lemuel Brown | 1852 |
| | bds. 119 Clark | 1853 |
| | h. 150 Dearborn | 1854 |
| DYE, Nathan, music teacher | | not in 1855-1856 |

\* \* \*

[12] "It is worthy of note that in the year 1854 the first music printed in Chicago from movable music type was set in the composing rooms of the Literary Budget by Joseph Cockroft ..." - Andreas, Alfred Thomas. History of Chicago. (Chicago, A. T. Andreas, 1884-1886) v1, p500

[13] No directory listing. Entry based on advertisement dated "Ja 12," Daily Chicago Times, March 5, 1858 ([1]:4)

[14] "Metropolitan Music Store! Opposite the Court House, Chicago, Ills. The subscriber begs to announce that he has fitted up and opened the above establishment, with a view of supplying the increasing requirements of the musical people of Chicago, and respectfully solicits a share of their patronage. The stock consists of Sheet Music and Instruction Books, American and Foreign, German songs, with English words. ... Extra Fine Italian Strings, Violins, Guitars, Flutes, Accordeons, Brass Instruments, and Musical Merchandise in general ... both for the wholesale and retail trade ... Boardman, Gray & Co.'s celebrated PIANOS ... Carhart, Needham & Co.'s MODEL MELODEONS; ... MELOPEANS ... W. J. Davis, No. 89 La Salle street" - Chicago Tribune, Dec. 27, 1855 ([4]:3, adv.)

[15] "The undersigned, having purchased the large stock of Sheet Music formerly owned by Mr. H. M. Higgins, are removing to their new store, No. 91 Washington St. ... De Motte Bros. ..." - Chicago Tribune, Aug. 23, 1867 ([1]:9, adv.)

| | | |
|---|---|---|
| DYE, Nathan, music teacher | 148 Dearborn st. N.Y. 10 y. | 1857 |
| DYE, N., teacher | h. 204 State | 1858 |
| DYE, Nathan, music teacher | 90 S. Halsted | 1859 |
| | h. ss. W. Lake near Oakley | 1860 |
| | h. W. Lake nr. Western av. | 1861 |
| DYE, Nathan, music teacher | | not in 1862 |
| DYE, Nathan, music teacher | h. ss. W. Lake n. Oakley | 1863-1865 |
| DYE, Nathan, local [sic] and instrumental music teacher | r. 917 W. Lake | 1866 |
| DYE, Nathan, music teacher and piano dealer | 104 Randolph, r. 917 W. Lake | 1867 |
| DYE, Nathan, music teacher | r. 917 W. Lake | 1868-1870 |
| | r. 323 Park av. | 1871-1872 |
| ELMORE, Theodore J., asst. bookkeeper, Root & Cady | 651 W. Lake | 1868 |
| | r. 1095 W. Lake | 1869-1870 |
| ELMORE, Theodore J., bkpr., Root & Cady | r. 17 Davis | 1871 |
| ELMORE, Theo. J., cashier, Root & Cady | r. 17 Davis | 1872 |
| ELMORE, Theo. J. & Co. (Theodore J. Elmore and ---) pianos, organs and musical mdse.[16] | 78 State | 1873 |
| ESTEY, Jacob (J. Estey & Co.) | r. Brattleboro, Vermont | 1865 |
| ESTEY, J. & Co. (Jacob Estey, S. M. Waite, Riley Burdett and Joel Bullard) Cottage organs and melodeons | 77, 79 and 81 Sedgwick | 1865 |
| FALK, Theodore, German teacher | bds. 120 Townsend | 1863-1864 |
| FALK, Theodore A., lithographer and teacher [of] music | h. 225 N. Wells | 1865 |
| FALK, Theodore | | not in 1866-1867 |
| FALK, Theodor, dealer in books and music | 156 Illinois, r. 342 N. Wells | 1868 |
| FALK, Theodore, drygoods and notions | 340 Larrabee, r. same | 1869-1870 |
| FALK, Theodore | | not in 1871 |
| FALK, Theodore, lithographer | r. 450 Catherine | 1872 |
| FALLIS, Sylvanus W., wood engraver, W. D. Baker | r. 238 Warren ave. | 1871 |
| FALLIS, S. W. (Baker & Co.) | | 1872 |
| FAULDS, D. P.[17] | | |
| FEULNER, Joseph, saloon | 450 S. Clark | 1858 |
| FEULNER, Joseph, bootmkr. | h. 154 Buffalo | 1859 |
| FEULNER, Joseph | | not in 1860 |
| FEULNER, Joseph, musician | h. 165 Buffalo | 1861 |
| FEULNER, Joseph, musical instruments | 163 Fourth av., h. same | 1862 |
| FEULNER, Joseph, musical instrument mkr. | 454 Clark, h. same | 1863 |
| FEULNER, Joseph, instrument repairer | 151 Randolph, h. 454 Clark | 1864 |
| FEULNER, Joseph, musician, Great West'n Light Guard Band | h. 460 Clark | 1865 |
| FEULNER, Joseph, saloon | 466 S. Clark, r. same | 1866 |
| FOOTE, J. Howard, importer of musical instruments and musical merchandise, at Reed's Temple of Music | 47 and 49 Dearborn, r. New York City | 1868 |
| FOOTE, J. Howard, importers of musical instruments, strings, etc. | 49 Dearborn, r. New York City | 1869-1870 |
| FOOTE, J. Howard, music importer and dealer | 49 Dearborn, r. Brooklyn | 1871 |
| FOOTE, J. Howard, musical instruments, importer and wholesale dealer | 9 S. Halsted | 1872 |

\*　　　\*　　　\*

[16] Started business Dec. 10, 1872, discontinued 1877. - Cf Elmore, Theodore James, comp. Family Memorials in Prose and Verse ... (Savannah, Morning News Steam Printing House, 1880) p. xii-xiii.

[17] No Chicago directory listing for this well-known Louisville firm has been found, but intermittent advertisements appeared in the Chicago Tribune between Sept. 25, 1862, and Apr. 22, 1864. A joint advertisement for W. M. Harlow & D. P. Faulds appeared Dec. 19, 1862 ([1]:8).

| | | |
|---|---|---|
| *FREEMAN, Benjamin [piano forte maker] | 166 Clark | 1866 |
| FREEMAN, Benjamin, piano forte mnfr. | r. 957 W. Madison | 1867-1868 |
| GEMMELL, John, lithographer | 132 Lake | 1857-1859 |
| GEMMELL, John, lithographer | | not in 1860-1866 |
| GEMMELL, John, lithographer and publisher | 123 Randolph, r. 150 Harrison | 1867 |
| | 123 Randolph, r. 80 N. Green | 1868 |
| GEMMELL, John, lithographer | r. 13 S. Green | 1869-1870 |
| FEMMEL [sic] J., publisher | r. 65 Clark | 1871 |
| GEMMEL, J., lithographer and publisher | r. 32 Gold | 1872 |
| GERARD, John B., surveyor, Ogden, Fleetwood & Co. | h. 203 Illinois | 1862-1864 |
| | room 14, 98 Washington | 1865 |
| GERARD, John B. (Ziegfeld, Gerard & Co.) | r. 239 Ontario | 1866 |
| GERARD, John B., clk., Ogden, Fleetwood & Co. | r. 239 Ontario | 1867-1868 |
| *GOLDSMITH, H. [piano forte dealer] | 91 Washington | 1870 |
| GOOLD, John E., clerk, Nathaniel Goold | bds. 1024 Prairie Ave. | 1870 |
| GOOLD, John E. (N. Goold & Son) | r. 1024 Prairie av. | 1871-1872 |
| GOOLD, Nathaniel, carpenter | house cor. Mich. and Division streets | 1848 |
| | h. corner Michigan and Dearborn | 1849-1851 |
| GOOLD, Nathaniel, carpenter | | not in 1852-1853 |
| GOULD, [sic] Nathaniel, carpenter | h. Prairie avenue | 1854-1855 |
| GOULD, [sic] N., traveling agent, Reed & Co. | b. 104 Monroe | 1856 |
| GOOLD, Nathaniel | | not in 1857 |
| GOOLD, Nathaniel, pianos [18] | [90 Lake street] h. Prairie av., c. Ringgold pl. | 1858 |
| GOOLD, Nathaniel, piano ware room [19] | 82 Lake, h. sw. cor. Prairie av. and Ringgold pl. | 1859 |
| | 115 Lake, h. Ringgold pl. nr. Prairie av. | 1860-1863 |
| GOOLD, Nathan, pianos and melodeons | 115 Lake, h. Prairie av. nr. 22d | 1864 |
| GOOLD, Nathaniel, piano fortes, melodeons | 99 Washington, r. 13 Cottage Grove av. | 1865 |
| GOOLD, Nathaniel, piano forte warerooms | 150 State, r. 13 Cottage Grove av. | 1866-1867 |
| | 150 State, r. 1024 Prairie av. | 1868-1870 |
| GOOLD, Nathaniel (N. Goold & Son) | r. 1024 Prairie av. | 1871-1872 |
| GOOLD, N. & Son, pianos | 137 and 139 State | 1871 |
| | 1024 Prairie av., late 137 and 139 State | 1871F |
| GOOLD, N. & Son (Nathaniel and John E. Goold) piano forte dlrs. | 13 Cottage Grove av. | 1872 |
| GOOLD, Thomas E., organ maker | r. 82 Chicago av. | 1870 |
| GREENE, Robert G., clerk, J. S. Greene [land agent] | | 1852 |
| GREENE, Robert G. | | not in 1853 |
| GREENE, R. G. (Mould & G.) | bds. Mrs. Sweet | 1854 |
| GREENE, R. G. music and pianofortes [20] | 74 Lake | 1855 |
| GREENE, R. G., music dealer | 74 Lake, h. 258 Michigan | 1856 |
| GREENE, R. G., musical merchandise | 75 Lake, h. 258 Wabash av. R. I. 4 y. | 1857 |
| GREENE, Robert G., real est. | 66 Randolph, h. 258 Wabash av. | 1858 |

\* \* \*

[18] Although Goold's business was primarily as a piano dealer, he also sold sheet music. Cf Chicago Tribune, July 26, 1858 (1:3, adv.), et seq. "New music. - ... Louis Staab has laid upon our table the 'Carrie Mazurka' published by Lee & Walker, Philadelphia, and by N. Goold, Lake Street, Chicago." - Ibid., Nov. 12, 1858 (1:2)

[19] First advertisement giving 82 Lake Street as address - Ibid., May 12, 1859 (1:6), reading in part: Sheet music and instruction books. A full and complete assortment for sale ... Piano tuning and repairing done ...

[20] First mention of R. G. Greene at 74 Lake Street: Daily Democratic Press, Aug. 20, 1855 ([2]:1)

| | | |
|---|---|---|
| *GROSS, Joseph A. [Music & musical instruments] | 117 S. Clarke | 1858 |
| HACKEL, Charles, organ builder | 369 Ohio | 1858 |
| HAECKHEL, Charles (Wolfram & Haeckhel) | h. 369 Ohio | 1859-1862 |
| | bds. 39 Green | 1863 |
| | h. Sigel nr. Sedgwick | 1864 |
| | h. 56 Sigel | 1865 |
| HAECKHEL, Charles (Wolfram & Haeckhel) | | not in 1866 |
| HAECKHEL, Charles (Wolfram & Haeckhel) | r. 61 Sigel | 1867 |
| | r. 209 Blackhawk | 1868 |
| HAECKEL, Charles, organ builder | r. 209 Blackhawk | 1869-1870 |
| HANNA, John B., librarian | 77 Dearborn, h. Barber bet. Jefferson & Des Plaines | 1863 |
| HANNA, John B., printer | 50 McCormick's bldg., r. nr. Jefferson | 1864 |
| | 191 Lake | 1865 |
| HANNA, John B., printer, James Barnet | 191 Lake, h. 113 Barber | 1866 |
| HANNA, John B., book and job printer | 48 Clark, r. 351 W. 12th | 1867 |
| HANNA, John B., printer | room 35, Reynold's blk. | 1868 |
| HANNA, John B. (Barnet & Hanna) | r. 139 Brown | 1869-1870 |
| HANNA, J. B., printer, Spalding & Lamonte [printers & stationers] | r. 139 Brown | 1871 |
| HANNA, John B., printer, Dean Bros. & Hoffman | r. 67 Waller | 1872 |
| HARLOW, William M., pianos and melodeons[21] | 54 Clark, h. St. Louis, Mo. | 1862 |
| HEALY, Patrick J. (Lyon & Healy) | h. 320 Hubbard | 1865 |
| HEALY, Patrick J., music dealer | h. 319 Hubbard | 1866 |
| HEALY, Patrick J. (Lyon & Healy) | h. 474 W. Taylor | 1867 |
| | r. 308 W. Madison | 1868 |
| | r. 415 W. Van Buren | 1869-1870 |
| | r. 335 S. Halstead | 1871 |
| | r. 148 S. Peoria | 1872 |
| HEINEMANN, William (Charles Shober & Co.) | r. 186 Superior | 1867-1868 |
| | r. 629 W. Madison | 1869 |
| HELMKAMP, G. A., Musical Instrument Maker | Jeff., bt. Ran[dolph] and Wab[ash] | 1849 |
| HELMKAMP, G. A., Musical Instrument Maker. Manufacturer of organs, piano fortes, guitars, violins, etc. | No. 51 Wells street | 1851 |
| HELMKAMP, Anthony G., Piano Manufacturer | 49 Randolph, h. cor. Division and Hamilton | 1852 |
| HENDRICKS, John, lithographer | 38 and 40 LaSalle, r. 133 Sedgwick | 1867 |
| HENTSCHEL, Charles, musical instrument maker, Hentschel & Martin | bds. 62 W. Randolph | 1867 |
| HENTSCHEL, Charles, musical instrument maker, Henry Martin | | 1868 |
| HENTSCHELL, Emil (Hentschell & Martin) | r. Wells | 1865 |
| | r. 210 E. Randolph | 1866 |
| | r. 62 W. Randolph | 1867 |
| HENTSCHELL, Emil | | not in 1868-1869 |
| HENTSHAL [sic] Emil | bds. 82 W. Lake | 1870 |
| HENTSCHEL, Emil | | not in 1871 |
| HENTSCHEL, Emil, musical instrument mkr. | r. 106 Archer av. | 1872 |
| HENTSCHELL & MARTIN (Emil Hentschell and Henry Martin) musical instruments | 218 Lake | 1865 |
| HENTSCHEL & MARTIN (Emil Hentschel & Henry Martin) manufs. brass musical instruments | 218 E. Lake up stairs | 1866 |
| HENTSCHEL & MARTIN (Emil Hentschel and Henry Martin) musical instrument mnfrs. | 218 Lake | 1867 |

\* \* \*

[21] A joint advertisement for W. M. Harlow and D. P. Faulds appeared in the Chicago Tribune, Dec. 19, 1862 (1:8)

| | | |
|---|---|---|
| HIGGINS, Adoniram J. (of H. Brothers) | 122 Superior st.  N.Y.  1 y. | 1856-1857 |
| HIGGINS, Adoniram J., music store | 84 Randolph, h. 122 Superior | 1858 |
| HIGGINS, Adoniram J. | | not in 1859-1860[22] |
| HIGGINS, A. Judson, music and instruments[23] | 40 Clark, h. 60 S. Des Plaines | 1861 |
| HIGGINS, A. Judson, com. mer. | h. 60 S. Des Plaines | 1862-1863 |
| HIGGINS, A. Judson | | not in 1864 |
| HIGGINS, A. J., physician | h. 130 Madison | 1865 |
| | 142 Clark, h. same | 1866 |
| HIGGINS, Hiram M. (of H. Brothers) | 61 N. Wells.  N.Y.  10 y. | 1856-1857 |
| HIGGINS, Hiram M., music | 84 Randolph, h. 91 N. Wells | 1858 |
| HIGGINS, Hiram M., dealer in musical instruments | 45 Lake, h. 91 N. Wells | 1859 |
| HIGGINS, Hiram M., sheet music and musical instruments | 117 Randolph, h. 91 N. Wells | 1860-1861 |
| HIGGINS, Hiram M., music dealer and publisher | 117 Randolph, h. 91 N. Wells | 1862 |
| HIGGINS, Hiram M., music publishing house | 117 Randolph, h. 91 N. Wells | 1863 |
| HIGGINS, Hiram M., music publisher | 117 Randolph, r. Hyde Park | 1864 |
| HIGGINS, Hiram M., music dealer | 117 Randolph, h. Kenwood station, Hyde Park | 1865 |
| HIGGINS, Hiram M., music dealer and publisher | 115 and 117 Randolph, h. Kenwood station, Hyde Pk. | 1866 |
| | 117 Randolph, h. Hyde Park | 1867 |
| HIGGINS, H. M., pianos, organs and musical instruments[24] | 122 S. Clark, r. Hyde Park | 1868 |
| HIGGINS, Hiram M., piano mnfr. and wine mer. | 122 Clark, r. 109 Kankakee av. | 1869 |
| HIGGINS, Hiram M., pianos | 150 Clark | 1870 |
| HIGGENS [sic] BROTHERS, music &c.[25] | 54 Randolph | 1855 |
| HIGGINS BROTHERS, music store | 54 Randolph st.  1 y. | 1856-1857 |
| | 84 Randolph | 1858 |
| HOOK, Moses (Warren & Hook) | 85 and 87 Clark | 1863 |
| HOOK, Moses | h. cor. Racine and Fullerton av. | 1864 |
| HOOK, Moses, com. mer. | r. Racine rd., c. Fullerton av. | 1865 |
| HOOK, Mrs. S. G., matron, Warren's music school | 85 and 87 Clark, h. same | 1863 |
| HORNER, Mrs. W. B., ladies' music store | 67 Randolph | 1853 |
| | 69 Randolph | 1854 |
| HORNER, Mrs. W. B, ladies' music teacher | 115 W. Madison | 1855 |
| JACKSON, Richard, organbuilder, Davies [sic] Jackson & Co. | r. 351 Hurlbut | 1871 |
| JACOBS, J. L., accordeons | 79 Lake | 1858 |
| KENNICOTT, John W., salesman, Lyon & Healy | r. 75 S. Morgan | 1871 |
| KENNICOTT, J. W., music store | 287 W. Madison, bds. 340 W. Washington | 1872 |
| KIMBALL, W. W. | h. 15 Edina pl. | 1858 |
| KIMBALL, William W., real estate agt. | 51 S. Clark | 1859 |
| KIMBALL, William W., pianoes [sic] and melodeons[26] | 95 Clark | 1860 |
| KIMBALL, William W., pianodealer | 99 Clark, bds. Stewart House | 1861 |
| KIMBALL, William W., dealer in pianos and melodeons, sole agt. for Alexander's organs | 99 Clark, bds. Sherman House | 1862 |

\* \* \*

[22] Although there are no directory listings for these years, the Tribune for Nov. 6, 1860 (1:7), told of his publishing and selling music at 49 Clark Street.

[23] Last advertisement: Ibid., Oct. 31, 1861 (4:1): succeeded by E. H. Patterson, Ibid., Nov. 19, 1861 (1:7).

[24] On May 13, 1863 (4:3), Higgins announced in the Tribune his removal to 122 South Clark Street, "having disposed of the sheet music department of his business."

[25] In "Names too late for Regular Insertion." An advertisement first appeared in the Democratic Press for July 28 (2:6).

[26] First advertisement found: Ibid., Nov. 7, 1859 (1:4).

| | | |
|---|---|---|
| KIMBALL, W. W., piano fortes and melodeons | 142 Lake, bds. Sherman House | 1863-1864 |
| KIMBALL, W. W., pianos, organs and melodeons | Crosby's Opera House, bds. Sherman House | 1865 |
| | Crosby's Opera House, bds. 611 Wabash av. | 1866 |
| | 63 Washington, r. 594 Wabash av. | 1867 |
| | 63 Washington, Crosby's Opera House; r. 610 Michigan Ave. | 1868-1871[27] |
| | Wabash av. cor. 13th | 1872 |
| KLEIN, Bernhard (F. A. Meinhold & Co.) | bds. 15 N. Clark | 1869-1870 |
| KLEIN, Bernard (Meinhold & Co.) | r. 163 Clark | 1871 |
| | r. 481 State | 1872 |
| KNAUER, August, pianomaker | r. 139 N. Clark | 1867 |
| KNAUER, B. (C. K. & Sons) | h. Clarke bt. Ohio and Ontario | 1851 |
| KNAUER, Bruns [sic] Piano maker | 133 N. Clarke | 1852 |
| KNAUER, Bruno, piano maker | | not in 1853-1857 |
| KNAUER, Bruno, piano mnfr. | 139 N. Clark | 1858 |
| KNAUER, Bruno, real estate broker | bds. 141 N. Clark | 1859 |
| KNAUER, Bruno, agt. | 141 N. Clark | 1860-1861 |
| KNAUER, Bruno, real estate agt. and notary public | 1 Ewing's blk., h. 141 N. Clark | 1862-1865 |
| KNAUER, Bruno (Herman Knauer & Co.) | 141 N. Clark | 1866 |
| | r. 332 Superior | 1867 |
| KNAUER, Bruno (Knauer Brothers and H. Knauer & Co.) | r. 332 Superior | 1868 |
| KNAUER, Bruno (Knauer Bros.) | r. 324 Superior | 1869-1870 |
| KNAUER, Bruno (H. Knauer & Co. and Knauer Bros.) | r 324 Superior | 1871 |
| KNAUER, Bruno (Knauer Bros.) | r. 324 Superior | 1872 |
| KNAUER, C., & Sons, Piano Manufacturers[28] | Clarke bt. Ohio and Ontario | 1851 |
| KNAUER, C. & Sons, Piano Manufacturers | | not in 1852 |
| KNAUER, C. & Son, piano forte makers | 131 North Clark | 1853 |
| KNAUER, Charles & Son, piano manufacturers | 131 North Clark | 1854-1856 |
| KNAUER & SON, piano maker | 147 N. Clark st. 7 y. | 1857 |
| KNAUER, C. & Son, piano mnfrs. | 139 and 141 N. Clark | 1858 |
| KNAUER, C. (C. K. & Sons) | h. Clarke bt. Ohio and Ontario | 1851 |
| KNAUER, Carl, Piano maker | 133 N. Clarke | 1852 |
| KNAUER, Charles (C. K. & Son) | h. 133 North Clark | 1853 |
| | h. 131 North Clark | 1854-1855 |
| KNAUER, Charles | | not in 1856 |
| KNAUER, Charles of C. K. & Son | 145 N. Clark st. | 1857 |
| KNAUER, Charles, piano mnfr. | 139 Clark | 1858 |
| | 141 N. Clark, h. same | 1859 |
| KNAUER, Charles (Bruno Knauer, agt.) | 141 N. Clark | 1860 |
| KNAUER, Charles | | not in 1861-1863 |
| KNAUER, Charles, pianomkr. | h. 141 N. Clark | 1864-1866 |
| KNAUER, E. (C. K. & Sons) | h. Clarke bt. Ohio and Ontario | 1851 |
| KNAUER, Edmund, Piano maker | 133 N. Clarke | 1852 |
| KNAUER, Edmond [sic] (C. K. & Son) | bds. 131 North Clark | 1853 |
| KNAUER, Edmund, music saloon | 184 Lake | 1854-1855 |
| KNAUER, Edmund | | not in 1856 |
| KNAUER, Edmund of C. K. & Son | 145 N. Clark st. Ger. 7 y. | 1857 |

\* \* \*

[27] Post-fire address: 610 Michigan Ave. - The Weekly Trade Circular 1 (Jan. 18, 1872) 13.

[28] "Chicago, Her Manufactures ... Piano Fortes. There are three manufactories of Piano Fortes in the city. Messrs. Phelps & Wiley, no. 11 [?] Dearborn street, H. & J. Stone, 17 North Clark street and C. Knauer, 131 North Clark street. They employ about fifteen persons, and manufacture annually about sixty pianos, at an average value of $250.00, making the aggregate value of Pianos annually made $15,000. They meet with a ready sale, being disposed of, as soon as finished. The purchasers are residents of Chicago, and ... neighboring counties." - Chicago Daily Tribune, Feb. 1, 1855 (4:7).

| | | |
|---|---|---|
| KNAUER, Edmund, piano mnfr. | 139 N. Clark | 1858 |
| KNAUER, Edmond [sic] house agent | 141 N. Clark | 1859 |
| KNAUER, Edmund (Knauer and Malcolm) | bds. 139 N. Clark | 1860-1861 |
| | room 1, Ewing's blk., h. 141 N. Clark | 1862-1866 |
| KNAUER, Edmund | | not in 1867 |
| KNAUER, Edmund (Knauer Brothers) | r. 332 Superior | 1868 |
| | r. 324 Superior | 1869-1870 |
| KNAUER, Edmond [sic] (H. Knauer & Co. and Knauer Bros.) | r. 324 Superior | 1871 |
| KNAUER, Edmund (Knauer Bros.) | r. 324 Superior | 1872 |
| KNAUER, Harman [sic] (C. K. & Sons) | h. Clarke bt. Ohio and Ontario | 1851 |
| KNAUER, Herman, Piano maker | 133 N. Clarke | 1852 |
| KNAUER, Herman | | not in 1853 |
| KNAUER, Herman (Charles K. & Son) | h. 131 North Clark | 1854-1855 |
| KNAUER, Herman | | not in 1856 |
| KNAUER, Herman of K. & Son | 145 N. Clark st. | 1857 |
| KNAUER, Herman, piano mnfr. | 139 N. Clark | 1858 |
| KNAUER, Herman, pianomkr. | bds. 141 N. Clark | 1859 |
| KNAUER, Herman, piano mnfr. | 139 and 141 N. Clark | 1860 |
| KNAUER, Herman, piano mkr. | h. 141 N. Clark | 1861 |
| KNAUER, Herman | | not in 1862-1864 |
| KNAUER, Harmon [sic] piano mnfr. | h. 141 N. Clark | 1865 |
| KNAUER, Herman (Herman Knauer & Co.) | r. 141 N. Clark | 1866 |
| | r. Superior | 1867 |
| | r. 332 Superior | 1868 |
| KNAUER, Herman (Knauer Bros.) | r. 324 Superior | 1869-1870 |
| KNAUER, Herman (H. Knauer & Co.) | r. 324 Superior | 1871 |
| KNAUER, H. (Knauer & Co.) | r. 324 Superior | 1872 |
| KNAUER, Herman & Co. (Herman Knauer and Bruno Knauer) piano manufacturers | 159 Kinzie | 1866-1868 |
| KNAUER, H. & Co. (Herman Knauer and ---) piano makers | 72 Lake | 1869-1870 |
| KNAUER, H. & Co. Chicago Piano Factory | 72 Lake | 1871 |
| KNAUER & CO. (H. Knauer and A. Hann) flour mers. | 190 N. Clark | 1872 |
| KNAUER & SON, piano maker | 147 N. Clark st. 7 y. | 1857 |
| KNAUER & MALCOLM (Edmund Knauer and Robert Malcolm) real est. agts. | 139 N. Clark | 1860 |
| | room 1, Ewing's blk. | 1861-1866 |
| KNAUER BROTHERS (Edmund and Bruno Knauer) realestate brokers | room 3, Uhlich's blk. | 1868 |
| KNAUER BROS. (Edmond [sic] and Bruno Knauer) realestate and money lenders | 3 Uhlich's blk., N. Clark, cor. Water | 1869-1871 |
| | room 2, 55 N. Clark | 1872 |
| KNIRSCH, Otto, lithographer | 162 Lake, h. 33 Newberry | 1865 |
| KNIRSCH, Otto (Chicago Lithographing Co.) | r. 174 Indiana | 1866 |
| KNIRSCH, Otto, practical lithographer | room 19, Reynold's blk. | 1867 |
| KNOPFEL, Gustavus C. (G. C. Knopfel & Co.) | | 1864-1869 |
| KNOPFEL, Gustavus C. | | not in 1870 |
| KNOPFEL, G. C., agent Hook's organs | 143 Clark | 1871 |
| *KNOPFEL, G. C. [musical instruments] | 980 Wabash av. | 1872 |
| KNOPFEL, G. C. & Co (Gustavus C. Knopfel, Thomas H. Condell and Julius Albrand) fancy groceries, fruits, etc. | 104 S. Water | 1868-1869 |
| KREUGER, Charles, musical instrument mkr. | 274 N. Franklin, h. same | 1859 |
| KUHN, Joseph, printer, Chas. Shober | bds. 74 State | 1864 |
| KUHN, Joseph, lith. printer, W. Engraving Co. | | 1865 |
| KUHN, Joseph | | not in 1866 |

| | | |
|---|---|---|
| KUHN, Joseph, lithographer | 114 Dearborn, r. Willow cor. Halsted | 1867 |
| | r. 26 Mohawk | 1868 |
| KUHN, Joseph, lithographer, Edward Mendel | r. 134 Sophia | 1869-1870 |
| *LAWINSKI, S. [music and musical instruments] | 536 State | 1870-1871 |
| | 538 State | 1872 |
| LEVINO, Emanuel (Louis Nelke & Co.) | | 1868 |
| LEWINO, Emanuel (Louis Nelke & Co.) | | 1869-1870 |
| LEWIS, William, clerk, Root & Cady | h. Wells bet. Division and Granger | 1863 |
| | h. cor. Indiana and LaSalle | 1864 |
| | r. 101 Halsted | 1865 |
| LEWIS, William, violinist | r. 101 S. Halsted | 1866-1867 |
| LEWIS, William, clerk, Root & Cady | r. Hyde Park | 1868-1872 |
| LEWIS, William (Root & Lewis) | r. Hyde Park | 1873-1874 |
| LEWIS, William (Root & Sons Music Co.) | r. Hyde Park | 1875 |
| LUHRSON [sic] F., manufacturer musical instruments | 170 Washington | 1852 |
| LUHRSEN, Friedrich, musical instrument repairer | 92 Wells, h. same | 1853 |
| LAURSEN [sic] Frederick, variety store | 92 Wells | 1854-1855 |
| LUHRSEN, Frederick, pianoforte maker | over Burhans & Smith's livery stable, h. 92 Wells | 1855 |
| *LUHRSEN, F. [piano fortes and musical instruments] | 117 S. Clark | 1856 |
| LUHRSEN, Frederick, music store | 117 Clark st. 1 y. | 1857 |
| LYON, G. W. | bds. Orient house | 1865 |
| LYON, George W. (Lyon & Healy) music store | cor. Washington & Clark, h. 142 Erie | 1866 |
| | rooms 116 Washington | 1867 |
| | r. 276 W. Randolph | 1868 |
| | r. 383 W. Monroe | 1869 |
| | r. Wabash av. cor. Wash[ington] | 1870 |
| | r. 390 Fulton | 1871 |
| | bds. 295 Fulton | 1872 |
| LYON & HEALY | | not in 1865[29] |
| LYON & HEALY (George W. Lyon, Patrick J. Healy) music publishers | cor. Clark and Washington [*104 S. Clark] | 1866 |
| | 116 Washington | 1867 |
| LYON & HEALY (George W. Lyon & Patrick J. Healy) importers of musical instruments | 116 Washington and 114 Clark | 1868-1869 |
| | 96, 98 and 100 Wabash av., and 20 Wash[ington] | 1870 |
| LYON & HEALY, music and musical goods | 150 Clark [Higgins' late store] | 1871 |
| | 287 W. Madison, late 150 Clark | 1871F |
| | Wabash av. se. cor. 16th | 1872 |
| | 162 State | 1873-1875 |
| MACKLETT, Herman, violinmkr. | r. 176 Randolph | 1871 |
| MARSH, Stephen W. & Sons, piano fortes, sheet music, etc. | 70 Lake | 1853 |
| MARSH, S. Wisner, piano tuner | 70 Lake | 1853 |
| MARSH, S. W. (Brabant & Co.) | 70 Lake | 1854 |
| MARSH, Stephen W., Metropolitan Music Store | 94 LaSalle | 1855 |
| MARSH, Stephen W. | | not in 1856 |
| MARSH, Stephen W. | Ann bet. Randolph & Washington Mass. 4 y. | 1857 |
| MARSH, Stephen W., pianos and music | h. 371 S. Clark | 1858 |
| MARSH, S. Wisner, pianoforte tuner, C. L. Watkins & Co. | h. 146 W. Jackson | 1859 |

\* \* \*

[29] First advertisement found: Chicago Tribune, Oct. 20, 1864 (1:7).

| | | |
|---|---|---|
| MARSH, Stephen W. | h. Madison bet. Reuben & Paulina | 1860 |
| MARSH, Stephen W. | | not in 1861-1866 |
| MARSH, S. W., pianofortes | office, Smith & Nixon's bldg., r. 281 S. Clinton | 1867 |
| MARTIN, Henry (Hentschell & Martin) | r. 368 Wells | 1865 |
| | r. 56 E. Hinsdale | 1866 |
| | r. 65 E. Hinsdale | 1867 |
| MARTIN, Henry, musical instrument mnfr. | 218 Lake, r. 22 Oakwood | 1868 |
| MARTIN, Henry, musical instrument maker | 55 W. Randolph, r. 22 Oakwood | 1869-1870 |
| MARTIN, H. M., music publisher | r. 246 Wabash | 1871 |
| MATHUSHEK'S Piano Forte Co. and Phelps and Goodman's organs and melodeons, Sidney W. Sea, gen. agt. | 109 Dearborn | 1869-1870 |
| MEINHOLD, F. A. & Co. (Theodore Meinhold & Bernhard Klein) mnfrs. and importers of musical instruments | 130 Clark | 1869-1870 |
| MEINHOLD, Theodore (F. A. Meinhold & Co.) | bds. 15 N. Clark | 1869-1870 |
| MEINHOLD, Theodore (Meinhold & Co.) | r. 163 Clark | 1871 |
| | r. 481 State | 1872 |
| MEINHOLD & CO., musical instruments | 163 Clark | 1871 |
| MEINHOLD & CO. (T. Meinhold and B. Klein) musical instruments | 481 State | 1872 |
| MENDEL, Edward, lithographer | 170 Lake | 1853 |
| MENDEL, Edward, lithographer and engraver | 170 Lake | 1854 |
| | 170 Lake, bds. 228 Randolph | 1855-1857 |
| | 162 Lake, h. Washington House | 1858 |
| | 19 Link's bldg., h. same | 1859 |
| | 162 Lake, h. same | 1860 |
| MENDELL [sic] Edward, lithographer and map publisher | Lake nw. corner LaSalle | 1861-1862 |
| MENDEL, Edward, lithographer | Lake, nw. c. LaSalle, h. 32 Warren | 1863 |
| MENDEL, Edward, lithographic engraver | 162 and 164 Lake, h. 32 Warren | 1864 |
| MENDEL, Edward, lithograph and steel engraving | 162 and 164 Lake, h. Wabash av., cor. 23rd | 1865-1866 |
| | 162 Lake, r. 1052 Wabash av. | 1867-1868 |
| | First National Bank bldg., State sw. cor. Washington, r. 1052 Wabash av. | 1869-1870 |
| | 104 State, r. 1054 Wabash | 1871 |
| | 22d ne. cor. State,[30] r. 1052 Wabash av. | 1872 |
| MERRILL, Hiram T., teacher of music and dealer in musical instruments | 113 Randolph, h. 114 S. Green[31] | 1863 |
| MERRILL, Hiram T. (Merrill & Brennan) | r. 114 S. Green | 1864-1865 |
| MERRILL, Hiram T. (H. T. Merrill & Co.) | r. 522 W. Washington | 1866 |
| MERRILL, Hiram T., music publisher and dealer in musical instruments | 119 Madison, h. 522 Washington | 1867 |
| MERRILL, Hiram T., musicstore | 119 and 121 Madison, r. 70 Honore | 1868 |
| | r. 70 Ashland av. | 1869 |
| MERRILL, H. T., music teacher | r. 70 Honore | 1870-1871 |
| MERRILL, H. T., organist | r. 70 Hanover | 1872 |
| MERRILL, H. T. & Co. (Hiram T. Merrill and ---) pianos and melodeons | 91 Washington | 1866 |
| MERRILL & BRENNAN (Hiram T. Merrill and J. H. Brennan) music dealers | 91 Washington | 1864 |

\* \* \*

[30] Address listed in The Weekly Trade Circular, 1 (Jan. 18, 1872) 13.
[31] First advertisement found: Chicago Tribune, Sept. 30, 1862 (1:7).

| | | |
|---|---|---|
| MERRILL & BRENNAN (Hiram T. Merrill & John H. Brennan) pianos and melodeons | 91 Washington | 1865 |
| MERRILL & BRENNAN (Hiram T. Merrill and John H. Brennan) music publishers and dealers in musical instruments | 91 Washington | 1866 |
| METROPOLITAN MUSIC STORE[32] | 94 LaSalle | 1855 |
| MOLTER, John, music teacher | h. 346 S. Wells | 1858 |
| | h. 130 Edina pl. | 1859 |
| | h. 401 Clark | 1860-1861 |
| | h. 450 State | 1862 |
| MOLTER, John, music teacher [*piano forte dealer][33] | 114 Randolph, h. same | 1863 |
| MOLTER, John, dealer in pianos and musical instruments | 104 Randolph, r. same | 1864 |
| MOLTER, John (Molter & Wurlitzer) | h. 91 N. Wells | 1865 |
| | h. Cottage Grove | 1866 |
| | h. ss. Ontario, bet. Clark and Dearborn | 1867 |
| | r. 196 Ontario | 1868 |
| | r. 241 Huron | 1869-1870 |
| *MOLTER, John [piano fortes] | 117 Randolph | 1871 |
| MOLTER, John, musical instruments | 194 W. Madison, late 117 Randolph | 1871F |
| | 120 W. Madison, r. 378 W. Randolph | 1872 |
| MOLTER, John, music | 120 W. Madison, r. 378 W. Randolph | 1873 |
| | 100 Madison, r. 255 Ontario | 1874 |
| MOLTER & WURLITZER (John Molter, Rudolph Wurlitzer, Cincinnati) importers of and dealers in musical instruments, &c. | 82 Dearborn[34] | 1865-1866 |
| MOLTER & WURLITZER (John Molter and Rudolph Wurlitzer) pianos, melodeons and organs | 111 Randolph | 1867 |
| MOLTER & WURLITZER (John Molter and Rudolph Wurlitzer) dealers in musical merchandise | 117 Randolph | 1868 |
| MOLTER & WURLITZER (John Molter & Rudolph Wurlitzer) music publishers and dealers in musical instruments | 117 Randolph | 1869 |
| MOLTER & WURLITZER (John Molter & Rudolph Wurlitzer) pianos, organs, etc. | 117 Randolph | 1870 |
| MOULD, B. K. of Brainard & M | res. Mrs. Merriam's | 1847 |
| | residence D. Hatch's | 1848-1849 |
| MOULD, Brooks K. | h. 107 State | 1851 |
| MOULD, Brook [sic] K., Music Store | 98 Lake, b. Matteson House | 1852 |
| | 98 Lake, h. cor. Clark and Van Buren | 1853 |
| MOULD, B. K. (M. & Greene) | h. 273 Clark | 1854 |
| MOULD, Brooks K., clerk, R. G. Green [sic][35] | h. Prairie av. s. of Monterey | 1855 |
| MOULD, B. K. (B. K. M. & Co.) | 70 Lake, h. Prairie av. | 1856 |
| | h. Prairie av. nr. Buena Vista st. O. 7 y. | 1857 |
| MOULD, Brooks K., music | 104 Lake, h. 532 Wabash av. | 1858 |
| MOULD, Brooks K. | | not in 1859-1861 |
| MOULD, B. R. [sic] com. mer. | under Briggs house, h. ws. Michigan av., bet. Rio Grande and Hardin pl. | 1862 |

\* \* \*

[32] In "Names too late for Regular Insertion." Listed elsewhere under S. W. Marsh.
[33] First advertisement: "New Music Store" - Chicago Tribune, Oct. 13, 1863 (1:8)
[34] Advertisement of Molter & Wurlitzer's removal from 136 Clark to 82 Dearborn - Chicago Tribune, May 9, 1865 (1:9).
[35] "Mould & Greene, 98 Lake" is listed in the Chicago Almanac for 1855.

| | | |
|---|---|---|
| MOULD, Brooks K. | h. Michigan av., nr. Bond | 1863 |
| | r. Michigan av., nw. c. 27th | 1864 |
| MOULD, Brooks K. | | not in 1865 |
| MOULD, B. K., bkpr. | 28 Market | 1866 |
| MOULD, B. K. & Co., musical instruments and music | 83 Lake st. 7 y. | 1857 |
| MOULD, E. C. | b. B. K. Mould's | 1851 |
| MOULD & GREENE, music and pianos | 98 Lake | 1854-1855 |
| MULLER, Gallus (Ziegfeld, Gerard & Co.) | r. 203 Illinois | 1866 |
| MULLER, Gallus | | not in 1867 |
| MULLER, Gallus, salesman, Molter & Wurlitzer | r. 203 Illinois | 1868 |
| MULLER, Gallus, bookkeeper, Molter & Wurlitzer | r. 239 Ontario | 1869-1870 |
| MULLER, Gallus, bkpr. | r. Lincoln av. bet. Franklin and Wisconsin | 1871 |
| NELKE, Louis, practical lithographer | 14 Clark | 1865 |
| NELKE, Louis, lithographer and engraver | 14 S. Clark, r. 111 Michigan | 1866 |
| | 14 S. Clark, r. 208 N. Wells | 1867 |
| NELKE, Louis (Louis Nelke & Co.) | r. 144 Ontario | 1868-1870 |
| NELKE, Louis (Nelke, Black & Co.) | r. 470 N. Clark | 1871 |
| NELKE, Louis, printer and engraver | 250 Milwaukee av., bds. 354 W. Indiana | 1872 |
| NELKE, Louis & Co. (Louis Nelke & Emanuel Levino) lithographers, engravers and printers | 14 Clark | 1868-1870 |
| NELKE, Black & Co., lithographers | 96 and 98 Randolph | 1871 |
| NEWELL, Augustus, mnfr. organ reeds | 77 Sedgwick, r. 375 Belden av. | 1871 |
| NIXON, Wilson K. (Smith & Nixon) | h. cor. Washington and Bishop pl. | 1864 |
| | h. 136 Wolcott | 1865 |
| | bds. Tremont House | 1866 |
| | r. 111 Pine | 1867-1868 |
| | r. 111 S. Sangamon | 1869-1870 |
| | r. 294 Erie | 1871 |
| PALMER, H. R., editor, Concordia, teacher of music[36] | room 9, 164 Randolph | 1866 |
| PALMER, H. R., publisher, The Concordia | room 38, Crosby's Opera House | 1867-1868 |
| | r. 353 W. Adams | 1869-1870 |
| PALMER, H. R., music composer | r. 353 W. Adams | 1871 |
| PALMER, H. R., music publisher | r. 333 W. Adams | 1872 |
| PATTERSON, Ezra H., bookkeeper, A. J. Higgins[37] | bds. 60 S. Des Plaines | 1861 |
| PATTERSON, Ezra H., accountant, Woodruff & Rosseter | bds. 60 S. Des Plaines | 1862 |
| PAYNE, John, printer Democratic Press | h. 165 Adams | 1855 |
| PAYNE, John | | not in 1856 |
| PAYNE, John, printer (Dem. Press) | 165 Adams st. Eng. 3 y. | 1857 |
| PAYNE, John, printer | h. 87 S. Halsted | 1858-1859 |
| | h. S. Des Plaines bet. W. Old and North | 1860 |
| | h. 166 W. Lake | 1861-1863 |
| PAYNE, John, music printer | 191 Lake, h. 166 W. Lake | 1864 |
| | room 7, 112 Randolph[38] | 1865 |
| | Loomis nr. W. Taylor, r. same | 1866 |
| PAYNE, John, printer | r. 296 Loomis | 1867 |
| PAYNE, John, printer, Root & Cady | r. Lake View | 1868 |

\* \* \*

[36] "A new monthly ... the Concordia has just been issued by H. R. Palmer, no. 164 $^1/_2$ Randolph St. ..." - Chicago Tribune, Jan. 4, 1866 (4:1)

[37] "E. H. Patterson, successor to A. J. Higgins" - advertisement, first appeared, Chicago Tribune, Nov. 19, 1861 (1:7)

[38] In "Alterations, Removals, etc." [too late for regular insertion]

| | | |
|---|---|---|
| PETERS, J. L., music publisher[39] | 117 Randolph, r. St. Louis | 1867 |
| PHELPS, Lyman, piano forte manufacturer | h. 102 Madison | 1853 |
| PHELPS, L. N. (P & Wiley) | bds. 121 Dearborn | 1854 |
| PHELPS, L. N., piano tuner | 72 State | 1855 |
| PHELPS, L. N. | | not in 1856-1858 |
| PHELPS, Lyman, piano fortes and melodeons | 132 Clark, bds. 218 Madison | 1859 |
| PHELPS, Lyman, piano fortes | 134 Clark, bds. Merchants' Hotel | 1860 |
| PHELPS, Lyman, pianoforte mnfr. | 166 Clark, bds. City Hotel | 1861 |
| PHELPS, Lyman, pianomkr. | 166 Clark, h. same | 1862 |
| PHELPS, Lyman, piano forte manufacturer | $126\frac{1}{2}$ Dearborn, bds City Hotel | 1863 |
| | $126\frac{1}{2}$ Dearborn, h. 166 Clark | 1864 |
| PHELPS, Lyman | | not in 1865 |
| PHELPS, Lemon [sic] piano forte manufacturer and dealer | r. 153 4th av. | 1866 |
| PHELPS, Samuel, piano forte maker | bds. 184 Washington | 1853 |
| PHELPS & WILEY, piano forte makers | 118 Dearborn | 1854 |
| PILCHER, Henry, organ builder | 52 N. Jefferson, h. 365 W. Lake | 1863 |
| PILCHER, Henry (Pilcher & Co.) | | 1864 |
| PILCHER, Henry (Pilcher & Chant) | r. 365 W. Lake | 1865 |
| PILCHER, Henry (Pilcher Brothers) | r. 365 W. Lake | 1866 |
| PILCHER, Henry, organ builder, Warren Root | r. 394 Warren | 1867 |
| PILCHER, Henry (Pilcher Bros.) | r. 858 W. Washington | 1868-1870 |
| PILCHER, Henry | | not in 1871 |
| PILCHER, Henry, mnfr. church organs | Washington, sw. cor. Western av., r. 856 Washington | 1872 |
| PILCHER, Thomas E., organ builder | r. $100\frac{1}{2}$ Ann | 1866 |
| PILCHER, William, organ builder | 52 N. Jefferson, h. 365 W. Lake | 1863 |
| PILCHER, William (Pilcher & Co.) | | 1864 |
| PILCHER, William | | not in 1865 |
| PILCHER, William (Pilcher Brothers) | r. Warren bet. Oakley and Western av. | 1866 |
| PILCHER, William, organ builder, Warren Root | r. 394 Warren | 1867 |
| PILCHER, William (Pilcher Bros.) | r. 856 W. Washington | 1868-1870 |
| PILCHER, William | | not in 1871 |
| PILCHER, William (Pilcher & Son) | r. 858 W. Washington | 1872 |
| PILCHER, W. H. (Pilcher & Son) | r. 858 W. Washington | 1872 |
| PILCHER & CHANT (Henry Pilcher and H. W. Chant) organ builders | 375 and 377 W. Randolph | 1865 |
| PILCHER & CO. (Henry and William Pilcher) organ builders | 377 and 379 Randolph | 1864 |
| PILCHER & SON (William and W. H. Pilcher) mnfrs. church organs | ws. Paulina bet. Milwaukee av. and Blackhawk | 1872 |
| PILCHER BROTHERS (Henry and William Pilcher) organ builders | 375 and 377 W. Randolph | 1866 |
| PILCHER BROTHERS (Henry and William Pilcher) organ builders | | not in 1867 |
| PILCHER BROS. (Henry and William Pilcher) organbuilders | W. Washington, cor. Western av. | 1868-1870 |
| PRESTON, J. [piano] repairer | 22 Kinzie | 1856 |
| PRESTON, James, piano forte mr. | 116 Dearborn | 1864 |
| PRESTON, James, pianoforte maker | 118 Dearborn | 1865 |
| PRESTON, James | | not in 1866 |
| PRESTON, James, piano mnfr. | 75 Market, r. 146 Market | 1867 |

\* \* \*

[39] Peters bought H. M. Higgins' catalog of publications and his stock of sheet music and books [Cf Ibid., May 29, 1867 (1:7, adv.)] and then in turn sold the stock of music to the De Motte brothers, retaining the publications. [Ibid., Aug. 23, 1867 (1:9, adv.)]

| | | |
|---|---|---|
| PRESTON, James, jr., pianomaker | 75 Market, r. 146 Market | 1867 |
| PRESTON, John, piano maker | h. 109 Madison | 1849 |
| | h. Kinzie near Wolcott | 1851 |
| PRESTON, John, Piano Manufacturer | Kinzie bt. Wolcott and Cass | 1852 |
| | h. 22 Kinzie | 1853-1855 |
| PRESTON, John, Piano Manufacturer | | not in 1856 |
| PRESTON, John, piano maker [or piano mnfr. or pianos] | 22 Kinzie Eng. 12 y. | 1857 |
| | h. 22 Kinzie | 1858 |
| | 116 Dearborn, h. same | 1859-1864 |
| | 118 Dearborn | 1865 |
| | 75 Market, cor. Washington | 1866 |
| | 75 Market, r. 146 Market | 1867-1868 |
| | 75 Market, r. same | 1869-1870 |
| | 259 Randolph, r. 146 Market | 1871 |
| | 259 Randolph, r. 155 S. Clinton | 1872 |
| PRESTON, Thomas, pianoforte maker, John Preston | 116 Dearborn | 1863-1864 |
| PRESTON, Thomas, wks. John Preston | bds. 118 Dearborn | 1865 |
| PRESTON, Thomas | | not in 1866 |
| PRESTON, Thomas, pianomaker | r. rear 768 State | 1867 |
| PRESTON, Thomas | | not in 1868 |
| PRESTON, Thomas, pianomaker, John Preston | r. 768 State | 1869-1870 |
| PRESTON, Thomas, mnfr. pianos | r. 155 S. Clinton | 1871 |
| PRESTON, Thomas, pianomkr. | r. 155 S. Clinton | 1872 |
| PRINCE, Charles F., agt. for George A. Prince | bds. 263 Illinois | 1859 |
| PRINCE, Charles F. | | not in 1860 |
| PRINCE, Charles F., agt., George A. Prince Co. | bds. 79 Dearborn | 1861 |
| | bds. Briggs House | 1862-1863 |
| | h. Dearborn bet. Lake & S. Water | 1864 |
| | 89 Washington, rooms 16 Dearborn | 1865 |
| PRINCE, Charles F. | | not in 1866-1868 |
| PRINCE, Charles F., agt., George A. Prince & Co. | 89 Washington, r. 104 Randolph | 1869-1870 |
| | r. 104 Randolph | 1871 |
| PRINCE, George A. (G. A. Prince & Co.) | h. at Buffalo, N. Y. | 1859-1869 |
| PRINCE, George A. & Co. (George A. Prince and Thomas Stephenson) melodeons | 110 Lake | 1859-1860 |
| PRINCE, George A. & Co. (George A. Prince and Thomas Stephenson) melodeon manfrs. | 82 Lake | 1861 |
| | 43 Lake | 1862 |
| | office, 43 Lake | 1863-1864 |
| PRINCE, George A. & Co. (George A. Prince and Thomas Stephenson) melodeon and organ manfrs. | 89 Washington | 1865 |
| PRINCE, George A. & Co., organs and melodeons | 89 Washington, r. Buffalo, N. Y. | 1866 |
| PRINCE, George A. & Co., Buffalo, Automatic organs and melodeons, George W. Vining, agt. | 89 Washington | 1867-1868 |
| PRINCE, George A. & Co. (George A. Prince and Charles E. Bacon) mnfrs. of organs and melodeons | 89 Washington | 1869-1870 |
| PRINCE, Geo. A. & Co., mnfrs. organs and melodeons | 98 Washington | 1871[40] |
| PROSSER, W. R., clerk, Wooster & Harmon's | | 1849 |
| PROSSER, W. R. | | not in 1851 |
| PROSSER, Wm. | h. sw. of Bulls Head | 1852 |
| PROSSER, W. R. at B. K. Mould's | bds. Mrs. Tucker | 1853 |

\* \* \*

[40] Post-fire address: 651 Wabash ave. - The Weekly Trade Circular, 1 (Jan. 18, 1872) 13

| | | |
|---|---|---|
| PROSSER, W. R., clerk, Mould & Greene | | 1854 |
| PROSSER, W. R., clerk, R. G. Greene | | 1855 |
| PROSSER, W. R. | | not in 1856-1858 |
| PROSSER, William R. | at 82 Lake, bds. 32 Washington | 1859 |
| PROSSER, William R., pianofortes | 115 Lake, bds. Washington bet. State and Wabash av. | 1860 |
| | 115 Lake, bds. State cor. Monroe | 1861 |
| PROSSER, William R., pianos and melodeons | 130 Clark, bds. 68 Monroe | 1862-1866 |
| | 130 S. Clark, bds. 109 Wabash av. | 1867 |
| | 130 Clark, bds. 68 Monroe | 1868 |
| PROSSER, William R., piano dealer | room 3, 165 Clark | 1869-1870 |
| PROSSER, William R., pianos and organs | 165 Clark | 1871 |
| REED, Alanson, piano dealer | 88 and 90 Randolph, h. cor. Ada and Prairie | 1863 |
| REED, Alanson H. [sic] Reed's Temple of Music, dealer in pianos, melodeons, organs, sheet music, &c. | 88 and 90 Randolph, h. cor. Ada and Prairie | 1864 |
| REED, Alanson (Reed's Temple of Music) | r. 509 Carroll | 1865-1866 |
| REED, Alanson (Alanson Reed & Son) | h. 409 W. Randolph | 1867 |
| | r. 27 Bishop ct., cor. W. Madison | 1868-1870 |
| | r. 45 24th | 1871-1872 |
| | r. Hinsdale | 1873-1875 |
| REED, Alanson H., clerk | 88 and 90 Randolph, h. cor. Ada and Prairie | 1863 |
| REED, Alanson, jr., clerk | 88 Randolph | 1864 |
| REED, Alanson H. (Reed's Temple of Music) | r. 509 Carroll | 1865-1866 |
| REED, Alanson H. (A. Reed & Sons) | r. 409 W. Randolph | 1867-1868 |
| | bds. 27 Bishop ct. | 1869-1870 |
| | r. 45 24th | 1871 |
| | r. 81 16th | 1872 |
| | r. Hinsdale | 1873-1874 |
| | r. 608 Michigan av. | 1875 |
| REED, Alanson & Sons (Alanson H. and John W.) dealers in pianos, melodeons, organs, sheet music &c. Temple of Music | 88 and 90 Randolph and 69 Dearborn | 1866 |
| REED, A. & Sons (Alanson, Alanson H. and John W. Reed) proprs., Reed's Temple of Music | 88 and 90 Randolph, and 69 Dearborn | 1867 |
| | 47 and 49 Dearborn | 1868-1871 |
| REED, A. & Sons (Alanson, Alanson H. and J. Warner Reed) pianos | 81 16th | 1872 |
| REED, A. & Sons (A., A. H., and J. W.) pianos and organs | Van Buren, sw. cor. Dearborn | 1873 |
| REED, A. & Sons (Alanson, Alanson H. and J. Warner) pianos, Reed's Temple of Music | Van Buren se. cor. Dearborn | 1874-1875 |
| REED, Cheney (R & Watkins) | h. 204 State | 1853-1854 |
| | h. 135 Michigan av. | 1855-1857 |
| REED, John W., clerk, Reed's Temple of Music | bds. Ada, nw. cor. Prairie | 1864 |
| REED, John W. (Reed's Temple of Music) | r. 509 Carroll | 1865-1866 |
| REED, John W. (Alanson Reed & Son) | h. 409 W. Randolph | 1867 |
| REED, J. Warner (A. Reed & Sons) | r. 409 W. Randolph | 1868 |
| REED, John W. (A. Reed & Sons) | bds. 27 Bishop ct. | 1869 |
| REED, J. Warner | bds. 27 Bishop st. [sic] | 1870 |
| REED, J. Warner (A. Reed & Sons) | r. 46 24th | 1871-1872 |
| REED, J. Warner | | not in 1873 |
| REED, J. Warner (A. Reed & Sons) | r. 586 Michigan av. | 1874 |
| | r. Hinsdale | 1875 |
| REED & WATKINS, piano forte warerooms | 51 Randolph | 1853-1854 |

| | | |
|---|---|---|
| REED & WATKINS, piano forte warerooms (Continued) | 49, 51 Randolph | 1855 |
| REED & WATKINS, piano and music store | 51 Randolph | 1856 |
| REED & WATKINS, Piano Forte and Melodeon Warehouse | 51 Randolph st. 4 y. | 1857 |
| REED'S TEMPLE OF MUSIC (Alanson Reed, Alanson H. Reed and John W. Reed) props. | 88 and 90 Randolph and 69 Dearborn | 1865-1867 |
| REED'S TEMPLE OF MUSIC [listed as such] | | not in 1868-1870 |
| REED'S TEMPLE OF MUSIC, A. Reed & Sons, proprs. Pianos, organs and melodeons | 47 and 49 Dearborn st. | 1871 |
| | 81 16th st. | 1871F |
| REED'S TEMPLE OF MUSIC [listed as such] | | not in 1872-1873 |
| REED'S TEMPLE OF MUSIC - A. Reed & Sons, proprs. | cor. Dearborn and Van Buren | 1874-1875 |
| REEN, Charles, lithographer | 106 Lake, h. 190 Ohio | 1858 |
| REEN & SHOBER, lithographers | 106 Lake | 1858 |
| REID, George H. (William T. Reid & Co.) | r. 136 W. Madison | 1872 |
| REID, William T., piano mnfr. | 136 W. Madison, h. same | 1859 |
| REID, William T. | | not in 1860 |
| REID, William T., piano mnfr. | 136 W. Madison | 1861 |
| REID, William T., pianoforte maker | 136 W. Madison, h. same | 1862-1864 |
| REID, William T., pianomkr. and repairer | 136 W. Madison | 1865 |
| REID, William T., piano-forte manufacturer | 136 W. Madison, r. same | 1866 |
| REID, William T., pianoforte mnfr. and repairer | 136 W. Madison, r. same | 1867 |
| REID, William T., pianotuner | r. 136 W. Madison | 1868 |
| REID, William T., pianoforte mnfr. | 136 W. Madison, r. same | 1869 |
| REID, W. T., pianoforte mnfr. | 136 W. Madison, r. same | 1870 |
| REID, W. T., piano repairer | 136 W. Madison | 1871 |
| REID, William T. (William T. Reid & Co.) | r. 136 W. Madison | 1872 |
| REID, W. T. & Co. (William T. and George H. Reid) piano mnfrs. | 136 W. Madison | 1872 |
| ROOT, Charles T., student | bds. 281 Wabash av. | 1866 |
| ROOT, Charles T. | | not in 1867-1869 |
| ROOT, Charles T., salesman, Root & Cady | r. 11 Groveland Park | 1871 |
| ROOT, Charles T., music dealer | r. 548 South Park av. | 1872 |
| ROOT, Charles T. (George F. Root & Sons) | bds. 548 South Park av. | 1873 |
| ROOT, Charles T. (Root & Sons) | r. 297 Michigan av. | 1874 |
| ROOT, Charles T., paperbarrels | bds. 548 South Park av. | 1875 |
| ROOT, Ebenezer T. (Root & Cady) | h. 15 Buffalo | 1859 |
| | h. 156 W. Adams | 1860 |
| ROOT, E. Towner (Root & Cady) | h. 156 W. Adams | 1861 |
| | h. 378 W. Madison | 1862-1865 |
| ROOT, E. Towner (Root & Cady) | | not in 1866 |
| ROOT, E. Towner (Root & Cady) | h. 49 Van Buren | 1867 |
| ROOT, Ebenezer T. (Root & Cady) | r. Hyde Park | 1868-1870 |
| | r. ws. Cornell nr. 52nd | 1871 |
| | r. Hyde Park | 1872 |
| ROOT, Ebenezer T. (Root & Lewis) | r. Hyde Park | 1873-1874 |
| ROOT, E. Towner (Root & Sons Music Co.) | r. Hyde Park | 1875 |
| ROOT, Frederick W., clerk, Root & Cady | bds. 276 W. Washington | 1864 |
| | bds. 281 Wabash av. | 1865-1868 |
| ROOT, Frederick W. | | not in 1869 |
| ROOT, F. W., musical composer, Root & Cady | | 1870 |
| ROOT, Frederick, professor of music | r. 11 Groveland Park | 1871 |
| ROOT, Frederick W. (George F. Root & Sons) | r. 548 South Park av. | 1872-1873 |
| ROOT, George F. (Root & Cady) | bds. 156 W. Adams | 1861 |
| | bds. 378 W. Madison | 1862 |

| | | |
|---|---|---|
| ROOT, George F. (Root & Cady) (Continued) | h. 276 W. Washington | 1863-1864 |
| | h. 281 Wabash av. | 1865-1868 |
| | r. Hyde Park | 1869 |
| | r. 67 Washington | 1870 |
| | r. 11 Groveland Park | 1871 |
| ROOT, George F. (George F. Root & Sons) | r. 548 South Park av. | 1872-1873 |
| ROOT, George F., pres., Chicago Musical College | 109 State | 1874 |
| ROOT, George F. (Root & Sons Music Co.) | r. 548 South Park av. | 1875 |
| ROOT, George F. & Sons (George F., W. A., F. W., and C. T.) music dealers | 750 Wabash av. | 1872 |
| | 283 Wabash av. | 1873 |
| ROOT, Warren (Root & Coon [provision dealers]) | r. 199 Park av. | 1866 |
| ROOT, Warren, organ builder | 375 and 377 W. Lake, r. Park av. nr. Robey | 1867 |
| ROOT, William A., clerk, Root & Cady | bds. 15 Buffalo | 1859 |
| ROOT, William A., bookkeeper, Root & Cady | bds. 156 Adams | 1860 |
| ROOT, William A. | | not in 1861 |
| ROOT, William A., bookkeeper, Root & Cady | bds. 378 W. Madison | 1862 |
| ROOT, William A., clerk | bds. 378 W. Madison | 1863-1864 |
| ROOT, William A. | | not in 1865 |
| ROOT, William A., clk., Root & Cady | bds. 378 W. Madison | 1866 |
| ROOT, William A., salesman, Root & Cady | bds. 192 Van Buren | 1867 |
| ROOT, William A., clerk, Root & Cady | r. 806 Wabash av. | 1868 |
| | bds. 874 Indiana av. | 1869 |
| ROOT, William A., salesman, Root & Cady | | 1870 |
| | r. 75 26th | 1871 |
| ROOT, W. A. (George F. Root & Sons) | r. 7 Scammon pl. | 1872 |
| | bds. 548 South Park av. | 1873 |
| ROOT, William A. (Root & Sons) | r. 1024 Michigan av. | 1874 |
| ROOT, William A. (Root & Sons Music Co.) | r. 1130 Indiana av. | 1875 |
| ROOT & CADY (Ebenezer T. Root and Chauncey M. Cady) music store[41] | 95 S. Clark | 1859 |
| ROOT & CADY (Ebenezer T. Root and Chauncy [sic] M. Cady) music publishers | 95 Clark | 1860 |
| ROOT & CADY (George F. and E. Towner Root and Chauncey M. Cady) music publishers and dealers | 95 Clark | 1861-1864 |
| ROOT & CADY (George F. and E. Towner Root and Chauncey M. Cady) pianos, cabinet organs, melodeons, music and musical instruments, whol. and retail | 67 Washington, Crosby's Opera bldg.[42] | 1865-1866 |
| ROOT & CADY (George F., Ebenezer T. Root and Chauncey M. Cady) musical instrument dealers | 67 Washington | 1867 |
| ROOT & CADY ... music and musical instruments and music publishers | 67 Washington, Opera House blk. | 1868-1871 |
| ROOT & CADY, musical instruments | 612 Michigan, late 67 Washington | 1871F |
| ROOT & CADY (E. T. Root, C. M. Cady and William Lewis) pianos, organs and musical instruments | 281 Wabash av. | 1872 |
| ROOT & LEWIS (E. T. Root and Wm. Lewis) music dealers | 262 State | 1873 |
| | 156 State | 1874 |

\* \* \*

[41] First announced in the Chicago Tribune, Dec. 9, 1858 (1:3); first advertisement, Ibid., Jan. 15, 1859 (1:7).

[42] "We have removed from 95 Clark Street to 67 Washington Street in Crosby's Opera House ... Root & Cady" - Ibid., May 17, 1865 (1:7, adv.).

| | | |
|---|---|---|
| ROOT & SONS (Wm A. & Chas. T.) music publishers & dealers | 109 State | 1874 |
| ROOT & SONS MUSIC CO. (C. C. Curtiss, manager) | 156 State | 1875 |
| ROOT & SONS MUSIC CO., The, music dealers (C. C. Curtiss, manager) | 156 State | 1876-1878 |
| ROTH, August (Shober & Roth, lithographers) | | not in 1860[43] |
| RUHLING, Adolph (of Vergho, R. & Co.) | 89 S. Water Ger. 5 y. | 1856-1857 |
| RUHLING, Adolf, fancy goods | 111 S. Water, h. May's Hotel | 1858 |
| RUHLING, Adolph (Vergho, Ruhling & Co.) | bds. Hotel May | 1859-1860 |
| | bds. Richmond House | 1861 |
| | bds. Matteson House | 1862-1863 |
| | bds. Sherman House | 1864 |
| | bds. Tremont House | 1865 |
| | r. Wells, bet. Water and Lake | 1866 |
| | r. 218 Ohio | 1867-1871 |
| | r. Europe | 1872 |
| SCHAAF, Adam, pianopolisher | r. 210 Randolph | 1871 |
| SCHAAF, Gotthard [house and sign] painter | 212 Twelfth, h. same | 1859-1861 |
| SCHAAF, Gotthard | | not in 1862 |
| SCHAAF, Gotthard, saloon | 212 W. 12th | 1863-1864 |
| SCHAAF, Gotlieb [sic] painter | h. 212 W. 12th | 1865 |
| SCHAAF, Gothold [sic] saloon keeper | 212 W. 12th, r. same | 1866 |
| SCHAAF, Gotthard, saloon | 212 W. 12th, r. same | 1867 |
| SCHAAF, Gotthard (G. Schaaf & Co.) | r. 44 Clybourn av. | 1868 |
| SCHAAF, Gotthart [sic] (G. Schaaf & Bros.) | r. 8 Oak | 1869 |
| SCHAAF, Gotthard, sec., Turner society, Vorwaerts | 212 W. 12 | 1870 |
| SCHAAF, G. & Bro. (Gotthard and John A. Schaaf) pianoforte makers | 71 N. Clark | 1868 |
| SCHAAF, G. & Bros. [sic] (Gotthart [sic] and John A. Schaaf) piano factory | 80 Ontario | 1869-1870 |
| SCHAAF, G. & Bros. | | not in 1871 |
| SCHAAF, John A. (Schaaf & Derry) | 575 N. Wells st. | 1867 |
| SCHAAF, John A. (G. Schaaf & Bro. and Schaaf & Derry) | r. 210 N. Dearborn | 1868 |
| SCHAAF, John A. (G. Schaaf & Bros.) | r. 210 N. Dearborn | 1869-1870 |
| SCHAAF & DERRY (J. A. Schaaf and H. Derry) furniture dealers | 71 N. Clark | 1867-1868 |
| *SCHAFF [sic] BROS. [piano fortes] | Clybourn av. sw. cor. N. Halstead | 1872 |
| SCHOMACKER, Henry C. (H. C. Schomacker & Co.) | r. 159 Clark | 1869-1870 |
| SCHOMACKER, H. C. & Co. (Henry C. Schomacker and George F. Cole) piano dealers | 159 Clark | 1869-1870 |
| SEA, Sidney W., land agent | r. Lake View | 1866 |
| SEA, Sidney W., real estate agt. | 122 Randolph | 1867-1868 |
| SEA, Sidney W., gen. agt., Mathushek's Piano-forte Co. and Real Estate and Merchandise Broker | 109 Dearborn, r. Lake View | 1869-1870 |
| SEA, S. W., real estate agt. | 21 LaSalle, r. 136 Elm | 1871 |
| SHOBER, Charles, lithographer | 106 Lake, h. Ohio n. N. Clark | 1858 |
| | 109 Lake, h. 146 Ontario | 1859 |
| SHOBER, Charles (Shober & Roth) | h. 89 Indiana | 1860 |
| SHOBER, Charles, lithographer | 109 Lake, h. 50 Division | 1861 |
| SHOBER, Charles, engraver and lithographic printer | 109 Lake, h. ns. Division, w. of Sedgwick | 1862 |
| SHOBER, Charles, lithographer | Lake, cor. Clark, h. Division, 4th w. Sedgwick | 1863 |
| | h. 346 N. Wells | 1864 |
| | 123 Lake, r. 346 N. LaSalle | 1865 |

\* \* \*

[43] The firm of Shober & Roth is listed.

| | | |
|---|---|---|
| SHOBER, Charles, lithographer (Continued) | Lake, cor. Clark, r. ws. Dearborn bet. Goethe and Schiller | 1866 |
| SHOBER, Charles (Charles Shober & Co.) | r. ws. Dearborn, bet. Goethe and Schiller | 1867 |
| | r. 502 N. Dearborn | 1868-1870 |
| SHOBER, Charles, lithographer and engraver | 108 and 110 Randolph, r. 502 N. Dearborn | 1871 |
| SHOBER, Charles (Charles Shober & Co.) | r. Belden av. cor. Belden pl. | 1872 |
| SHOBER, Charles & Co. (Charles Shober and William Heinemann) lithographers and engravers | Lake, se. cor. Clark | 1867 |
| | room 21, 132 Lake | 1868 |
| | 119 to 125 Lake, cor. Clark | 1869-1870 |
| SHOBER, Charles & Co. | | not in 1871[44] |
| SHOBER, Charles & Co. (Charles Shober and Edward Carqueville) proprs., Chicago Lithographing Co. | 73 W. Washington | 1872 |
| SHOBER & ROTH (Charles Shober and August Roth) lithographers | 109 Lake | 1860 |
| SIMON, Richard, musical instruments | 60 N. Clark, h. Clark bet. Indiana and Ontario | 1865 |
| SIMON, Richard | | not in 1866-1869 |
| *SIMON, Richard [music and musical instruments] | 209 Clark | 1870 |
| SMITH, James R. (Smith & Nixon) | h. Cincinnati, Ohio | 1864-1870 |
| SMITH, James R. | | not in 1871 |
| SMITH, H. [sic] R. (Smith & Nixon) | Wabash av. se. cor. 16th | 1872 |
| SMITH & NIXON (James R. Smith and Wilson K. Nixon) pianoforte dealers | sw. cor. Washington and Clark | 1864-1865 |
| | 104 S. Clark | 1866 |
| SMITH & NIXON (James R. Smith and Wilson K. Nixon) general agents for Steinway & Son's pianos | 116 Washington and 114 Clark | 1867 |
| SMITH & NIXON (James R. Smith and W. K. Nixon) pianoforte dealers | Clark cor. Washington | 1868-1869 |
| *SMITH & NIXON [piano dealers] | 98 and 100 Wabash av. | 1870 |
| SMITH & NIXON, gen. agts. for Steinway & Sons' pianos | 150 Clark | 1871 |
| SMITH & NIXON (H. [sic] R. Smith and W. K. Nixon) pianos | Wabash av. se. cor. 16th | 1872 |
| STEPHENSON, Thomas (G. A. Prince & Co.) | h. at Buffalo, N. Y. | 1859-1866 |
| STONE, Frederick W. (H. Stone & Co.) | h. 231 N. Clark | 1865 |
| STONE, Frederick W. (Stone Bros. & Co.) | bds. ns. Ohio, bet. LaSalle and Clark | 1866-1867 |
| STONE, Frederick W., pianomaker | r. 703 Carroll | 1868 |
| STONE, Frederick W., pianotuner | r. 611 W. Indiana | 1869-1870 |
| STONE, Frederick W. | | not in 1871 |
| STONE, Frederick, pianomkr., Julius Bauer & Co. | r. 305 22d | 1872 |
| STONE, H. [piano fortes] | 19 N. Clark | 1856 |
| STONE, H , piano maker | 19-21 N. Clark Prus. 4 y. | 1857 |
| STONE, H. | | not in 1858 |
| STONE, Henry, pianomkr. | 19 N. Clark, h. 203 N. Clark | 1859 |
| STONE, Henry, piano mfr. | 19 N. Clark, h. 174 Indiana | 1860 |
| | 26 N. Clark, h. ns. W. Indiana bet. N. Curtis and N. May | 1861 |

\* \* \*

[44] Post-fire address: 7 and 9 S. Jefferson St. Cf The Weekly Trade Circular, 1 (Jan. 18, 1872) 13.

| | | |
|---|---|---|
| STONE, Henry, piano mfr. (Continued) | 26 N. Clark up stairs, h. 233 W. Indiana | 1862 |
| | room 4, Ewing's blk., h. 233 W. Indiana | 1863-1864 |
| STONE, Henry (H. Stone & Co.) | h. 231 N. Clark | 1865 |
| STONE, Henry, pianofortemaker | r. 158 Ohio | 1866-1867 |
| STONE, Henry | r. 158 Ohio | 1868 |
| STONE, Henry, pianomaker | r. 158 Ohio | 1869-1870 |
| STONE, Henry, piano mnfr. | 158 Ohio | 1871 |
| STONE, H. & Co. (Henry and Frederick W. Stone) piano makers | room 23, Ewing's block, 26 N. Clark | 1865 |
| STONE, H. & J., piano makers ... Chicago piano forte manufactory | cor. Clark and North Water | 1853 |
| | 17 North Clark | 1854 |
| | 179 N. Clark | 1855 |
| STONE BROS. & CO. (Henry and Frederick W. Stone) piano manfrs. | 23 Ewing's blk., 26 N. Clark | 1866 |
| STONE BROS. & CO. (Henry and Frederick W. Stone and ---) piano mnfrs. | 23 Ewing's blk., 26 N. Clark | 1867 |
| STORY, H. L., dealer in organs, Reed's Temple of Music | 47 and 49 Dearborn, r. 481 W. Madison | 1868 |
| STORY, H. L. (H. L. Story & Co.) | r. Randolph, bet. Elizabeth and Ann | 1869-1870 |
| | r. 392 W. Randolph | 1871 |
| STORY, H. L. (Story & Camp) | r. 547 W. Monroe | 1872 |
| STORY, H. L. & Co. (H. L. Story and I. N. Camp) organs and melodeons | 47 Dearborn | 1869-1870 |
| STORY, H. L. & Co., organs and melodeons | 47 Dearborn | 1871 |
| STORY & CAMP (H. L. Story and I. N. Camp) organs | 409 W. Randolph | 1872 |
| TEUFEL, Robert, lithographic printer | h. 55 W. Washington | 1864-1865 |
| TEUFEL, Robert, lithographer | r. 55 W. Washington | 1866 |
| TEUFEL, Robert (Robert Teufel & Co.) | 87 S. Jefferson | 1867 |
| TEUFEL, Robert & Co. (Robert Teufel and W. F. Dieffenbacher) lithographers and publishers | room 67, 127 Clark | 1867 |
| TRAVERS, George W., carriagemkr., Morgan ne. cor. W. Randolph and music dealer | 277 W. Randolph, bds. 289 W. Lake | 1859 |
| *TRUBY, John W. [music and musical instruments] | 372 State | 1870 |
| TRUBY, J. W., musical instruments | 372 State | 1871 |
| Van ALLEN, David S., piano maker | 166 Clark, h. same | 1863 |
| Van ALLEN, David S., foreman, W. B. Fowler [furniture] | bds. 259 Canal | 1864 |
| VERGHO, Chas. (of V., Ruhling & Co.) | 89 S. Water st. Ger. $2\frac{1}{2}$ y. | 1857 |
| VERGHO, Charles, fancy goods | 111 S. Water, h. Tremont House | 1858 |
| VERGHO, Charles (Vergho, Ruhling & Co.) | bds. Revere House | 1859 |
| | bds. Hotel May | 1860 |
| | h. 90 Sedgwick | 1861-1863 |
| | h. 213 Chicago av. | 1864 |
| | h. 215 Chicago av. | 1865-1869 |
| VERGHO, Charles | | not in 1870 |
| VERGHO, Charles (Vergho, Ruhling & Co.) and Consul for Bavaria and Wurtemburg | r. 680 Sedgwick | 1871 |
| VERGHO, Charles (Vergho, Ruhling & Co.) and sec., Novelty Mnfg. Co. | | 1872 |
| VERGHO, Ruhling & Co. [fancy goods] | cor. S. Water and Dearborn | 1856 |
| VERGHO, Ruhling & Co., Fancy Goods, Cutlery, &c. | 89 S. Water st. | 1857 |
| VERGHO, Ruhling & Co., fancy goods | 111 S. Water and 9 S. Dearborn | 1858 |
| VERGHO, Ruhling & Co. (Charles Vergho & Adolf Ruhling) importers of variety goods [novelty goods, musical instruments] | 111 S. Water cor. Dearborn | 1859 |
| VERGHO, Ruhling & Co., Fancy Goods, Cutlery, &c. | 89 S. Water st. | 1860 |

| | | |
|---|---|---|
| VERGHO, Ruhling & Co., fancy goods | 110 Lake | 1861-1862 |
| | 104 Lake | 1863 |
| VERGHO, Ruhling & Co. (Charles Vergho, Adolph Ruhling and ---) fancy goods, whol. and retail | 104 Lake | 1864 |
| VERGHO, Ruhling & Co. (Charles Vergho, Adolph Ruhling) fancy goods, toys and musical instruments | 104 Lake | 1865 |
| VERGHO, Ruhling & Co. (Charles Vergho and Adolph Ruhling) English, French and German fancy goods, toys, baskets and musical instruments | 104 Lake | 1866-1868 |
| VERGHO, Ruhling & Co. (Charles Vergho, Adolph Ruhling and ---) importers of fancygoods and musical instruments | 104 Lake | 1869-1870 |
| VERGHO, Ruhling & Co., importers | 104 Lake, will remove 1st Jan. to 138, 140 and 142 State | 1871 |
| VERGHO, Ruhling & Co. (Charles Vergho, Adolph Ruhling and ---) toys, fancy goods and baskets, whol. and ret. | 138, 140 and 142 State | 1872 |
| VINING, George W., agent, Geo. A. Prince & Co. | 89 Washington | 1866 |
| | 89 Washington, r. Fulton, nw. cor. Paulina | 1867 |
| | 89 Washington, r. 40 Walnut | 1868 |
| WAITE, Silas M. (R. Burdett & Co.) | r. Brattleboro, Vt. | 1869-1871 |
| WANGEMAN, Hugo (R. & H. Wangeman) | 202 E. Lake, up stairs, bds. Schall House | 1866 |
| | rooms 131 Dearborn | 1867-1868 |
| | r. 180 S. Green | 1869-1870 |
| WANGEMAN, Hugo, wood engraver, W. D. Baker | r. 180 S. Green | 1871 |
| WANGEMAN, Hugo, engraver on wood | 42 W. Madison, r. 144 N. Ada | 1872 |
| WANGEMAN, Rudolph (R. & H. Wangeman) | 202 E. Lake, up stairs, bds. Schall House | 1866 |
| | rooms 131 Dearborn | 1867-1868 |
| | r. 180 S. Green | 1869-1870 |
| WANGEMAN, R. & H. (Rudolph Wangeman and Hugo Wangeman) manfrs. and repairers, musical instruments | 202 E. Lake, up stairs | 1866 |
| WANGEMAN, R. & H (Rudolph and Hugo Wangeman) musical instruments | 131 Dearborn | 1867-1870 |
| WARREN, Edwin R. (Warren & Co.) | h. 126 S. Clark | 1859 |
| | h. 170 Clark | 1860 |
| WARREN, E. R. (E. R. Warren & Co.) | h. 85 Clark | 1861-1862 |
| WARREN, Edwin R. (Rev.) (Warren & Hook) | h. 85 Clark | 1863 |
| WARREN, Edwin R. (Rev.) (E. R. Warren & Co.) | 85 Clark | 1864-1865 |
| WARREN, Edwin R., melodeons and pianos | 85 Clark, office, 53 Dearborn, r. same | 1866-1867 |
| WARREN, E. R. & Co. (---) piano and melodeon warerooms | 85 Clark | 1861-1862 |
| WARREN, E. R. & Co. (Edwin R. Warren and Moses Hook) piano and melodeon wareroom | 85 and 87 Clark | 1863 |
| WARREN, E. R. & Co., piano forte dealers | 85 Clark | 1864 |
| WARREN, E. R. & Co. (Edwin R. Warren and ---) pianofortes and melodeons | 85 Clark | 1865 |
| WARREN & CO. (Edwin R. Warren and ---) pianofortes and melodeons | 126 S. Clark | 1859 |
| | 170 Clark | 1860 |
| WARREN'S MUSIC SCHOOL, Rev. Edwin R. Warren, principal | 170 Clark | 1860 |

| | | |
|---|---|---|
| WARREN'S MUSIC SCHOOL, Rev. Edwin R. Warren, principal (Continued) | 85 Clark | 1861-1862 |
| | 85 and 87 Clark | 1863-1864 |
| WARREN'S NORMAL ACADEMY OF MUSIC | 85 Clark | 1865 |
| WARREN'S NORMAL ACADEMY OF MUSIC, E. R. Warren, proprietor | 85 Clark | 1866-1867 |
| WATKINS, C. L. (Reed & W.) | bds. 204 State | 1853-1854 |
| | bds. C. Reed | 1855 |
| | 51 Randolph, h. 135 Michigan av. | 1856 |
| | h. 135 Michigan av. Vt. 4 y. | 1857 |
| WATKINS, C. L. | | not in 1858 |
| WATKINS, Chauncey L. (C. L. Watkins & Co.) | h. 151 Michigan | 1859 |
| WATKINS, Chauncey L. (Watkins & Summerfield [lawyers]) | h. 141 W. Washington | 1860 |
| WATKINS, Chauncey L., notary public | 93 Randolph, h. 141 W. Washington | 1861 |
| WATKINS, C. L & Co., pianofortes | 67 Randolph | 1858 |
| WATKINS, C. L. & Co. (Chauncey L. Watkins and ---) agents for T. Gilbert & Co.'s pianos | 124 Lake | 1859 |
| WILDER, F. O. & Co., Melodeon Manufacturers | 67 Randolph | 1852 |
| WILDER, F. O. & Co. | | not in 1853-1860 |
| WILDER, Frederick O., pianomkr. | h. ss. W. Madison bet. Leavitt and Hoyne | 1861 |
| | bds. 96 Adams | 1862 |
| WILEY, --- (Phelps & Wiley) | | not in 1854 |
| *WILEY & CO. [piano forte manufacturer] | 120 Dearborn | 1855 |
| WILLSON, John, salesman | h. ss. Fulton, bet. Robey and Lincoln | 1862 |
| WILLSON, John | | not in 1863-1864 |
| WILLSON, John (Ziegfeld & Willson) | 69 Dearborn, h. 221 Madison | 1865 |
| WILLSON, John, bkpr. | S. Water bet. Franklin and Wells, h. 221 Madison | 1866 |
| WOLCOTT, James H., with Kimball & Wolcott [com. mer.] | h. 11 N. Curtis | 1862-1864 |
| WOLCOTT, James H. | | not in 1865-1867 |
| WOLCOTT, James H., pianos, organs and melodeons | 55 Washington, r. 251 Park av. | 1868 |
| WOLCOTT, James H., pianofortes | 99 State, r. 251 Park av. | 1869-1870 |
| WOLCOTT, James H., agt., Decker Bros. pianos | 161 State, r. 251 Park | 1871 |
| WOLCOTT, James H. | r. 251 Park av. | 1872 |
| WOLFRAM, Herman, organ manufacturer | h. 2 Ohio | 1855 |
| WOLFRAM, Herman | | not in 1856 |
| WOLFRAM, Kermann [sic] organ builder | 2 Ohio st. Ger. 1 y. | 1857 |
| WOLFRAM, Herman, organ builder | h. 369 Ohio | 1858 |
| WOLFRAM, Herman (Wolfram & Haeckhel) | h. 369 Ohio | 1859-1862 |
| | bds. 39 Green | 1863 |
| | h. ns. Sigel bet. N. Wells and Franklin | 1864 |
| | h. 125 Sigel | 1865-1866 |
| | r. 129 Sigel | 1867-1868 |
| WOLFRAM, Herman, organ builder | 129 Sigel, r. same | 1869-1871 |
| | r. 68 Kramer | 1872 |
| WOLFRAM & HACKEL [sic] organ builders | 369 Ohio | 1858 |
| WOLFRAM & HAECKHEL (Herman Wolfram & Charles Haeckhel) organ builders | 369 Ohio | 1859-1862 |
| | 471 and 473 N. Wells | 1863-1865 |
| | 497 and 499 N. Wells | 1865-1866 |
| | 129 Sigel | 1867-1868 |
| WOOD, Samuel A., music and plate printer | 112 Randolph | 1865 |
| WOODBURY, Manley | 158 State | 1855 |
| WOODBURY, A. [sic] printer | h. 347 Clark | 1856 |

| | | |
|---|---|---|
| WOODBURY, Manley A. | | not in 1857 |
| WOODBURY, Manley A., engraver | h. 63 Edina pl. | 1858 |
| WOODBURY, Manley A., stencil cutter | Clark cor. Randolph | 1859 |
| WOODBURY, Manney [sic] A., engraver and stencil cutter | 65 Clark, h. 135 Jackson | 1860 |
| | 65 Clark, h. 170 Clark | 1861 |
| WOODBURY, Manly [sic] A., engraver | h. 170 Clark | 1862 |
| WOODBURY, Manley A., engraver, Root & Cady | h. 248 Clark | 1863 |
| | h. 232 Clark | 1864 |
| | h. 190 Clark | 1865 |
| WOODBURY, Manley A., music engraver, Root & Cady | r. 709 State | 1866 |
| WOODBURY, M. A., music engraver | room 18, 77 Dearborn, r. 156 Quincy | 1867-1870 |
| WOODBURY, Manley A., engraver | r. 9 Grant | 1871 |
| ZIEGFELD, Florence (Ziegfeld & Willson) | r. 96 Ohio | 1865 |
| ZIEGFELD, Florence (Ziegfeld, Gerard & Co.) | r. 298 Chicago av. | 1866 |
| ZIEGFELD, F., professor, Chicago Conservatory of Music | room 2, Opera House, h. 298 Chicago av. | 1867 |
| ZIEGFELD, Florence, music teacher. | r. 298 Chicago av. | 1868 |
| | room 2, Opera House, r. 298 E. Chicago av. | 1869-1870 |
| ZIEGFELD, Florence, director, Chicago Academy of Music | 1 Crosby Opera House, r. 298 Superior | 1871 |
| ZIEGFELD, Florence | | not in 1872 |
| ZIEGFELD, Ferdinand [sic] music teacher | r. 493 Wabash av. | 1873 |
| ZIEGFELD, Florence, director, Chicago Musical College | r. 493 Wabash av. | 1874-1876 |
| ZIEGFELD & WILLSON (Florence Ziegfeld & John Willson) sheet music, musical instruments and music publishers [45] | 69 Dearborn | 1865 |
| ZIEGFELD, Gerard & Co. (Florence Ziegfeld, John B. Gerard and Gallus Muller) music publishers and brass and silver instrument manufacturers | 133 Dearborn and 83 and 85 Madison (or 133 Dearborn and 98 Washington) | 1866 |

\* \* \*

[45] First advertisement found: Chicago Tribune, Apr. 24, 1865 (1:7); last advertisement appeared Ibid., Aug. 17, 1865 (1:8), followed by ads of Florence Ziegfeld on Oct. 17-18 and Dec. 1-2, 1865.

BIBLIOGRAPHY

PRIMARY SOURCES

Root & Cady's publications, both sheet music and books, listed individually elsewhere.
Copyright ledgers (manuscript) for the District Courts of Illinois, later Northern Illinois, 1818-1872, and Massachusetts, 1839-1868. Rare Book Room, Library of Congress.

BOOKS AND PAMPHLETS

Biographical Sketches of the Leading Men of Chicago. Chicago: Wilson, Peirce & Co., 1876.
Biographical Sketches of the Leading Men of Chicago, Written by the Best Talent of the Northwest. Chicago: Wilson & St. Clair, 1868.
Chicago. A Strangers' and Tourists' Guide to the City of Chicago, Containing Reminiscences of Chicago in the Early Day; An Account of the Rise and Progress of the City. Chicago: J. S. Thompson, 1866.
COOK, Frederick Francis. Bygone Days in Chicago; Recollections of the "Garden City" of the Sixties. Chicago: A. C. McClurg & Co., 1910.
Fourth Annual Review of the Commerce, Railroad and Manufactures of Chicago, for the Year 1855. Compiled from Several Articles Published in the Daily Democratic Press. Chicago: Democratic Press Steam Printing House, 1856.
GUYER, Isaac D. History of Chicago; Its Commercial and Manufacturing Interests and Industry. Chicago: Church, Goodman & Cushing, 1862.
HIGGINS, H. M., firm, music publishers, Chicago. Quarterly Circular of H. M. Higgins Music Publishing House. Chicago [1863?]
Hyde Park, Illinois. Report for the Year 1869. Chicago: Rand, McNally & Co., 1869.
KIRKLAND, Caroline, ed. Chicago Yesterdays; A Sheaf of Reminiscences. Chicago: Daughaday and Co., 1919.
Lyon & Healy, firm, music publishers, Chicago. Seventy-five Years of Everything Known in Music. [Chicago] Lyon & Healy, Inc., c1940.
Out-of-town; Being a Descriptive, Historical and Statistical Account of the Suburban Towns and Residences of Chicago. Chicago: Western News Co., 1869.
ROOT, Frederick Woodman. An American Basis of Musical Criticism; An Essay Read Before the Chicago Literary Club. [n.p., n.d.] (From the Musical Visitor)
ROOT, George Frederick. The Story of a Musical Life; An Autobiography. Cincinnati: The John Church Co., c1891.
RYAN, Thomas. Recollections of an Old Musician. London: Sands & Co., 1899.
UPTON, George Putnam. Musical Memories; My Recollections of Celebrities of the Half Century, 1850-1900. Chicago: A. C. McClurg & Co., 1908.
WHITTLE, Daniel W., ed. Memoirs of Philip P. Bliss ... Contributions by Rev. E. P. Goodwin, Ira D. Sankey, Geo. F. Root. N. Y.: A. S. Barnes & Co., 1877.
ZELL, T. Ellwood, & Co., Chicago. A Guide to the City of Chicago. Chicago: T. E. Zell & Co., 1868.

ARTICLES

"George F. Root, Singer, Teacher, Composer and Patriot," [Memorial Issue] The Presto, 12 (Aug 15 1895) [9]-10.
[Letter from C. M. Cady] Dwight's Journal of Music, 13 (Aug 7 1858) 150-51.
MATHEWS, William Smythe Babcock. "Geo. F. Root, Mus. Doc.," Music, 8 (Sept 1895) 502-9.
[Obituary of G. F. Root] The Presto, 12 (Aug 8 1895) [9]
PARTON, James. "Chicago," Atlantic Monthly, 19 (Mar 1867) 325-45.
ROOT, George Frederick. "Madame Patti and the Old Songs," Music, 1 (Mar 1892) [428]-31.
STONE, Henry. "A Song in Camp," The Century Magazine, 35 (Dec 1887) 320.
"[Trade] To Honor Geo. F. Root," The Presto, 12 (Aug 8 1895) [16]A.
UPTON, George Putnam. "The Musical Progress of Chicago," Western Monthly, 3 (Feb 1870) 122-8.
---- "The Musician of the 'People,'" The Presto, 12 (Aug 15 1895) 10.

## BIBLIOGRAPHIES

Board of Music Trade of the United States of America. *Complete Catalogue of Sheet Music and Musical Works Published by the Board of Music Trade of the United States of America, 1870.* N. Y.: The Board of Music Trade, 1871.

BRAINARD, S., Sons, music publishers, Cleveland. *The Musician's Guide; A Descriptive Catalogue of Sheet Music, Music Books, and the Most Celebrated Composers ... Embracing, Beside the Original Publications of Root & Cady, the Following Well-known Catalogues of Sheet Music: George P. Reed, Henry Tolman, Nathan Richardson, H. Oakes, Russell & Richardson, Russell & Tolman, Henry Tolman & Co., Mason & Hamlin, Ziegfeld, Gerard & Co., Russell & Fuller, H. T. Merrill & Co.* Cleveland: S. Brainard's Sons [1872]

## CHICAGO CITY DIRECTORIES

1843 FERGUS, Robert. ... *Directory of the City of Chicago, Illinois for 1843* ... Chicago: Fergus Printing Co., 1896. (Fergus' Historical Series, no. 28)

1846 *Norris' Chicago Directory for 1846 & 47* ... Chicago: Geer & Wilson, 1846.

1847 *Norris' Chicago Directory for 1847-48, being the sixth year of publication.* Chicago: J. H. Kedzie, 1847.

1848 *Norris' Chicago Directory for 1848-49* ... Published by J. W. Norris and L. S. Taylor. Chicago: Eastman & McClellan, printers, 1848.

1849 *Chicago City Directory and Annual Advertiser, for 1849-50* ... by O. P. Hatheway & J. H. Taylor. Chicago: Jas. J. Langdon, printer, 1849.

1850 No directory for 1850 being listed or known in the Chicago Public Library, the Chicago Historical Society, the University of Illinois Library, or the Library of Congress, it seems likely that none was issued.

1851 *Danenhower's Chicago City Directory for 1851* ... Chicago: W. W. Danenhower, 1851.

1852 *Udall & Hopkins' Chicago City Directory for 1852 & 53* ... 1st annual ed. Chicago: Udall & Hopkins, 1852.

1853 *Hall & Smith's Chicago City Directory for 1853-54* ... 2d annual ed. Chicago: R. Fergus, printer, 1853.

1854 *Hall & Co.'s Chicago City Directory and Business Advertiser. For 1854-55.* Chicago: R. Fergus [c1854]

1855 1855-6. *The Chicago City Directory and Business Advertiser.* 4th annual ed. ... E. H. Hall, comp. Chicago: R. Fergus, 1855.
*The Chicago Almanac and Advertiser for the year 1855*, comp. ... by E. H. Hall. Chicago: Chicago Printing Co. [c1855]

1856 *Case & Co.'s Chicago City Directory for the year ending June first, 1857.* John Gager, comp. Chicago: J. Gager & Co., 1856.
*Hall's Business Directory of Chicago* Published ... on the first of November, 1856. Chicago: 1856.

1857 *Gager's Chicago City Directory, for the year ending June 1st, 1857* [sic] comp. by John Gager ... Vol. 1. Chicago: J. Gager & Co., 1858.

1858 *D. B. Cooke & Co.'s Directory of Chicago for the year 1858* ... Comp. by Tanner, Halpin & Co. Chicago: D. B. Cooke & Co., 1858.

1859 *D. B. Cooke & Co.'s City Directory for the year 1859-60* ... Comp. by R. B. Kennedy & Co. Pub. ... after ... May 1st. Chicago: D. B. Cooke & Co., 1859.
*Smith & Du Moulin's Chicago City Directory for the year ending May 1, 1860.* Chicago: Smith & Du Moulin [c1859]

1860 *D. B. Cooke & Co.'s Chicago City Directory, for the year 1860-61* ... Comp. by T. M. Halpin & Co. Chicago: D. B. Cooke & Co., 1860.

1861- *Halpin & Bailey's Chicago City Directory, for the year 1861-62.*
1863 [- 1863-64] Comp. by T. M. Halpin. Chicago: Halpin & Bailey, 1861-63.

1864 *Halpin's seventh annual ed., Chicago City Directory, 1864-5* ... Chicago: T. M. Halpin & Co., 1864.

John C. W. Bailey's Chicago City Directory for the year 1864-5 ... Chicago: J. C. W. Bailey, 1864.
1865 Halpin's eighth annual Chicago City Directory, 1865-6 ... Chicago: T. M. Halpin, 1865.
J. C. W. Bailey & Co.'s Chicago City Directory for the year 1865-6 ... Comp. by James T. Hair ... Chicago: J. C. W. Bailey, 1865.
1866 John C. W. Bailey's Chicago City Directory for the year 1866-67 ... Chicago: 1866.
Edwards' Annual Director to the ... City of Chicago ... 1866. Chicago: R. Edwards, 1866.
1867 John C. W. Bailey's Chicago City Directory, Vol. X for 1867-8 ... pub. after ... May first ... Chicago: J. C. W. Bailey, 1867.
1867-Edwards' Annual Directory to the ... City of Chicago for 1867-68.
1873 [1873-74] Chicago: R. Edwards, 1867-73.
1871F Edwards' Chicago Directory ... up to Dec. 12, 1871. Fire ed. Chicago: R. Edwards, 1871.
1874-The Lakeside Annual Directory of the City of Chicago ... 1874-5.
1875 [-1875-6] Chicago: Williams, Donnelly & Co., 1874-75.

### CLEVELAND CITY DIRECTORIES

1837 MacCABE, Julius P. Bolivar. A Directory of the Cities of Cleveland & Ohio, for the years 1837-38 ... Cleveland: Sanford & Lott, Book & Job Printers, 1837.
1845 PEET, Elijah. Peet's General Business Directory of ... Cleveland ... for ... 1845-6. Cleveland: Sanford & Hayward, Printers, 1845.
1846 ---- ---- Cleveland: Printed by Smead & Cowles, 1846.
1853 Knight & Parsons' Business Directory of the City of Cleveland ... Cleveland: E. G. Knight & Co., 1853.
1857 Boyd's Cleveland City Directory ... 1857. Comp. by William H. Boyd. Cleveland: 1857.
1861 J. H. Williston & Co.'s Directory of the City of Cleveland ... for 1861-2. Cleveland: B. Franklin Print., 1861.

### NEWSPAPERS AND PERIODICALS

Atlanta (Ga.) Constitution, June 17, 19, 1889.
The American Monthly Musical Review, and Choir Singers' Companion, 1 (1850)
Brainard's Musical World, 1-13, 17 (1864-77, 1880), passim.
Chicago Daily Journal, 1851-63, passim.
Chicago Daily Tribune, 1855-56, July, 1858-March, 1872, passim.
The Chicago Magazine of Fashion, Music and Home Reading, 2 (Oct-Dec 1871)
Chicago Musical Review, 1 (1866)
Chicago Times, April-December, 1856, 1858, passim.
Church's Musical Visitor, 1-26 (1871-87), passim.
The Daily Democratic Press, Chicago, 1851-56, passim.
The Metronome, (Boston), 1 (1871)
Music Trade Review, 1-11 (1875-80), passim.
The Musical Independent, 1-4 (Nov 1868-Jan 1873)
Musical People, 7 (1883)
New York Musical Review and Choral Advocate, 6-12 (1855-65)
Peters' Musical Monthly, 2-4 (1868-70)
The Presto, 6-13 (1889-96), passim.
Publishers' and Stationers' Weekly Trade Circular, 1-2 (1872-73)
Publishers' Weekly, 3-4 (1873-74)
The Song Journal (Detroit), 1 (1871)
The Song Messenger of the Northwest, 1-13 (1864-75)

SECONDARY SOURCES

BOOKS AND PAMPHLETS

ALLEN, Orrin Peer. The Descendants of Nicholas Cady of Watertown, Mass. Palmer, Mass.: C. B. Fiske, 1910.
ANDREAS, Alfred Thomas. History of Chicago. From the Earliest Period to the Present Time. Chicago: A. T. Andreas, 1884-86.
---- History of Cook County, Illinois. Chicago: A. T. Andreas, 1884.
AYARS, Christine Merrick. Contributions to the Art of Music in America by the Music Industries of Boston, 1640-1936. N. Y.: The H. W. Wilson Co., 1937.
BRAINARD, Lucy Abigail. The Genealogy of the Brainerd-Brainard Family in America, 1649-1908. [Hartford?] Hartford Press, 1908.
CHASE, Gilbert. America's Music: from the Pilgrims to the Present. Rev., 2nd ed. N. Y.: McGraw-Hill [c1966]
CLARKE, Louise Brownell. The Greenes of Rhode Island. N. Y.: 1903.
COLBERT, Elias. Chicago. Historical and Statistical Sketch of the Garden City: A Chronicle of Its Social, Municipal, Commercial and Manufacturing Progress, from the Beginning Until Now. Chicago: P. T. Sherlock, 1868.
---- and CHAMBERLIN, Everett. Chicago and the Great Conflagration. Cincinnati: C. F. Vent, 1871.
COMSTOCK, John Moore. The Congregational Churches of Vermont and Their Ministry, 1762-1942. St. Johnsbury, Vt.: The Cowles Press, Inc., 1942.
EHRENTHAL, Wilhelm. Das Kutschkelied auf der Seelenwanderung. Forschungen über die Quellen des Kutschkeliedes im grauen Alterthume nebst alten Texten und Uebersetzungen in neuere Sprachen. Mit einer Hieroglyphen-Tafel. Hrsg. zum Besten der Deutschen Invalidenstiftung. Leipzig: F. A. Brockhaus, 1871.
FISHER, William Arms. One Hundred and Fifty Years of Music Publishing in the United States. An Historical Sketch with Special Reference to the Pioneer Publisher, Oliver Ditson Company, Inc., 1783-1933. Boston: O. Ditson Co., Inc., 1933.
FITE, Emerson David. Social and Industrial Conditions in the North During the Civil War. Reprint ed. N. Y.: P. Smith, 1930.
FLEMING, Herbert Easton. Magazines of a Market-Metropolis: Being a History of the Literary Periodicals and Literary Interests of Chicago. Chicago: The University of Chicago Press, 1906.
GILBERT, Paul Thomas. Chicago and Its Makers; A Narrative of Events from the Day of the First White Man to the Inception of the Second World's Fair. Chicago: F. Mendelsohn, 1929.
GOODSPEED, Edgar J. History of the Great Fires in Chicago and the West. N. Y.: H. S. Goodspeed & Co., 1871.
HANBY, Brainerd Oaks. The Remarkable Life of a Song Writer. Cynthiana, Ind.: Argus Printing and Publishing Co., 1938.
HARWELL, Richard B. Confederate Music. Chapel Hill: The University of North Carolina Press, c1950.
HIGGINS, Katharine Chapin. Richard Higgins ... and His Descendants. Worcester, Mass.: Printed for the Author, 1918.
HOWARD, John Tasker. Our American Music. N. Y.: T. Y. Crowell Co., 1939.
---- Stephen Foster, America's Troubadour. N. Y.: T. Y. Crowell Co., 1934.
JONES, F. O. Handbook of American Music and Musicians. New ed. Buffalo: C. W. Moulton, 1877.
MATHEWS, William Smythe Babcock. A Hundred Years of Music in America. Chicago: G. L. Howe, 1889.
MOSES, John. Illinois, Historical and Statistical. Chicago: Fergus Printing Co., 1889-92.
PIERCE, Bessie Louise. A History of Chicago. Vol. 1-2. N. Y.: A. A. Knopf, 1937-40.
REDWAY, Virginia Larkin. Music Directory of Early New York City. N. Y.: The New York Public Library, 1941.

Regan Printing House, Chicago. Story of Chicago in Connection with the Printing Business. Chicago: Regan Ptg. House, 1912.
RICH, Arthur Lowndes. Lowell Mason, the Father of Singing Among the Children. Chapel Hill: The University of North Carolina Press, 1946.
ROOT, James Pierce. Root Genealogical Records, 1600-1870. N. Y.: Anthony & Co., 1870.
SPILLANE, Daniel. History of the American Pianoforte, Its Technical Development and the Trade. N. Y.: D. Spillane, 1890.
STATON, Kate E., ed. Old Southern Songs of the Period of the Confederacy: the Dixie Trophy Collection. N. Y.: S. French, c1926.
THORSON, Theodore W. A History of Music Publishing in Chicago, 1850-1960. Evanston, Ill.: 1961. (University Microfilms, Ann Arbor, Mich. [Publication] 62-874) Ph. D. dissertation, Northwestern University.
[WILLIAMS, Rudolph] The New Church and Chicago, A History. Chicago: W. B. Conkey Co., 1906.
WORK, Henry Clay. Songs ... Compiled by Bertram G. Work. N. Y.: J. J. Little & Ives Co. [188-?]
WRIGHT, John Stephen. Chicago: Past, Present, Future. Chicago: Western News Co., 1868.
Writers' Program, Ohio. Westerville in the American Tradition. Columbus, O.: F. J. Heer Printing Co., 1940.


## PUBLICATIONS OF EDUCATIONAL INSTITUTIONS

Alpha Delta Phi. The Alpha Delta Phi, 1832-1882. [Boston] By the Fraternity, 1882.
CHASE, Theodore R. The Michigan University Book, 1844-1880. Detroit: Richmond, Backus & Co., 1881.
Chicago Musical College. Catalogue of the Chicago Musical College. Chicago: Evening Post and Job Printing Rooms, 1872.
COOK, John Williston and McHUGH, J. V. A History of the Illinois State Normal University, Normal, Illinois. Normal, Ill. [Pantagraph Printing and Binding Establishment] 1882.
Illinois. State Normal University, Normal. Semi-Centennial History of the Illinois State Normal University, 1857-1907. Prepared under the Direction of a Committee of the Faculty. [Normal? Ill.; c1907]
Michigan. University. Regents' Proceedings ... 1837-1864. Ann Arbor: The University, 1915.
Oberlin College. General Catalogue of Oberlin College, 1833-1908. Oberlin, O.: The College, 1909.
---- Triennial Catalogue of the Officers and Students in Oberlin Collegiate Institute, 1848-9. Oberlin, O.: J. M. Fitch, 1848.
Union Theological Seminary, New York. Alumni Catalogue ... 1836-1926. N. Y.: 1926.


## BIBLIOGRAPHIES

Boston. Athenaeum. Confederate Literature: A List of Books and Newspapers, Maps, Music and Miscellaneous Matter Printed in the South During the Confederacy ... Prepared by Charles N. Baxter and James M. Dearborn. Boston: The Boston Athenaeum, 1917.
BYRD, Cecil K. Bibliography of Illinois Imprints, 1814-58. Chicago: The University of Chicago Press, 1966.
DICHTER, Harry and SHAPIRO, Elliott. Early American Sheet Music, Its Lure and Its Lore. N. Y.: R. R. Bowker Co., 1941.
Historical Records Survey. Check List of Chicago Ante-Fire Imprints, 1851-1871. (American Imprints Inventory, No. 4) Chicago: The Historical Records Survey, 1938.

Historical Records Survey, District of Columbia. *Bio-Bibliographical Index of Musicians in the United States of America from Colonial Times* ... Washington: Music Division, Pan American Union, 1941.

SCOTT, Franklin William. *Newspapers and Periodicals of Illinois, 1814-1879.* Revised and enlarged ed. (Collections of The Illinois State Historical Library, Vol. 45. Springfield, Ill.: The Trustees of the Illinois State Historical Library, 1910.

## ARTICLES

BIRDSEYE, George W. "American Song Composers. George F. Root of Chicago." *New York Musical Gazette*, 1 (July 1867) 65.

---- "America's Song Composers ... II. George F. Root." *Potter's American Monthly*, 12 (Feb 1879) 145-8.

---- "America's Song Composers ... IV. Henry C. Work." *Potter's American Monthly*, 12 (Apr 1879) 284-8.

COOKE, D. B. "My Memories of the Book Trade." *Publisher's Weekly*, 9 (Mar 18 1876) 379.

COONLEY, Lydia Avery. "George F. Root and His Songs." *New England Magazine*, 19 (Jan 1896) [554]-70.

ENGEL, Lehman. "Songs of American Wars." *Modern Music*, 19 (Mar-Apr 1942) 147-52.

EPSTEIN, Dena J. "The Battle Cry of Freedom." *Civil War History*, 4 (Sept 1958) 307-18.

GALBREATH, Charles B. "Song Writers of Ohio. Benjamin Russel Hanby, Author of 'Darling Nelly Gray.'" *Ohio Archaeological and Historical Publications*, 14 (1905) 180-215.

HOVEY, Charles E. "A Schoolmaster's Story." *The Schoolmaster*, 2 (Nov 1869) 83.

MOTOYOSI-SAIZAU. "L'Armée Japonais." *Le Monde Moderne*, 1 (Apr 1895) 568-74.

INDEX

This index includes the usual citations of names, places, subjects and titles of compositions which are discussed in the text. Moreover, to permit reference to works for which only the title is known, it also includes all titles of Root & Cady publications, listed chronologically in Appendix A.

For sheet music publications a composer index is given in Appendix B, and a subject index in Appendix C.

Abbott, Jacob, 18
Abbott's School for Young Ladies, New York, 18, 24
Absence, 126
Absent Mary, 103
The Academy Vocalist, 19
Adalida Polka, 98
Adams, C. R., 27, 100
Addio. Madrid, 1851, 139
Adelaide, 13
Adelina Polka, 123
Adoration Polka, 121
The Advance, 28
Agawam Quickstep, 94, 98
Agnes by the River, 113
L'Agréable Reverie, 133
An Aid to Congregational Singing, 144
Alexandria, Va., 44
The Alice Polka, 134
All Hail! Live Innocent and Purely. See Salva Dimora Casta.
All Hail the Reign of Peace, 99
All Hail to Ulysses! 96
All in the Golden Prime of May, 122
All Rights for All! 106
Allie, 121
Alpine Bells, 94, 102
The Alpine Glee Singer, 4
The Alps, Marche de Bravoura, 70
Always of Thee, 127
Amateur March, 93
Amelia Mazurka, 7
American Antiquarian Society, 95
Amitie pour Amitie, 65, 111
Among the Angels, 116
And He's Got the Money Too, 115
Andover, Mass., 81
Andy Veto, 102
The Angel Choir, 113
Angel Mary, 96
Angel Nellie, 100
Angel Nettie Bane, 124
Angels Beckon Me! 134
Angels Guard Her Dreams Tonight, 108
The Angels Took Jennie Away. See Jennie's Gone Home.
Anguera, Antonio de, Soldier's Dream Polka Militaire, 7
  Wau-Bun Galop, 7
The Annie Huger Galop, 129
Annie Laurie, 93, 104
Annie Snow, 123
The Antique Ring, 120
Anyhow, 108
Apfelblüthen Walzer, 70
The Apology, 95
Apothecaire et Perruquier, 125
April Shower Polka Redowa, 97
Aria alla Scozzese, 94

Army Regulations for Drum, Fife and Bugle, 44, 143
Arnold, Isaac Newton, 46
Aroldo, 133
The Artillery Galop, 113
The Artist's Dream. See Reve d'Artist.
Asheville, N. C., 29-30
At Sunrise, 127
At the Beautiful Gate, 121
At the Golden Gate, 101
Atlanta, Ga., 29-30
Atlanta (Grand Victory March), 114
L'Attacca Quickstep, 92
Auld Lang Syne, 105, 109
Ave Maris Stella, 139
Away! Away! the Track Is White, 103
Away on the Prairie Alone, 100

Babcock, W. B., Funeral March, 65
Baby Blue-Eyes, 134
Baby Goes Alone, 115
Babylon Is Fallen! 51, 95, 96
Baby's Gone to Sleep, 103, 113, 115
Baby's Sweet Sleep, 127
Bach, Ch., & Co., Milwaukee, 84
Bach, Johann Sebastian, 58, 77, 80
Bach & Kuschbert, Milwaukee, 84
Il Bacio, 100
Baker, Benjamin Franklin, 17n, 68
Baker (engraver), Chicago, 37, 38
Balatka, Hans, 27
Balfe, Michael William, Then You'll Remember Me, 53
Un Ballo in Maschera, 133
Baltimore (place of publication), 3
Banks, Gen. Nathaniel, 45
The Banner of the Fatherland, 79, 124
Banquet Polka, 116
Barbe Bleue, 110, 125
Barker, T. T., Boston, 5
Barrus, H. G., 68; Lament of the Irish Lover, 53
The Barry Schottische, 103, 106
Base Ball, 124
Battiste, ---- 58
The Battle Cry of Freedom, 17, 43, 46-48, 49, 94, 95, 98, 133
The Battle of Manassas, 101
Bauer, Julius, 22, 33, 35, 44
Bauer, Julius, & Co., 57, 59
Baumbach, Adolph, 78; arr., Beauties of the Opera, 70
Les Bavards, 125
Bayly, Thomas Haynes, No, Ne'er Can Thy Home Be Mine, 53
Be a Man, 108
Be Sure to Call as You Pass By, 91
Beads Man Polka, 106

223

Beardslee, Jerome, 80
Beauties of the Opera, 70
Beautiful Angels, 122
Beautiful Child of Song, 51
Beautiful Hands, 113
The Beautiful Maiden Just Over the Way, 91
Beautiful Rose, 93, 95
Beautiful Spirit of Song, 113
Beautiful Starlight, 122
Because He Loved Me So, 133
Becker, Paul, Andante and Scherzo, 60
Bedford, J. D., & Co., New York, 4
The Bee March, 130
The Bee Song, 98
Beethoven, Ludwig van, 58, 77;
    Adelaide, 13
    sonatas, 80
Behind the Jessamine, 126
Believe Me If All Those Endearing Young
    Charms, 123
La Belle Brunette, Valse, 122
La Belle Hélène, 70, 108, 125
Belle of Lincoln Park, 129
Belles de Chicago, 115
Belles of Chicago, 120
Bells of Sabbath Morning, 116, 127
Ben Bolt's Reply, 68
Beneath the Loved One's Window, 101
Benny Havens, 113
Benteen, Frederick D., Baltimore, 3
Bergen, Edgar, 46
Bergmann, Carl, 57
Berlioz, Hector, 18
Bermuda's Fairy Isle, 92
Berry, T. S., New York, 5
Bertha Louise, 97
Bessie Jayne, 106
Bessie Lee, the Highland Lassie, 128
Bessie's Trust, 120
Betsy Jane Polka, 102
Beyond, 125
Bibliography of Illinois Imprints, 1814-58, 4
Bird of the Mountain, 127
Birds in the Night, 126
Birds of the Forest Waltz, 93
Bisco, 62
Blackmar, A. E., New York, 11
Blanche Waltz Melodieuse, 91
Blessner, Gustav, 61
Bliss, Philip Paul, 19
    Jolly Jonathan and His Notional Naburs,
        84
    Mr. Lordly and I, 72
Bloomington, Ill., 26
The Blue Bells of Scotland, 109
Blue Beard, 129
The Blue Bird, 144
Blushing Rose Polka, 112

Board of Music Trade, 6, 7, 12, 29, 48n, 77
    1865 meeting, 52, 62
    1866 meeting, 77
    1869 meeting, 77
Board of Music Trade Catalogue. See Com-
    plete Catalogue of Sheet Music and
    Musical Works ...
The Boat Ride, 130
The Bob-o-link, 37
Bonapo, 125
Bonnie Annie Lee, 124
The Bonnie Bright Eyes of Somebody, 124
Bonnie Dundee, 123
Bonnie Marguerita, 110
Bonnie Venture Waltz, 99
Boone, L. S., 27
Boston, 18, 20, 21, 25, 27, 37, 70, 71, 77;
    (place of publication) 5, 6, 7, 8,
    34, 36, 38, 48n, 80, 81
Boston firms, 62-71
Boston Academy of Music Chorus, 18
Boston Brigade Band, 63
Boston Musical Gazette, 17
Boston Musical Journal, 17
The Boston Musical Times, 34
Boston public schools singing classes, 18
Boulanger, Opera House Drawing March, 60
The Boy at the Fountain, 135
Bow Down Thine Ear, 112
Brabant, Herbert, 6
Brabant & Co., 6
Bradbury, William B., 4, 24, 25, 48-49
    Jubilee, 35
    Key Note, 58
Bradley, C. J. M., Ben Bolt's Reply, 68
Brainard, Henry Mather, 3, 4
Brainard, Silas, 3
Brainard & Mould, 3
Brainard Bros., Cincinnati, 29
Brainard's Musical World, 82
Brainard's (S.) Sons, Cleveland, 29, 58, 61,
    71, 78, 81, 84
Brass bands, 34
Brauer, Fr., The Youth's Musical Friend, 84
Brave Battery Boys, 122
Brave Boys Are They, 9, 49
Break, Break, Break, 123
Brennan, John H., 12
Bridal Flowers for the Piano, 120
Briggs House, Chicago, 22
Briggs House Classical Concerts, 22, 36
Briggs House Polka, 37, 91
Brigham, Clarence S., 95
Bright Eyes Waltz, 112
The Broken Band, 103
The Brook, 114, 125
Brother in the Army, 98
Brother, Tell Me of the Battle, 97, 98, 99

Brothers of the Mystic Tie, 113
Brown, George W., 13, 84
Browne, Elizabeth (Higgins)  See Jackson,
     Elizabeth (Higgins)
Bryan Hall, Chicago, 43, 44
Buck, Dudley, Easter Morning, 84
The Buckskin Bag of Gold, 120
Budding of the Tones, 96
Buffalo and Erie Co. (N. Y.) Public Library,
     4, 78, 95, 100n
The Bugle Call, 49, 52, 143
Burditt, B. A., The Dennis Quick Step, 63
     Major Train's Quick Step, 63
The Buttonwood Tree at the Door, 4
Bygone Days in Chicago, 38n
Byrd, Cecil, Bibliography of Illinois Imprints,
     1814-58, 4

The Cabinet Organ Companion, 143
Cady, Abigail Brainerd, 23
Cady, C. M. (firm) New York, 29
Cady, Chauncey Marvin, 23-30, 82-83
     Cady's Popular Home Songs, 25
     Minnehaha Glee Book, 25, 48
     O'er the Billow, 25
     Three Angel Visitants, 25
     We Meet Upon the Level, 37, 38
Cady, Cornelius Sidney, 23
Cady, Harriette, 23, 28
Cady, Oliver, 23
Call 'Em Names, Jeff, 94
Call Me Darling, Darling Call Me, 119
Call Me Pet Names, 100
Call Me When Breakfast Is Ready, 118
Camelia Polka, 120
Camp, Isaac N., 22n
Camp Schottische, 114
Camp Song of the Chicago Irish Brigade, 92
Camps, Tramps, & Battlefields, 72, 99
Can the Soldier Forget? 97
Canton, O., 24
Captain Jinks, 112
The Captive Bird, 91
Carl Pretzel Waltz, 129
Carlotta Galop, 123
Carrickfergus Schottische, 103
La Cascade de Roses, 109
The Cascade of Pleasure, 120
Cast Thy Burden on the Lord, 112
Castanet Waltz, 127
Cattle Bell at Evening, 100
Cawthorne, N., 60
Central City Polka, 97
C'era un Re di Thule, 97
Chandler, F. Stevens, They Blossom There Up
     There, 61
Chandler & Curtiss, Chicago, 22, 83
Le Chant du Depart, 119

Chant National des Croates, 139
Chapel Gems for Sunday Schools, 144
Charlie Schottische, 101
The Charm, 146
Chase Among the Roses, 121
Le Château à Toto, 125
Chicago. Board of Education, 48
     Court House Square, 33
     fire, 1871, 3, 80
     First Congregational Church, 26
     first music book, 48
     first music journal, 6
     first music publisher, 4-5
     first music store, 3
     streets, level of, 33
Chicago Academy of Sciences, 28
Chicago Historical Society, 51, 95
Chicago Light Guard Band, 37, 44
The Chicago Mazurka, 99
Chicago Music Store, 3, 4
Chicago Musical College, 20
Chicago Musical Institute, 28
The Chicago Musical Review and Flower-
     Queen, 8-9, 21, 24, 25, 49
Chicago Musical Union, 21, 22, 23, 25, 26-27
Chicago Musical Union Academy, 22, 27
Chicago Philharmonic Society, 5, 6
Chicago Post & Mail Co., 29
Chicago Schottische, 126
Chicago Theological Seminary, 27
Chicago. World's Columbian Exposition,
     1893, 22
Chickering, Jonas, 65
Childhood Songs, 116
The Children in the Grave Yard, 127
The Chinaman's Farewell.  See Tin-ni-min-
     ni-win-kum-ka.
Christian Hymn and Tune Book, 146
Christmas Cheer, 111
Christmas Chime Carol & Hymn, 100
Christy's Minstrels, introduce Kingdom
     Coming, 45
Church, John, Cincinnati, 7, 11, 71
---- & Co., 81
Church of the New Jerusalem (Swedenborgian),
     22
Cincinnati (place of publication), 5, 29, 38, 81
Cincinnati Air Line Railroad Galop, 93, 102
The City Railway Galop, 62
Civil War, 43-53; outbreak, 19, 39, 43-44;
     close, 57
---- music, 20; songs, 43-48, 49, 51, 52, 57,
     59
Clapp, C. C., & Co., Boston, 5
Clark, James G., The Bob-o-link, 37
     A Collection of Ballads, Duetts and Quar-
          tettes Sung by Ossian's Bards, 68
     I Love My Home, 37

Clark, James G. (Continued)
  Indian Mother's Lullaby, 68
  Rock of Liberty, 68
Clark's School Visitor, 51
Clear Cold Water, 24
Cleveland, 3-4, 24, 58 (place of publication) 29, 81
Les Cloches du Monastère, 94, 109
La Clochette de l'Esperance Schottisch, 133
Columbians, 7
Columbia's Call, 102, 105
Columbia's Guardian Angels, 96
Come Again Sweet Holiday, 126
Come Home, Father, 52, 97, 98, 99, 102
Come on this Silent Night, 102
Come, Said Jesus' Sacred Voice, 96
Come to Me, Dearest, 118
Come to Me, Gentle Sleep, 135
Come to Me Memories Olden, 110
Come Where the Morning Is Breaking, 72, 102
Come Where the South Wind Wanders, 121
Come While the World Lies Dreaming, 105
Comedy Galop, 70
The Coming of Day, 104
Commencement March, 109
Complete Catalogue of Sheet Music and Musical Works Published by the Board of Music Trade of the United States of America, 1870, 5-7, 12, 68, 70, 77
Comrade, All Around Is Brightness, 98, 99
Con Anima Polka, 102
Concert Polka Mazurka, 119
The Concordia (music journal), 61
Confederacy, pirated editions in, 9, 49
Confederate lines, 45
The Conservatory Waltz, 125
Continental Railroad Chorus. See Crossing the Grand Sierras.
The Contraband, 45
Converse, Charles C., 24
Cook, Frederick Francis. Bygone Days in Chicago, 38n
Copyright records, 4, 36-37, 53, 63-70, 84; Washington central depository, 84
Coquette Mazurka, 94
Coquette Waltz, 97
Coralline Mazurka Brillante, 110
La Corinna, 5
The Cork Leg, 53
Corn Flower Valse, 109
Corn Is King! 12, 61, 94
The Coronation of the Rose. See The Flower Queen (cantata)
The Coronet, 143
Corporal Schnapps, 96
The Cottage in the Wood, 106
Counting Seeds. See One I Love, Two I Love.
Cousin John, 107, 111

Cramer, Henri, Il Desiderio, varied, 70
The Crimson Glow of Sunset Fades, 128
Crispino e la Comare, Gems from, 101
Croquet, 122
Crosby, Albert, 57
Crosby, Frances, 23
Crosby, Uranus H., 57
Crosby Opera House, 57, 60, 61, 79, 80
Crosby's Opera House Waltz, 98
The Crossing Sweeper, 111
Crossing the Grand Sierras, 121
Crowding Awfully, 102
Crown of Roses Waltz, 128
The Crown of Sunday School Songs, 146
Cruel, Cruel Men, 117
Crystal Showers, 113
Cupid and Mammon, 107
Curiosity Galop, 127
A Curious Circumstance, 60
Currie, William H., 6, 49
Cycloid Polka, 99
Czar and Zimmermann Pot Pourri, 97

D. C. Mazurka, 103, 105
Dad's a Millionaire! 101
Daisy Deane, 43, 95, 96, 102
Damenwahl Polka, 121
Daniel, 19, 21
Darling Blue Eyed Mell, 121
Darling Ella, 116
Darling Jenny Lee. See The Little Gem.
Darling Little Eva Ray, 128
Darling Nelly Gray, 19
Dash Away Galop, 127
Daughter of the Isles, 123
Davis, E. C., Song of Night, 4
Dawning of the Better Day, 115
The Day Is Cold, 123
The Day Is Ended, 127
De Day ob Liberty's Comin', 94, 95
Daylight, 102
Days That Are Gone! 110
The Days That Are No More, 122
The Days When We Were Young, 51, 95
De Anguera, Antonio. See Anguera, Antonio de.
Dear Little Barefeet, I've Counted Your Toes, 123
Dear Mother the Battle Is Over, 12
The Dear Ones All at Home, 92
The Dear Sweet Bells of Memory, 127
Dearborn Waltz, 101
Dearest, Good Night, 6
Death of the Robin, 92
Degenhard, Charles G., 60
Delisser & Procter, New York, 34
The Dell of Roses, 113
Delusion Mazurka Characteristique, 93

DeMotte, A. Huyler, 11
DeMotte, Edgar M., 11
DeMotte, T. G., music publisher, Chicago, 11
DeMotte, Thomas G., 11
DeMotte Brothers, Chicago, 10-11
Dempster, William R., 64
    The Lament of the Irish Emigrant, 63
The Dennis Quick Step, 63
De Passio, Mr., 22
Des Moines City Waltz, 97
Il Desiderio, 70, 100
Der Deutsche Knabe. See The German Youth.
Les Deux Anges, 103, 139
Dew Drop Mazurka, 70
Dew Pearls Waltz, 121
Did the Loved One Return? 103
Dillon Schottische, 111
Dinna Ye Hear the s'Logan? 102
Dinorah, 102
Ditson, Oliver, Boston, 5, 7, 11, 12, 25, 48n, 59, 62-63, 70, 80
Dixie, 45, 105
Do They Love Us Yet? 6
Dobmeyer, J. J., & Co., St. Louis, 11
Doeb & Strengson, Toledo, 100
Don Giovanni, 102, 110
Donau Walzer, 114
Donna e Mobile, 109
Don't Be Sorrowful, Darling, 11
Don't Stay Late To-Night, 134
Douglas, Stephen A., 28
The Dove, 144
Down Brakes, 121
Down by the Brook at the End of the Lane, 110
The Down Easter's Journey. See Out West.
Drake, A. E., The Buttonwood Tree at the Door, 4
Dream on, Lillie, 92, 95
Dreaming, Ever Dreaming, 109
Dreams of Heaven, 123
Drifting Leaflets, 119
The Drunkard's Wife to Her Husband. See Touch Not the Fair Cup, Though It Sparkles.
Dubois & Stoddard, Boston, 62
Dwight's Journal of Music, 25, 49
Dyhrenfurth, Julius, 4
Dynamicon, 58

Easter Morning, 84, 122
Eclairs Occidentals. See Flashes from the West.
Ecstasy, 108
Ehrenthal, Wilhelm, Das Kutschkelied auf der Seelenwanderung, 79
Eichberg, Julius, 61
Ekaton Waltzes, 122
Eleanore Waltzes, 123
Election campaign, spring, 1863, 47
The Elements of Musical Composition, 61

Elgin, Ill., 24
Elkhorn, Wis., 8
Ella Bell, 113
Ella Schottische, 134
Elliott, D. H., 57
Ellsworth, Elmer E., 38, 44
Ellsworth Requiem, 44
Ellsworth Requiem March, 92
Ellsworth Zouave & National Lancers' Greeting Grand March, 101
Emancipation Proclamation, disapproval of, 47, 48
----manuscript of, 51
Emerald Schottisch, 7
Emery, Stephen A., Apfelblüthen Walzer, 70
    Menuet, 70
    Polonaise, 70
Emilie Waltz, 130
Emita Redowa, 122
Emma May. See Linden Bowers.
Emmeline Mazurka de Salon, 122
The Enchantress Schottisch, 93
Engaged, 133
The Ensign of Glory, 93
Ernani, 133
Ervie Morie, 124
Estey Organ Co., 29-30
L'Etoile Galop, 115
Etta Mazurka, 100
Evangelical Hymns, 4
Evening, 91
Evening. See also Soir.
Evening Bells, 96
Evening Chimes, 129
Evening Prayer, 110
Eventide, 95
Ever in Dreams, 118
Ever of Thee, 91
Ever With Me, 111
Excursion Schottische, 129
Excuse Me! Schottische, 126

Faces I See in My Dreams, 128
Faces to Memory Dear, 105
Fairy Bridal Polka, 121
Fairy Footsteps Waltz, 101
Fairy Nora Loves Me, 99
Fairy Polka Redowa, 92
Fairy Ring, 97
The Famous Grecian Bend, 13
Fancy Free Polka Characteristique, 126
Farewell Beloved Friends, Farewell, 127
Farewell False Heart, 11
Farewell, Father, Friend and Guardian, 99, 133
Fashionable Waltz. See Valse a la Mode.
Father Abraham's Reply to the 600,000, 94
Father, Come Down With the Stamps, 103

Father, Dear Father, Come Home With Me Now.
    See Come Home, Father.
Father Will Settle the Bill, 121, 124
Fatherless, 124
Father's Come Home, 99
Faulds, D. P., Louisville, 7, 28, 38
Faust Caprice de Concert, 107
Faust Pot Pourri, 105
Feather Polka, 134
Feather Waltz, 113
Fétis, François Joseph, 24
Field, William A., Comedy Galop, 70
The Fields of Home, 97
La Fille du Regiment, 109
The Fire Brigade Quickstep, 91
Fireman's Marching Song, 101
Fireside Harmonies ... for the Mason & Hamlin
    Cabinet Organ, 61, 107
First Blossom Waltz, 112
First Bud Waltz, 112, 126
First Dreams, 112
First Finger Waltz, 112
The First Gun Is Fired! May God Protect the Right!
    43-44, 53, 92
The First Love Dream, 94, 95
Fisherman, Fisherman, Over the Sea, 120
The Fitzpatrick Polka, 129
Five Finger Waltz, 130
Five C'clock in the Morning, 103, 114
Flag of the Fearless and Free, 49
Flashes from the West, 127
Floating Clouds, 133
Floating on the Lake, 104
Floating on the Wind, 94, 102
Floraline Shore, 111
Florance, George A., The Pet Polka, 37, 38
The Flower Girl, 70
Flower of the West, 120
The Flower Queen (cantata), 8, 18-19
----(music journal) 6, 8, 24, 49
Flowers of Beauty Schottische, 105, 120
The Fly-Away Waltz, 127
Fly, Birdling, Through the Verdant Wood, 109
Fly Love to Me, 129
Flying Trapese. See The Man on the Flying
    Trapese.
Foes and Friends, 101
Follow the Drum, 98
Fond Heart, oh, Think of Me, 121
For President, Ulysses Grant, A Smoking His
    Cigar, 107
For You! 120
The Forest Choir, 144
The Forest Requiem, 37, 71, 91
Forest Temple, 100
Forget Me Not, 123
Fort Sumter, S. C., bombardment, 43

The Fortune Daisy, 123
Forward, Boys, Forward, 44, 92
La Forza del Destino, 98
Foster, Stephen C., 19
    Beautiful Child of Song, 51
    Mine Is the Mourning Heart, 51
The Founder of Notre Dame, 105
Fountain in the Sunlight, 100
Foutrill, Henry, Dear Mother the Battle Is
    Over, 12
Fra Diavolo, 98, 110
Fradel, Charles, 61
Franco-Prussian war, 79
Franz, Robert, 22, 59
    O Wert Thou in the Cauld Blast, 36
Fraternity March, 107
Free as Air Quickstep, 129
The Freedman's Song. See Now Den! Now
    Den!
Freedom's Harvest Time, 100
Freiberg, Fred, arr., Skating Waltz, 60
French D. A., '63 Is the Jubilee, 51
Frisbie, Henrie L., The Stars and Stripes,
    the Flag of the Free, 44
From the Bosom of the Waters, 129
Fry, William Henry, 28
Fuchsia Galop, 120
Fuller, ----, Boston, 62, 65
The Fundamental Technics of Piano Playing,
    144
Funeral March to the Memory of Abraham
    Lincoln, 104

Gade, Niels Wilhelm, 58
Gaetana Mazurka, 129
La Gaillarde, 91
Gala Day, 100
Galena, Ill., 61
Garden City Polka, 5
Garry Owen, 123
Gather 'Round the Table, 110
Gathering Home, 112, 119, 139
La Gazetier Polka, 100
Geh' zur Ruh'. See Repose.
Gems from France and Italy with English
    Translations, 70
General Fremont's March, 93
Gen. Grant's March, 93
Genl. Lyon's Battle March, 93
Gen. McClernand's Grand March, 94
General Sherman's Grand Atlanta March, 104
Geneviève de Brabant, 125
Gentle Naiad, 117
The German Youth, 116
Gird on! Gird on! 108, 134
The Girl for Me, 107
The Girl With the Auburn Tress, 121

The Girls at Home, 93
Girls, Don't Fool with Cupid, 120
Give the Boy a Chance, 121
Glad to Get Home, 65
The Glory, 81, 146
Glory! Glory! 100, 101
Glory Immortal.  See Oh Gloria.
Go Ask My Wife, 115
God Bless Our Brave Young Volunteers, 44, 92
God Save the Nation! 94
Göckerwitz, F., Boston, 37
Goldbeck, Robert, 84
The Golden Crown, 62
Golden Dream, 100
The Golden Dreamland, 125
Golden Leaves of Autumn, 114
Golden Memories, 109
The Golden Morn, 118
Golden Ringlets, 111
Gondellied, 100
Gone! 121
Gone to Heaven, 115, 134
Good Bye Jeff! 98, 99
Good Bye Johnnie, 110
Good Bye Old Glory, 99
Good Luck, 124
Goodfellow, G. G., 60
Goold, Nathaniel, 22, 59
Gordon, S. T., & Son, New York, 11, 69;
    purchase of Tolman's music books, 62
Gottschalk, Louis Moreau, 18, 21
Gould, J. E., Philadelphia, 5
Gould, Nathaniel.  See Goold, Nathaniel.
Gouttes d'Eau, 139
Grace Methodist Episcopal Church, Chicago, 60
Grad aus dem Wirthshaus.  See Out of the Tavern.
Graded Songs for Day Schools, 145, 146
Graff, George P., Lilly Day, 6, 7
Grafted into the Army, 94, 95, 96
Grand Galop Chromatique, 106
Grand Girard Mazurka, 101
Grand Instrumental Medley, 101
Grand March from Tannhauser, 91
Grand Polonaise, 109, 114
Grand Rally of Freemen, Chicago, 28
A Grand Vocal Medley, 100
Grand Waltz for the Guitar, 104
La Grande Duchesse, 110, 125
Grandfather Darling, 125
Grandfather's Clock, 29, 52
Grandma, 116
Grandmother Told Me So, 95
Grandmother's Cot, 125
The Grant Songster, 145
Grau, Jacob, Italian opera troupe, 57
Gray Distance Hid Each Shining Sail, 97
Greene, R. G., music publisher, 6, 49; melodeon
    manufacturer, 6

Greene, Robert Gorton, 5-6; relations with
    B. K. Mould, 5-6
Greene & Walker, Boston, 37
La Grenadille Waltzes, 118
Grief and Song, 70
Griffith Gaunt Schottische, 103
Griggs, S. C., & Co., Chicago, 4
Grosvenor Library, Buffalo.  See Buffalo and
    Erie County (N. Y.) Public Library.
Grover's German opera troupe, 57
Gruss an die Heimath.  See Home Greeting.
Guests of the Heart, 114
The Gum Tree Canoe, 68
Guyer, I. D., History of Chicago, 38

Haines (Miss) School for Young Ladies, 18
Hall, Thomas J., 77
Hall, Wm., & Son, New York, 6, 21, 24,
    33, 34, 38, 62, 77
Hallie Lee, 103
Hambaugh, James S., Stars and Stripes
    Schottisch, 53
Hanby, Benjamin R., 19, 43; Darling Nelly
    Gray, 19, 43
    Ole Shady, 43
Hanby, Rev. William, 43
Hancock Light Infantry, Boston, 63
Handel, George Frederick, 77; Messiah, 27
Hanky Panky Polka, 127
Hans and Hanne Polka, 118
Hansbrough, W., 27
The Happy Daughters, 120
Happy Days of Yore, 93
Happy Dreams, 98
Harding, W. N. H., 5, 7, 61, 95
Hark! The Vesper Hymn Is Stealing, 109
The Harp of Katie Bell, 121
The Harp That Once Thro' Tara's Halls, 124
Have Courage My Boy to Say No, 126
Have Ye Sharpened Your Swords? 92
Haydn, Joseph, Sonata, piano, 77
The Haymakers, 19, 22, 35
Haynes, James E., Farewell False Heart, 11
Hazel Dell, 19
Healy, Patrick J., 11
Hear the Cry That Comes Across the Sea! 134
The Heart Bowed Down, 109
Heart Hymns for the New Life, 145
Heart to Heart and Soul to Soul, 122
The "Heathen Chinee," 126
The Heather Bells, 101
Hecaton Waltzes.  See Ekaton Waltzes.
Heigh Ho! I'm in Want of a Beau! 116
He'll Soon Propose, 117
Hempsted, H. N., Milwaukee, 38, 100
Henrietta Mazurka, 123
Her Bright Smile Haunts Me Still, 98, 100, 101
Her Letter.  See Poverty Flat.

Here in This Moonlit Bower, 91
Hero's March, 60
Hertel, J. W., Adrian, Mich., 100
He's Comin' Again, 95
He's Gone! 119
Hesse, Adolf Friedrich, 58
L'Heure de la Prière, 93
Higgins, A. J., Chicago, 7-9
Higgins, Adoniram Judson, 7-9; Mabel Clare, 9
Higgins, Elizabeth. See Jackson, Elizabeth (Higgins)
Higgins, H. M., Chicago, 7, 9-10, 12, 13, 25, 45, 48, 59
Higgins, Hiram Murray, 7-10, 22, 28n; income, 52
Higgins, Libbie. See Jackson, Elizabeth (Higgins)
Higgins, Thomas Metcalf, 7, 8
Higgins Brothers, Chicago, 6, 7-9, 24, 25, 35, 49
Higgins family, 7
Higgins' Patriotic Glee Book, 49
Highland Gems, 123
His Voice Still Speaks to Me, 101
A History of Music Publishing in Chicago, 1850-1960, 4
Ho! Westward Ho! 110
Hoard, L. D., Dearest, Good Night, 6
  Long Years Have Passed, 6
  Nocturne, 7
Hold the Fort! 134
Holden Guards Schottische, 94
Home Again Returning, 103
Home Far Away, 91, 95
Home Greeting, 118
Home Run Galop, 105
Home, Sweet Home, 109
Home's Harmony, 109
Homeward, 114
Honor to Sheridan, 106
Hope on the Unseen Shore, 120
Hovey, Gen. C. E., 25
How It Marches, the Flag of the Union, 99, 133
How Sweet the Thought, 111
How Sweetly She's Sleeping, 121
How to Put the Question, 122
Howard, Frank, 62, 77
Howe, Elias, Jr., Boston, 68
Howe & Tolman, Boston, 68
Hubbard, Charles P., 62; Come Where the Morning Is Breaking, 72
Hubbard, James M., Love, Sweet Love Is Everywhere, 51
Huguenot Captain Polka, 103
A Hundred Years Hence, 115
Huneman, Julius, 13
Hunting Tower. See When Ye Gang Awa, Jamie.
Huntington, F. J., New York, 24
Hurrah for General Grant! 107
Hurrah Polka, 108

Hutchinson, Judson, If I Were a Voice, 64
Hyde Park, Ill., 10, 23, 28
Hyde Park Hotel, 28
The Hyde Park Polka, 100

I Am Weary and Faint in the Battle of Life! 124
I Ask No More, 103, 106
I Can Not Forget, 115
I Cannot Forget Thee, 129
I Don't Sing 'Cause I Can't, 122
I Dream of the Beautiful Past, 129
I Feel I'm Growing Old, Dear Wife, 118
I Have No Mother Now, 8
I Heard the Voice of Jesus Say, 123
I Know a Lovely Maiden, 117
I Love My Home, 37
I Love the Charming Autumn, 102
I Love to Think of Thee, 124
I Met Her at the Mat-inee, 117
I Never Kiss and Tell, 92
I Stand Beside a Lonely Grave, 127
I Stand on Memory's Golden Shore, 96
I Stood Before Her Portrait, 96
I Wait for Thy Coming, My Darling! 110
I Wonder Why He Comes Not, 99
I'd Mourn the Hopes That Leave Me, 108
Ida Waltz, 108
Idlewild Mazurka, 135
Idol of My Heart, 120
The Idol of the Day. See Par Excellence.
Idyls of the Prairie, 113
If I Only Knew it Came from Paris, 115
If I Were a Voice, 64
If Maggie Were My Own! 108, 133
If Papa Were Only Ready! 107
If You Love Me, Say So! 117
If You'll Promise Not to Tell, 122
I'll Leave it all to You, 125
I'll Tell You Why, 118
Illini Polka, 96
Illinois Grand March, 98
Illinois music copyright registrations, 4, 36, 37, 53, 61, 84
Illinois. 19th Regiment Band, 44
----State Board of Education, 25, 26
----State Normal University, 23, 25-26
----University. Library, 6, 11, 37, 38, 95
I'm Always Your Lovin' Katreen, 105
I'm Dying Far from Those I Love, 97
I'm Hame Again. See Bonnie Annie Lee.
I'm Happy Tonight, 118
I'm in Love, 115
I'm Married! 116
I'm Queen of the Night, 104
I'm Such a Nice Young Man, 115
I'm Thinking of Our Youth, Tom, 104
Imitation of the Banjo, 122

Impatience, 105
Impromptu Brilliante, 110
In a Horn, 102
In Dreams of My Childhood, 119
In Memoriam, Quartette on the Death of Abraham
    Lincoln, 62
In Memory of Abraham Lincoln, 99
In the Valley of the West, 101
In the Woods, 105
In Those Bright Eyes, 112
Indian Mother's Lullaby, 68
Indianapolis, 24
Invitation to the Galop, 120
Invitation to the Waltz, 119
Irish Diamonds, 123; no. 2, 124
The Irresistible Schottische, 126, 127
Is There Room Among the Angels? 113
Is Your Heart Still the Same to Me, My Darling?
    102
Isabella Waltz, 123
I'se on de Way, 97
It, 121
It Is an Age of Progress! 108
It Is Better Farther On, 125
It's Not Poor Mother's Fault, 111
It's True, 'Twas in the Papers, 124
I've Got a Baby, 118
Ivison & Phinney, New York, 4
Ixion Medley, 118

Jackson, Elizabeth (Higgins), 7
    My Barefoot Boy, 7
    Songs of Affection, 7
    Thy Spirit Will Ever Be Near, 7
    The Valentine; or, The Spirit of Song, 7
Jackson, Ernest Higgins, 7
Jackson, Leonora, 7
Jamie's Awa', 120
Janet's Choice, 127
Japanese marching song resembling Tramp,
    Tramp, Tramp, 52
Jeannette and Jeannot, 53
Jennie's Gone Home, 120
Jenny Brown and I, 95
Jenny Lyle, 103
Jenny Wade, the Heroine of Gettysberg, 98
Jerome Jenkins, 118
Jeunesse Polka, 134
Jewett, J. P., & Co., Boston, 34
Jimmy's Wooing, 92
Joachim, Joseph, 7
Joanna Dear, My Jo, 111
John Brown Song, 47, 93, 133
John Chinaman, 119
Johnny Is a Farmer Boy, 122
Johnny Schmoker, 95
Johnson, Artemas Nixon, 17, 18
Johnson, Mrs. D. C., 62

Jolly Jonathan and His Notional Naburs, 139
Josephine Waltz, 118
Joy Bells Polka, 100
La Joyeuse Polka, 122
Julie Polka, 103
Just After the Battle, 97, 98, 99
Just Before the Battle, Mother, 48n, 49, 51,
    96, 97, 99

Kathleen Mavourneen, 92
Katie Waiting at the Door, 127
Katrina's Story. See I'm Always Your Lovin'
    Katreen.
Keep a Brave Heart Still, 97
Keep Straight Ahead, 117
Keep the Ball A-rolling, 110
Keller, M., Grief and Song, 70
    Unbidden Tears, 70
Kimball, Almira R. See Root, Almira R.
    (Kimball)
Kimball, W. W., Chicago, 22, 35, 57, 59
Kimball Piano and Organ Co., 30
Kind Friends One & All, 37
Kind Smiles for All, 108, 133
The King of Thule. See C'era un Re di
    Thule.
Kingdom Coming, 28n, 43, 45-46, 48n, 49,
    93, 94, 95, 96, 99
The Kingdom Has Come, 45
Kinzie, Mrs. John H., Wau-Bun, 7
The Kiss. See Il Bacio.
Kiss Me Good Night, 122
Kiss Me Mother, Kiss Your Darling, 97, 99,
    105, 114
Kiss Me When I Come Home, 115
Kitty Clyde's Grave. See Thou Wilt Come
    Never More to the Stream.
Kitty McCree O'Tessell, 125
Kitty McKay, 115
Kitty More, 104
Kitty Ryder, 92
Kitty Vane and I, 135
Knight, Joel, Evangelical Hymns, 4
The Knight's Farewell, 113
Knox, E., The Melodious Songster, 4
El Kohinoor Polka, 127
Das Kuckuck Lied. See Song of the Cuckoo.
Kücken, Friedrich Wilhelm, Barcarole, 53
Das Kutschkelied, 79
Kutschke's War-song, 79, 128

Lablache, Luigi, 18
Ladies' Choice Polka. See Damenwahl Polka.
Ladies' Favorite Polka, 119
The Lafner Waltz, 93
Lake Forest Mazurka, 128
Lake Shore Mazurka, 101
The Lament of the Irish Emigrant, 63

Lament of the Irish Lover, 53
The Land o' the Leal, 114
The Land of the Loving, 117
The Land That Is Fairer Than Day, 122
The Language of Love. See Le Parlate d'Amor.
Lashed to the Mast, 103
The Last Words of Maximilian. See Poor Carlotta.
The Latch String at the Door, 133
The Latest Polka, 126
Laura Anna, 105
Lay Me Down and Save the Flag! 97, 99
Leaf by Leaf the Roses Fall, 120
The Leaves Around Me Falling, 123
Leavitt, Trow & Co., New York, 18
Le Carpentier, Adolph, 53
Lee, A. H., 57
Lee, Julius, 77
Lee, Robert E., surrender, 47
Lee & Walker, Philadelphia, 77
Lefébure-Wély, Louis James Alfred, 53
Lempster, N. H., 3
Lend a Kind Helping Hand to the Poor, 103
Let Me Dream of Home and Loved Ones, 105
Let Me Go! 103
Let Us Forget the Past, 103
Let Woman Vote! 106
Lewis, William, 22, 58, 78, 80, 83
----& Son, Chicago, 58
Liberty Bird, 99
Library of Congress, 6, 17, 53, 63, 95
Liebeswonne. See Love's Delight.
Life's Dream Is O'er, 114
The Light Auburn Curl, 111
Light Guard Band, Chicago. See Chicago Light Guard Band.
Light Guard Polka, 6
Light Guard Schottisch, 6, 108
Lighte, Newton & Bradbury pianos, 8
Lightly Rocking, 129
Lilla Is an Angel Now, 101
Lillie of the Snowstorm, 101
Lillie Schottische, 101
Lilly, Edward, Little Ella's Song to Her Angel Brother, Charlie, 60
Lilly Brook, 37, 71, 91
Lilly Dale, 48n
Lilly Day, 6, 7
Lily-Bell, the Culprit Fay, 145
Lily Queen Waltz, 123
Lincoln, Abraham, 34, 43, 62; 2d call for troops, 46; Emancipation Proclamation, 51
Linda di Chamounix, 109
Linden Bowers, 104
Linden Waltz, 130
Lindsay, Charles M., Hero's March, 60
The Linnet, 144
Lippert, Henry E., La Corinna, 5
    Rescue Grand March, 5

Lischen et Fritzchen, 125
List! the Evening Breeze Is Stealing, 91
List to Me, 114
Little Alice, 97
The Little Angel, 117
Little Barefoot, 116, 117, 119
The Little Boot Black, 107, 112
Little Bother, 117
The Little Carnival, 129
Little Dimpled Hands, 116
The Little Drummer Boy's March, 97, 113
Little Ella's Song to Her Angel Brother, Charlie, 60
Little Elma's Waltz, 118
Little Flirt Waltz, 129
The Little Gem, 109
Little Hattie Harvey, 112
Little Maggie May, 125
Little Major, 51, 94, 95, 96
The Little Octoroon. See Glory! Glory!
The Little Ones at Home, 113
Little Pet Schottische, 125, 126
Little Robin Tell Kitty I'm Coming, 128
Little Shoes and Stockings, 116
The Little Stone Cot in the Dell, 112
Little Stub Toe Polka, 110
Little Sunshine, 113, 134
The Little Wanderer's Song, 112
Lizzie, the Lass of the Brown Wavy Hair, 122
Lob, Otto, 13; A Curious Circumstance, 60
    Kutschke's War-song, 79
Loeschhorn, Albert, Tarantelle, 51
The Lovely Tear, 128
Long, Mrs. J. H., 27
Long, Peter, Western Harp, 4
Long Ago, 102
Long Branch, N. J., 77
Long Years Have Passed, 5
Longing for the Shore, 96
Longman, Edwin H., The City Railway Galop, 62
Look Me in the Eye Johnny, 123
Look Out Upon the Stars, 108
Lora Vale, 97, 112, 119
The Lord Is My Shepherd, 112
The Lord My Pasture Shall Prepare, 126
Lorena, 9, 11
Lost Lomie Laine, 106
Lottie in the Lane, 96
Lottie's All the World to Me, 102
Louisville (place of publication) 4, 7, 38
Love Among the Roses, 115, 120, 121
Love in May, 100, 120
Love, Sweet Love Is Everywhere, 51, 96
Love's Delight, 100
Love's Flirtation, Polka Brillante, 122
Loving Little Lou, 129
Loving Thee Ever, 133

Low in the Dust, 37
Loyal Leagues, 49
Lucia di Lammermoor, 109
Lumbard, Mr., 22, 43
Lumbard, Frank, 46
Lumbard, Jules G., 36n; introduces The Battle
    Cry of Freedom, 46
Luna Polka, 102
Lyon, George Washburn, 11, 22n
Lyon & Healy, Chicago, 11-12, 22n, 58, 79, 80

Ma Belle Polka Redowa, 94
Mabel! 102, 106
Mabel Clare, 9
Mabel Waltzes, 102, 129
McClellan, Gen. George, 44
MacEvoy, Charles, arr., The Pet Polka, 37
McLean Co., Ill., 25
Maggie Blair, 117
Magoun, Thomas P. J., 62
Maiden's Prayer, 92, 114
Major Anderson's March, 92
Major Train's Quick Step, 63
Make Home Beautiful, 126
Making Love by Moonlight, 121
Making Love While on the Ice, 115
The Man on the Flying Trapese, 112
The Man Who Got the Cinder in His Eye, 102
Mara March, 127
March de la Reine, 139
March on! March on! 97
Marching Home! 121
Marching Through Georgia, 52, 98, 99
Marechal, A., Do They Love Us Yet? 6
Marie, 124
Marie Quadrilles, 122
Marrie Polka-Mazurka, 91
Marsh, S. W., Chicago, 6
Martha, 102, 109
Martin, T. W., Chicago, 84
Mary of the Glen Waltz, 130
Mary Polka Redowa, 127
Mason, Lowell, 18, 19, 20, 24, 25, 48-49;
    Sabbath Hymn and Tune Book, 34, 36
Mason, William, 24; Amitié pour Amitié, 65
Mason & Hamlin, Boston & New York, 36, 61,
    73, 78; organs 81, 82
Mason & Law, New York, 24
Mason Brothers, New York, 19, 34, 35, 36, 58
The Masonic March, 98
The Masons' Dirge, 101
The Masons' Holiday, 101
The Masons' Home, 101
Massachusetts copyright records, 63-70
The Master's Gold Year, 125
Mathews, W. S. B., 78, 82; "Music in the
    Interior," 79
Matin, 122

Matinée Polka, 98
Maudie Moore, 96, 99
May Breeze Variations Brillante, 98
May March, 134
May Queen Quadrille, 99
Medora, 122
Meet Me Just at Twilight, 118, 134
Melodies of the Moonlight Harmonists, 6
Melodious Songster, 4
Memories' Graves. See In Dreams of My
    Childhood.
Memories of Home, 135
Mendel, lithographer, 99n
Mendelssohn-Bartholdy, Felix, 58, 69
Mercantile Association, Chicago, 28
Mercer Street Church, New York, 18
Mercy's Dream (chromo), 57
Merrill, H. T., Chicago, 12
Merrill, Hiram T., 12, 61-62
    Corn Is King! 12, 61
    The Golden Crown, 62
    In Memoriam, Quartette on the Death
        of Abraham Lincoln, 62
    Merrill's Sabbath School Songs, 62
    The Music Teacher's Register, 62
    Take Your Gun and Go, John, 44-45
Merrill, H. T., & Co., Chicago, 12, 61,
    78, 84
Merrill & Brennan, Chicago, 12, 59, 61, 71
Merrill's Sabbath School Songs, 62
Merry Christmas, 134
The Merry Sleigh-Ride, 130
Messiah, 27
Metropolitan Hall, Chicago, 21, 22
Michigan Schottische, 92
Michigan. University, 23
Mid-day, 113
The Midnight Stars, 120
The Midnight Winds, 105
The Midnight Zephyrs, 120
Mill Wheel Polka, 130
Miller & Curtis, music printers, New York,
    48
The Miller's Song, 100
Millie Clair, 117
The Million Dollar Waltz, 115
Milwaukee (place of publication), 38, 84
Mind Your Own Bread and Butter, 111
Mine Is the Mourning Heart, 51, 95
Mine Own, 92
Minnehaha Glee Book, 25, 48
Minnesota State Teachers' Convention, 50
Minnesota, the Lily of the West, 113
Minnie Munroe, 117
Miriam's Song of Triumph, 112
Miserere, 106
Mr. Lordly and I, 72, 102
La Mode, 126

Moelling, Theodore, 62
Mollenhauer, ----, Spharen Polka, 65
Molter, John, 13, 84; The Famous Grecian Bend, 13
    The Patriotic Glee Book, 10, 13
Molter & Wurlitzer, Chicago, 13, 84
Moment Polka, 93
Mona's Reverie, 111
Monroeville, O., 24
Monsieur et Madame Denis, 125
Monticello Waltz, 116
Moonlight on the Billow, 134
Moonlight Vespers, 108
Morning. See Martin.
Morning Star Waltz, 100
Morris, Jack C., Publishing Activities of S. C. Griggs & Co., 1848-1896, 4
Mother, Blame Me Not for Loving, 94
Mother, Oh Sing to Me of Heaven, 72, 92
Mother's Request. See Good Bye Johnnie.
Mother's Room, 125
Mother's Waiting for Her Children, 120
Mott, Mrs. Margaret M., 95
Mould, Brooks K., arrival in Chicago, 3; first publication, 4-5; relations with R. G. Greene, 5-6; new store, 6-7; return to Cleveland, 7; disposal of plates, 7
Mould, B. K., & Co., Chicago, 6-7
Mould, Edmond C., 3, 4
Mould, Henry J., 3
Mould, H., & Sons, Cleveland, confectioners, 3, 4
Mould & Greene, Chicago, 5-6
Mould & Numsen, Cleveland, confectioners, 4
The Mountains of Life, 113
Mozart, Wolfgang Amadeus, 77, 80
Murfreesboro, Tenn., 47
Murray, James R., 43, 77, 81; Song Messenger editor, 50
    Daisy Deane, 43
    Pity the Homeless; or, Burnt Out, 81
    Prussia, Gird Thy Sons for Battle! 79
The Museum Polka, 98
Music in America (prize essay), 24
The Music of the Sea, 101
The Music Teacher's Register, 62
The Musical Album March, 102
Musical Bon-Bons, 119
Musical Celebrities (game), 50
Musical conventions, 17, 19, 20, 24, 25, 34, 48
Musical Curriculum, 52, 80, 143; rev. ed., 81
The Musical Drama, 65
Musical Education Society, Boston, 17
The Musical Fountain, 144
The Musical Garland, 116
The Musical Gift, 63
The Musical Independent, 12

Musical instruments
    Accordions, 3, 10, 33, 34, 78, 82
    Banjos, 33
    Bugles, 38, 44
    Cabinet organs, 58, 61
    Clarinets, 3
    Concertinas, 33
    Cornets, 33, 34
    Cornopeans, 33
    Cymbals, 34
    Double basses, 78
    Drums, 10, 34, 38, 44, 78
    Dulcimers, 78
    Fifes, 34, 44
    Flageolets, 3, 78
    Flutes, 3, 33, 34, 58, 78
    Flutinas, 10, 33, 34
    Guitars, 10, 33, 34, 78, 82
    Harmoniums, 11, 36
    Horns, brass post, 3
    Melodeons, 4, 5, 6, 10, 11, 33, 34, 35, 38
    Metronomes, 78
    Organs, 10, 11, 33, 34, 80, 82, 83
    Pianos, 4, 5, 8, 10, 12, 13, 34, 35, 38, 51, 58, 80, 82, 83
    Piccolos, 78
    Pitch pipes, 33
    Saxhorns, 34
    Seraphines, 34
    Tamborines, 33, 78
    Tuning forks, 3
    Violins, 3, 5, 10, 33, 34, 58, 78, 82
    Violoncellos, 5, 10, 78
    Zithers, 78
Musical Review and Choral Advocate. See New York Musical Review and Choral Advocate.
Musical Union. See Chicago Musical Union
The Musician's Guide, 77-78
My Angel Spirit Bride, 104
My Barefoot Boy, 7, 119
My Beau That Went to Canada, 99
My Cottage Home, Dear Mother, 72, 92, 95
My Faith Looks up to Thee, 123
My Father's Fireside, 61
My Heart Is Far Over the Sea, 116
My Heart Is Like a Silent Lute, 92
My Home Is on the Prairie, 37, 71, 91
My Landlady's Pretty Little Daughter, 117
My Lily, 110
My Love and I, 122
My Loved One's Grave, 134
My Madeline, 110
My Margaret, 107
My Mother Bids Me Bind My Hair, 108, 111
My Mother She Is Sleeping, 37, 91
My Mother's Farewell Kiss, 118

My Mother's Song, 117
My Native Hills, 117
My Soul Shall Know Thine in That Beautiful Land.
    See The Mountains of Life.
My Thoughts Are Far Away, 111
My Thoughts Are of Thee, 135
Myrtle Wreath, 105

Nabucodonosor, 108, 133
Name Me in Thy Prayer, 112, 134
Nasby's Lament Over the New York Nominations,
    113
The Nation's Hero Grand March, 111
Nellie Lost and Found, 93, 95, 112
Nellie Ray, 98
Nevins, William, Army Regulations for Drum,
    Fife and Bugle, 44, 143
The New Skedaddle, 94
New Temperance Melodist, 34
New York (place of publication), 5, 24, 29, 34,
    36, 38
New York Musical Review and Choral Advocate,
    21, 24
New York Musical Review and Musical World, 49
New York Public Library, 4, 10, 68, 95, 100n
New York (State) Institution for the Blind, 18
Newark, N. J., Public Library, 95
Newberry Library, 95
Newman, M. H., & Co., New York, 4
Newman & Ivison, New York, 4
Newport, R. I., 77
Niagara Falls, N. Y., 77
Nichols, M. O., 58
A Night of Love, 113
Nightfall at Home, 108, 134
The Nilsson Waltz, 134
9th Missouri Quickstep, 93
No Letters from Home! 120
No, Ne'er Can Thy Home Be Mine, 53
Nora MacRae, 116
Norah Darling Don't Believe Them, 91
Normal, Ill., 26, 27
Normal Musical Institute, 19
North and South, 99
North Reading, Mass., 17, 21
Northmen, Awake, 106
Northwestern Rifles March, 93
Northwestern Sanitary Fair, 51
Not at all Like Me!  See The Photograph.
Not for Thy Beauty, 115
Notes for the Music Library Assn., 39
Novello, London, 34
Now Den! Now Den! 100
Now from Labor and from Care, 112
Now, Moses, 100
Une Nuit d'Amour.  See A Night of Love.
Numerical Harp, 4
The Nun, 123

Oh, Are Ye Sleeping Maggie, 36, 91, 103
O Bring My Darling Back to Me, 128
Oh! Bury the Brave Where They Fall, 96
O, Come, O, Come with Me!  See Undine's
    Song.
O, Come You from the Battle-field? 96
O Come You from the Indies? 92
O Father Take My Hand, 124
Oh, Gloria, 97
Oh, Haste on the Battle!  94
Oh, He Kissed Me When He Left Me, 96
O Hush Thee, My Babie, 122
Oh! Lady Fair, I Dream of Thee, 111
O Linger No Longer, 111
Oh, Louie Is My Fair One, 103
O Lux Beati Trinitas, 139
O Moonlight Deep and Tender, 123
O My Charming Elfie May, 53
O Quam Suavis Est, 139
Oh, Say to My Spirit, Thy Bride Will I Be,
    126
Oh Scorn Not Thy Brother, 8
O Set My Heart at Rest, 105
Oh! Share My Cottage Gentle Maid, 3
Oh! Sing with the Birds, 118
O, Soft Sleep the Hills, 104
Oh, Sorosis! 111, 134
O, Summer Moon, 116
O Take Me to Thy Heart Again, 98, 116
O Vos Omnes, 139
O Wert Thou in the Cauld Blast, 36
O, Worship the Lord, 105
O, Wrap the Flag Around Me, Boys, 93, 95
O Ye Tears! O Ye Tears! 94, 95, 103
Oakes, H., Boston.  See Oakes, William
    H., Boston.
Oakes, William H., Boston, 62, 64, 78
Oberlin College, 23
Oberlin Seminary, 23
Ocean House Polka Redowa, 108
Octoroon Schottische, 105
O'er My Little Brother's Grave, 124
O'er the Billow, 25
Oesten, Theodore, 53
Off for a Holiday, 130
Offenbach, Jacques, Orpheus, Fantasie, 73
    Selections from La Belle Hélène, 70
Often in Dreams I'm Roaming, 110
Ogden, W. A., 62
O'Googerty's Wedding, 117
Ohio State Musical Assn., 24
Oil-do-ra-do, 98
Ola, 106
The Old Brown Cot, 96
The Old Cabin Home, 68
The Old Church Bells, 112
The Old Church Choir, 105
The Old Clock in the Corner, 130

Old Folk's Love Song, 118
Old Friends, 110
Old Friends and True Friends, 108, 112
Old Glory and U. S. Grant, 134
The Old Hickory Cane, 117
The Old House Far Away, 95
The Old Kitchen Floor, 123
Old Sayings, 116
Old Settlers' Harmonic Society, Chicago, 3
The Olive of Love, 127
Olivet College March, 104
On Land and Sea, 128
On, On, On, the Boys Came Marching, 98, 99
On the Banks of the Pearl, 125
On the Beautiful Blue Danube Waltz, 129
On the Danube. See Donau Walzer.
On the Field of Battle, Mother. See Just Before the Battle, Mother.
One by One, 96
The One Horse Galop, 123
One I Love, Two I Love, 135
Only, 128
Only a Part, 120
Only a Waiting Maid, 111
Only Four, 106
Only Love Me, 128
Only Waiting, 37, 71, 91
Open the Gates, 122
L'Opéra dans le Salon, 133
Opera House Drawing March, 60
Orange Blossom Mazurka, 120
Orient, N. Y., 24
Oriole Waltz, 97
Orphée aux Enfers, 125
Orpheus Fantasie, 73, 112
Osbourn, J. G., engraver, Chicago, 37
Osbourn & Strail, Chicago, 3
Our Angel Child, 135
Our Blue Eyed Darling, 126
Our Captain's Last Words, 93
Our Comrade Has Fallen, 94
Our Folks Schottische, 126
Our Nation's Captain, 97
Our Own, 120
Our Protective Union, 101
Our Song Birds, 144
Our Turn Is Coming, 126
Out of the Tavern, 107
Out On the Shore, 127
Out West, 101
Over the Dancing Waves, 130
Over the Sea, 68
The Owl in the Ruin. See Watcher Gray.
Oxford, O., 24

Pacific Glee Book, 77, 146
The Pagoda Waltz, 129
Paine, T., The Old Cabin Home, 68

The Palm, 81, 146
Palmer, H. R., Chicago, 61
Palmer, Horatio Richmond, 61
    The Elements of Musical Composition, 61
    My Father's Fireside, 61
    The Song Queen, 61
    They Blossom There Up There, 61
Palmer's Normal Collection of Sacred Music, 146
Palmer's System of Teaching the Rudiments of Vocal Music in Classes, 61
Panis Angelicus Fit Panis Hominum, 139
Papa, Help Me Across, 124
The Papillion, 128
Par Excellence, 121
Parker, J. C. D., The Musical Drama, 65
Le Parlate d'Amor, 97
Parlor Skating Schottische, 98
Parnassus, 120
Parting Song, 103
Passing Away, 106, 108, 133
Passing Through the Fire, 81, 135
Passion Flower Waltzes. See La Grenadille Waltzes.
The Past We Can Never Recall, Jamie, 107, 119
Patiently Waiting, 125
The Patriotic Glee Book, 10, 13
The Patriot's Prayer, 97
Patterson, Ezra H., Chicago, 9
Patti, Adelina, 20
Pebble Polka, 113
La Périchole, 125
Persley, George. See Brown, George W.
The Pet Polka, 37, 38, 91
Peters, C. F., edition, 80
Peters, J. L., St. Louis, 10, 11
Peters, W. C., Cincinnati, 28
Peters, W. C., & Sons, Cincinnati, 38
Le Petit Tambour, 109
Phelps, Minnie A., 62
The Phi Gamma Delta March, 118
Philadelphia (place of publication) 5, 77
Philander Brown, the Ill-used Young Man, 115
Philharmonic Society. See Chicago Philharmonic Society.
The Photograph, 105
Piano Pictures, 84, 129
Pic Nic Waltz, 104
The Picture on the Wall, 97
Pilgrim's Night-March, 114
Pining for the Old Fireside, 101
Pirated editions, Confederate, 9, 49
Pistorius, Hermann Alexander, Das Kutschkelied, 79
Pity the Homeless; or, Burnt Out, 81
Plagge, Christoph, Garden City Polka, 5
Les Plaisirs de la Valse. See Belles de Chicago.

236

Plate numbers, 36-37, 39, 53, 59-73, 83-84
Playing for a Wife. See Queen of Hearts.
Please, Father, Let Us in! See Lillie of the Snowstorm.
La Pluie de Météores, 126
A Poem of Life, 120
The Polish Refugee, 139
Polka Gracieuse, 92
Polka Grotesque, 110
Pond, H. Augustus, The Buttonwood Tree at the Door, 4
Pond Lilly Schottisch, 108
Le Pont des Soupirs, 125
The Pony Ride, 130
Poor Broken Heart, 105
Poor Carlotta! 105
Poor Jack Brown, 107
Poor Kitty Popcorn, 133
Poor Little Blind Maggie, 134
Poor Mother! Willie's Gone, 98
Popping Corn, 111
The Popular Piano Instructor, 19
Les Postillons Valse, 99
Poverty Flat, 121
Prairie Queen Quadrilles, 118
Praise God from Whom All Blessings Flow, 47
Pray for Me! 122
Precious to Thee, 122
Presidential campaign, 1860, 34
----election, 1864, 47
The President's Emancipation March, 94
The President's Grave, 98
The Prettiest Girl in Town, 114
The Pride of the Dell, 121
Prince & Co. melodeons, 33, 34, 35
La Princesse de Trebizonde, 125
Prison Duet from Trovatore, 109
The Prize, 146
Pro Phundo Basso. See Bliss, Philip Paul.
Pro Phundo Basso, 110
Profit and Loss, 117
Promesse, 124
The Promised Land Tomorrow, 117
Prussia, Gird Thy Sons for Battle! 79, 124
Public domain, pieces in, 39, 53, 71, 84
Public school music, 20, 48
Pulling Hard Against the Stream, 126
Put Me in My Little Bed, 126
Put up the Bars, 104

Quarterly Circular of H. M. Higgins Music Publishing House, 10
Queen of Hearts, 116
Qui Vive! 125
The Quiet Days When We Are Old, 37
Quintillian, Marcus Fabius, 24
Quit That, 135

Racine, Wis., 24
Rain on the Calm Lake, 104
Rally for the Leader, 134
Ratcliffe, F. W., Louisville, 4
Recollections of a Music Box, 123
Recruiting songs, 44
The Red Bird, 144
Reed, Alanson, Chicago, 12-13, 60; income, 52
Reed, Alanson, & Sons, Chicago, 13, 58
Reed, Alanson H., 13
Reed, George P., Boston, 18, 62-63, 65, 69, 71-72, 78; copyright registrations, 63
Reed, G. P., & Co., Boston, 6, 63-64, 66
Reed, John Warner, 13
Reed & Co., Boston, 64
Reed's Temple of Music, Chicago, 13, 60
Reeves, Sims, 18
Remembered, 121
Repose, 113, 128
Rescue Grand March, 5
Rêve d'Artist, 134
The Revelers' Chorus, 100
Revue et Gazette Musicale de Paris, 24
Richards, Brinley, 53
Richardson, Nathan, Elements of Music at Sight, 65
    The Modern School for the Pianoforte, 64
    The Popular Piano Instructor, 19
Richardson, Nathan, Boston, 8, 19-20, 62, 64-65, 66, 69, 77, 78
Richmond House Polka, 37, 91
Rigoletto, 109, 133
Ring the Bell, Watchman! 98, 99
Rinck, Johann, 58
Rippling Rill Polka, 104
Rippling Wave Schottische, 127
Ristori Grande Valse, 102
Ritters Abschied. See The Knight's Farewell.
Riverside Mazurka, 129
Riverside Polka, 124
The Rivulet, 101
The Robert Brierly Schottisch, 97, 102
Roberto il Diavolo, 109
Robert's Return from the War. See O Come You from the Indies?
The Robin, 144
Robinson Crusoe, 125
Rock Me to Sleep, Mother, 4, 92, 94
Rock of Ages, 112
Rock of Liberty, 68
Roe Stephens Music Co., Detroit, 11
Romeo and Juliet, 107, 110
Room for One More, 104
Root, Almira R. (Kimball), 22
Root, Charles T., 81
Root, Ebenezer Towner, 20-23, 28, 36, 80, 83; arrival in Chicago, 4, 21; marriage, 22, 28; income, 52

Root, Ebenezer Towner (Continued)
    Slumber Gentle Lady, 62
Root, E. T., & Sons, Chicago, 22-23
Root, Frank K., 22
Root, Frederick Ferdinand, 17, 20
Root, Frederic Woodman, 81 Orpheus Fantasie, 73
    Pacific Glee Book, 77
    Piano Pictures, 84
Root, George F., 8, 11, 17-20, 77, 81, 82, 83; attitude toward composition, 19, 43; approach to publishing, 19-20; a layman's musician, 20; compositions, 20, 23, 24, 34, 71; enters Root & Cady, 35; 1st war song, 43; endorses emancipation, 48; contributions to The Song Messenger, 49; war songs, 49; income, 52
----The Academy Vocalist, 19
    The Banner of the Fatherland, 79
    The Battle Cry of Freedom, 17, 43, 46-48, 49
    Camps, Tramps & Battlefields, 72
    Clear Cold Water, 24
    Daniel, 19, 21
    The First Gun Is Fired! May God Protect the Right! 43-44, 53
    The Flower Queen, 18-19
    The Forest Requiem, 37, 71
    Forward, Boys, Forward, 44
    From the Ruins Our City Shall Rise, 81
    Glad to Get Home, 65
    The Glory, 81
    God Bless Our Brave Young Volunteers, 44
    The Haymakers, 19, 22, 35
    Hazel Dell, 19
    Just Before the Battle, Mother, 48n, 49, 51
    Kind Friends One & All, 37
    Lilly Brook, 37, 71
    Low in the Dust, 37
    Mother, Oh Sing to Me of Heaven, 72
    Musical Curriculum, 52, 80; rev. ed., 81
    My Cottage Home, Dear Mother, 72
    My Home Is on the Prairie, 37, 71
    My Mother She Is Sleeping, 37
    Oh, Are Ye Sleeping Maggie, 36
    Only Waiting, 37, 71
    Passing Through the Fire, 81
    The Quiet Days When We Are Old, 37
    Rock Me to Sleep Mother, 4
    Rosalie, the Prairie Flower, 48n, 62
    See the Sky Is Darkling, 62
    The Silver Lute, 48-49, 53, 81
    Softly She Faded, 37, 71
    Tramp, Tramp, Tramp, 17, 43, 48n, 52
    The Vacant Chair, 17, 48n, 49, 51
    Within the Sound of the Enemy's Guns, 51
    Ye Have Done it Unto Me, 81
    The Young Ladies' Choir, 18
Root, George F., & Sons, Chicago, 22, 81-83
Root, Sarah Flint, 17, 20

Root, Walter R., 22
Root, William A., 57, 81
Root & Cady, Chicago, 13, 19, 27; successors to H. M. Higgins, 10; aids Lyon & Healy, 12; first advertisement, 33; original investment, 33; stock, 34; advertisements, 33-36, 44-45; early publications, 36-38; first catalog, 39; war songs, 43-48; output in 1864, 52; purchase of presses, 52; scope of catalog, 52; St. Paul branch store, 57; move to Crosby Opera House, 57; new store, 58; sales, 1865-66, 58-59; post-war publications, 59; absorption of other firms, 60; purchase of Tolman catalog, 70-73; issues The Musician's Guide, 77-78; baseball team, 79; expansion, 78-79; dissolution, 20, 22, 29, 80-81; sale of catalogs, 81-82; bankruptcy, 83; reorganized firm, 29, 80
Root & Cady's Collection of Popular Songs, Duetts, Trios &c. by Various Composers, 53
Root & Cady's Eclectic Piano Forte Instructor, 143
Root & Lewis, Chicago, 22, 83
Root & Sons Music Co., Chicago, 22, 83
Root's Guide for the Piano Forte, 143
Rory O'More, 124
Rosalie, the Prairie Flower, 48n, 62
La Rose, 108
Rose Waltz, 120
The Rosebud Polka Rondo, 91
Rosemary Crown, 95
Rosy Hours, 118
Rossini, Gioacchino Antonio, 3; Semiramide, 5 Sombre Forêt, 65
    William Tell, trio from, 22
Rubinstein, Anton, 58
Ruck Waltz, 104
La Ruisseau. See The Rivulet.
The Ruler in Peace and the Leader in War, 110
Russell, George D., Boston, 62, 63, 65, 69
Russell & Fuller, Boston, 65, 66, 77, 78
Russell & Patee, Boston, 100n
Russell & Richardson, Boston, 65, 66, 69, 77, 78, 101
Russell & Tolman, Boston, 34, 36-37, 38, 62, 65, 66-69, 77, 78, 101
The Rustic Lassie Polka, 130
Rutgers Female Institute, New York, 18, 22

Sabbath Hymn and Tune Book, 34
Sabbath Morn, 111
The Sabbath Morning, 105
Sacred Lyrics, 145
Sadly the Bells Toll the Death of the Hero, 44

Sadly To-night I Am Dreaming, 119
Safely Through Another Week, 111
Saffery, E. C., The Union Volunteers, 44
Sag Harbor, N. Y., 24, 30
Sailing into Dreamland, 107
St. Louis, Mo., 10, 11
St. Paul, Minn., 57
St. Paul Waltz, 97, 112, 121
Sally Ann's Away! 103
Sally Port Polka, 116
Salva Dimora Casta, 97
San Souci Galop, 100
Sans Souci, Marche Triumphal, 123
Sanders, Robert L., 46
San Diego, Calif., 10
Sandusky, O., 24
Santa Lucia, 106
Sara Neighed! 133
Savior Breathe an Evening Blessing, 97, 110
Saviour When in Dust, to Thee, 118
School Lyrics, 145
Schubert, Franz Peter, 9, 28, 80; Serenade, 22
Schumann, Robert Alexander, 28, 58, 59, 80, 105
Secondary imprints, 4, 5, 6, 36, 38
The Secret, 91
See the Sky Is Darkling, 62
Send the Little Ones Happy to Bed, 128
Seven Girls and No Man, 119
The Seven Sounds (music journal), 62
Shabona Schottisch, 96
Shades of Evening, 68
Shadow Waltz, 94
Shadows of the Past, 111
Shadows on the Stream, 116
Shakesperian Grand March, 104
Shaking of Hands, 104
Shall I Ever See My Boy! 134
Sharpshooter's March, 97
She Has Such Winning Ways, 111
She Shines in Honor Like a Star, 121
She Sleeps Beneath the Elms, 96
Sheffield, Mass., 17, 20
Shells of Ocean, 94, 109
Sherman House, Chicago, 33
Sherman House Polka Redowa, 92
The Ship That Never Return'd, 99
Shooting Star Galop di Bravura, 101
The Short Girl Dressed in Green, 110
Shower of Meteors. See La Pluie de Météores.
Shower Waltz, 115
Shrival, R. G., Oh! Share My Cottage Gentle Maid, 3
Shun the Broad Road, 113, 117
Sibylla Valse, 116
The Sigh, 101
Silent Evening, 93, 95
The Silver Clarion, 145
Silver Lake Waltz, 108

The Silver Lute, 48-49, 50, 52, 53, 81, 143, 144
Silver Star Waltz, 114
Silver Whistle, 111
Silvery Ripples Waltz, 130
Since the Day I Signed the Pledge, 104
Sing, Birdie, Sing, 103, 109
Sing Me to Sleep, Father, 100
Sing Softly, Love, 96
Sing to Me Dear Sister, 124
The Singing Bird or Progressive Music Reader, 4
The Singing Skewl, 116
Singular Dreams, 95
Sister in Heaven, 128
Sister Maggie, 91
Sister May, 110
Sit Thee Down Beside Me Nannie, 125
'63 Is the Jubilee, 51, 94, 95
Skating Polka, 92
The Skating Quadrille, 93
Skating Waltz, 60, 104
Slaves, 43, 45-46
Sleep, Baby, Sleep, 94
Sleeping for the Flag, 96, 99
Sleigh Bells Mazurka, 116
Sleigh Ride Galop, 100, 106, 109
Sleighing with the Girls, 96
Slumber Gentle Lady, 62
Slumber Song from L'Africaine, 100
The Smile Polka Gracieuse, 101
Smith, Thomas, & Son, New York, 4
Smith & Nixon, Chicago, 11, 12, 59
Smith Schottische, 116
Snipkins (role), 22
The Snow-Bird, 144
Snow-flakes, 112, 134
Social Waltz, 116
Sodowa March, 121
Soft Breezes in the Solemn Night, 102
Softly Fall the Silvery Moonbeams, 128
Softly She Faded, 37, 71, 91
Sogni d'Amore, 105
Soir, 122
Soldier's Dream Polka Militaire, 7
Soldier's Dream Song, 93, 95
Soldier's Friend Polka Quickstep, 96
Soldier's Home Medley, 98
The Soldier's Last Request, 109, 117
The Soldier's Pet. See Poor Kitty Popcorn.
Sombre Forêt, Romance from Wm. Tell, 65
Some Day When I Am Far Away, 117
Some People Think Only of Money, 118
Some Sweet Day, 119
Somebody's Waiting Down in the Dell, 126
Somewhere, 116, 119
Somnambula, 102
Sonatas, 77, 78, 80

Song King, 80, 81
Song Messenger of the Northwest, 21, 43, 48, 49, 50, 52, 81-83
Song of a Thousand Years, 51, 95, 97
The Song of Blanche Alpen, 94
Song of Night, 4
Song of the Cuckoo, 107
Song of the Egyptian Girl, 92, 95
Song of the Fairies, 130
Song of the Negro Boatman, 93
Song of the Redman, 107
The Song Queen, 61, 81
Songs for the New Life, 77, 145
Songs of Affection, 7
Songs of Summer, 126
Songs of the Free Masons, 101
Songs That We Never Forget, 114, 119
The Songs We Sang upon the Old Camp Ground, 102
La Sonnambula, 124
Sontag, Henriette, 18
Sophia Polka, 96
Sophia Waltz, 101
Sound the Loud Timbrel. See Miriam's Song of Triumph.
Sounds from Home, 110
Sounds from Mexico, 110
Sounds from the Old Camp Ground, 133
South Carolina, secession, 43
Souvenir de l'Africaine, 101
Souvenir de Paris, 120
Sparkle Schottische, 110
Sparkling Dew Polka, 128
The Sparkling Schottische, 109
Sparkling Wavelets, 130
Spharen Polka, 65
Spingler Institute, New York, 24
The Spirit of Song, 7
The Spring at the Foot of the Hill, 107
Spring Style Schottisch, 93
Springfield Polka, 94
Staab, Franz, Amelia Mazurka, 7
    I Have No Mother Now, 8
    Light Guard Polka, 6
    Light Guard Schottisch, 6
    Valse Brillante, 6, 7
Stand Up for Uncle Sam, My Boys, 93, 95
Star Polka, 98
Starry Night, 100
Starry Waves, 118
Stars and Stripes Schottisch, 53, 93
The Stars and Stripes, the Flag of the Free, 44, 92
The Star Spangled Banner, 35, 105
Starved in Prison, 133
Steinway & Sons, New York, 12
Steinway pianos, 11, 33, 34
The Stevens March, 105
Stewart, I. L., The Western Sunday School Psalmody, 4

Still I Love Thee, 110
Still Thy Tumult, Wild, Wild Waves! 134
Stone's River, battle of, 47
The Stream of Time, 120
Studio Polka, 116
Sturges Rifles, 44
Such Is Fashion, 119
The Sugar Plum Waltz, 130
Summer Bloom Waltz, 119
Summer Night Schottisch, 104
Summer's Sweets Shall Bloom Again, 107
Sunlight to the Soul, 121
The Sunny South, 129
Sunrise, 113
Sunset, 113
Susie Had a Mocking Bird, 127
Swedenborg, Emanuel, 20
Sweet Buried Friend of Mine, 101
The Sweet By and By, 122
Sweet Ethelinda, 119
Sweet Molly Matilda Jane, 120
Sweet Robin Waltz, 126
The Sweet Times Were the Old, 118
Sweetly, Softly, 129
The Sweetness of Thy Smile, 120
Sweets to the Sweetest, 119
Swinging in the Trees, 130

Take Back the Heart, 114
Take Me from My Little Bed, 126, 130
Take Your Gun and Go, John, 44-45, 93, 95
The Tanner and the Blue, 113
Tantum Ergo, 139
Taps (bugle call), 105
Tarantelle, 51, 96
Taylor, Woodbury M., 29
Te Deum Laudamus, 112, 120
Teachers Songs, 143
A Tear for the Comrade That's Gone, 133
Telephone, 29
The Temperance Band. See Gird on! Gird on!
The Temperance Ship, 128
Templar March, 106
Temple, M. L., 57
Terrace Hill Waltz, 130
A Terrible War with Nobody Hurt, 122
Testament Hymns, 145
Thalberg, Sigismond, 77
That Little Church Around the Corner, 127, 134
That Little Room Up Stairs, 113
Then and Now, 125
Then You'll Remember Me, 53, 110
There! I Told You So, 124
There Is No Heart, 110
There Is No One Like a Mother, 103
There's a Darling Girl I Know, 118
There's a Void in Our Household, 115
There's Always a Welcome for Thee, 117

There's Music in My Heart, Love, 103
There's No Such Beau as Mine, 116
There's Sunshine After Rain, 122, 134
They Blossom There Up There, 61
They Buried Her under the Old Elm Tree, 8
They Have Broken up Their Camps, 99, 133
They Tell Me Thou Art Sleeping, 104
Thinking of Home Polka, 104
This Beautiful World That We Live In, 115
Thomas, J. P., Shades of Evening, 68
Thornton, ---- 62
The Thorough Base School, 145
Thorson, Theodore W., History of Music Publishing in Chicago, 1850-1960, 4
Those Wildering Eyes of Thine, 121
Thou Art My Own, 128
Thou Everywhere, 109
Thou Wilt Come Never More to the Stream, 92
Three Angel Visitants, 25
Thy Spirit Will Ever Be Near, 7, 119
Tiger Polka, 93
The Time for Love, 117
The Tin Wedding, 118
Tin-ni-min-ni-win-kum-ka, 120
'Tis Finished! 99, 133
'Tis the Heart Makes the Home, 114
'Tis Lone on the Waters, 124
To Whom Shall We Give Thanks, 109
Tobey, A. B., Sadly the Bells Toll the Death of the Hero, 44
Together, 124
Tolman, Henry, 62, 66-68, 69, 77, 78, 100
Tolman, Henry, & Co., Boston, 59, 61, 62, 64, 69-70, 73, 78, 84
Tolman & Co., Boston, 48n
"Tolman catalogue," 61, 71, 77
Tommy Dodd, 111
Tommy's Return, 108
Tomorrow, 124
Too Genteel You Know! 134
Torrent Song, 123
Touch Not the Fair Cup, Though It Sparkles, 101
Touch the Keys Softly, 103, 112
Touches of Little Hands, 127
Tramp, Tramp, Tramp, 17, 21, 43, 48n, 52, 98, 99, 112, 133
Traumgewebe, 121
Traviata, 102
Tread Lightly Ye Comrades, 94, 95
Treasures, 106
Treasures of the Past, 116
Tremont House, Chicago, 47
Tremont House Polka, 37, 91
Tribute of Affection, 105
Tripping Through the Barley, 116
The Triumph, 81, 145
Trois Temps Polka Mazurka, 121
Tromb-al-ca-zar, 125

Il Trovatore, 57, 102
Truax, D. A., Cincinnati, 5
The Trumpet of Glory, 127, 130
The Trumpeter, 109
Trumps, 124
Trust Me Cathleen, 124
Try, John! Try, John! 115
Turner March, 105
'Twas After Twelve When You Came Home, 111

Ueberall Du. See Thou Everywhere.
Unbidden Tears, 70
Uncle Joe's Hail Columbia, 94
Uncle Sam, 133
Uncle Sam's Funeral, 97
Under the Arbor, 120
Under the Beautiful Stars, 117
Underfoot, 123
Underground Railroad, 43
Undine, 107, 133
Undine's Song, 107
Union Charitable Society, Chicago, 22
The Union Pacific, 118
Union Theological Seminary, New York, 19, 21, 23
The Union Volunteers, 44, 92, 95
U. S. Agricultural Society Fair, 28, 34
U. S. Sanitary Commission, 51
University of Illinois. See Illinois. University.
The Unseen City, 117
Up in a Balloon, 117, 134
Upside Down Galop, 121
Upton, George, Musical Memories, 3, 10, 27, 57

Vaas, A. J., 27; Briggs House Polka, 37
    Ellsworth Requiem, 44
    Richmond House Polka, 37
    Tremont House Polka, 37
    Zouave Cadets Quickstep, 35, 37-38, 44
The Vacant Chair, 17, 48n, 49, 51, 93, 95, 96
The Vale of Romance, 120
The Valentine; or, The Spirit of Song, 7
The Valley of Chamouni, 99
Valse a la Mode, 111
Valse Brillante, 6, 7
Vaschetti, C., The Flower Girl, 70
Vedrai Carino, 106
The Velocipede, 114
Velocipede Polka, 114
Velocipede Waltz, 115
Velocipedia, 114, 115
Venzano Valse, 93
Verdi, Giuseppe, Il Trovatore, 57
Vert-Vert, 125
Vertrees, W. A., Numerical Harp, 4

A Very Bad Cold, 113
A Vesper Song for Our Volunteers' Sisters, 95
Viardot, Pauline, 18
Vicksburg Is Taken, Boys, 97, 99
Victoire Galop Militaire, 109
Viola Schottisch, 97
Viva La Prussia! 79, 124
A Voice from the Ocean, 130
The Voice That I Love, 115
La Volta, 104
The Volunteer's Grave.  See Tread Lightly Ye Comrades.
Vose piano, 51
Vote It Right Along, 115

Wait, My Little One, Wait, 124
Waiting at the Old Linden Tree.  See Angel Nellie.
Waiting for Angels to Come, 115
Wake! Lady Wake! 91
Wake Nicodemus, 98, 99
Walk! Walk! Walk! 113
Wallace, William Vincent, 21
Wandering in the Greenwood, 130
War songs, 43-48, 49
Warbling of the Birds, 96
Warblings at Eve, 100, 109
Ward, S. A., printer, Chicago, 37
Warren, A. E., Dew Drop Mazurka, 70
Washington and Lincoln, 97
Watcher Gray, 114
Watching for Pa, 95
Water in the Moonlight, 102
Wau-Bun Galop, 7
The Way It's Done, 110
We Are Coming from the Cotton Fields, 98
We Are the Boys that Fear No Noise, 130
We Are Traveling on Together, 104
We Meet Upon the Level, 37, 38, 91
We Praise Thee.  See Te Deum Laudamus.
We Shall Miss You Dearest Brother, 97
Webb, George James, 18
Weber, Karl Maria von, 80
Webster, Joseph Philbrick, 8, 9, 10, 11; Don't Be Sorrowful, Darling, 11
    Lorena, 9, 11
    Oh Scorn Not Thy Brother, 8
    They Buried Her under the Old Elm Tree, 8
Webster, William C., 8, 24, 49
Wein, Weib und Gesang, 125
Welcome Schottische, 116
Welcome Song of the 40th Wisconsin Volunteers, 97
Welcome to Spring, 91
We'll Fight it out Here on the Old Union Line, 134
We'll Go Down Ourselves, 94
We'll Have to Get the Style, 133
We'll Have to Mortgage the Farm, 120
We're Waiting for Father! 104, 133
Wesleyan Sacred Harp, 34

Western Harp, 4
Western Journal of Music, 6, 49
Western Sunday School Psalmody, 4
Westport, N. Y., 23
What Is the Use of Our Being Unhappy? 126
What Might Have Been, 110
What Shall I Ask for Thee? 105, 119
What Shall the Harvest Be? 121
What Then! 118
Wheelock pianos, 30
When Grandmama Is Gone, 114
When I Am Gone, 118
When I Courted Mary Ann, 126
When I Lie Dreaming, 108, 112
When Mother Fell Asleep, 113
When My Ship Comes In! 103, 109
When Sue and I Went Skating, 111
When the Birds Come in Spring, 115
When the Clover Was in Bloom, 121
When the Dear Ones Gather at Home, 129
When the Evening Star Went Down, 101
When the Roses Bud and Blossom, 118
When the Swallows Homeward Fly, 91
When Thou'rt Lonely Think of Me, 122
When We've Nothing Else to Do, 118
When Will My Darling Boy Return? 97
When We Sleep Beneath the Daisies, 128
When Ye Gang Awa, Jamie, 114
When You & I Were Young, Maggie, 107, 119
When You Told Me the Tale of Your Love, 116
Where Are the Dear Friends of Childhood? 117
Where Are You Going? 125
Where Go You, Pretty Maggie? 107
Where Little Baby Rests, 124
Where the Firelight Gleams at Home, 119
Where the Woodland Birdlings Warble, 127
Where'er the Heart to True Heart Beats, 123, 124
Whippoorwill, 123
White, Edward L., The Musical Gift, 63
    Yankee Doodle with Variations, 64
White, Smith & Perry, Boston, 81
White Fawn March, 112
White Fawn Schottische, 112
Whitmore, Florence, Emerald Schottisch, 7
Who Comes Dar? 98
Who Shall Rule This American Nation? 101
The Whole Story, 129
Who'll Save the Left? 95
Who's to Blame? 116
Why Doesn't He Speak? 124
Why Don't He Write? 117
Why Not? 110
Why Not I? 129
Wide Awake Clubs, 34
Wigwam, Chicago, 22, 28, 44
Will You Come to Meet Me, Darling? 96, 98
Will You Wed Me Now I'm Lame, Love? 96

Willeford, William H., Collection of Psalms, Hymns and Spiritual Songs, 4
William Tell March, 126
Willie's Coming Home, 117
Willie's Wooing, 119
Willow Farm, 17
Willow Song, 123
Wimmerstedt, A. E., 60, 62
Wine, Wife & Song Waltz, 129
Wingfield Schottisch, 94
Winkle, Pip, 60
Winnemore, A. F., The Gum Tree Canoe, 68
Winter Flowers, 114
Within the Sound of the Enemy's Guns, 51, 96
Woman Is Going to Vote, 106
Won't You Tell Me Why, Robin? 118
Woodbury, Isaac B., 24, 68
Work, Alanson, anti-slavery activities, 43
Work, Henry Clay, 19, 28n, 29, 43; editor of The Song Messenger, 49-50; war song, 49; attitude toward tune alteration, 50; removed as editor, 50
    Babylon Is Fallen, 51
    Brave Boys Are They! 9, 49
    Come Home, Father, 52
    The Days When We Were Young, 51
    Grandfather's Clock, 29, 52
    Kingdom Coming, 28n, 43, 45-46, 48n, 49
    Little Major, 51
    Marching Through Georgia, 52
World War II, 43
Would I? 118
Would You Could Meet Me To-night, 121

The Wounded Boy at Kenesaw, 98
Wurlitzer, Rudolph, Cincinnati, 13, 84
Wyman, Addison P., The Alps, Marche de Bravoura, 70
Wyndham Polka, 129

Yankee Doodle with Variations, 64
Ye Banks and Braes o' Bonnie Doon, 123
Ye Have Done It unto Me, 81, 135
Yes, Dearest, I'll Love Thee, 124
Yes, We Will Be True to Each Other, 103, 106
Young American Galopade, 116
Young Eph's Jubilee, 100
Young Girl of the Period, 117
The Young Ladies' Choir, 18
Young Man of the Period, 117
Y. M. C. A., 28
Young Men's Christian Association Hymns, 146
Your Name! The Honey Bee Is Humming It, 94, 100
Youth Polka. See Jeunesse Polka.
The Youth's Musical Friend, 84

Les Zephyrs du Matin, 91
Ziegfeld, Florenz, 13, 60
Ziegfeld, F., & Co., Chicago, 60
Ziegfeld & Gerard, Chicago, 13, 59, 60
Ziegfeld, Gerard & Co., Chicago, 61, 78
Ziegfeld & Willson, Chicago, 13, 60
Zimenia, 121
Zouave Cadets Quickstep, 35, 37-38, 44, 91
Zouaves, 44